A Title Guide
to the Talkies,
1975 through 1984

by

ANDREW A. AROS

(As conceived by Richard B. Dimmitt)

The Scarecrow Press, Inc.
Metuchen, N.J., & London
1986

Library of Congress Cataloging-in-Publication Data

Aros, Andrew A., 1944–
    A title guide to the talkies, 1975 through 1984.

    Includes index.
    1. Moving-pictures--Catalogs. I. Dimmitt,
Richard B. (Richard Bertrand). Title guide to the
talkies. II. Title.
PN1998.A6695 1986   016.79143'75   85-27682
ISBN 0-8108-1868-X

For

ROCK HUDSON

and the thousands who have had
their stars dimmed by A.I.D.S.

INTRODUCTION

With the publication of this volume, the "Title Guide" series stretches from the advent of the "talkies" in 1928 to the space age, a period of more than fifty-five years. In that period of time we have had a depression, a world war, political upheavals, social unrest, and the threat of nuclear war.

Through this all, the movies have reflected the timbre of the times and have shown us what is happening, even in areas halfway around the world. That is one of the particular feats of magic those flickering images can perform for us. They can extend our world and our personal experiences far beyond the commonplace.

The age of great films is not dead; the best are yet to be made. Just glance through some of the titles covered in this volume, and you'll see what I mean.

There are many more novelizations (filmscripts turned into books to capitalize on a film's success) published now than ever before, but finding information on them is becoming increasingly difficult since they rarely stay in print beyond the few short months that a film is in release. Occasionally, some titles become "classics," but quickly lose that status when the book is out of print.

For the inexhaustible resources of the Los Angeles County Public Library, I am truly grateful. I have found many obscure and hard-to-find novelizations in their extensive paperback collections throughout their service area. Also, the West Covina Library has an excellent series of reference works that made this job easier.

Finally, I offer my thanks to John Pearson of the Orange County Public Library for his suggestions on the manuscript.

Andrew A. Aros
Diamond Bar, CA
October 1985

ABBREVIATIONS USED IN THE BOOK

BFI — Monthly Film Bulletin. British Film Institute, London.

FD — Film Directors. Singer, Michael, ed. Beverly Hills: Lone Eagle Publications; 1984.

HR — Hollywood Reporter (daily).

LACOPL — Los Angeles County Public Library.

LAT — Los Angeles Times (daily).

NYT — New York Times (daily).

Q — International Motion Picture Almanac (annual). New York: Quigley Publishing Co.

V — Variety (Hollywood & New York editions).

W — Screen World (annual). Willis, John, ed. New York: Crown Publishers.

A TITLE GUIDE TO THE TALKIES,
1975-1984

1. AARON LOVES ANGELA. (Columbia-1975-Gordon Parks-R).
Original screenplay by Gerald Sanford. (Q, W)

2. ABDUCTION. (Venture-1975-Joseph Zito-R). Screenplay by
Kent E. Carroll, based on "Black Abductor" by Harrison
James. (W)

3. ABIGAIL LESLIE IS BACK IN TOWN. (Monarch-1975-Joe
Sarno-X). Screenplay written by Joe Sarno. (W)

4. ABSENCE OF MALICE. (Columbia-1981-Sydney Pollack-PG).
Screenplay by Kurt Luedtke. (BFI, HR, LAT, Q, V, W)

5. ABSOLUTION. (Enterprise Pictures-1981-Anthony Page-N/R).
Screenplay by Anthony Shaffer. (V)

6. ABUSE. (Cinevista-1983-Arthur J. Bressan Jr.-N/R).
Screenplay by Arthur J. Bressan Jr. (V)

7. ACAPULCO GOLD. (R. C. Riddel-1978-Burt Brickerhoff-PG).
Screenplay written by Don Enright and O'Brian Tomalin. (W)

8. THE ACCUSER. (Parafrance-1977-Jean-Louis Bertuccelli-N/R).
Screenplay by Rene-Victor Pilhes, Stephen Becker, Jean-
Louis Bertucelli, from the book by Rene-Victor Pilhes. (V)

9. ACE OF ACES. (Gaumont/Cerito Rene Chateau-1982-Gerard
Oury-N/R). Screenplay by Gerard Oury and Daniele Thompson. (V)

10. ACES HIGH. (Cinema Shares-1979-Jack Gold-N/R). This
screenplay by Howard Barker was based on the play Journey's
End by R. C. Sheriff; Brentano's, 1929, 204p. (LACOPL, W)

11. ACROSS THE GREAT DIVIDE. (Pacific International-1976-
Stewart Raffill-G). Screenplay by Stewart Raffill. (W)

12. ACT OF AGGRESSION. (Joseph Green-1975-Gerard Pires-R).
Screenplay written by Gerard Pires and Jean-Patric Manchette,
based on the novel The Shrewsdale Exit by John Buell; Farrar,
1972, 279p. (LACOPL, W)

13. ADAM AND NICOLE. (United Pictures-1976-Trevor Wrenn-X). No writing credits given. (W)

14. ADIOS AMIGO. (Atlas Films-1976-Fred Williamson-PG). Screenplay by Fred Williamson. (W)

15. THE ADVENTURE OF SHERLOCK HOLMES' SMARTER BROTHER. (20th Century-Fox-1975-Gene Wilder-PG). Gene Wilder wrote this original screenplay. (Q, W)

16. THE ADVENTURES OF BUCKAROO BANZAI: ACROSS THE 8th DIMENSION. (20th Century-Fox-1984-W. D. Richter-PG). Screenplay authored by Earl MacRauch. (V)

17. THE ADVENTURES OF FRONTIER FREMONT. (Sun Classic-1976-Richard Friedenberg-G). Screenplay credited to David O'Malley. (W)

18. THE ADVENTURES OF PICASSO. (Dome Productions-1980-Tage Danielsson-N/R). Screenplay by Hans Alfredson and Tage Danielsson. (W)

19. THE ADVENTURES OF PINOCCHIO. (G. G. Communications-1978-Jesse Vogel-G). Screenplay by Albert D'Angelo, based on the novel by Carlo Collodi; Macmillan, 1969. (LACOPL, W)

20. THE ADVENTURES OF STARBIRD. (Cougar-1978-Jack Hively-G). Alex Grunberg wrote this original screenplay. (W)

21. THE ADVENTURES OF THE WILDERNESS FAMILY. (Pacific International Enterprises-1975-Stewart Raffill-G). Stewart Raffill wrote this original screenplay. (W)

22. AFFAIR. (Intercontinental-1976-Andree Marchand-X). Screenplay by Elisabeth Reclair. (W)

23. AFFAIR AT AKITSU. (Shochiku Productions-1980-Yoshishiga Yoshida-N/R). Screenplay by Yoshishiga Yoshida. (V)

24. AFFAIRE IN RIO DE JANEIRO. (Hollywood International-1975-Carlos Tobalina-X). Written by Carlos Tobalina. (W)

25. THE AFFAIRS OF JANICE. (Leisure Time-1976-Zebedy Colt-X). Screenplay written by Zebedy Colt. (W)

26. THE AFFAIRS OF ROBIN HOOD. (Lima-1981-Richard Kanter-R). No screenplay credit available. (W)

27. AGAINST A CROOKED SKY. (Doty-Dayton-1975-Earl Bellamy-G). Screenplay by Douglas C. Stewart and Eleanor Lamb. (W)

28. AGAINST ALL ODDS. (Columbia-1984-Taylor Hackford-R).
    Screenplay by Eric Hughes, based on the 1947 film Out of the
    Past by Daniel Mainwaring; Build My Gallows High, novel by
    Daniel Mainwaring; Morrow, 1946, 213p. (HR, LACOPL, LAT,
    NYT, V)

29. AGATHA. (Warner Bros.-First Artists-1979-Michael Apted-PG).
    Screenplay by Kathleen Tynan and Arthur Hopcraft, based on
    a story by Kathleen Tynan. (V, W)

30. THE AGE OF THE MEDICI. (Audio/Brandon-1979-Roberto
    Rossellini-N/R). This original screenplay was written by
    Roberto Rossellini, Luciano Scaffa, and Marcella Mariani. (W)

31. AGENCY. (Jensen Farley-1981-George Kaczender-R). A
    screenplay by Noel Nynd, based on the novel by Paul Gottlieb.
    (LAT, W)

32. THE AGONY AND ECSTASY OF MICHAEL, ANGELO AND
    DAVID. (No credits available-1976-X). (W)

33. AGUIRRE, THE WRATH OF GOD. (New Yorker-1977-Werner
    Herzog-N/R). An original screenplay by Werner Herzog.
    (NYT, W)

AHAVA ILEMETH see THE SECRET OF YOLANDA

34. AIRPLANE! (Paramount-1980-Jim Abrahams, David Zucker,
    Jerry Zucker-PG). An original screenplay by Jim Abrahams,
    David Zucker, and Jerry Zucker. (HR, LAT, V, W)

35. AIRPLANE II: THE SEQUEL. (Paramount-1982-Ken Finkleman-
    PG). Screenplay written by Ken Finkleman. (LAT, V, W)

36. AIRPORT '77. (Universal-1977-Jerry Jameson-PG). Michael
    Scheff and David Spector wrote the screenplay, from a story
    by H. A. L. Craig and Charles Kuenstle, inspired by the
    film Airport, based on the novel by Arthur Hailey; Doubleday,
    1968. (LACOPL, NYT, Q, V)

37. ALAMBRISTA! (Filmhaus-1979-Robert M. Young-N/R). Orig-
    inal screenplay by Robert M. Young. (W)

38. THE ALCHEMIST. (Video Form Pictures-1981-Charles Band-
    N/R). Alan J. Adler wrote this original screenplay. (BFI)

39. ALEX AND THE GYPSY. (20th Century-Fox-1976-John Korty-
    R). The screenplay was authored by Lawrence B. Marcus,
    based on the novella The Bailbondsman by Stanley Elkin.
    (NYT, W)

40. ALEXANDER THE GREAT. (RAI RETE 2/ZDF Anghelopulos-1980-Theodoros Anghelopulos-N/R). An original screenplay written by Theodoros Anghelopulos. (V)

41. ALEXANDRIA ... WHY? (Misr International-1979-Youssef Chahine-N/R). Youssef Chahine and Mohsen Zayed wrote this original screenplay. (V)

42. ALICE DOESN'T LIVE HERE ANYMORE. (Warner Bros.-1975-Martin Scorsese-PG). An original screenplay by Robert Getchell; novelization by Robert Getchell; Warner Books, 1975, 142p. (HR, LACOPL, NYT, W)

43. ALICE IN THE CITIES. (Bauer International-1977-Wim Wenders-N/R). An original screenplay by Wim Wenders and Veith der Furstenberg. (NYT, W)

44. ALICE, OR THE LAST ESCAPADE. (Filmel/PHPG-1977-Claude Chabrol-N/R). Claude Chabrol wrote this original screenplay. (V)

45. ALICE, SWEET ALICE. (Allied Artists-1977-Alfred Sole-N/R). An original screenplay by Rosemary Ritvo and Alfred Sole. (V, W)

46. ALIEN. (20th Century-Fox-1979-Ridley Scott-R). Screenplay credited to Dan O'Bannon; novelization by Alan Dean Foster; Warner Books, 1979, 270p. (HR, LACOPL, LAT, NYT, V, W)

47. ALIEN CONTAMINATION. (Cannon Group-1983-Lewis Coates aka Luigi Cozzi-R). Original screenplay written by Lewis Coates (aka Luigi Cozzi). (V, W)

48. ALIEN ENCOUNTER. (Group I Films-1979-Edward Hunt-G). Edward Hunt and Stanton Friedman wrote the screenplay. (W)

49. THE ALIEN FACTOR. (Cinemagic Visual Effects-1978-Donald M. Dohle-N/R). Screenplay written by Donald M. Dohle. (V, W)

50. ALIEN THUNDER. (Cinerama-1975-Claude Fournier-PG). No screenplay credit available. (W)

THE ALL-AMERICAN VIXEN see THE ALL-AMERICAN WOMAN

51. THE ALL-AMERICAN WOMAN. (Manuel S. Conde-1976-Mark Haggard-X). Screenplay written by Mark Haggard. (W)

52. ALL CREATURES GREAT AND SMALL. (EMI-1975-Claude Whatham-N/R). Screenplay written by Hugh Whittmore, from the book by James Herriot; St. Martin's Press, 1972, 422p. (LACOPL, W)

53. ALL NIGHT LONG. (Essex-1976-Alan B. Colberg-X). No
     screenplay credits given. (W)

54. ALL NIGHT LONG. (Universal-1981-Jean-Claude Tramont-R).
     An original screenplay by W. D. Richter. (HR, LAT, V, W)

55. ALL OF ME. (Universal-1984-Carl Reiner-PG). A screenplay
     by Phil Alden Robinson, adapted by Henry Olek from the
     novel by Ed Davis. (V)

56. ALL RIGHT, MY FRIEND. (Toho-1983-Ryu Murakami-N/R).
     Screenplay written by Ryu Murakami, based on his original
     story. (V)

57. ALL SCREWED UP. (New Line Cinema-1976-Lina Wertmuller-
     PG). An original screenplay by Lina Wertmuller. (NYT, Q,
     W)

58. ALL THAT JAZZ. (20th Century-Fox-1979-Bob Fosse-R). An
     original screenplay by Robert Alan Aurthur and Bob Fosse;
     novelization by H. B. Gilmour; Jove, 1979. (HR, LACOPL,
     LAT, NYT, Q, V, W)

59. ALL THE MARBLES. (MGM/United Artists-1981-Robert
     Aldrich-R). An original screenplay by Mel Frohman. (LAT,
     V, W)

60. ALL THE PRESIDENT'S MEN. (Warner Bros.-1976-Alan J.
     Pakula-PG). William Goldman wrote the screenplay, based on
     the book of the same title by Carl Bernstein and Bob Wood-
     ward; Simon & Schuster, 1974, 349p. (HR, LACOPL, LAT,
     NYT, Q, V, W)

61. ALL THE RIGHT MOVES. (20th Century-Fox-1983-Michael
     Chapman-R). An original screenplay by Michael Kane. (V)

62. ALL THE YOUNG WIVES. (International Cinefilm-1975-Mike
     Ripps-R). No screenplay credits given. (W)

63. ALL THINGS BRIGHT AND BEAUTIFUL. (World Northal-1978-
     Eric Till-G). A screenplay by Alan Plater, based on the book
     by James Herriot; St. Martin's Press, 1974, 378p. (LACOPL,
     W)

64. ALLEY CAT. (Film Ventures International-1984-Eduardo Pal-
     mos, Victor Ordonez, Al Valletta-R). An original screenplay
     by Robert E. Waters. (V)

65. ALLIGATOR. (Group I Films-1980-Lewis Teague-R). A
     screenplay written by John Sayles, from a story by John
     Sayles and Frank Ray Perilli. (BFI, V, W)

66. ALMOST HUMAN. (Joseph Brenner-1981-Umberto Lenzi-R).
No screenplay credits given. (V, W)

67. AN ALMOST PERFECT AFFAIR. (Paramount-1979-Michael
Ritchie-PG). Walter Bernstein and Don Peterson wrote the
screenplay based on a story by Michael Ritchie and Don
Peterson. (HR, LAT, V, W)

68. ALMOST SUMMER. (Universal-1978-Martin Davidson-PG). An
original screenplay by Judith Berg, Sandra Berg, Martin
Davidson, and Marc Reid Rubel. (HR, V)

69. ALOHA, BOBBY AND ROSE. (Columbia-1975-Floyd Mutrux-
PG). An original screenplay by Floyd Mutrux. (HR, LAT,
NYT, Q, V, W)

70. ALONE IN THE DARK. (New Line Cinema-1982-Jack Sholder-
R). An original screenplay written by Jack Sholder. (LAT,
V, W)

71. ALPHA BETA. (Cine III-1976-Anthony Page-PG). A screenplay by E. A. Whitehead, based on his play. (NYT, W)

72. ALPHABET CITY. (Atlantic-1984-Amos Poe-R). Screenplay
by Gregory K. Heller and Amos Poe, from a story by Gregory
K. Heller, and with additional dialog by Robert Seidman. (V)

73. ALTERED STATES. (Warner Bros.-1980-Ken Russell-R). A
screenplay by Sidney Aaron, from a novel by Paddy Chayefsky;
Harper & Row, 1978. (LACOPL, V, W)

AMADA AMANTE see BELOVED LOVER

74. AMADEUS. (Orion-1984-Milos Forman-PG). Screenplay written
by Peter Shaffer, based on his play; Harper & Row, 1981,
128p. (BFI, HR, LACOPL, LAT, V)

AMANTI MIEI see CINDY'S LOVE GAMES

75. THE AMATEUR. (20th Century-Fox-1982-Charles Jarrott-R).
Screenplay by Robert Littell and Diana Maddox, based on
Robert Littell's novel of the same name; Simon & Schuster,
1981, 252p. (LACOPL, V)

76. THE AMAZING DOBERMANS. (Golden Films-1976-Byron
Chudnow-G). Screenplay written by Michael Kraike, William
Goldstein, and Richard Chapman, from a story by Michael
Kraike and William Goldstein. (V)

77. THE AMAZING DR. JEKYLL. (Webster-1976-Tim McCoy-X).
No writing credits given. (W)

78. THE AMAZING LOVE SECRET. (Topar-1975-Tom Parker-R).
No writing credits given. (W)

79. THE AMBASSADOR. (Cannon-1984-J. Lee Thompson-N/R).
A screenplay written by Max Jack, based on Elmore Leonard's
novel 52 Pick Up; Delacorte Press, 1974, 254p. (LACOPL, V)

80. AMERICAN DREAMER. (Warner Bros.-1984-Rick Rosenthal-PG).
A screenplay written by Jim Kouf and David Greenwalt, from
a story by Ann Biderman. (V)

81. THE AMERICAN FRIEND. (New Yorker-1977-Wim Wenders-
N/R). Screenplay written by Wim Wenders, based on the
novel Ripley's Game by Patricia Highsmith; Knopf, 1974, 267p.
(LACOPL, NYT, Q, V, W)

82. THE AMERICAN GAME. (World Northal-1979-Jay Freund &
David Wolf-PG). Screenplay written by Jay Freund and David
Wolf. (W)

83. AMERICAN GIGOLO. (Paramount-1980-Paul Schrader-R). An
original screenplay by Paul Schrader; novel by Timothy Harris
and Paul Schrader, Delacorte Press, 1979, 212p. (HR,
LACOPL, LAT, NYT, Q, V, W)

84. AMERICAN HOT WAX. (Paramount-1978-Floyd Mutrux-PG).
Screenplay by John Kaye. (HR, NYT, V, W)

85. AMERICAN NIGHTMARE. (Mano Films Ltd.-1984-Don
McBrearty-N/R). Screenplay by John Sheppard, from a story
by John Gualt and Steven Blake. (V)

86. AMERICAN NITRO. (Cannon-1979-Bill Kimberlin-PG). No
screenplay credit given. (W)

87. AMERICAN POP. (Columbia-1981-Ralph Bakshi-R). Screenplay credited to Ronni Kern. (LAT, V, W)

88. THE AMERICAN SUCCESS COMPANY. (Columbia-1979-William
Richert-PG). William Richert and Larry Cohen co-authored the
screenplay, based on a story by Larry Cohen. (V, W)

89. AMERICAN TABOO. (Steve Lustgarten Productions-1984-Steve
Lustgarten-N/R). Screenplay by Steve Lustgarten. (V)

90. AN AMERICAN WEREWOLF IN LONDON. (Universal-1981-John
Landis-R). Original screenplay by John Landis. (HR, LAT,
V, W)

91. AMERICANA. (David Carradine and Skip Sherwood
Production-1981-David Carradine-N/R). Screenplay written
by Richard Carr. (V)

92.   AMERICATHON. (United Artists-1979-Neil Israel-PG).
      Screenplay by Neil Israel, Michael Mislove, Monica Johnson,
      from a story by Neil Israel, Peter Bergman and Philip Proc-
      tor. (V, W)

93.   AMIN; THE RISE AND FALL. (International Film Marketing-
      1982-Sharad Patel-R). Uncredited screenplay. (LAT, W)

94.   THE AMITYVILLE HORROR. (American International-1979-
      Stuart Rosenberg-R). Screenplay by Sandor Stern, based
      on the book by Jay Anson; Bantam Books, 1978, 269p.
      (LACOPL, LAT, NYT, V, W)

95.   AMITYVILLE 3-D. (Orion-1983-Richard Fleischer-PG).
      Screenplay by William Wales. (LAT, V)

96.   AMITYVILLE II: THE POSSESSION. (Orion-1982-Damiano
      Damiani-R). Tommy Lee Wallace wrote the screenplay, based
      on the book Murder in Amityville by Hans Holzer; Dorchester
      Publishing Co., 1982, 288p. (HR, LACOPL, LAT, Q, V, W)

      AMOR BANDIDO see OUTLAW LOVE

97.   AMOR DE PERDICAO. (Joseph Papp-1981-Manoel de Oliveira-
      N/R). Screenplay by Manoel de Oliveira. (W)

98.   THE AMOROUS ADVENTURES OF DON QUIXOTE AND SANCHO
      PANZA. (Burbank International-1976-Raphael Nussbaum-R).
      Script by Raphael Nussbaum, Ed Woodworth, Al Bukzin. (W)

      L'AMOUR A MORT see LOVE UNTO DEATH

      UN AMOUR DE SWANN see SWANN IN LOVE

      L'AMOUR PAR TERRE see LOVE ON THE GROUND

99.   THE AMSTERDAM KILL. (Golden Harvest-1977-Robert
      Clouse-R). Screenplay by Robert Clouse and Gregory Tiefer.
      (NYT, V, W)

100. AMUCK. (Group 1-1978-R). No production credits available.
      (W)

101. AMY. (Buena Vista-1981-Vincent McEveety-G). This original
      screenplay was authored by Noreen Stone. (LAT, V, W)

      EL ANACORETA see THE ANCHORITE

102. THE ANCHORITE. (Incine and Hispano Fox-1977-Juan
      Estelrich-N/R). A screenplay written by Juan Estelrich and
      Rafael Azcona. (V)

103. ... AND JUSTICE FOR ALL. (Columbia-1979-Norman Jewison-R). Screenplay by Valerie Curtin and Barry Levinson. (HR, LAT, NYT, Q, V, W)

104. AND NOW MY LOVE. (Avco Embassy-1975-Claude Lelouch-PG). Claude Lelouch and Pierre Uytterhoeven wrote the screenplay. (NYT, Q, W)

105. AND THE SHIP SAILS ON. (Franco Cristaldi-1983-Federico Fellini-N/R). Original story and screenplay by Federico Fellini and Tonino Guerra. (HR, LAT, V, W)

106. ANDREA. (Group 1-1979-Leopold Pomes-R). No screenplay credits available. (W)

107. ANDROID. (New World Pictures-1982-Aaron Lipstadt-R). Screenplay written by James Reigle and Don Opper, based on an original idea by Will Reigle. (V, W)

108. ANGEL. (Motion Picture of Ireland-1982-Neil Jordan-N/R). Screenplay written by Neil Jordan. (V)

109. ANGEL. (New World-1984-Robert Vincent O'Neil-R). Screenplay by Robert Vincent O'Neil and Joseph M. Cala. (V)

110. THE ANGEL ABOVE AND THE DEVIL BELOW. (Martoni Enterprises-1975-X). Screenplay by Jon Cutaia. (W)

111. ANGEL OF H.E.A.T. (Studios Pan Image-1983-Myrl A. Schreibman-R). Helen Sanford authored this original screenplay. (V)

112. ANGEL ON FIRE. (Essex-1976-Roberta Findley-X). No screenplay credit available. (W)

113. ANGELA. (Classic Films and Canafox Films-1984-Boris Sagal-N/R). Screenplay by Charles Israel. (V)

114. ANGELO, MY LOVE. (Cinecom-1983-Robert Duvall-N/R). An original screenplay written by Robert Duvall. (LAT, V)

115. ANGELS. (Boxoffice International-1976-Spencer Compton-R). Drew Abrams, Richard Power, Spencer Compton, and Ed Margulies wrote this original screenplay. (W)

116. ANGI VERA. (New Yorker-1980-Pal Gabor-N/R). Screenplay written by Pal Gabor, from a novel by Endre Veszi. (W)

117. ANITA, SWEDISH NYMPHET. (Cambist-1975-Torgny Wickman-X). Torgny Wickman wrote the screenplay. (W)

DE ANNA see THE ANNA

118. THE ANNA. (Olga Madsen Production-1983-Erik van Zuylen-N/R). Written by Erik van Zuylen. (V)

119. ANNA KARENINA. (Corinth-1979-Margarita Philihina-N/R). Screenplay by Bavov Arbhin, based on the novel by Leo Tolstoy; Bobbs-Merrill, 1978, 870p. (LACOPL, LAT, W)

120. ANNE DEVLIN. (Aeon Films-1984-Pat Murphy-N/R). Screenplay by Pat Murphy. (V)

121. ANNIE. (Map-1976-Massimo Dellamano-X). Based on a story by Annie Belle. (W)

122. ANNIE. (Columbia-1982-John Huston-PG). Screenplay by Carol Sobieski, based on the stage play with a book by Thomas Meehan, music by Charles Strouse, and lyrics by Martin Charnin. (HR, LAT, NYT, Q, V, W)

123. ANNIE HALL. (United Artists-1977-Woody Allen-PG). An Academy Award-winning original screenplay by Woody Allen and Marshall Brickman. (HR, LAT, NYT, Q, V, W)

124. THE ANONYMOUS AVENGER. (Hallmark-1976-Enzo G. Castellari-R). Screenplay written by Dino Maiuri and Massimo DeRita. (W)

125. ANOTHER COUNTRY. (Orion Classics-1984-Marek Kanievska-PG). Screenplay by Julian Mitchell, based on his play; Limelight Editions, 1984. (LACOPL, LAT, V)

126. ANOTHER MAN, ANOTHER CHANCE. (United Artists-1977-Claude Lelouch-PG). Screenplay by Claude Lelouch. (NYT, Q, W)

127. ANOTHER TIME, ANOTHER PLACE. (Umbrella Films-1983-Michael Radford-N/R). Screenplay by Michael Radford, based on the novel by Jessie Kesson. (BFI, V)

128. ANTARCTICA. (TLC Films-1984-Koreyoshi Kurahara-G). Tatsuo Nogami, Ken Saji, Toshiro Ishido, and Koreyoshi Kurahara share screenplay credit. (V)

129. ANTI-CLOCK. (International Film Exchange-1980-Jane Arden and Jack Bond-N/R). Screenplay by Jane Arden. (V, W)

130. ANXIOUS TO RETURN. (China Film Export & Import Corporation-1980-Li Jun-N/R). Screenplay by Li Keyi. (V)

131. ANY WHICH WAY YOU CAN. (Warner Bros.-1980-Buddy Van

Horn-PG). Stanford Sherman wrote the screenplay, based on characters created by Jeremy Joe Kronsberg. (V, W)

132. ANYONE BUT MY HUSBAND. (Anonymous-1975-Robert Norman-X). No screenplay credit given. (W)

133. APE. (Worldwide Entertainment-1976-Paul Leder-PG). Paul Leder and Reuben Leder wrote this original screenplay. (V, W)

APOCALIPSIS CANIBAL see NIGHT OF THE ZOMBIES (1983)

134. APOCALYPSE NOW. (United Artists-1979-Francis Coppola-R). Screenplay by John Milius and Francis Coppola. (HR, LAT, NYT, Q, V, W)

135. THE APPLE. (Cannon Group-1980-Menahem Golan-PG). Screenplay by Menahem Golan, based on a story by Coby and Iris Recht. (V, W)

136. THE APPLE DUMPLING GANG. (Buena Vista-1975-Norman Tokar-G). Screenplay by Don Tait, based on a book by Jack M. Bickham; Doubleday, 1971, 189p. (HR, LACOPL, LAT, NYT, Q, V, W)

137. THE APPLE DUMPLING GANG RIDES AGAIN. (Buena Vista-1979-Vincent McEveety-G). A screenplay by Don Tait, based on characters created by Jack M. Bickham. (HR, LAT, V, W)

138. THE APPLE GAME. (Argent Arts/Entertainment Marketing-1980-Vera Chytilova-R). An original screenplay authored by Vera Chytilova and Kristina Vlachova. (W)

139. THE APPLE WAR. (Svenska-1975-Tage Danielsson-N/R). Screenplay by Hans Alfredson and Tage Danielsson. (W)

140. ARABIAN ADVENTURE. (EMI Films-1979-Kevin Connor-N/R). Screenplay written by Brian Hayles. (V, W)

141. ARABIAN NIGHTS. (United Artists-1980-Pier Paolo Pasolini-N/R). Screenplay written by Pier Paolo Pasolini. (W)

L'ARGENT see THE MONEY (1983)

142. AROUND THE WORLD WITH JOHNNY WADD. (Cunard-1975-X). No additional production credits available. (W)

143. THE ARREST. (Serge Fradkoff-1982-Raphael Rebibo-N/R). Screenplay by Raphael Rebibo. (W)

144. ARTHUR. (Orion/Warner Bros.-1981-Steve Gordon-PG). An
      original screenplay by Steve Gordon. (HR, LAT, NYT, Q,
      V, W)

      ASALTO EN TIJUANA see ASSAULT ON TIJUANA

145. THE ASCENT. (Mosfilm-1977-Larissa Shepitko-N/R). Screen-
      play written by Yuri Klepikov and Larissa Shepitko. (LAT,
      NYT, V)

146. ASHANTI. (Columbia-1979-Richard Fleischer-R). Stephen
      Geller wrote the screenplay based on the novel Ebano by
      Alberto Vazquez Figueroa. (V, W)

147. ASHES AND EMBERS. (Mypheduh Films-1982-Haile Gerima-
      N/R). Screenplay authored by Haile Gerima. (W)

148. ASSAULT ON AGATHON. (Nine Network/Jensen International-
      1976-Laslo Benedek-N/R). Screenplay by Alan Caillou, based
      on his novel of the same title. (V, W)

149. ASSAULT ON PRECINCT 13. (Turtle Releasing Org.-1976-
      John Carpenter-R). Screenplay written by John Carpenter.
      (V, W)

150. ASSAULT ON TIJUANA. (Filmadora S.A./Metropolitan's
      Million Dollar Prods.-1984-Alfredo Gurrola-N/R). Screenplay
      by Jorge Patino and Abe Glazer. (V)

151. THE ASSISTANT. (International Film Exchange-1982-Zoro
      Zahon-N/R). Zoro Zahon, and Ondrej Sulaj wrote the screen-
      play, based on a novel by Ladislav Ballek. (V, W)

152. THE ASSOCIATE. (Warner/Columbia-1979-Rene Gainville-
      N/R). Screenplay written by Rene Gainville and Jean-Claude
      Carriere, from the novel My Partner, Mister Davis by Jenaro
      Prieto. (LAT, V, W)

153. THE ASTRAL FACTOR. (Cougar-1978-John Floria-PG).
      Arthur Pierce and Earle Lyon authored the screenplay. (W)

154. THE ASTROLOGER. (Republic Arts-1975-Craig Denney-R).
      Screenplay written by Dorothy June Pidgeon. (W)

155. THE ASTROLOGER. (Interstar-1979-Jim Glickenhaus-R). No
      screenplay credit given; based on a novel by John Cameron;
      Random House, 1972, 309p. (LACOPL, W)

156. ASYA. (Corinth-1982-Josef Heifitz-N/R). Screenplay by
      Josef Heifitz, from a novel by Ivan Turgenev. (W)

157. ASYLUM OF SATAN. (Studio 1-1975-William Girdler-PG).
Screenplay written by William Girdler. (W)

158. AT LONG LAST LOVE. (20th Century-Fox-1975-Peter
Bogdanovich-G). An original screenplay written by Peter
Bogdanovich. (HR, LAT, NYT, W)

159. AT THE EARTH'S CORE. (American International-1976-Kevin
Connor-PG). Milton Subotsky wrote the screenplay, based
on a novel by Edgar Rice Burroughs; Dover, 1963. (HR,
LACOPL, LAT, NYT, W)

160. ATLANTIC CITY. (Paramount-1981-Louis Malle-R). An original screenplay by John Guare. (HR, LAT, Q, V, W)

161. ATOR. (Comworld Pictures-1982-David Hills-PG). An original screenplay written by David Hills. (LAT, V)

ATRAPADOS see TRAPPED

162. ATTACK OF THE KILLER TOMATOES. (NAI Entertainment-
1978-John DeBello-PG). Costa Dillon, Steve Peace, and John
De Bello shared screenplay credit. (V, W)

163. THE ATTIC. (Atlantic-1980-George Edwards-R). An original
screenplay by Tony Crechales and George Edwards. (W)

AU NOM DE TOUS LES MIENS see FOR THOSE I LOVED

164. AUDREY ROSE. (United Artists-1977-Robert Wise-PG).
Screenplay written by Frank De Felitta, based on his novel
of the same name; Putnam, 1982, 374p. (HR, LACOPL, LAT,
Q, NYT, V, W)

165. AUGUSTINE OF HIPPO. (Entertainment Marketing Corp.-
1979-Roberto Rossellini-N/R). Roberto Rossellini, Marcella
Mariani, Luciano Scaffa, and Carlo Cremona authored this
screenplay. (W)

166. AUTHOR! AUTHOR! (20th Century-Fox-1982-Arthur Hiller-
PG). Israel Horovitz wrote this original screenplay. (V)

167. THE AUTOBIOGRAPHY OF A FLEA. (Mitchell Bros. Film
Group-1977-Sharon McNight-X). Screenplay by Sharon
McNight and William Boyer. (V, W)

168. AUTOPSY. (Joseph Brenner-1978-Armando Crispini-R).
Screenplay credits not available. (W)

169. AUTUMN BORN. (North American Pictures-1983-Lloyd A.

Simandl-N/R). Screenplay by Sharon Christensen, Shannon
Lee, and Ihor Procak. (V)

170. AUTUMN MARATHON. (International Film Exchange-1979-
Georgy Danelia-N/R). Screenplay by Alexander Volodin. (W)

171. AUTUMN SONATA. (New World Pictures-1978-Ingmar Berg-
man-PG). An original screenplay by Ingmar Bergman. (NYT,
V)

172. AVALANCHE. (New World Pictures-1978-Corey Allen-PG).
Claude Pola and Corey Allen shared credit for this original
screenplay. (V, W)

173. AVALANCHE EXPRESS. (20th Century-Fox-1979-Mark
Robson-PG). A screenplay by Abraham Polonsky, based on
the novel by Colin Forbes; Dutton, 1977. (HR, LACOPL, V,
W)

174. AN AVERAGE MAN. (Cineriz-1977-Mario Monicelli-N/R). An
original screenplay by Sergio Amidei and Mario Monicelli. (V)

175. THE AVIATOR'S WIFE. (New Yorker-1981-Eric Rohmer-N/R).
An original screenplay written by Eric Rohmer. (LAT, W)

176. THE AWAKENING. (Orion-1980-Mike Newell-R). Allan Scott,
Chris Bryant, and Clive Exton based their screenplay on the
novel The Jewel of Seven Stars by Bram Stoker; Harper,
1904. (LACOPL, Q, V, W)

177. THE AWAKENING OF ANNIE. (Atlas-1976-Zygmunt
Sulistrowski-X). Written by Zygmunt Sulistrowski. (W)

178. AXE. (New American Film-1983-Frederick R. Friedel-R). An
original screenplay written by Frederick R. Friedel. (V)

179. BABY BLUE MARINE. (Columbia-1976-John Hancock-PG). An
original screenplay by Stanford Whitmore. (HR, LAT, NYT,
Q, V, W)

180. BABY DOLLS. (Coast Films-1982-Mel Welles-R). Buck Flower
and John Goff co-authored the screenplay. (W)

181. BABY, IT'S YOU. (Paramount-1982-John Sayles-R). A
screenplay written by John Sayles, based on a story by Amy
Robinson. (HR, LAT, V, W)

182. BABYLON. (National Film Finance-1980-Franco Rosso-N/R).
Martin Stellman and Franco Rosso are credited with the writing of this original screenplay. (V)

183. BACHELOR PARTY. (20th Century-Fox-1984-Neal Israel-R).
      Screenplay written by Neal Israel and Pat Proft, from a
      story by Bob Israel. (V)

184. BACK ROADS. (Warner Bros.-1981-Martin Ritt-R). An orig-
      inal screenplay by Gary Devore. (HR, LAT, Q, V, W)

185. BAD BOYS. (Universal-1983-Richard Rosenthal-R). Richard
      DiLello wrote this original screenplay. (BFI, HR, LAT, V,
      W)

186. THE BAD BUNCH. (Dimension-1976-Greydon Clark-R).
      Original screenplay by Greydon Clark and Alvin L. Fast. (W)

187. BAD MAN'S RIVER. (Scotia International-1975-Eugenio
      Martin-PG). No screenplay credits available. (W)

188. THE BAD NEWS BEARS. (Paramount-1976-Michael Ritchie-
      PG). An original screenplay by Bill Lancaster. (HR, NYT,
      Q, W)

189. THE BAD NEWS BEARS GO TO JAPAN. (Paramount-1978-
      John Barry-PG). An original screenplay by Bill Lancaster.
      (NYT, V, W)

190. THE BAD NEWS BEARS IN BREAKING TRAINING. (Para-
      mount-1977-Michael Pressman-PG). Paul Brickman wrote the
      screenplay, based on characters created by Bill Lancaster.
      (HR, LAT, NYT, V)

191. BAD TIMING/A SENSUAL OBSESSION. (World Northal-1980-
      Nicholas Roeg-N/R). An original screenplay written by Yale
      Udoff. (Q, V, W)

192. THE BAILIFF OF GRIEFENSEE. (Condor-1979-Wilfried
      Bollinger-N/R). Screenplay by Wilfried Bollinger and Gerold
      Spaeth, from the novel by Gottfried Keller. (V)

193. BAKER'S HAWK. (Doty-Dayton-1976-Lyman D. Dayton-G).
      Dan Greer and Hal Harrison Jr. wrote the screenplay, based
      on the novel by Jack Bickham; Doubleday, 1974, 233p.
      (LACOPL, V, W)

      LE BAL see THE BALL

194. THE BALL. (AMLF-1983-Ettore Scola-N/R). A screenplay by
      Ettore Scola, Ruggero Maccari, Jean-Claude Penchenat, Furio
      Scarpelli, based on the stage production of the Theatre du
      Campagnol, from an original idea by Jean-Claude Penchenat.
      (V)

195. THE BALLAD OF GREGORIO CORTEZ. (Embassy-1983-Robert M. Young-PG). Screenplay written by Robert M. Young, from the book With His Pistol in His Hand by Americo Paredes; University of Texas Press, 1958. (HR, LACOPL, LAT)

196. THE BALLAD OF NARAYAMA. (Toei-1983-Shohei Imamura-N/R). A screenplay by Shohei Imamura, based on the novel by Shichiro Fukazawa. (V)

197. THE BALTIMORE BULLET. (Avco Embassy-1980-Robert Ellis Miller-PG). A screenplay by John F. Brascia and Robert Vincent O'Neil. (Q, V, W)

198. BAMBINA. (Buckley Bros.-1976-Alberto Lattuada-R). Ottavio Jemma, Alberto Lattuada, and Bruno Di Geronimo collaborated on the writing of this screenplay. (W)

199. BAMBOO HOUSE OF DOLLS. (Peppercorn-Wormser-1976-No Director Credit Given-R). No screenplay credits available. (W)

200. THE BANDITS. (Lone Star-1979-Robert Conrad and Alfredo Zacharias-PG). No screenplay credits available. (W)

201. BANISHED. (Toho-1978-Masahiro Shinoda-N/R). No screenplay credits available; based on a novel by Tsutomu Minagami, adapted, by Jeiji Hasebe and Masahiro Shinoda. (V, W)

202. BARBAROSA. (Universal Associated Films-1982-Fred Schepisi-PG). Screenplay written by William D. Wittliff. (BFI, LAT, V, W)

203. BARN OF THE NAKED DEAD. (Twin World-1976-Alan Rudolf-R). An original screenplay by Gerald Cormier. (W)

204. BARNEY. (Columbia-1977-David S. Waddington-N/R). Screenplay by Colin Drake. (V)

205. BAROCCO. (Robert A. McNeil-1980-Andre Techine-N/R). An original screenplay written by Andre Techine. (NYT, W)

206. BARRACUDA. (Republic-1979-Harry Kerwin-PG). Screenplay written by Wayne Crawford and Harry Kerwin. (W)

207. BARRY LYNDON. (Warner Bros.-1975-Stanley Kubrick-PG). Screenplay written by Stanley Kubrick, based on the novel by William Makepeace Thackeray; Tempo Books, 1975, 312p. (HR, LACOPL, LAT, NYT, Q, V, W)

208. BASKET CASE. (Analysis-1982-Frank Henenlotter-N/R). An original screenplay by Frank Henenlotter. (BFI, V, W)

17   Bastien

209. BASTIEN, BASTIENNE. (Les Films Moliere-1979-Michel
Andrieu-N/R). Screenplay written by Michel Andrieu. (V)

210. BATTLE BEYOND THE STARS. (New World-1980-Jimmy T.
Murakami-PG). Screenplay by John Sayles, from a story by
John Sayles and Anne Dyer. (V, W)

211. BATTLESTAR GALACTICA. (Universal-1979-Richard A.
Colla-PG). Screenplay by Glen A. Larson; novelization by
Glen A. Larson and Robert Thurston; Berkley, 1978, 244p.
(LACOPL, W)

212. BATTLETRUCK. (New World-1982-Harley Cokliss-PG). An
original screenplay by Irving Austin, Harley Cokliss, and
John Beech. (LAT, V, W)

213. THE BAWDY ADVENTURES OF TOM JONES. (Universal-1976-
Cliff Owen-R). Screenplay written by Jeremy Lloyd, based
on the musical Tom Jones; from the novel by Henry Fielding;
Dodd, 1967. (LACOPL, NYT, Q, W)

214. BAY BOY. (Orion-1984-Daniel Petrie Jr.-N/R). Screenplay
written by Daniel Petrie Jr. (V)

215. BEACH BLANKET BANGO. (Freeway-1975-Morris Deal-X).
Screenplay by Pete Turner. (W)

216. THE BEACH GIRLS. (Crown International Pictures-1982-Pat
Townsend-R). Patrick Duncan authored this original screenplay. (LAT, V, W)

217. BEACH HOUSE. (New Line-1982-John Gallagher-PG). An
original screenplay by Marino Amoruso and John Gallagher.
(W)

218. THE BEAR. (Embassy-1984-Richard Sarafian-PG). Michael
Kane wrote this original screenplay; novelization by Richard
Woodley; Pocket Books, 1984. (HR, LACOPL, LAT, V)

219. BEAR ISLAND. (Columbia-1980-Don Sharp-PG). Screenplay
by Don Sharp, David Butler, and Murray Smith, based on the
novel by Alistair MacLean. (V, W)

220. THE BEAST WITHIN. (MGM/United Artists-1982-Philippe
Mora-R). A screenplay by Tom Holland, based on the novel
of the same name by Edward Levy; Arbor House, 1981, 69p.
(LACOPL, LAT, V, W)

221. THE BEASTMASTER. (MGM/United Artists-1982-Don
Coscarelli-PG). A screenplay by Don Coscarelli and Paul
Pepperman. (BFI, LAT, V, W)

222.   BEAT STREET. (Orion-1984-Stan Lathan-PG). A screenplay by Andy Davis, David Gilbert, Paul Golding, from a story by Steven Hager. (V)

223.   BEATLEMANIA. (American Cinema-1981-Joseph Manduke-PG). Conceived and designed by Bob Gill and Robert Rabinowitz. (V, W)

224.   BEAU PERE. (New Line Cinema-1981-Bertrand Blier-N/R). An original screenplay by Bertrand Blier. (W)

225.   BEAUTY AND THE BEAST. (IFEX-1983-Juraj Herz-N/R). Screenplay written by Juraj Herz, from a story by Frantisek Haubin and Ota Hofman. (W)

226.   THE BEES. (New World-1978-Alfredo Zacharias-PG). Alfredo Zacharias wrote this original screenplay. (V, W)

227.   BEGGING THE RING. (Colin Gregg Films-1979-Colin Gregg-N/R). An original screenplay written by Colin Gregg and Hugh Stoddart. (V)

228.   BEHIND CONVENT WALLS. (Trust International-1978-Walerian Borowczyck-N/R). Screenplay written by Walerian Borowczyck, based on a short story by Stendhal. (V)

229.   BEHIND LOCKED DOORS. (Boxoffice International-1975-Charles Romine-R). Screenplay written by Charles Romine and Stanley H. Brasloff. (W)

230.   THE BEING. (BFV-1983-Jackie Kong-R). An original screenplay by Jackie Kong. (LAT, V, W)

231.   BEING THERE. (United Artists-1979-Hal Ashby-PG). Screenplay by Jerzy Kosinski, based on his novel; Harcourt, 1970, 142p. (LACOPL, Q, V, W)

232.   THE BELL JAR. (Avco Embassy-1979-Larry Peerce-R). Screenplay by Marjorie Kellogg, based on the novel by Sylvia Plath; Faber, 1966, 258p. (LACOPL, Q, V, W)

233.   BELLS OF AUTUMN. (Sovexportfilm-1980-Vladimir Gorikker-N/R). A screenplay by Alexander Volodin, based on the poem by Alexander Pushkin. (V)

234.   BELOVED LOVER. (Luiz Carlos Barreto-1979-Bruno Barreto-N/R). An original screenplay by Jose Louzeiro and Leopoldo Serran. (V)

235.   BELOW THE BELT. (Atlantic Releasing-1980-Robert Fowler-R). Screenplay written by Robert Fowler and Sherry Sonnett,

from the novel <u>To Smithereens</u> by Rosalyn Drexler; New
American Library, 1972, 187p. (BFI, LACOPL, V, W)

236. THE BELSTONE FOX. (Cine III-1976-James Hill-G). Screenplay written by James Hill, based on "The Ballad of the
Belstone Fox" by David Rook. (W)

237. BENEATH THE MERMAIDS. (Sirens-1976-Frank Renfroe-X).
Screenplay by Ned Weston and Frank Renfroe. (W)

238. BENEATH THE VALLEY OF THE ULTRAVIXENS. (RM Films-
1979-Russ Meyer-N/R). Screenplay written by R. Hyde and
B. Callum, from a story by Russ Meyer. (V, W)

239. THE BERMUDA TRIANGLE. (Schick Sunn Classics-1979-
Richard Friedenberg-G). Screenplay by Stephen Lord, from
the book by Charles Berlitz; Doubleday, 1974, 203p.
(LACOPL, V, W)

240. THE BEST. (Group I-1979-M. Guerin-R). No screenplay
credits available. (W)

241. THE BEST DEFENSE. (Paramount-1984-Willard Huyck-R).
Screenplay by Gloria Katz and Willard Huyck, based on
Robert Grossbach's novel <u>Easy and Hard Ways Out</u>; Harper's
Magazine Press, 1975, 245p. (HR, LACOPL, V)

242. BEST FRIENDS. (Crown International-1975-Noel Nosseck-R).
An original screenplay by Arnold Somkin. (W)

243. BEST FRIENDS. (Warner Bros.-1982-Norman Jewison-PG).
An original screenplay written by Valerie Curtin and Barry
Levinson. (BFI, W)

244. THE BEST LITTLE WHOREHOUSE IN TEXAS. (Universal-
1982-Colin Higgins-R). Screenplay by Larry L. King, Peter
Masterson, and Colin Higgins, based on the stage-play book
by Larry L. King and Peter Masterson; Samuel French, n.d.
(BFI, HR, LACOPL, LAT, Q, V, W)

245. THE BEST WAY. (Specialty-1978-Claude Miller-N/R). Luc
Beraud and Claude Miller wrote this original screenplay.
(NYT, W)

246. BETRAYAL. (20th Century-Fox-1983-David Jones-R).
Screenplay written by Harold Pinter, based on his play;
Grove Press, 1979. (BFI, LACOPL, LAT, V)

247. THE BETSY. (Allied Artists-1978-Daniel Petrie Jr.-R).
William Bast and Walter Bernstein wrote this screenplay,
based on the novel by Harold Robbins; Trident Press, 1971,
502p. (HR, LACOPL, NYT, V, W)

248. BETTER LATE THAN NEVER. (Warner Bros.-1983-Bryan
      Forbes-PG). An original screenplay by Bryan Forbes. (W)

249. BETWEEN MIRACLES. (Damon International-1979-Nino
      Manfredi-N/R). Screenplay by Nino Manfredi, Leo Benvenuti,
      Piero De Bernardi, from a story by Nino Manfredi. (W)

250. BETWEEN THE COVERS. (International Producers-1975-X).
      No production credits available. (W)

251. BETWEEN THE LINES. (Midwest Films-1977-Joan Micklin
      Silver-R). A screenplay and story by Fred Barron. (NYT,
      V, W)

252. BEVERLY HILLS COP. (Paramount-1984-Martin Brest-R).
      Screenplay by Daniel Petrie Jr., based on a story by Danilo
      Boch and Daniel Petrie Jr. (HR, LAT, NYT, V)

253. BEYOND AND BACK. (Sunn Classic Pictures-1978-James L.
      Conway-G). A screenplay by Stephen Lord, based in part
      on the book by Ralph Wilkerson; Melodyland Productions,
      1977, 175p. (LACOPL, NYT, V, W)

254. BEYOND DEATH'S DOOR. (Sunn Classic Pictures-1979-
      Henning Schellerup-PG). Screenplay uncredited; based on
      book by Maurice Rawlings; T. Nelson, 1978, 173p. (LACOPL,
      W)

255. BEYOND EROTICA. (Joseph Brenner-1980-Jose Maria Forque-
      R). An original screenplay by Hermongenes Sainz and Jose
      Maria Forque. (W)

256. BEYOND EVIL. (IFI-SCOPE III-1980-Herb Freed-R). Paul
      Ross and Herb Freed wrote the screenplay, which was based
      on a story by David Baughn. (V, W)

257. BEYOND FULFILLMENT. (Essex-1976-Billy Thornberg-X).
      No screenplay credit given. (W)

258. BEYOND REASONABLE DOUBT. (Satori-1983-John Laing-
      N/R). David Yallop wrote the screenplay, based on his book.
      (W)

259. BEYOND THE DARKNESS. (Mid-Broadway-1976-Michael
      Wlater-R). An original screenplay by August Reiger. (W)

260. BEYOND THE DOOR. (Film Ventures International-1975-
      Oliver Hellman-R). Richard Barrett authored this original
      screenplay. (NYT, Q, W)

261. BEYOND THE DOOR #2. (Film Ventures International-1979-

Mario Bava-R). Lamberto Bava and Franco Barbieri wrote
this original screenplay. (W)

262. BEYOND THE LIMIT. (Paramount-1983-John Mackenzie-R).
A screenplay by Christopher Hampton, based on the novel
The Honorary Consul by Graham Greene; Simon and Schuster,
1973, 315p. (BFI, HR, LACOPL, LAT, V, W)

263. BEYOND THE POSEIDON ADVENTURE. (Warner Bros.-1979-
Irwin Allen-PG). Screenplay by Nelson Gidding, based on
the novel by Paul Gallico; Delacorte Press, 1978, 237p. (BFI,
HR, LACOPL, LAT, V, W)

264. BEYOND THE REEF. (Universal-1981-Frank C. Clark-PG).
Screenplay by Louis LaRusso II and Jim Carabatsos, based
on the novel Tikoyo and His Shark by Clement Richer; Knopf,
1951. (LACOPL, NYT, V, W)

265. BIDDY. (Sands Film-1983-Christine Edzard-N/R). Screenplay written by Christine Edzard. (V)

266. BIG ABNER. (Evart Industries-1976-X). No production
credits available. (W)

267. THE BIG BRAWL. (Warner Bros.-1980-Robert Clouse-R).
Robert Clouse wrote the screenplay, from a story by Robert
Clouse and Fred Weintraub. (V, W)

268. THE BIG BUS. (Paramount-1976-James Frawley-PG). Screenplay written by Fred Freeman and Lawrence J. Cohen. (NYT,
Q, W)

269. THE BIG CHILL. (Columbia-1983-Lawrence Kasdan-R). An
original screenplay written by Lawrence Kasdan and Barbara
Benedek. (HR, LAT, V)

270. THE BIG FIX. (Universal-1978-Jeremy Paul Kagan-PG).
Screenplay written by Roger L. Simon, based on his novel;
Straight Arrow Books, 1973, 183p. (LACOPL, NYT, Q, V, W)

271. BIG MEAT EATER. (Palace Pictures-1982-Chris Windsor-
N/R). Screenplay by Phil Savath, Laurence Keane, Chris
Windsor, with additional dialogue by Gisele Villeneuve. (BFI)

272. THE BIG RED ONE. (United Artists-1980-Samuel Fuller-PG).
An original screenplay by Samuel Fuller. (Q, V, W)

273. THE BIG SCORE. (Almi Films-1983-Fred Williamson-R). An
original screenplay written by Gail Morgan Hickman. (LAT,
V, W)

274. THE BIG SLEEP. (United Artists-1978-Michael Winner-R).
      Screenplay by Michael Winner, based on a novel by Raymond
      Chandler; World Publishing Co., 1939. (HR, LACOPL, NYT,
      V, W)

275. BIG THUMB. (Filmpeople Inc.-1977-Richard Lipton-X).
      Screenplay by Carl Stone and David Newburge. (V)

276. BIG WEDNESDAY. (Warner Bros.-1978-John Milius-PG).
      Screenplay written by John Milius and Dennis Aaberg; novel-
      ization by Dennis Aaberg; Bantam, 1978. (LACOPL, NYT,
      Q, W)

277. A BIGGER SPLASH. (Buzzy Enterprises-1975-Jack Hazan-
      N/R). Screenplay written by Jack Hazan and David Mingay.
      (BFI, W)

278. THE BILLION DOLLAR HOBO. (International Picture Show-
      1978-Stuart E. McGowan-G). An original screenplay written
      by Stuart E. McGowan, Tim Conway, and Roger Beatty. (W)

279. BILLY IN THE LOWLANDS. (Theatre Company of Boston-
      FTF Inc.-1979-Jan Egleson-N/R). An original screenplay
      written by Jan Egleson. (V, W)

280. BILLY JACK GOES TO WASHINGTON. (Taylor-Laughlin
      Distribution Co.-1977-T. C. Frank aka Tom Laughlin-N/R).
      An original screenplay written by Frank and Teresa Cristina
      (aka Tom Laughlin and Delores Taylor), adapted from the
      screenplay Mr. Smith Goes to Washington by Sidney Buchman,
      based on a story by Lewis R. Foster. (V, W)

281. THE BINGO LONG TRAVELING ALL-STARS AND MOTOR
      KINGS. (Universal-1976-John Badham-PG). A screenplay
      by Hal Barwood and Matthew Robbins, based on the novel by
      William Brashler; Harper, 1973, 244p. (HR, LACOPL, NYT,
      Q, V, W)

282. THE BIRCH INTERVAL. (Gamma III-1976-Delbert Mann-PG).
      A screenplay by Joanna Crawford, from her novel; Houghton,
      1964. (NYT, Q, W)

283. THE BIRCH WOOD. (No Distributor Given-1981-Andrzej
      Wajda-N/R). An original screenplay by Jaroslaw Isaszkiewica.
      (W)

      BIRDS OF A FEATHER see LA CAGE AUX FOLLES

284. BIRDS, ORPHANS AND FOOLS. (Golden-1976-Juri Jakubisko-
      R). Juri Jakubisko wrote this story and screenplay. (W)

285. BIRDY. (Tri-Star-1984-Alan Parker-R). Screenplay by
      Sandy Knopf and Jack Behr, based on the novel by William
      Wharton; Knopf, 1978, 309p. (HR, LACOPL, LAT, NYT, V)

286. BIRGITT HAAS MUST BE KILLED. (Frank Moreno-1982-
      Laurent Heynemann-N/R). Screenplay by Pierre Fabre,
      Laurent Heynemann, and Caroline Huppert. (LAT, W)

287. THE BISHOP'S BEDROOM. (Titanus-1977-Dino Risi-N/R).
      Screenplay by Leo Benvenuti and Piero DeBernardi, with the
      collaboration of Piero Chiara and Dino Risi. (V)

288. THE BITCH. (Brent Walker Productions-1979-Gerry O'Hara-
      R). Screenplay by Gerry O'Hara, based on a novel by
      Jackie Collins; Pocket Books, 1984, 256p. (LACOPL, V)

289. THE BITE. (808 Pictures-1975-Jerry Denby-X). No screen-
      play credit available. (W)

290. BITE THE BULLET. (Columbia-1975-Richard Brooks-PG).
      An original screenplay by Richard Brooks. (NYT, W)

291. THE BITTER TEARS OF PETRA VON KANT. (New Yorker-
      1976-Rainer Werner Fassbinder-N/R). An original screenplay
      by Rainer Werner Fassbinder. (W)

292. BITTERSWEET LOVE. (Avco Embassy-1976-David Miller-R).
      Adrian Morrall and D. A. Kellogg authored this screenplay.
      (NYT, Q, V, W)

293. BLACK AND SILVER. (BFI-Great Britain-1981-William and
      Marilyn Raban-N/R). William and Marilyn Raban wrote this
      screenplay based on the story The Birthday of the Infanta by
      Oscar Wilde; Macmillan, 1929. (BFI, LACOPL)

294. BLACK AND WHITE LIKE DAY AND NIGHT. (New Yorker-
      1981-Wolfgang Petersen-N/R). An original screenplay written
      by Jochen Wedgartner and Karl Heinz Willschrei. (LAT, NYT,
      W)

295. THE BLACK BIRD. (Columbia-1975-David Giler-PG). A
      screenplay by David Giler, from a story by Don M. Mankie-
      wicz and Gordon Cotler; novelization by Alexander Edwards;
      Warner Books, 1975, 141p. (LACOPL, NYT, Q, W)

296. THE BLACK CAT. (World Northal-1984-Lucio Fulci-R). A
      screenplay by Biagio Proietti and Lucio Fulci, from a story
      by Biagio Proietti, based on a story by Edgar Allan Poe in
      Complete Stories and Poems; Doubleday, 1966. (LACOPL, V)

297. THE BLACK DRAGON'S REVENGE. (Howard Mahler-1975-

Tommy Foo Ching-R). An original screenplay written by
Norbert Albertson. (W)

298. THE BLACK GESTAPO. (Bryanston-1975-Lee Frost-R).
      Screenplay written by Lee Frost and Wes Bishop, from a
      story by Ronald K. Goldman, Lee Frost and Wes Bishop. (W)

299. BLACK HEAT. (Independent International-1976-Al Adamson-
      R). No screenplay credits available. (W)

300. THE BLACK HOLE. (Buena Vista-1979-Gary Nelson-PG). A
      screenplay by Jeb Rosebrook and Gerry Day, based on a
      story by Jeb Rosebrook, Bob Barbash, and Richard Landau;
      novelization by Alan Dean Foster; Ballantine, 1979. (HR,
      LACOPL, LAT, Q, V, W)

301. BLACK JACK. (Kestral-1979-Kenneth Loach-N/R). A screen-
      play by Kenneth Loach, from the novel by Leon Garfield;
      Pantheon, 1968, 192p. (LACOPL, V)

302. BLACK JOY. (Elliott Kastner/Arnon Milchan Release-1977-
      Anthony Simmons-N/R). An original screenplay by Jamal Ali
      and Anthony Simmons, from a play by Jamal Ali. (V)

303. BLACK LITTER. (El Iman-1977-Manuel Gutierrez Aragon-
      N/R). An original screenplay by Manuel Gutierrez Aragon
      and Jose Luis Borau. (V)

304. BLACK LOLITA. (Parliament-1975-Stephen Gibson-R).
      Stephen Gibson and Mike Brown wrote this original screen-
      play. (W)

305. THE BLACK MARBLE. (Avco Embassy-1980-Harold Becker-
      PG). Screenplay written by Joseph Wambaugh, from his
      novel; Delacorte Press, 1978, 354p. (LACOPL, V, W)

306. BLACK MOON. (20th Century-Fox-1975-Louis Malle-R).
      Screenplay by Louis Malle and Ghislain Uhry, with additional
      dialogue by Joyce Bunuel. (NYT, Q, W)

307. BLACK OAK CONSPIRACY. (New World-Bob Kelljan-R).
      Screenplay written by Hugh Smith and Jesse Vint, from a
      story by Hugh Smith. (V)

308. THE BLACK PIRATE. (Cineriz-1977-Sergio Sollima and Al-
      berto Silvestri-N/R). No screenplay credits given. (V)

309. BLACK SHAMPOO. (Dimension-1976-Greydon Clark-R). An
      original screenplay by Alvin L. Fast and Greydon Clark. (W)

310. BLACK SOCKS. (Cineprobe-1975-Ronald Sullivan-X). An
      original screenplay by Joel Gross. (W)

311.   THE BLACK STALLION. (United Artists-1979-Carroll Ballard-
       G). Melissa Mathison, Jeanne Rosenberg, and William D.
       Wittliff wrote this screenplay based on the novel by Walter
       Farley; Random House, 1941. (HR, LACOPL, LAT, Q, V, W)

312.   THE BLACK STALLION RETURNS. (MGM/UA-1983-Robert
       Dalva-PG). Screenplay by Richard Kletter and Jerome Kass,
       based on the novel by Walter Farley; Random House, 1945,
       245p. (HR, LACOPL, LAT, V)

313.   BLACK STARLETT. (Omni-1975-Chris Munger-R). A screen-
       play by Howard Ostroff, from a story by Daniel B. Cady.
       (W)

314.   BLACK STREETFIGHTER. (New Line-1976-Timothy Galfas-
       N/R). An original screenplay by Tim Kelly and Melvyn
       Frohman. (W)

315.   BLACK SUNDAY. (Paramount-1977-John Frankenheimer-R).
       Screenplay by Ernest Lehman, Kenneth Ross, and Ivan Mof-
       fat, based on a novel by Thomas Harris; Putnam, 1975, 318p.
       (LACOPL, NYT, Q, W)

316.   BLACK TRASH. (Cinematic-1978-Chris Rowley-R). Screen-
       play written by Bima Stagg. (W)

317.   BLACKJACK. (SES International-1978-John Evans-R). An
       original screenplay by John Evans. (W)

318.   BLACKOUT. (New World-1978-Eddy Matalon-R). Screenplay
       by John C. W. Saxton, based on a story by John Dunning
       and Eddy Matalon. (V, W)

319.   THE BLADE MASTER, ATOR THE INVINCIBLE. (New Line
       Cinema-1984-David Hills-PG). A screenplay by David Hills.
       (V)

320.   BLADE RUNNER. (Warner Bros.-1982-Ridley Scott-R). A
       screenplay by Hampton Fancher and David Peoples, based on
       the novel Do Androids Dream of Electric Sheep by Philip K.
       Dick; Doubleday, 1968. (BFI, LACOPL, LAT, V)

321.   BLAISE PASCAL. (Entertainment Marketing-1980-Roberto
       Rossellini-N/R). A screenplay written by Marcella Mariani,
       Luciano Scaffa, and Roberto Rossellini. (W)

322.   BLAME IT ON RIO. (20th Century-Fox-1984-Stanley Donen-
       R). A screenplay written by Charlie Peters and Larry Gel-
       bart. (V)

323.   BLAME IT ON THE NIGHT. (Tri-Star Pictures-1984-Gene
       Taft-PG-13). A screenplay by Len Jenkin. (V)

324. BLAST. (New World-1976-Frank Arthur Wilson-R). An
original screenplay written by Frank Arthur Wilson. (W)

325. BLAZING STEWARDESSES. (Independent International-1975-
Al Adamson-R). No screenplay credits available. (W)

DIE BLECHTROMMEL see THE TIN DRUM

326. BLIND DATE. (Omega Pictures-1984-Nico Mastorakis-N/R).
An original screenplay by Nico Mastorakis. (V)

327. BLIND RAGE. (Trans World Films-1978-Efren C. Pinon-R).
A screenplay written by Jerry Tirazona and Leo Fong. (V,
W)

328. THE BLONDE CONNECTION. (Hampton International-1975-R).
No production credits available. (W)

329. BLOOD AND GUNS. (Movietime-1979-Giulio Petroni-R). No
screenplay credits available.

330. BLOOD AND GUTS. (Ambassador Films-1978-Paul Lynch-
N/R). A screenplay by Joseph McBride, William Gray, and
John Hunter, from an original story by Joseph McBride. (V)

331. BLOOD BEACH. (Jerry Gross-1981-Jeffrey Bloom-R). Jeffrey Bloom wrote this screenplay from an original story by
Jeffrey Bloom and Steven Nalevansky. (LAT, V, W)

332. BLOOD FEUD. (AFD-1980-Lina Wertmuller-R). An original
screenplay written by Lina Wertmuller. (W)

333. BLOOD IN THE STREETS. (Independent International-1975-
Sergio Sollima-R). The screenplay was a collaborative effort
by Arduino Maiuri, Massimo DeRita, and Sergio Sollima. (W)

334. THE BLOOD OF HUSSAIN. (Parindah Films-1980-Jamil
Dehlavi-N/R). An original screenplay by Jamil Dehlavi. (V)

335. BLOOD SIMPLE. (River Road-1984-Joel Coen-N/R). Joel
Coen and Ethan Coen authored this original screenplay. (V)

336. BLOOD, SWEAT AND FEAR. (Cinema Shares-1975-N/R). No
production credits available. (W)

337. BLOOD TIDE. (21st Century Distribution-1982-Richard
Jefferies-R). A screenplay written by Richard Jefferies.
(V, W)

338. BLOOD WATERS OF DR. Z. (Capital Productions-1982-Don
Barton-PG). An original screenplay by Lee Larew and Ron
Kivett. (V, W)

339. BLOOD WEDDING. (Libra-1981-Carlos Saura-N/R). Antonio
     Artero wrote the screenplay, based on the play by Federico
     Garcia Lorca, adapted by Alfredo Manas in Three Tragedies;
     New Directions, 1955. (BFI, LACOPL, LAT, W)

340. BLOODBROTHERS. (Warner Bros.-1978-Robert Mulligan-R).
     A screenplay by Walter Newman, based on the novel by
     Richard Price; Houghton Mifflin, 1976, 271p. (LACOPL, NYT,
     Q, V, W)

341. BLOODEATERS. (Parker National-1980-Chuck McCann-R).
     A screenplay by Chuck McCann. (V, W)

342. BLOODSUCKING FREAKS. (Troma-1982-Joel M. Reed-R).
     An original screenplay written by Joel M. Reed. (V, W)

343. BLOODY KIDS. (Palace Pictures-BFI-1979-Stephen Frears-
     N/R). An original screenplay by Stephen Poliakoff. (BFI)

344. BLOW OUT. (Filmways-1981-Brian De Palma-R). An original
     screenplay by Brian De Palma. (V, W)

345. BLOW TO THE HEART. (1982-Gianni Amelio-N/R). A
     screenplay by Gianni Amelio and Vincenzo Cerami, from a
     story by Gianni Amelio. (BFI)

346. BLOWDRY. (Great Exploitations-1976-Laser Scepter-X). An
     original screenplay by Sam Kitt. (V)

347. THE BLUE BIRD. (20th Century-Fox-1976-George Cukor-G).
     A screenplay written by Hugh Whitemore and Alfred Hayes,
     based on The Blue Bird by Maurice Maeterlinck; Dodd, 1925,
     211p. (LACOPL, NYT, Q, W)

348. BLUE COLLAR. (Universal-1978-Paul Schrader-R). Paul
     Schrader and Leonard Schrader wrote the screenplay, sug-
     gested by source material by Sydney A. Glass; novelization
     by Leonard Schrader; Bantam Books, 1978, 149p. (LACOPL,
     NYT, Q, V, W)

349. BLUE COUNTRY. (Gaumont-1978-Jean-Charles Tacchella-PG).
     Screenplay by Jean-Charles Tacchella. (NYT, W)

350. THE BLUE LAGOON. (Columbia-1980-Randal Kleiser-R).
     Screenplay by Douglas Day Stewart, based on the novel by
     Henry DeVere Stacpoole; Blue Lagoon Publishers, 1980, 193p.
     (HR, LACOPL, V, W)

351. BLUE MONEY. (Crown International-1975-Alain-Patrick
     Chappuis-R). No screenplay credits available. (W)

352. BLUE SKIES AGAIN. (Warner Bros.-1983-Richard Michaels-
      PG). An original screenplay by Kevin Sellers. (LAT, V)

353. BLUE SUNSHINE. (Cinema Shares-1978-Jeff Lieberman-R).
      Jeff Lieberman wrote this original screenplay. (W)

354. BLUE THUNDER. (Columbia-1983-John Badham-R). An orig-
      inal screenplay by Dan O'Bannon and Don Jakoby. (BFI,
      LAT, V)

355. THE BLUES BROTHERS. (Universal-1980-John Landis-R).
      A screenplay written by Dan Aykroyd and John Landis. (V,
      W)

356. BOARDWALK. (Atlantic Releasing Corp.-1979-Stephen
      Verona-N/R). A screenplay by Stephen Verona and Leigh
      Chapman. (Q, V, W)

357. THE BOAT. (Bavaria Atelier Film Production-1981-Wolfgang
      Petersen-N/R). A screenplay written by Wolfgang Petersen,
      based on the novel of the same title by Lothar-Guenther
      Buchheim; Knopf, 1975, 463p. (BFI, LACOPL, LAT, Q, V,
      W)

358. THE BOAT IS FULL. (Quartet-1981-Markus Imhoof-N/R).
      Markus Imhoof wrote this original screenplay. (LAT, W)

359. BOBBIE JO AND THE OUTLAW. (American International-
      1976-Mark L. Lester-R). A screenplay by Vernon Zimmer-
      man. (NYT, Q, W)

360. BOBBY DEERFIELD. (Columbia-1977-Sydney Pollack-PG).
      A screenplay by Alvin Sargent, based on the novel Heaven
      Has No Favorites by Erich Maria Remarque; Harcourt, 1961.
      (LACOPL, NYT, Q, V)

361. THE BOD SQUAD. (Film Ventures International-1976-R).
      No production credits available. (W)

      BODAS DE SANGRE see BLOOD WEDDING

362. BODY AND SOUL. (Cannon Group-1981-Geroge Bowers-R).
      An original screenplay by Leon Isaac Kennedy. (BFI, LAT,
      V, W)

363. BODY DOUBLE. (Columbia-1984-Brian De Palma-R). A
      screenplay by Robert J. Avrech and Brian De Palma, from a
      story by Brian De Palma. (V)

364. BODY HEAT. (Ladd/Warner Bros.-1981-Lawrence Kasdan-R).
      An original screenplay by Lawrence Kasdan. (BFI, LAT, V,
      W)

365. BODY ROCK. (New World Pictures-1984-Marcelo Epstein-PG-
      13). An original screenplay by Desmond Nakano. (LAT, V)

366. THE BODYGUARD. (Aquarius-1976-Simon Nuchtern-R). No
      screenplay credits available. (W)

367. THE BODYGUARD. (IFEX/Sovesportfilm-1982-Ali Khamrayev-
      N/R). An original screenplay written by Ali Khamrayev.
      (LAT, W)

368. BOESMAN AND LENA. (New Yorker-1976-Ross Devenish-
      N/R). Screenplay written by Athol Fugard, from his play;
      Oxford University Press, 1978, 299p. (LACOPL, NYT, W)

369. BOGARD. (L-T Films-1975-Timothy Galfas-X). An original
      screenplay by Tim Kelly and Melvyn Frohman. (W)

370. BOLERO. (Double 13-1982-Claude Lelouch-N/R). An original
      screenplay by Claude Lelouch. (W)

371. BOLERO. (Cannon Group-1984-John Derek-N/R). This orig-
      inal screenplay was written by John Derek. (V)

372. LE BON PLAISIR. (MK2-1984-Francis Girod-N/R). A screen-
      play authored by Francis Girod and Francoise Giroud, based
      on her novel; Mazarine, 1983, 297p. (LACOPL, V)

373. BON VOYAGE, CHARLIE BROWN (AND DON'T COME BACK).
      (Paramount-1980-Bill Melendez-G). Screenplay by Charles M.
      Schulz, based on his "Peanuts" characters. (V, W)

374. BONJOUR AMOUR. (Atlantic-1978-Roger Andrieux-N/R). An
      original screenplay by Roger Andrieux and Jean Marie Besnard.
      (NYT, W)

375. LES BONS DEBARRAS. (International Film Exchange-1981-
      Francis Mankiewicz-N/R). An original screenplay by Rejean
      Ducharme. (W)

376. THE BOOB TUBE. (Independent International-1975-X). No
      additional production credits available. (W)

377. THE BOOBY HATCH. (Constellation-1976-Rudy Ricci and
      John Russo-X). Screenplay by Rudy Ricci and John Russo.
      (W)

378. THE BOOGENS. (Jensen Farley-1982-James L. Conway-R).
      Screenplay by David O'Malley and Bob Hunt, from a story by
      Tom Chapman and David O'Malley. (LAT, W)

379. THE BOOGEY MAN. (Jerry Gross Organization-1980-Ulli
      Lommel-R). An original screenplay by Ulli Lommel. (V, W)

DAS BOOT see THE BOAT

380. THE BORDER. (Universal-1982-Tony Richardson-R). An original screenplay by Deric Washburn, Walon Green, and David Freeman. (BFI, HR, V, W)

381. BORDERLINE. (AFD-1980-Gerrold Freedman-PG). Steve Kline and Gerrold Freedman wrote this original screenplay. (BFI, Q, V, W)

UN BORGHESE PICCOLO PICCOLO see AN AVERAGE MAN

382. BORN AGAIN. (AVCO Embassy-1978-Irving Rapper-PG). Walter Bloch wrote the screenplay, from the book by Charles Colson; Chosen Books, 1976. (LACOPL, Q, V, W)

383. BORN TO RAISE HELL. (Marathon-1975-Roger Earl-X). No screenplay credits available. (W)

384. THE BOSOM FRIEND. (Euro-Centrafilm Release-1982-Dimitri Frenkel Frank-N/R). An original screenplay written by Dimitri Frenkel Frank. (V)

385. BOSS LADY. (Lima-1982-Chris Warfield-R). An original screenplay written by John Hayes. (W)

386. BOSS NIGGER. (Dimension-1975-Jack Arnold-PG). An original screenplay by Fred Williamson. (NYT, W)

387. THE BOSS' SON. (New American Cinema-1978-Bobby Roth-N/R). Bobby Roth wrote this original screenplay. (V, W)

388. BOTH WAYS. (Douglas-1975-Jerry Douglas-X). No screenplay credits given. (W)

389. THE BOTTOM LINE. (Silverstein-1978-Georges Lautner-R). An original screenplay by Francis Veber. (W)

390. BOULEVARD NIGHTS. (Warner Bros.-1979-Michael Pressman-R). Desmond Nakano wrote this original screenplay; novelization by Dewey Gram; Warner, 1979, 222p. (LACOPL, Q, V, W)

391. BOUND FOR GLORY. (United Artists-1976-Hal Ashby-PG). A screenplay by Robert Getchell, based on the autobiography of Woody Guthrie; Dutton, 1968, 430p. (LACOPL, NYT, Q, V, W)

392. THE BOUNTY. (Orion-1984-Roger Donaldson-PG). A screenplay written by Robert Bolt, based on the book Captain Bligh and Mr. Christian by Richard Hough; Dutton, 1972, 320p. (HR, LACOPL, LAT, NYT, V)

393. THE BOUNTY-HUNTER. (Tricontinental-1978-Sergio Giral-
     N/R). An original screenplay by Sergio Giral and Jorge
     Sotolongo. (W)

394. BOXOFFICE. (Josef Bogdanovich-1982-Josef Bogdanovich-
     N/R). An original screenplay by Josef Bogdanovich. (V, W)

395. A BOY AND HIS DOG. (LGJAF-1975-L. Q. Jones-N/R).
     An original screenplay by L. Q. Jones, based on the novella
     by Harlan Ellison. (LAT, NYT, W)

396. THE BOYS FROM BRAZIL. (20th Century-Fox-1978-Franklin
     J. Schaffner-R). Heywood Gould wrote the screenplay, based
     on the novel by Ira Levin; Random House, 1976, 275p.
     (LACOPL, NYT, Q, V, W)

397. THE BOYS IN COMPANY C. (Columbia-1978-Sidney J. Furie-
     R). An original screenplay by Rick Natkin and Sidney J.
     Furie. (HR, LAT, NYT, Q, V, W)

     BOZSKA EMA see THE DIVINE EMMA

398. BRADY'S ESCAPE. (Satori-1984-Pal Gabor-N/R). An origi-
     nal screenplay by William W. Lewis, from a story by Pal
     Gabor. (V)

399. BRAINSTORM. (MGM-1983-Douglas Trumbull-PG). A screen-
     play by Robert Stitzel and Philip Frank Messina, from a story
     by Bruce Joel Rubin. (BFI, LAT, V)

400. BRAINWAVES. (Motion Picture Marketing-1983-Ulli Lommel-
     PG). Ulli Lommel wrote the screenplay, with additional dia-
     log by Buz Alexander and Suzanne Love. (V)

401. BRANNIGAN. (United Artists-1975-Douglas Hickox-PG). A
     screenplay by Christopher Trumbo, Michael Butler, William P.
     McGivern, and William Norton, from a story by Christopher
     Trumbo and Michael Butler. (NYT, Q, W)

402. THE BRASS RING. (E. O. Productions-1975-Martin Beck-
     PG). An original screenplay by Grey Lynelle. (W)

403. BRASS TARGET. (United Artists/MGM-1978-John Hough-PG).
     Alvin Boretz wrote the screenplay, based on the novel The
     Algonquin Project by Frederick Nolan; Morrow, 1974, 222p.
     (LACOPL, NYT, Q, V, W)

404. BREAD AND CHOCOLATE. (World Northal-1978-Franco
     Brusati-N/R). An original screenplay by Franco Brusati,
     Iaia Fiastri and Nino Manfredi, based on a story by Franco
     Brusati. (NYT, Q, W)

405.   BREAK OF DAY. (GUO Films-1976-Ken Hannam-N/R).   A
       screenplay written by Cliff Green. (V)

406.   BREAKER BREAKER. (American International-1977-Don
       Hulette-PG). An original screenplay written by Terry
       Chambers; novelization by E. M. Corder; Pocket Books, 1977,
       205p. (HR, LACOPL, LAT, NYT, V, W)

407.   BREAKER MORANT. (New World/Quartet-1980-Bruce Beres-
       ford-N/R). A screenplay written by Bruce Beresford, Jona-
       than Hardy, and David Stevens, based on a play by Kenneth
       Ross. (Q, W)

408.   BREAKFAST IN BED. (William Haugse-1978-William Haugse-
       N/R). An original screenplay by William Haugse. (W)

409.   BREAKHEART PASS. (United Artists-1976-Tom Gries-PG).
       A screenplay by Alistair MacLean, from his novel; Doubleday,
       1974, 178p. (LACOPL, NYT, W)

410.   BREAKIN'. (MGM/UA & Cannon Group-1984-Joel Silberg-PG).
       A screenplay by Charles Parker, Allen DeBevoise, and Gerald
       Scaife, from a story by Charles Parker and Allen DeBevoise.
       (V)

411.   BREAKIN' 2, ELECTRIC BOOGALOO. (Tri-Star-1984-Sam
       Firstenberg-PG). Screenplay by Jan Ventura and Julie
       Reichert, based on characters created by Charles Parker and
       Allen DeBevoise. (LAT, V)

412.   BREAKING AWAY. (20th Century-Fox-1979-Peter Yates-PG).
       A screenplay by Steve Tesich; novelization by Joseph Howard;
       Warner, 1979, 191p. (LACOPL, Q, V, W)

413.   BREAKING GLASS. (Paramount-1980-Brian Gibson-PG).   An
       original screenplay by Brian Gibson. (LAT, W)

414.   BREAKING POINT. (20th Century-Fox-1976-Bob Clark-R).
       A screenplay by Roger E. Swaybill and Stanley Mann, from a
       story by Roger Swaybill. (W)

415.   BREAKOUT. (Columbia-1975-Tom Gries-PG). A screenplay
       by Howard B. Kreitsek, Marc Norman, and Elliott Baker, based
       on a novel by Warren Hinckle, William Turner, and Eliot
       Asinof. (W)

416.   BREAKTHROUGH. (Maverick Pictures-1981-Andrew McLaglen-
       PG). An original screenplay by Tony Williamson. (V, W)

417.   THE BREAKUP. (New Line Cinema-1975-Claude Chabrol-
       N/R). A screenplay by Claude Chabrol, based on the novel
       by Charlotte Armstrong. (W)

418. BREATHLESS. (Orion-1983-Jim McBride-R). A screenplay
by L. M. Kit Carson and Jim McBride, based on the script
for A Bout de Souffle, a 1959 film written by Jean-Luc Godard, with a story by Francois Truffaut. (BFI, HR, LAT, V)

419. A BREED APART. (Orion-1984-Philippe Mora-N/R). An
original screenplay by Paul Wheeler. (V)

420. A BRIDGE TOO FAR. (United Artists-1977-Richard Attenborough-PG). William Goldman wrote the screenplay, based
on the book by Cornelius Ryan; Simon & Schuster, 1974,
670p. (HR, LACOPL, NYT, Q, V, W)

421. A BRIEF VACATION. (Allied Artists-1975-Vittorio De Sica-
PG). Screenplay by Cesare Zavattini, from a story by
Rodolfo Sonego. (NYT, V)

422. BRIMSTONE AND TREACLE. (United Artists Classics-1982-
Richard Loncraine-R). Original screenplay by Dennis Potter. (BFI, LAT, V, W)

423. THE BRINK'S JOB. (Universal-1978-William Friedkin-PG).
Screenplay by Walon Green, based on the book by Noel Behn;
Putnam, 1977. (HR, LACOPL, NYT, Q, V, W)

424. BRITANNIA HOSPITAL. (Universal-1982-Lindsay Anderson-
R). Screenplay by David Sherwin. (BFI, LAT, V, W)

425. BROADWAY DANNY ROSE. (Orion-1984-Woody Allen-PG).
An original screenplay by Woody Allen. (V)

426. BROKEN ENGLISH. (Audieff Inc.-1984-Michi Gleason-N/R).
A screenplay written by Michi Gleason. (V)

427. BROKEN SKY. (Scandinavia Today-1982-Ingrid Thulin-N/R).
Screenplay credits not available. (W)

428. BRONCO BILLY. (Warner Bros.-1980-Clint Eastwood-PG).
Screenplay written by Dennis Hacklin. (Q, V, W)

429. BRONTE. (A Charlotte Ltd. Partnership-1984-Delbert Mann-
N/R). William Luce wrote this original screenplay. (V)

430. THE BRONTE SISTERS. (Gaumont-1979-Andre Techine-N/R).
A screenplay written by Andre Techine, Pascal Bonitzer, and
Jean Gruault. (V)

431. THE BROOD. (New World Pictures-1979-David Cronenberg-
R). An original screenplay by David Cronenberg. (V, W)

432. THE BROTHER FROM ANOTHER PLANET. (An A-Train Films

Production-1984-John Sayles-N/R). An original screenplay
written by John Sayles. (V)

433. BROTHERHOOD OF DEATH. (Downtown-1976-Bill Berry-R).
Screenplay written by Bill Berry, from a story by Ronald K.
Goldman. (W)

434. BROTHERS. (Warner Bros.-1977-Arthur Barron-R). A
screenplay by Edward and Mildred Lewis. (NYT, Q, V)

435. BROTHERS AND SISTERS. (British Film Institute-1980-
Richard Woolley-N/R). An original screenplay by Richard
Woolley and Tammy Walker. (V)

436. THE BROTHERS KARAMAZOV. (Columbia-1980-Ivan Pyriev-
N/R). A screenplay written by Ivan Pyriev, based on the
novel by Fyodor Dostoyevsky; Norton, 1976, 887p. (LACOPL,
W)

437. BRUBAKER. (20th Century-Fox-1980-Stuart Rosenberg-R).
Screenplay by W. D. Richter, suggested from a book by
Thomas Murton and Joe Hyams. (LACOPL, Q, V, W)

438. BRUCE LEE AND I. (Pacific Grove-1975-Bruce Lee-R). No
screenplay credits available. (W)

439. BRUCE LEE-SUPER DRAGON. (Allied Artists-1976-R). No
production credits available. (W)

440. BRUCE VS. THE BLACK DRAGON. (Ark Films-1978-R). No
production credits available. (W)

441. BRUTAL JUSTICE. (Aquarius-1978-Bert Lenzi-R). An original screenplay by Bert Lenzi. (W)

442. BUCK ROGERS IN THE 25TH CENTURY. (Universal-1979-
Daniel Haller-PG). A screenplay by Glen A. Larson and
Leslie Stevens. (LAT, Q, V, W)

443. BUCKSTONE COUNTY PRISON. (Film Ventures International-
1979-Jimmy Huston-R). An original screenplay by Tom
McIntyre. (W)

444. BUCKTOWN. (American International-1975-Arthur Marks-R).
Screenplay written by Bob Ellison. (NYT, W)

445. BUDAPEST TALES. (Hungarofilm-1982-Istvan Szabo-N/R).
Screenplay written by Istvan Szabo. (W)

446. BUDDING LOVE. (Prodis-1977-Roger Andrieux-N/R). A
screenplay by Roger Andrieux and Jean-Marie Benard. (V)

447. BUDDY BUDDY. (MGM/United Artists-1981-Billy Wilder-R).
Screenplay by Billy Wilder and I. A. L. Diamond, based on a
play and story by Francis Veber. (BFI, LAT, V, W)

448. THE BUDDY HOLLY STORY. (Columbia-1978-Steve Rash-PG).
A screenplay by Robert Gittler, from a story by Steve Rash
and Fred Bauer; novelization by Robert Gittler; Ballantine,
1978. (HR, LACOPL, LAT, NYT, Q, W)

449. THE BUDDY SYSTEM. (20th Century-Fox-1984-Glenn Jordan-
PG). A screenplay by Mary Agnes Donoghue. (V)

450. BUFFALO BILL AND THE INDIANS, OR SITTING BULL'S
HISTORY LESSON. (United Artists-1976-Robert Altman-PG).
A screenplay by Robert Altman and Alan Rudolph, based on
the play Indians by Arthur Koppit; Hill & Wang, 1964, 81p.
(HR, LACOPL, LAT, NYT, Q, V, W)

451. BUFFALO RIDER. (Starfire-1978-George Lauris-PG). No
screenplay credits available. (W)

452. BUG. (Paramount-1975-Jeannot Szwarc-PG). A screenplay
by William Castle and Thomas Page, based on The Hephaestus
Plague by Thomas Page; Putnam, 1973, 191p. (LACOPL,
NYT, Q, W)

453. THE BUGS BUNNY / ROAD RUNNER MOVIE. (Warner Bros.-
1979-Chuck Jones-N/R). Screenplay written by Mike Maltese
and Chuck Jones. (W)

454. BUGS BUNNY SUPERSTAR. (Hare Raising Films-1975-Larry
Jackson-N/R). Screenplay credits not given. (W)

455. BUGS BUNNY'S 3RD MOVIE: 1001 RABBIT TALES. (Warner
Bros.-1982-David Detiege, Art Davis, Bill Perez-G). A
screenplay from stories by John Dunn, David Detiege, and
Friz Freleng. (V, W)

456. BUGSY MALONE. (Paramount-1976-Alan Parker-G). Screenplay originally written for the screen by Alan Parker. (NYT,
Q, W)

457. THE BULL BUSTER. (Cinemagic-1975-PG). No production
credits given. (W)

458. BULLSHOT. (A Handmade Films-1983-Dick Clement-N/R).
A screenplay by Ron House, Diz White and Alan Shearman.
(BFI, V)

459. BULLY. (Maturo Image Corp.-1978-Peter H. Hunt-PG). A
screenplay by Jerome Alden. (V, W)

460. BURIED ALIVE. (Aquarius Releasing-1984-Joe D'Amato aka
     Aristide Massaccesi-N/R). An original screenplay written by
     Ottavio Fabbri. (V)

461. THE BURNING. (A Filmways Release-1981-Tony Maylam-R).
     A screenplay by Peter Lawrence and Bobby Weinstein, based
     on a story by Harvey Weinstein, Tony Maylam and Brad Grey.
     (V, W)

462. BURNOUT. (Crown International-1979-Graham Meech-
     Burkestone-PG). A screenplay by Martin J. Rosen. (W)

463. BURNT OFFERINGS. (United Artists-1976-Dan Curtis-PG).
     A screenplay by William F. Nolan and Dan Curtis, based on
     the novel by Robert Marasco; Delacorte, 1973, 277p. (HR,
     NYT, Q, W)

464. BUSH MAMA. (Tricontinental-1979-Haile Gerima-N/R). No
     screenplay credits given. (W)

465. THE BUSHIDO BLADE. (Trident-1981-Tom Kotani-R). A
     screenplay by William Overgard. (V, W)

466. BUSTIN' LOOSE. (Universal-1981-Oz Scott-R). A screen-
     play by Roger L. Simon, adapted by Lonne Elder III, from a
     story by Richard Pryor. (V, W)

467. BUTCH AND SUNDANCE: THE EARLY DAYS. (20th Century-
     Fox-1979-Richard Lester-PG). Screenplay by Allan Burns,
     based on chracters created by William Goldman; novelization
     by William Goldman. (HR, LACOPL, Q, V, W)

468. BUTTERFLY. (Analysis Films-1982-Matt Cimber-R). A
     screenplay by John Goff and Matt Cimber, based on the
     novel The Butterfly by James M. Cain, adapted by Matt
     Cimber. (BFI, LAT, V, W)

469. BY DESIGN. (Atlantic-1982-Claude Jutra-N/R). Screenplay
     written by Joe Wiesenfeld, Claude Jutra, and David Eames.
     (LAT, W)

470. BYE-BYE BRAZIL. (Carnaval/Unifilm-1980-Carlos Diegues-
     N/R). Screenplay written by Carlos Diegues. (LAT, W)

471. C. B. HUSTLERS. (Rochelle-1978-Stuart Segall-R). John
     Alderman and John Goff wrote the screenplay, from a story
     by Martin Gatsby. (W)

472. C. B. MAMAS. (Mitchell Brothers-1976-James Mitchell and
     Artie Mitchell-X). No screenplay credit given.

473. C. H. O. M. P. S. (American International-1980-Don Chaffey-
G). A screenplay by Dick Robbins, Duane Poole and Joseph
Barbera, from a story by Joseph Barbera. (V, W)

474. C. H. U. D. (New World Pictures-1984-Douglas Creek-R).
A screenplay by Parnell Hall. (V)

475. C. O. D. (Lone Star Pictures International-1983-Chuck
Vincent-PG). A screenplay written by Chuck Vincent, Rick
Marx, and Jonathan Hannah, from a story by Wolfgang von
Schiber. (V)

476. CABOBLANCO. (Avco Embassy-1981-J. Lee Thompson-R).
Mort Fine and Milton Gelman co-authored this screenplay.
(LAT, V, W)

477. CADDIE. (Atlantic Releasing Corp-1981-Donald Crombie-
N/R). An original screenplay by Joan Long. (W)

478. CADDYSHACK. (Orion/Warner Bros.-1980-Harold Ramis-R).
A screenplay by Brian Doyle-Murray, Harold Ramis, and
Douglas Kenney. (V, W)

479. CAFE EXPRESS. (Summit Feature Distributors-1981-Nanni
Loy-N/R). An original story and screenplay by Nanni Loy.
(LAT, V, W)

480. LA CAGE AUX FOLLES. (United Artists-1979-Edouard
Molinaro-R). A screenplay and adaptation by Edouard
Molinaro, Marcello Danon, Jean Poiret, based on a play by
Jean Poiret. (HR, LAT, V, W)

481. LA CAGE AUX FOLLES II. (United Artists-1981-Edouard
Molinaro-R). A screenplay by Francis Veber, from a story
by Francis Veber, Jean Poiret, and Marcello Danon. (LAT,
V, W)

482. CAGED FURY. (Saturn International Pictures-1984-Cirio H.
Santiago-R). An original screenplay by Bobby Greenwood.
(V)

483. CAGED WOMEN. (Motion Picture Marketing-1984-Vincent
Dawn aka Bruno Mattei-R). An original screenplay by P.
Molteni and Oliver Lemat. (V)

484. CAL. (Warner Bros.-1984-Pat O'Connor-N/R). A screenplay
by Bernard MacLaverty, based on his novel; G. Braziller,
1983, 170p. (LACOPL, V)

485. CALIFORNIA DREAMING. (American International-1979-John

Hancock-R). A screenplay written by Ned Wynn. (Q, V, W)

486. CALIFORNIA SUITE. (Columbia Pictures-1978-Herbert Ross-PG). A screenplay by Neil Simon, based on his play; Random House, 1977. (LACOPL, V, W)

487. CALIGULA. (Penthouse Films-1980-Giovanni Tinto Brass-X). The screenplay, though uncredited, was written by Gore Vidal, adapted from his own story. (BFI, LAT, V, W)

488. CALL HIM MR. SHATTER. (Avco Embassy-1975-Michael Carreras-R). Don Houghton wrote the screenplay. (W)

489. CALL ME ANGEL SIR! (Jill Ross-1976-Kiki Young-X). A screenplay by E. Von Eaton. (W)

490. CALL OF THE WILD. (Constantin-1975-Ken Annakin-PG). Hubert Frank and Tibor Reves wrote the screenplay, based on a novel by Jack London; Macmillan, 1963, 128p. (LACOPL, W)

491. CALLAN. (Cinema National-1975-Don Sharpe-PG). A screenplay by James Mitchell, from his novel A Red File for Callan; Simon & Schuster, 1969, 173p. (HR, LACOPL, W)

492. THE CAMEL BOY. (Yoram Gross Film-1984-Yoram Gross-N/R). A screenplay by Yoram Gross and John Palmer. (V)

493. CAMERA BUFF. (New Yorker-1983-Krzysztof Kieslowski-N/R). An original screenplay by Krzysztof Kieslowski. (W)

494. CAMMINACAMMINA. (Gaumont-1983-Ermanno Almi-N/R). Ermanno Almi wrote the screenplay. (V)

495. CAN I DO IT ... TIL I NEED GLASSES? (National-American Entertainment Corp.-1979-I. Robert Levy-R). A screenplay by Mike Callie and Mike Price, based on an original story by Mike Callie and I. Robert Levy. (V)

496. CAN SHE BAKE A CHERRY PIE? (International Rainbow Pictures-1983-Henry Jaglom-N/R). A screenplay written by Henry Jaglom. (LAT, V)

497. CANDLESHOE. (Buena Vista-1978-Norman Tokar-G). A screenplay by David Swift and Rosemary Anne Sisson, based on Christmas at Candleshoe by Michael Innes; Dodd, 1953. (LACOPL, Q, W)

498. CANDY LIPS. (Honeypot-1976-Cecil B. Damill-X). No screenplay credit given. (W)

499. THE CANDY TANGERINE MAN. (Moonstone-1975-Matt Cimber-R). A screenplay written by George Theakos. (W)

500. CANDY'S CANDY. (Variety-1976-Renau Pieri-X). A screenplay by Renau Pieri. (W)

CANICULE see DOG DAY

501. CANNERY ROW. (United Artists-1982-David S. Ward-PG). A screenplay written by David S. Ward, based on John Steinbeck's novels Cannery Row--Viking, 1945, 208p.--and Sweet Thursday--Viking, 1954, 273p. (BFI, LACOPL, LAT, V)

502. CANNIBALS IN THE STREETS. (Almi Cinema 5-1982-Anthony M. Dawson aka Antonio Margheriti-R). A screenplay by Antonio Margheriti and Jimmy Gould, from a story by Jimmy Gould. (V, W)

503. CANNONBALL. (New World-1976-Paul Bartel-PG). An original screenplay by Paul Bartel and Donald C. Simpson. (W)

504. THE CANNONBALL RUN. (20th Century-Fox-1981-Hal Needham-PG). An original screenplay by Brock Yates. (LAT, Q, V, W)

505. CANNONBALL RUN II. (Warner Bros./Golden Harvest-1984-Hal Needham-PG). A screenplay by Harvey Miller, Hal Needham, and Albert S. Ruddy, based on characters created by Brock Yates. (V)

506. CAN'T STOP THE MUSIC. (Associated Film Distributors-1980-Nancy Walker-PG). An original screenplay by Bronte Woodward and Allan Carr. (V, W)

507. CANTATA DE CHILE. (Tricontinental-1978-Humberto Solas-N/R). An original screenplay by Humberto Solas, with the collaboration of Patricio Manns, Manuel Payan, Orlando Rojas, and Jorge Herrera. (W)

508. THE CANTERBURY TALES. (United Artists-1980-Pier Paolo Pasolini-N/R). A screenplay by Pier Paolo Pasolini, based on Geoffrey Chaucer's Canterbury Tales; Random House, 1964, 332p. (LACOPL, W)

509. CAPONE. (20th Century-Fox-1975-Steve Carver-R). A screenplay by Howard Browne. (Q, W)

510. CAPRICORN ONE. (Warner Bros.-1978-Peter Hyams-PG). A screenplay by Peter Hyams. (Q, V, W)

511. CAPTAIN LUST. (Anonymous Releasing Triumvirate-1977-

Beau Buchanan-X). A screenplay by Steven Barry and Beau
Buchanan. (V)

512. THE CAPTURE OF BIGFOOT. (Studio Film Corp.-1979-Bill
      Rebane-PG). A screenplay by Ingrid Neumayer and Bill
      Rebane. (W)

513. THE CAR. (Universal-1977-Elliot Silverstein-PG). A screen-
      play by Dennis Shryack and Michael Butler. (Q, V, W)

514. CAR WASH. (Universal-1976-Michael Schultz-PG). An origi-
      nal screenplay written by Joel Schumacher. (Q, W)

515. CARAVAN TO VACCARES. (Bryanston-1976-Geoffrey Reeve-
      PG). A screenplay by Paul Wheeler, based on the novel by
      Alistair MacLean; Doubleday, 1970, 259p. (HR, LACOPL, Q,
      V, W)

516. CARAVANS. (Universal-1978-James Fargo-PG). A screen-
      play by Nancy Voyles Crawford, Thomas A. McMahon, and
      Lorraine Williams, based on the novel by James A. Michener;
      Fawcett, 1973, 438p. (HR, LACOPL, LAT, V, W)

517. CARBON COPY. (Avco Embassy-1981-Michael Schultz-PG).
      An original screenplay by Stanley Shapiro. (LAT, Q, V, W)

518. CARDIAC ARREST. (Film Ventures International-1980-Murray
      Mintz-PG). An original screenplay written by Murray Mintz.
      (W)

519. CARELESS. (Senilita-1982-Mauro Bolognini-N/R). No screen-
      play credit given; based on a novel by Italo Svevo. (W)

520. THE CARHOPS. (NMD-1980-Peter Locke-R). A screenplay
      by Paul Ross and Michael Blank. (W)

521. CARMEN. (Emiliano Piedra-1983-Carlos Saura-N/R). A
      screenplay by Carlos Saura. (LAT, V)

522. CARNAL HAVEN. (Troy Benny-1975-Troy Benny-X). A
      screenplay written by Troy Benny. (W)

523. CARNAL MADNESS. (Rainbow-1975-Gregory Corarito-R).
      No screenplay credits given. (W)

524. CARNIVAL. (International Film Exchange-1982-T. Lioznova-
      N/R). Screenplay written by A. Rodionova and T. Lioznova.
      (W)

525. CARNIVAL MAGIC. (Krypton Corp-1982-Al Adamson-N/R).
      A screenplay by Mark Weston and Bob Levine. (V)

526. CARNIVAL OF BLOOD. (Monarch-1976-Leonard Kirtman-PG).
      No screenplay credits available. (W)

527. CARNY. (United Artists-1980-Robert Kaylor-R). Thomas
      Baum wrote the screenplay, based on a story by Phoebe
      Kaylor, Robert Kaylor, and Robbie Robertson. (BFI, Q, V,
      W)

528. CARO MICHELE. (Libra-1978-Mario Monicelli-N/R). A
      screenplay by Suso Cecchi D'Amico and Tonino Guerra,
      based on a novel by Natalia Ginzburg. (W)

529. CARRIE. (United Artists-1976-Brian De Palma-R). A
      screenplay by Lawrence D. Cohen, based on the novel by
      Stephen King; Doubleday, 1974, 199p. (HR, LACOPL, LAT,
      V, W)

530. CARRY ON EMMANUELLE. (Hemdale International-1978-
      Gerald Thomas-N/R). Lance Peters wrote this original
      screenplay. (V)

531. CARRY ON ENGLAND. (Rank-1976-Gerald Thomas-N/R).
      Jack Seddon and David Pursall wrote this screenplay. (V)

532. THE CARS THAT EAT PEOPLE. (New Line-1976-Peter Weir-
      PG). No screenplay credit given. (W)

533. CASANOVA. (Universal-1976-Federico Fellini-R). A screen-
      play by Federico Fellini and Bernardino Zapponi, liberally
      interpreted from The Story of My Life by Giacomo Casanova.
      (NYT, Q, V, W)

534. THE CASE AGAINST FERRO. (Specialty-1980-Alain Corneau-
      N/R). A screenplay by Alain Corneau and Daniel Boulanger.
      (W)

535. CASEY'S SHADOW. (Columbia-1978-Martin Ritt-PG). A
      screenplay by Carol Sobieski, based on the short story
      "Ruidoso" by John McPhee; novelization by Burton Wohl;
      Bantam, 1978. (LACOPL, Q, V, W)

536. CASOTTO. (Medusa Film-1980-Sergio Citti-N/R). A screen-
      play by Sergio Citti and Vincenzo Cerami. (V)

537. THE CASSANDRA CROSSING. (Avco Embassy-1977-George
      Pan Cosmatos-R). A screenplay written by Tom Mankiewicz,
      Robert Katz, and George Pan Cosmatos, from a story by
      Robert Katz and George Pan Cosmatos. (V)

538. THE CASTLE OF FU MANCHU. (International Cinema-1975-
      Jess Franco-PG). Peter Welbeck wrote this original screen-
      play. (W)

539. CAT AND MOUSE. (Quartet-1978-Claude Lelouch-PG).
     Screenplay written by Claude Lelouch. (W)

540. THE CAT FROM OUTER SPACE. (Buena Vista-1978-Norman
     Tokar-G). Ted Key wrote this original screenplay; noveliza-
     tion by Ted Key; Pocket Books, 1978. (LACOPL, V, W)

541. CAT MURKIL AND THE SILKS. (Gamma III-1976-John
     Bushelman-R). William C. Thomas wrote this screenplay.
     (W)

542. CAT PEOPLE. (Universal-1982-Paul Schrader-R). A screen-
     play written by Alan Ormsby, based on the story by DeWitt
     Bodeen. (HR, LAT, Q, V, W)

543. THE CATAMOUNT KILLING. (Hallmark-1975-Krzysztof
     Zanussi-N/R). A screenplay written by Julian and Sheila
     More, based on I'd Rather Stay Poor by James Hadley Chase.
     (W)

544. CATHERINE & CO. (Warner Bros.-1976-Michel Boisrond-R).
     A screenplay written by Leo L. Fuchs and Catherine Breillat,
     based on a novel by Edouard DeSegonzac. (Q, W)

545. CATHY'S CURSE. (21st Century-1980-Eddy Matalon-R). No
     screenplay credits available. (W)

546. CATTLE ANNIE AND LITTLE BRITCHES. (Universal-1981-
     Lamont Johnson-PG). A screenplay by David Eyre and
     Robert Ward, based on a screen story by Robert Ward, from
     his novel; Morrow, 1978, 240p. (LACOPL, LAT, Q, V, W)

547. THE CAULDRON OF DEATH. (Film Ventures International-
     1979-R). A screenplay written by Joe Maesso. (W)

548. CAVEMAN. (United Artists-1981-Carl Gottlieb-PG). A screen-
     play by Rudy DeLuca and Carl Gottlieb. (LAT, Q, V, W)

549. CEDDO. (New Yorker Films-1978-Ousmane Sembene-N/R).
     An original screenplay by Ousmane Sembene. (BFI, W)

550. CELESTE. (New Yorker-1982-Percy Adlon-N/R). A screen-
     play by Percy Adlon, based on Monsieur Proust by Celeste
     Albaret. (BFI, LAT, W)

551. CELINE AND JULIE GO BOATING. (New Yorker Films-1978-
     Jacques Rivette-N/R). A screenplay by Jacques Rivette,
     Eduardo de Gregorio, Juliet Berto, Dominique Labourier,
     Bulle Ogier, and Marie-France Pisier. (W)

552. THE CENSUS TAKER. (Argentum Prods.-1984-Bruce Cook-

N/R). A screenplay written by Bruce Cook and Gordon Smith. (V)

553. C'EST LA VIE ROSE. (Distelfilm Berlin-1977-Hans-Christian Stenzel-N/R). Screenplay written by Hans-Christian Stenzel, with dialog by Joerg Fauser. (V)

554. CHAINED HEAT. (Jensen Farley-1983-Paul Nicolas-R). A screenplay written by Vincent Mongol and Paul Nicolas. (LAT, V, W)

555. THE CHALLENGE. (CBS Theatrical Films-1982-John Frankenheimer-R). Screenplay written by Richard Maxwell and John Sayles. (BFI, LAT, Q, V, W)

556. CHALLENGE OF DEATH. (Henry Tan-1979-R). No production credits available. (W)

557. CHALLENGE OF THE DRAGON. (Cannon-1975-R). No production credits available. (W)

558. CHALLENGE TO WHITE FANG. (Premiere-1975-Lucio Fulci-PG). A screenplay written by Albert Silvestri, based on a story by Jack London. (W)

559. CHAMELEON. (Jon Jost-Rising Sun-1978-Jon Jost-N/R). A screenplay by Bob Glaudini and Jon Jost. (V)

560. THE CHAMP. (UA/MGM-1979-Franco Zeffirelli-PG). Walter Newman wrote the screenplay from a story by Frances Marion. (HR, Q, V, W)

561. CHAMPAGNE FOR BREAKFAST. (Lima-1981-Chris Warfield-R). A screenplay by John Hayes. (BFI, V)

562. CHAMPIONS. (Embassy-1984-John Irvin-PG). A screenplay by Evan Jones, based on the book Champion's Story by Bob Champion and Jonathan Powell; Coward, McCann & Geoghegan, 1982. (HR, LACOPL, LAT, V)

563. CHAN IS MISSING. (Wayne Wang-1982-Wayne Wang-N/R). Screenplay by Wayne Wang; Bamboo Ridge Press, 1984, 80p. (LAT, V)

564. CHANEL SOLITAIRE. (United Film Distribution-1981-George Kaczender-R). A screenplay by Julian More, from the novel by Mme. Claude Delay. (BFI, V, W)

565. A CHANGE OF SEASONS. (20th Century-Fox-1980-Richard Lang-R). A screenplay by Erich Segal, Ronni Kern, Fred Segal, from a story by Erich Segal and Martin Ransohoff. (Q, V, W)

566.   THE CHANGELING. (Associated Film Distribution-1980-Peter
       Medak-R). A screenplay by William Gray, from a story by
       Russell Hunte. (W)

567.   THE CHANT OF JIMMIE BLACKSMITH. (New Yorker-1980-
       Fred Schepisi-N/R). A screenplay by Fred Schepisi, from a
       novel by Thomas Keneally; Viking Press, 1972, 178p.
       (LACOPL, W)

568.   THE CHAPERONE. (Mirage-1975-Jaacov Jaacovi-X). No
       screenplay credit given. (W)

569.   CHAPTER TWO. (Columbia-1979-Robert Moore-PG). A
       screenplay by Neil Simon, based on his play of the same
       title; Random House, 1979, 132p. (HR, LACOPL, Q, V, W)

570.   CHARIOTS OF FIRE. (Ladd Co./Warner Bros.-1981-Hugh
       Hudson-PG). A screenplay by Colin Welland; novelization by
       W. J. Weatherby; Dell, 1981. (HR, LACOPL, LAT, Q, V, W)

571.   THE CHARITY BALL. (1976-X). No production credits
       available. (W)

572.   CHARLES AND LUCIE. (Nu-Image Film-1980-Nelly Kaplan-
       N/R). A screenplay by Nelly Kaplan, Jean Chapot, and
       Claude Makovski. (W)

573.   CHARLESTON. (Analysis Films-1978-Marcello Fondato-PG).
       A screenplay by Elio Scardamaglia and Marcello Fondato.
       (V, W)

574.   CHARLIE AND THE HOOKER. (Group I Films-1979-Emmanuele
       Summers-R). No screenplay credit given. (W)

575.   CHARLIE CHAN AND THE CURSE OF THE DRAGON QUEEN.
       (American Cinema-1981-Clive Donner-PG). Stan Burns and
       David Axelrod wrote the screenplay, from a story by Jerry
       Sherlock. (LAT, V, W)

576.   CHARLOTTE. (Gamma III-1975-Roger Vadim-X). No screen-
       play credit given. (Q, W)

577.   LE CHAT. (Joseph Green-1975-Pierre Granier-Deferre-N/R).
       A screenplay by Pierre Granier-Deferre and Pascal Jardin,
       based on the novel Cat by Georges Simenon; Harcourt, 1967.
       (LACOPL, W)

578.   CHATTER-BOX. (American International-1977-Tom De Simone-
       R). A screenplay by Mark Rosin and Norman Yonemoto, from
       a story by Tom De Simone. (V)

579. THE CHEAP DETECTIVE. (Columbia-1978-Robert Moore-PG).
A screenplay by Neil Simon; novelization by Robert Grossbach. (HR, LACOPL, Q, V, W)

580. CHEAPER TO KEEP HER. (American Cinema-1980-Ken
Annakin-R). An original screenplay by Timothy Harris and
Herschel Weingrod. (LAT, V, W)

581. CHECK MY OIL, BABY. (French-1976-Norbert Terry-X).
No screenplay credits given. (W)

582. CHECKERED FLAG OR CRASH. (Universal-1978-Alan Gibson-
PG). A screenplay by Michael Allin. (W)

583. CHEECH & CHONG STILL SMOKIN'. (Paramount-1983-Thomas
Chong-R). Thomas Chong and Richard Cheech Marin wrote
this original screenplay. (HR, LAT, V)

584. CHEECH AND CHONG'S NEXT MOVIE. (Universal-1980-
Thomas Chong-R). Screenplay written by Thomas Chong and
Richard Cheech Marin. (Q, V, W)

585. CHEECH & CHONG'S NICE DREAMS. (Columbia-1981-Thomas
Chong-R). A screenplay by Thomas Chong and Richard
Cheech Marin. (HR, LAT, Q, V, W)

586. CHEECH AND CHONG'S THE CORSICAN BROTHERS. (Orion-
1984-Thomas Chong-R). An original screenplay written by
Richard Cheech Marin and Thomas Chong. (LAT, V)

587. CHEERLEADERS' BEACH PARTY. (Cannon-1978-Alex E.
Goitein-R). A screenplay written by Chuck Vincent. (W)

588. CHEERLEADERS' WILD WEEKEND. (Dimension-1979-Jeff
Werner-R). A screenplay by D. W. Gilbert and Jason
Williams. (W)

589. CHEESE. (1976-Alan West-X). No production credits given.
(W)

LES CHEMINS DE L'EXIL see THE ROADS OF EXILE

590. CHER VICTOR. (Peppercorn-Wormser-1976-Robin Davis-PG).
No screenplay credits given. (W)

591. THE CHESS PLAYERS. (Creative Films-1978-Satyajit Ray-
N/R). A screenplay by Satyajit Ray. (W)

592. CHESTY ANDERSON, U. S. NAVY. (Atlas-1976-Ed Forsyth-
R). A screenplay by Paul Pompian and H. F. Green. (W)

593.   THE CHICKEN CHRONICLES. (Avco Embassy-1977-Francis
        Simon-PG). A screenplay by Paul Diamond. (Q, W)

594.   LA CHIENNE. (Ajay-1976-Jean Renoir-N/R). A screenplay
        by Jean Renoir and Andre Girard, from the novel by Georges
        de la Fouchardiere. (LAT, W)

        THE CHILD see KILL AND GO HIDE

595.   A CHILD IS A WILD YOUNG THING. (Skinner-1976-Peter
        Skinner-N/R). Screenplay written by Peter Skinner. (W)

596.   CHILD UNDER A LEAF. (Cinema National-1975-George
        Bloomfield-R). A screenplay written by George Bloomfield.
        (W)

597.   THE CHILDREN. (World Northal-1980-Max Kalmanowicz-R).
        A screenplay by Carlton J. Albright and Edward Terry. (W)

598.   CHILDREN OF BABYLON. (Joden-1980-Lennie Little-White-
        N/R). An original screenplay by Lennie Little-White. (V,
        W)

599.   CHILDREN OF RAGE. (LSV Productions-1975-Arthur Allan
        Seidelman-PG). A screenplay by Arthur Allan Seidelman,
        based on a story by Arthur Allan Seidelman and Anna Laura.
        (W)

600.   THE CHILDREN OF SANCHEZ. (Lone Star Pictures-1978-Hall
        Bartlett-R). A screenplay by Cesare Zavattini and Hall
        Bartlett, from the book by Oscar Lewis; Random House, 1961,
        449p. (LACOPL, V)

601.   CHILDREN OF THE CORN. (New World Pictures-1984-Fritz
        Kiersch-R). A screenplay written by George Goldsmith,
        based on a story by Stephen King. (V)

602.   CHILDREN OF THE EARTH. (A. S. Elan Film Production-
        1984-Lalla Mikkelsen-N/R). A screenplay written by Lalla
        Mikkelsen, based on the novel by Arvid Hanssen. (V)

        CHILLY SCENES OF WINTER see HEAD OVER HEELS

603.   CHINA GIRL. (Variety-1975-Paolo Uccello-X). An original
        screenplay by Edwin Brown. (W)

604.   THE CHINA SYNDROME. (Columbia-1979-James Bridges-PG).
        Mike Gray, T. S. Cook, and James Bridges wrote this origi-
        nal screenplay; novelization by Burton Wohl. (HR, LACOPL,
        LAT, Q, V, W)

605. CHINESE BLUE. (Melody-1975-John Chang-X). No screen-
      play credits available. (W)

606. THE CHINESE MACK. (Ellman Enterprises-1976-Herman Hsu-
      R). No screenplay credits available. (W)

607. CHINESE ROULETTE. (New Yorker-1977-Rainer Werner
      Fassbinder-N/R). An original screenplay by Rainer Werner
      Fassbinder. (W)

608. CHINO. (Intercontinental-1976-John Sturges-PG). A screen-
      play written by Clair Huffaker, based on the novel The Val-
      dez Horses by Lee Hoffman; Doubleday, 1967. (LACOPL, W)

      A CHOICE OF ARMS see CHOICE OF WEAPONS

609. CHOICE OF WEAPONS. (Parafrance-1981-Alain Corneau-N/R).
      A screenplay by Alain Corneau and Michel Grisolia. (LAT, V)

610. CHOIRBOYS. (Universal-1977-Robert Aldrich-R). Christopher
      Knopf wrote the screenplay, based on the novel by Joseph
      Wambaugh; Delacorte Press, 1975, 346p. (HR, LACOPL, Q,
      V, W)

611. CHOOSE ME. (Island Alive-1984-Alan Rudolph-N/R). An
      original screenplay written by Alan Rudolph. (V)

612. CHORUS CALL. (Entertainment Ventures-1979-Antonio
      Shepherd-R). An original screenplay by Antonio Shepherd.
      (W)

613. THE CHORUS GIRLS. (Independent International-1978-
      Eugene Martin-R). No screenplay credits given. (W)

614. THE CHOSEN. (American International-1978-Alberto De
      Martino-R). A screenplay by Sergio Donati, Aldo De Mar-
      tino, and Michael Robson. (W)

615. THE CHOSEN. (Edie and Ely Landau-1981-Jeremy Paul
      Kagan-N/R). Screenplay written by Edwin Gordon, based
      on the novel by Chaim Potok; Simon and Schuster, 1976.
      (BFI, LACOPL, LAT, V)

616. CHRIST STOPPED AT EBOLI. (Franklin Media-1979-
      Francesco Rosi-N/R). Francesco Rosi, Tonino Guerra, Raf-
      faele La Capria wrote the screenplay, based on the book by
      Carlo Levi; Farrar, 1963, 268p. (BFI, LACOPL, W)

617. CHRISTIAN THE LION. (Scotia American-1976-James Hill &
      Bill Travers-G). No screenplay credits given. (V)

618. CHRISTIANE F. (New World-1982-Ulrich Edel-N/R). Screenplay by Herman Weigel, based on the book by Kai Hermann
and Horst Rieck. (BFI, LAT, W)

619. CHRISTINE. (Columbia-1983-John Carpenter-R). A screenplay by Bill Phillips, based on the novel by Stephen King;
Viking Press, 1983, 526p. (HR, LACOPL, LAT, V, W)

CHRISTMAS EVIL see YOU BETTER WATCH OUT

620. A CHRISTMAS STORY. (MGM/UA-1983-Bob Clark-PG). A
screenplay by Jean Sheppard, Leigh Brown, and Bob Clark;
adapted from the novel In God We Trust, All Others Pay
Cash by Jean Sheppard; Doubleday, 1966. (HR, LACOPL,
LAT, V)

621. CHRISTY. (Independent-1976-No Director Credit Given-X).
No screenplay credits given. (W)

622. CHRONICLE OF A LATIN-AMERICAN SUBVERSIVE. (Alfa
Films International-1976-N/R). Screenplay written by Jose
Ignacio Cabrujas, Luis Correa, and Mauricio Walerstein. (V)

623. CHU CHU AND THE PHILLY FLASH. (20th Century-Fox-
1981-David Lowell Rich-PG). A screenplay by Barbara Dana,
from a story by Henry Barrow. (LAT, Q, V, W)

624. CHUQUIAGO. (Ukamau Productions-1978-Antonio Eguino-
N/R). An original screenplay by Oscar Soria. (V, W)

CHUVAS DE VERAO see A SUMMER RAIN

625. CINDERELLA. (Group I-1977-Michael Pataki-X). A screenplay by Frank Roy Perilli. (V)

626. CINDY'S LOVE GAMES. (1979-Aldo Grimaldi-N/R). An
original screenplay by Aldo Grimaldi. (BFI)

627. LE CINEMA DE PAPA. (Columbia Films-1979-Claude Berri-
N/R). A screenplay by Claude Berri. (W)

628. CIRCLE OF IRON. (Avco Embassy-1979-Richard Moore-R).
A screenplay by Stirling Silliphant and Stanley Mann, based
on a story by Bruce Lee, James Coburn, and Stirling Silliphant; novelization by Robert Weverka; Warner, 1979, 221p.
(LACOPL, V, W)

629. CIRCLE OF TWO. (Film Consortium of Canada-1980-Jules
Dassin-N/R). Thomas Hedley wrote the screenplay, based
on A Lesson in Love by Marie Terese Baird; Houghton, 1973,
221p. (LACOPL, V)

630. CISKE THE RAT. (Concorde Film-1984-Guido Pieters-N/R).
      A screenplay by Karin Loomans, based on the novel by Piet
      Bakker. (V)

      CITIZEN'S BAND see BREAKER BREAKER

      LA CITTA DELLE DONNE see CITY OF WOMEN

631. THE CITY GIRL. (Moon Pictures-1984-Martha Coolidge-N/R).
      A screenplay by Judith Thompson and Leonard-John Gates,
      based on a story by John MacDonald and Martha Coolidge.
      (V)

632. CITY HEAT. (Warner Bros.-1984-Richard Benjamin-PG).
      Screenplay by Sam O. Brown (aka Blake Edwards) and
      Joseph C. Stinson, from a story by Sam O. Brown. (HR,
      LAT, V)

633. CITY LOVERS. (TeleCulture Inc.-1982-Barney Simon-N/R).
      A screenplay by Barney Simon, from a story by Nadine
      Gordimer. (LAT, V)

634. CITY NEWS. (Zi/Fi Prods.-1982-David Fishelson and Zoe
      Zinman-N/R). A screenplay by David Fishelson and Zoe
      Zinman. (V)

      CITY OF THE WALKING DEAD see NIGHTMARE

635. CITY OF WOMEN. (Gaumont/New Yorker-1981-Federico
      Fellini-N/R). A screenplay by Federico Fellini, Bernardino
      Zapponi, and Brunello Rondi. (LAT, Q, V, W)

636. CITY ON FIRE. (Avco Embassy-1979-Alvin Rakoff-R). A
      screenplay by Jack Hill, David P. Lewis, and Celine
      LaFreniere. (Q, W)

637. CLAIR DE FEMME. (Atlantic-1980-Costa-Gavras-N/R). A
      screenplay by Costa-Gavras, based on a novel by Romain
      Gary; Gallimard, 1977, 168p. (LACOPL, W)

638. THE CLAMDIGGER'S DAUGHTER. (Monarch-1975-Roberta
      Findlay-X). A screenplay by Roberta Findlay. (W)

639. CLARENCE AND ANGEL. (Gardner-1981-Robert Gardner-
      N/R). A screenplay by Robert Gardner. (BFI, W)

640. CLARETTA AND BEN. (Aquarius Films-1983-Gian Luigi
      Polidoro-N/R). A screenplay by Rafael Azcona, Leo Ben-
      venuti, Piero de Bernardi, and Gian Luigi Polidoro, from a
      story by Gian Luigi Polidoro. (V)

641.   CLASH OF THE TITANS. (United Artists-1981-Desmond
       Davis-PG). An original screenplay by Beverley Cross;
       novelization by Alan Dean Foster; Warner Books, 1981, 304p.
       (LACOPL, LAT, Q, V, W)

642.   CLASS. (Orion-1983-Lewis John Carlino-R). A screenplay
       by Jim Kouf and David Greenwalt; screenplay supervisor,
       Luca Kouimelis. (BFI, HR, LAT, V, W)

643.   THE CLASS OF MISS MACMICHAELS. (Brut Productions-
       1978-Silvio Narizzano-N/R). A screenplay by Judd Bernard,
       based on the novel by Sandy Hutson.

644.   CLASS OF 1984. (Guerrilla High-1982-Mark Lester-N/R).
       A screenplay by Tom Holland, John Saxton, and Mark Lester,
       from a story by Tom Holland. (BFI, LAT, V, W)

645.   CLEOPATRA JONES AND THE CASINO OF GOLD. (Warner
       Bros.-1975-Chuck Bail-R). An original screenplay by Wil-
       liam Tennant, based on characters created by Max Julien.
       (Q, W)

646.   THE CLIMAX OF BLUE POWER. (F. C. Perl-1976-F. C.
       Perl-X). No screenplay credits given. (W)

647.   CLOAK AND DAGGER. (Universal-1984-Richard Franklin-PG).
       A screenplay by Tom Holland, from a story by Cornell Wool-
       rich. (LAT, V)

648.   THE CLOCKMAKER. (Joseph Green-1976-Bertrand Tavernier-
       N/R). A screenplay by Bertrand Tavernier, from the novel
       by Georges Simenon. (W)

649.   THE CLONUS HORROR. (Group I-1979-Robert S. Fiveson-R).
       A screenplay by Myrl A. Schreibman and Robert S. Fiveson.
       (W)

650.   CLOSE ENCOUNTERS OF THE THIRD KIND. (Columbia-1977-
       Steven Spielberg-PG). A screenplay by Steven Spielberg;
       novel by Steven Spielberg; Dell, 1977, 256p. (HR, LACOPL,
       LAT, NYT, Q, V, W)

651.   CLOSE SHAVE. (Tobann International-1981-Robert Hendrick-
       son-R). An original screenplay by Ronald Collier and Robert
       Hendrickson. (W)

652.   THE CLOSET CASANOVA. (Belladonna-1979-Ted Roter-R).
       A screenplay by Peter Balakoff and Belinda Balakoff. (W)

653.   CLOUD DANCER. (Blossom Pictures-1980-Barry Brown-PG).
       A screenplay by William Goodhart, based on a story by Barry
       Brown, Daniel Tamkus, and William Goodhart. (V)

654. THE CLUB. (Roadshow-1982-Bruce Beresford-N/R). A screenplay by David Williamson. (W)

655. COACH. (Crown International-1978-Bud Townsend-R). A screenplay by Stephen Bruce Rose and Nancy Larson, based on an idea by Mark Tenser. (HR, V, W)

656. COAL MINER'S DAUGHTER. (Universal-1980-Michael Apted-PG). A screenplay by Tom Rickman, based on the autobiography of Loretta Lynn, written with George Vescey; Regnery, 1976, 204p. (HR, LACOPL, LAT, Q, V, W)

657. COAST TO COAST. (Paramount-1980-Joseph Sargent-PG). An original screenplay by Stanley Weiser. (V, W)

658. COCAINE COWBOYS. (International Harmony-1979-Ulli Lommel-R). An original screenplay by Ulli Lommel, S. Compton, T. Sullivan, and V. Bockris. (W)

659. THE COCKTAIL HOSTESSES. (S.C.A.-1976-A. C. Stephen-R). No screenplay credit given. (W)

660. COCKTAIL MOLOTOV. (Alexandre Filmoso-1981-Diane Kurys-N/R). An original screenplay by Diane Kurys. (LAT, W)

661. THE COED MURDERS. (NMD-1980-Massimo Dallamano-R). No screenplay credits given. (W)

662. COLD CUTS. (Parafrance-1980-Bertrand Blier-N/R). An original screenplay by Bertrand Blier. (V)

663. COLD HOMELAND. (Triangel Film-1978-W. Werner Schaefer-N/R). A screenplay by Peter Steinbach and W. Werner Schaefer. (V)

664. COLD RIVER. (Pacific International Enterprises-1982-Fred G. Sullivan-PG). A screenplay by Fred G. Sullivan, based on a novel by William Judson; Mason & Lipscomb, 1974, 213p. (LACOPL, V, W)

665. THE COLD ROOM. (Manson International-1984-James Dearden-N/R). An original screenplay by James Dearden. (V)

666. THE COLLEGIATES. (MSW-1975-Carter Stevens and Robert Josephs-X). No screenplay credits given. (W)

667. COLONEL DELMIRO GOUVEIA. (Embrafilme-1979-Geraldo Sarno-N/R). An original screenplay by Geraldo Sarno and Orlando Senna. (W)

COLONEL OF THE SERTAO see COLONEL DELMIRO GOUVEIA

COLPIRE AL CUORE see BLOW TO THE HEART

668. COMA. (United Artists-1978-Michael Crichton-PG). Michael
      Crichton wrote the screenplay, based on the novel by Robin
      Cook; Little Brown, 1977, 306p. (HR, LACOPL, LAT, Q, V,
      W)

669. COME BACK TO THE FIVE AND DIME, JIMMY DEAN, JIMMY
      DEAN. (Mark Goodson/Viacom-1982-Robert Altman-PG). A
      screenplay by Ed Graczyk, based on his play. (BFI, LAT,
      V)

670. COME HOME AND MEET MY WIFE. (S. J. International-1975-
      Mario Monticelli-R). No screenplay credits given. (W)

671. COMEBACK. (V. Vietinghoff/Rocco Film Project-1982-Christel
      Buschmann-N/R). An original screenplay by Christel Busch-
      mann. (V)

672. THE COMEBACK. (Lone Star Pictures International-1982-
      Pete Walker-R). A screenplay by Murray Smith. (V, W)

673. THE COMEBACK TRAIL. (Dynamite Entertainment-Rearguard
      Prods.-1982-Harry Hurwitz-N/R). A screenplay by Harry
      Hurwitz, from a story by Roy Frumkes, Robert J. Winston,
      and Harry Hurwitz; additional material by Chuck McCann,
      Robert Staats, Irwin Corey, and Henny Youngman. (V, W)

674. COMES A HORSEMAN. (United Artists-1978-Alan J. Pakula-
      PG). A screenplay by Dennis Lynton Clark. (HR, LAT, Q,
      V, W)

675. COMFORT AND JOY. (Universal-1984-Bill Forsyth-N/R). An
      original screenplay by Bill Forsyth. (V)

676. COMIN' AT YA! (Filmways-1981-Ferdinando Baldi-R). A
      screenplay by Lloyd Battista, Wolf Lowenthal, and Gene
      Quintano, from a story by Tony Petitto. (LAT, V, W)

677. COMING ATTRACTIONS. (National-American-1979-Ira Miller-
      R). A screenplay by Varley Smith, Ian Praiser, Ira Miller,
      and Royce D. Applegate. (W)

678. COMING HOME. (United Artists-1978-Hal Ashby-R). A
      screenplay by Waldo Salt and Robert C. Jones, based on a
      story by Nancy Dowd. (HR, LAT, Q, V, W)

679. THE COMMITMENT. (Borden-1976-Richard Grand and Louis
      A. Shaffner-PG). A screenplay by Andrew Laskos, Louis A.
      Shaffner, and Richard Grand, from a story by Barbara Grand.
      (V)

COMMUNION see ALICE, SWEET ALICE

680. THE COMPANY OF WOLVES. (ITC-1984-Neil Jordan-N/R).
      A screenplay by Angela Carter and Neil Jordan, from an
      original story by Angela Carter. (V)

681. THE COMPETITION. (Columbia-1980-Joel Oliansky-PG). A
      screenplay by Joel Oliansky, from a story by Joel Oliansky
      and William Sackheim. (HR, LAT, Q, V, W)

682. THE CON ARTISTS. (S. J. International Pictures-1981-Serge
      Corbucci-PG). No screenplay credits given. (W)

683. CONAN THE BARBARIAN. (Universal-1982-John Milius-R).
      A screenplay by John Milius and Oliver Stone, based on the
      character created by Robert E. Howard; novelization by L.
      Sprague De Camp and Lin Carter; Bantam Books, 1982, 181p.
      (HR, LACOPL, LAT, V, W)

684. CONAN THE DESTROYER. (Universal-1984-Richard Fleischer-
      PG). A screenplay by Stanley Mann, from a story by Roy
      Thomas and Gerry Conway, based on the character created
      by Robert E. Howard. (V)

685. THE CONCORDE--AIRPORT '79. (Universal-1979-David Lowell
      Rich-PG). A screenplay by Erich Roth, from a story by
      Jennings Lang, inspired by the film Airport, based on the
      novel by Arthur Hailey. (HR, Q, V, W)

686. THE CONCRETE JUNGLE. (Pentagon-1982-Tom De Simone-R).
      A screenplay by Alan J. Adler. (BFI, LAT, V, W)

687. CONDORMAN. (Buena Vista-1981-Charles Jarrott-PG). A
      screenplay by Marc Stirdivant, suggested by the novel The
      Game of X; novelization by Joe Claro; Scholastic Inc., 1981,
      131p. (LACOPL, LAT, Q, V)

688. CONDUCT UNBECOMING. (Allied Artists-1975-Michael
      Anderson-PG). A screenplay by Robert Enders; play by
      Barry England; Samuel French, n.d. (LACOPL, Q, W)

689. CONFESSIONS FROM A HOLIDAY CAMP. (Columbia-1977-
      Norman Cohen-N/R). A screenplay written by Christopher
      Wood (aka Timothy Lea), based on the novel of the same title
      by Timothy Lea. (V)

690. CONFESSIONS OF A TEENAGE PEANUT BUTTER FREAK.
      (Freeway-1976-Gerald Graystone-X). Zachary Youngblood
      and Gerald Graystone are credited with this original screen-
      play. (W)

691. THE CONFESSIONS OF AMANS. (Bauer International-1977-
     Gregory Nava-N/R). A screenplay by Gregory Nava and
     Anna Thomas. (W)

692. CONFIDENCE. (New Yorker-1981-Istvan Szabo-N/R). A
     screenplay by Istvan Szabo, from a story by Istvan Szabo and
     Erika Szanto. (BFI, LAT, W)

693. CONFRONTATION. (New Yorker-1976-Rolf Lyssy-N/R). A
     screenplay by Rolf Lyssy and George Janett. (W)

694. CONQUEST. (United Film Distribution Co.-1984-Lucio Fulci-
     R). A screenplay by Gino Capone, Jose Antonio de la Loma
     Sr., and Carlos Vasallo, from a story by Giovanni Di Clemente.
     (V)

695. THE CONSEQUENCE. (Libra-1979-Wolfgang Petersen-N/R).
     A screenplay by Alexander Ziegler and Wolfgang Petersen,
     from a book by Alexander Ziegler. (W)

696. THE CONSPIRACY OF TORTURE. (Athena-1976-L. Fulci-R).
     No screenplay credits given. (W)

697. CONSTANT FACTOR. (New Yorker-1983-Krzysztof Zanussi-
     N/R). Screenplay by Krzysztof Zanussi. (W)

698. CONTINENTAL DIVIDE. (Universal-1981-Michael Apted-PG).
     An original screenplay written by Lawrence Kasdan. (BFI,
     HR, LAT, Q, V, W)

699. THE CONTRACT. (International Producers-1975-Claude
     Mulot-R). A screenplay by Albert Kantoff, Edgar Oppen-
     heimer, and Claude Mulot. (W)

700. CONTRACT. (New Yorker-1981-Krzysztof Zanussi-N/R). An
     original screenplay by Krzysztof Zanussi. (BFI, LAT, W)

701. CONVENTION GIRLS. (EMC-1978-Joseph Adler-R). An orig-
     inal screenplay by T. Gertler. (W)

702. CONVERSATION PIECE. (New Line-1976-Luchino Visconti-R).
     A screenplay by Suso Checchi D'Amico, Enrico Medioli, and
     Luchino Visconti. (W)

703. CONVOY. (United Artists-1978-Sam Peckinpah-R). B. W. L.
     Norton wrote the screenplay based on a song by C. W.
     McCall. (Q, V, W)

704. CONVOY BUDDIES. (Film Ventures International-1978-Arthur
     Pitt-PG). No screenplay credits available. (W)

705. COOLEY HIGH. (American International-1975-Michael Schultz-
      PG). An original screenplay by Eric Monte. (Q, W)

706. COONSKIN. (Bryanston-1975-Ralph Bakshi-R). A screenplay
      written by Ralph Bakshi. (Q, W)

707. CORNBREAD, EARL AND ME. (American International-1975-
      Joe Manduke-PG). A screenplay by Leonard Lamensdorf.
      (Q, W)

      CORNETTI A COLAZIONE see COUNTRY NURSE

708. THE CORRUPTION OF CHRIS MILLER. (Lanir-1975-Juan
      Antonio Bardem-R). A screenplay by Santiago Moncada. (W)

709. CORVETTE SUMMER. (United Artists-1978-Matthew Robbins-
      PG). An original screenplay by Hal Barwood and Matthew
      Robbins. (Q, W)

710. COTTON CLUB. (Orion-1984-Francis Coppola-R). Screen-
      play by William Kennedy and Francis Coppola, story by Wil-
      liam Kennedy, Francis Coppola, and Mario Puzo, suggested
      by the book by James Haskins; Random House, 1977, 169p.
      (HR, LACOPL, LAT, NYT, V)

711. COUNSELOR AT CRIME. (Joseph Green-1975-Alberto De
      Martino-R). An original screenplay by Alberto De Martino,
      Vincenzo Mannino, and Adriano Bolzoni. (W)

712. COUNT DRACULA AND HIS VAMPIRE BRIDE. (Dynamite
      Entertainment-1978-Alan Gibson-R). An original screenplay
      written by Don Houghton.

713. COUNT THE WAYS. (Evolution Enterprises-1976-Ann Perry-
      X). Screenplay by Ann Perry. (V)

714. COUNTDOWN AT KUSINI. (Columbia-1978-Ossie Davis-PG).
      Ossie Davis, Ladi Ladebo, and Al Freeman Jr. wrote the
      screenplay, from a story by John Storm Roberts. (Q, W)

715. COUNTERFEIT COMMANDOS. (Aquarius-1981-Enzo G.
      Castellari-R). A screenplay by Sergio Grieco. (V)

716. COUNTRY. (Buena Vista-1984-Richard Pearce-PG). A
      screenplay by William D. Wittliff. (LAT, V)

717. COUNTRY BLUE. (General Films-1975-Jack Conrad-R). No
      screenplay credits given. (W)

718. COUNTRY HOOKER. (Boxoffice International-1975-Lou Gwinn-
      X). No screenplay credits given. (W)

719. COUNTRY NURSE. (Cannon-1980-Alan W. Cools-N/R). An original screenplay by Luigi Petrini. (BFI)

720. COUP DE GRACE. (Cinema 5-1978-Volker Schlondorff-N/R). A screenplay by Genevieve Dormann, Margarethe Von Trotta, and Jutta Bruckner, based on the novel by Marguerite Yourcenar; Farrar, Straus and Cudahy, 1957, 151p. (LACOPL, LAT, W)

721. COUP DE SIROCCO. (New Line Cinema-1981-Alexandre Arcady-N/R). A screenplay by Jan and Daniel Saint-Hamon and Alexandre Arcady, from a novel by Daniel Saint-Hamon. (LAT, W)

COUP DE TETE see HOTHEAD

722. COUP DE TORCHON. (Parafrance-1981-Bertrand Tavernier-N/R). A screenplay by Bertrand Tavernier and Jean Aurenche, from the novel Pop. 1280 by Jim Thompson. (BFI, LAT, V)

723. COUPLES. (Sombrero-1976-Claude Goddard-X). No screenplay credit given. (W)

724. COURAGE. (Sandy Howard/Adams Apple Film-1984-Robert L. Rosen-N/R). A screenplay by Ronny Cox and Mary Cox. (V)

LE COURAGE DES AUTRES see THE COURAGE OF OTHERS

725. THE COURAGE OF OTHERS. (Inafri-1984-Christian Richard-N/R). Screenplay written by Christian Richard. (V)

726. THE COUSIN. (Cambist-1976-Aldo Lado-R). No screenplay credits given. (W)

727. COUSIN ANGELICA. (New Yorker-1977-Carlos Saura-N/R). A screenplay by Rafael Azcona and Carlos Saura. (W)

728. COUSIN, COUSINE. (Libra-1976-Jean-Charles Tacchella-R). An original screenplay by Jean-Charles Tacchella. (Q, W)

729. COVER GIRL MODELS. (New World-1975-Cirio Santiago-R). An original screenplay by Howard R. Cohen. (W)

730. COVERGIRL. (New World-1984-Jean-Claude Lord-R). A screenplay by Charles Dennis. (V)

731. COVERT ACTION. (21st Century-1980-Romolo Guerrieri-R). No screenplay credits given. (W)

732. CRACKERS. (Universal-1984-Louis Malle-PG). A screenplay by Jeffrey Fiskin, suggested by the film Big Deal on Madonna Street written by Suso Cecchi D'Amico, Mario Monicelli, Agenore Incrocci, and Furio Scarpelli. (V)

733. CRAZY MAMA. (New World-1975-Jonathan Demme-PG). A screenplay by Robert Thom, from a story by Francis Doel. (Q, V, W)

734. THE CREATURE FROM BLACK LAKE. (Howco International-1976-Joy Houck, Jr.-PG). Jim McCullough Jr. wrote this original screenplay. (W)

735. THE CREATURE WASN'T NICE. (Creatures Features-1981-Bruce Kimmel-PG). An original screenplay by Bruce Kimmel. (V, W)

736. THE CREATURES FROM BEYOND THE GRAVE. (Howard Mahler-1980-Kevin Connor-PG). A screenplay written by Robin Clarke and Raymond Christodoulou. (W)

737. THE CREEPER. (Coast-1980-Peter Carter-R). An original screenplay by Ian Sutherland. (W)

738. CREEPSHOW. (United Film Distribution-1982-George Romero-R). A screenplay written by Stephen King; novelization by Stephen King; New American Library, 1982. (BFI, LACOPL, LAT, V, W)

739. CRIME AND PASSION. (American International-1976-Ivan Passer-R). A screenplay by Jesse Laskey Jr. and Pat Silver. (LAT, W)

740. CRIME AND PUNISHMENT. (Artkino-1975-Lev Kulijanov-N/R). A screenplay by Nikolai Fisurovsky and Lev Kulijanov, based on the novel by Fyodor Dostoyevsky; Dodd, Mead, 1963, 484p. (LACOPL, W)

741. CRIME AT PORTA ROMANA. (Titanus-1980-Bruno Corbucci-N/R). A screenplay by Mario Amendola and Bruno Corbucci. (V)

742. CRIME BOSS. (Cinema Shares International-1976-Alberto De Martino-PG). No screenplay credits given. (W)

743. CRIMEBUSTERS. (United Artists-1979-E. B. Clucher-PG). An original screenplay by E. B. Clucher. (W)

744. CRIMES OF PASSION. (New World Pictures-1984-Ken Russell-N/R). A screenplay by Barry Sandler. (V)

745. CRIMES OF THE FUTURE. (Emergent Films-1984-David Cronenberg-N/R). Screenplay by David Cronenberg. (V)

746. THE CRIPPLED MASTERS. (New Line-1982-Joe Law-R). No screenplay credits given. (W)

CRONICA DE UN SUBVERSIVO LATINO-AMERICANO see CHRONICLE OF A LATIN-AMERICAN SUBVERSIVE

747. CROSS COUNTRY. (MGM/UA-1983-Paul Lynch-R). A screenplay by John Hunter and William Gray, based on the novel by Herbert Kastle; Delacorte Press, 1975, 355p. (HR, LACOPL, LAT, V)

748. CROSS CREEK. (Universal-1983-Martin Ritt-PG). A screenplay by Calene Young, based on the memoirs of Marjorie Kinnan Rawlings; Scribner's, 1942, 368p. (HR, LACOPL, LAT, V)

749. CROSS OF IRON. (EMI Films-1977-Sam Peckinpah-R). A screenplay by Julius J. Epstein and Herbert Asmodi, based on the book by Willi Heinrich; Bobbs, 1956, 456p. (HR, LACOPL, LAT, Q, V, W)

750. CROSSED SWORDS. (Warner Bros.-1978-Richard Fleischer-PG). A screenplay by George MacDonald Fraser, Berta Dominguez, and Pierre Spengler, based on the novel "The Prince and the Pauper" by Mark Twain; Heritage Press, 1964, 221p. (HR, LACOPL, LAT, Q, W)

751. CRUEL STORY OF YOUTH. (New Yorker Films-1984-Nagisa Oshima-N/R). Original screenplay by Nagisa Oshima. (V)

752. CRUISIN' 57. (Toby Ross-1975-Toby Ross-X). No screenplay credits given. (W)

753. CRUISING. (United Artists-1980-William Friedkin-R). A screenplay by William Friedkin, based upon a novel by Gerald Walker. (LAT, Q, V, W)

754. CRY FOR CINDY. (Cindy-1976-Wendy Lions-X). Dean Rogers wrote this original screenplay. (W)

755. CRY OF THE PENGUINS. (British Lion-EMI-1975-Al Viola-N/R). A screenplay by Anthony Shaffer, from a novel by Graham Billing, Forbush and the Penguins; Holt, 1965. (LACOPL, W)

756. CRY ONION. (Joseph Green-1980-Enzo G. Castellari-PG). A screenplay by Luciano Vincenzoni and Sergio Donati. (W)

757. CRY TO THE WIND. (Sebastian International-1979-Robert W. Davison-G). An original screenplay by Daiv James Nielsen. (W)

758. CUBA. (United Artists-1979-Richard Lester-R). A screenplay by Charles Wood; novelization by Karji; Pocket Books, 1979, 218p. (LACOPL, Q, V, W)

759. CUJO. (Warner Bros.-1983-Lewis Teague-R). A screenplay by Don Carlos Dunaway and Lauren Currier, based on the novel by Stephen King; Viking Press, 1981, 309p. (HR, LACOPL, LAT, V, W)

760. CURSE OF THE PINK PANTHER. (MGM/UA-1983-Blake Edwards-PG). A screenplay by Blake Edwards and Geoffrey Edwards. (LAT, V)

761. CURTAINS. (Jensen Farley-1982-Jonathan Stryker aka Richard Ciupka-R). A screenplay written by Robert Guza Jr. (BFI, LAT, V)

CUTTER AND BONE see CUTTER'S WAY

762. CUTTER'S WAY. (United Artists-1981-Ivan Passer-R). A screenplay by Jeffrey Alan Fiskin, based on the novel by Newton Thornburg; Little, Brown, 1976. (BFI, HR, LACOPL, LAT, Q, V, W)

763. THE CYCLE. (Icarus/Dispodex International-1979-Darius Mehrjui-N/R). A screenplay by Golan H. Saedi and Darius Mehrjui, based on the story "Garbage Dump" by G. H. Saedi. (W)

764. CYNTHIA'S SISTER. (Boxoffice International-1975-Arnold Baxter-N/R). A screenplay by Michael Hardy. (W)

765. D. C. CAB. (Universal-1984-Joel Schumacher-R). An original screenplay by Joel Schumacher, from a story by Topper Carew and Joel Schumacher. (HR, LAT, V, W)

766. DADDY'S DEADLY DARLINGS. (Aquarius-1984-Marc Laurence-R). An original screenplay by F. A. Foss aka Marc Laurence. (V)

767. DAFFY DUCK'S MOVIE: FANTASTIC ISLAND. (Warner Bros.-1983-Friz Freleng-G). Screenplay by John Dunn, David Detiege, and Friz Freleng. (V)

768. DAISY CHAIN. (Joseph Green-1980-Ralph Olsen and Ralph Thiel-PG). A screenplay by Ed Marcus and Joe Juliano. (W)

769. DAMIEN--OMEN II. (20th Century-Fox-1978-Don Taylor-R).
Screenplay by Stanley Mann and Michael Hodges; novelization
by Joseph Howard, Signet Books, 1978, 199p. (HR, LACOPL,
LAT, NYT, Q, V, W)

770. DAMNATION ALLEY. (20th Century-Fox-1977-Jack Smight-
PG). Screenplay by Alan Sharp and Lukus Heller, from the
novel by Roger Zelazny; Putnam, 1969, 157p. (LACOPL,
NYT)

771. THE DANCE OF DEATH. (Paramount-1979-David Giles-G). A
screenplay by C. D. Lecock, from the play by August Strindberg in Five Plays of Strindberg; Anchor, 1960, 351p.
(LACOPL, W)

772. DANGEROUS DAVIES--THE LAST DETECTIVE. (ITC/Inner
Circle-1981-Val Guest-N/R). Screenplay by Val Guest and
Leslie Thomas, from a novel by Leslie Thomas. (V)

773. DANIEL. (Paramount-1983-Sidney Lumet-R). Screenplay by
E. L. Doctorow, from his novel The Book of Daniel; Random House, 1971, 303p. (HR, LACOPL, LAT, V)

774. DANISH PASTRIES. (Mature-1975-Finn Karlsson-X). Peter
Hallmark wrote the screenplay. (W)

775. DAN'S MOTEL. (Jerry R. Barrish-1982-N/R). An original
screenplay by Jerry R. Barrish. (W)

776. DANTON. (Triumph/Columbia-1983-Andrzej Wajda-PG). A
screenplay by Jean-Claude Carriere, based on the play The
Danton Affair by Stanislawa Przybyszewska. (BFI, LAT, V)

777. DARE-DEVIL'S TIME. (Jadran Film-1977-Vladimir Tadej-N/R).
Screenplay by Branko Copic, Arsen Diklic, Vlastimir Radovan-
ovic, and Valdimir Tadej. (V)

778. THE DARK. (Film Ventures-1979-John Budd Cardos-R). An
original screenplay by Stanford Whitmore. (V, W)

779. THE DARK CRYSTAL. (Universal-1982-Jim Henson-PG).
A screenplay by David Odell, from a story by Jim Henson.
(V)

780. THE DARK END OF THE STREET. (First Run Features-1981-
Jan Egleson-N/R). An original screenplay by Jan Egleson.
(V, W)

781. DARK SUNDAY. (Intercontinental-1978-Jimmy Huston-R).
Howard Lee wrote this original screenplay. (W)

782. DARKTOWN STRUTTERS. (New World-1975-William Witney-
PG). A screenplay written by George Armitage. (NYT, W)

783. DARLINGS! (Meteor Film/The Movies-1984-Ruud van Hemert-
N/R). Screenplay by Ruud van Hemert. (V)

784. DAUGHTERS! DAUGHTERS! (Steinmann-Baxter-1975-Moshe
Mizrahi-PG). Screenplay by Moshe Mizrahi and Shai K.
Ophir. (NYT, W)

785. DAVID. (Kino International-1982-Peter Lilienthal-N/R).
Screenplay by Peter Lilienthal, Jurek Becker, Ulla Zieman,
from a novel by Joel Konig. (W)

786. DAWN OF THE DEAD. (United Film Distribution-1979-George
A. Romero-R). An original screenplay by George A. Romero.
(HR, Q, V, W)

787. DAWN OF THE MUMMY. (Harmony Gold-1981-Frank Agrama-
N/R). Daria Price, Ronald Dobrin, and Frank Agrama wrote
this original screenplay. (V, W)

788. THE DAY AFTER HALLOWEEN. (Group 1 Interntional-1981-
Simon Wincer-R). A screenplay by Chris and Everett DeRoche.
(V, W)

789. THE DAY IT CAME TO EARTH. (Howco International-1979-
Harry Z. Thomason-PG). An original screenplay by Paul
Fisk. (W)

790. DAY OF THE ANIMALS. (Film Ventures-1977-William Girdler-
PG). An original screenplay by William Norton and Eleanor E.
Norton; novelization by Donald Porter; Ballantine, 1977.
(LACOPL, NYT, V)

791. THE DAY OF THE LOCUST. (Paramount-1975-John Schlesin-
ger-R). A screenplay by Waldo Salt, based on the novel by
Nathanael West; Bantam Books, 1963, 139p. (HR, LACOPL,
NYT, Q, V, W)

792. DAY OF THE WOMAN. (Cinemagic Pictures-1978-Meir Zarchi-
R). An original screenplay by Meir Zarchi. (V, W)

793. THE DAY THE LORD GOT BUSTED. (American Films-1976-
Burt Topper-PG). Screenplay written by Burt Topper. (W)

794. THE DAY TIME ENDED. (Compass International/Manson
International-1980-John Bud Cardos-PG). Wayne Schmidt,
J. Larry Carroll, and David Schmoeller, wrote this original
screenplay. (V, W)

795. DAYS OF FURY. (Picturemedia Ltd.-1980-Fred Warshofsky-
      PG). A screenplay by Fred Warshofsky. (W)

796. DAYS OF HEAVEN. (Paramount-1978-Terrence Malick-PG).
      Terrence Malick wrote this original screenplay. (HR, LAT,
      NYT, Q, V, W)

797. DAYS OF WATER. (Tricontinental-1978-Manuel Octavio Gomez-
      N/R). Screenplay by Manuel Octavio Gomez, Bernabe Hernan-
      dez, and Julio Garcia Espinosa. (W)

798. THE DAYDREAMER. (Joseph Green-1976-Pierre Richard-PG).
      A screenplay by Pierre Richard and Andre Ruellan. (W)

799. DEAD AND BURIED. (Avco Embassy-1981-Gary A. Sherman-
      R). A screenplay by Ronald Shusett and Dan O'Bannon,
      based on a story by Jeff Millar and Alex Stern. (LAT, V, W)

800. DEAD KIDS. (Greater Union Organization-1981-Michael
      Laughlin-N/R). An original screenplay by Michael Laughlin
      and William Condon. (V)

801. DEAD MEN DON'T WEAR PLAID. (Universal-1982-Carl Reiner-
      PG). A screenplay by Carl Reiner, George Gipe, and Steve
      Martin. (V)

802. DEAD ON ARRIVAL. (CalAm Artists-1979-Charles Martin-R).
      Screenplay by Charles Martin. (W)

803. THE DEAD ZONE. (Paramount-1983-David Cronenberg-R).
      Screenplay by Jeffrey Boam, based on the novel by Stephen
      King; Viking Press, 1979, 426p. (LACOPL, LAT, V)

804. THE DEADLY ANGELS. (World Northal-1979-R). No produc-
      tion credits available. (W)

805. DEADLY BLESSING. (United Artists-1981-Wes Craven-R).
      Glenn M. Benest, Matthew Barr, and Wes Craven wrote the
      screenplay, based on a story by Glenn M. Benest and Matthew
      Barr. (LAT, Q, V, W)

806. DEADLY ENCOUNTER. (First American Films-1979-R. John
      Hugh-R). Original screenplay written by R. John Hugh.
      (W)

807. DEADLY EYES. (Warner Bros.-1983-Robert Clouse-R).
      Screenplay by Charles Eglee, based on a novel by James
      Herbert. (W)

808. THE DEADLY FEMALES. (Donwin-1976-Donovan Winter-N/R).
      Screenplay written by Donovan Winter. (V)

809. DEADLY FORCE. (Embassy-1983-Paul Aaron-R). Screenplay
      written by Ken Barnett, Barry Schneider, and Robert Vincent
      O'Neil. (LAT, V, W)

810. DEADLY GAMES. (Monterey Films-1983-Scott Mansfield-R).
      Screenplay by Scott Mansfield. (V)

811. DEADLY HERO. (Avco Embassy-1976-Ivan Nagy-R). George
      Wislocki wrote this original screenplay. (NYT, Q, W)

812. THE DEADLY SPAWN. (21st Century Distribution-1983-
      Douglas McKeown-R). Screenplay by Douglas McKeown, from
      a story by Ted Bohus, John Dods, and Douglas McKeown,
      with additional dialog by Tim Sullivan. (V, W)

813. DEAL OF THE CENTURY. (Warner Bros.-1983-William
      Friedkin-PG). Screenplay by Paul Brickman. (LAT, V)

814. DEAR BOYS. (Sigma Films-1980-Paul de Lussanet-N/R).
      Chiem van Houweninge and Paul de Lussanet wrote the screen-
      play, based on the novels Taal der Liefde, Lieve Jongens,
      and Lieve Leven by Gerard Reve. (BFI, V)

815. DEAR DEAD DELILAH. (Southern Star-1975-John Farris-R).
      John Farris wrote this original screenplay. (W)

816. DEAR DETECTIVE. (Cinema 5-1978-Philippe De Broca-N/R).
      Screenplay by Philippe De Broca, and Michel Audiard, based
      on the novel Le Frelon by Jean-Paul Rouland and Claude
      Olivier. (NYT, W)

      DEAR INSPECTOR see DEAR DETECTIVE

817. DEAR MR. WONDERFUL. (Lilienthal-1983-Peter Lilienthal-
      N/R). An original screenplay by Sam Koperwas. (W)

818. DEAR PAPA. (AMLF-1979-Dino Risi-N/R). Screenplay by
      Bernardino Zapponi, Marco Risi, and Dino Risi. (V)

819. DEATH COLLECTOR. (Epoch-1976-Ralph DeVito-R). Screen-
      play written by Ralph DeVito. (NYT, V, W)

820. DEATH DIMENSION. (Movietime-1978-Al Adamson-R).
      Screenplay written by Harry Hope. (W)

821. DEATH FORCE. (Caprican Three-1978-Cirio H. Santiago-R).
      Howard Cohen wrote this original screenplay. (W)

822. DEATH GAME. (Levitt-Pickman-1977-Peter Traynor-R).
      Screenplay written by Anthony Overman and Michael Ronald
      Ross. (V)

823. DEATH HUNT. (20th Century-Fox-1981-Peter Hunt-R).
      Screenplay by Michael Grais and Mark Victor. (LAT, Q, V,
      W)

824. DEATH IS MY TRADE. (WDR-Cologne and Iduna Film-1977-
      Theodor Kotulla-N/R). Screenplay by Theodor Kotulla, based
      on a novel by Robert Merle, Le Mort est mon Metier. (V)

825. DEATH JOURNEY. (Atlas-1976-Fred Williamson-R). The
      original story and screenplay were written by Abel Jones.
      (W)

826. DEATH KNOCKS TWICE. (Horizon-1975-Harold Philipp-R).
      No screenplay credits given. (W)

827. DEATH MACHINES. (Crown International-1976-Paul Kyriazi-
      R). Joe Walders and Paul Kyriazi wrote the screenplay, from
      an original screen story by Joe Walders. (W)

828. THE DEEP. (Columbia-1977-Peter Yates-PG). A screenplay
      by Peter Benchley and Tracy Keenan Wynn, from the novel
      by Peter Benchley; Doubleday, 1976, 301p. (NYT, Q, V)

829. DEEP JAWS. (Manuel S. Conde-1976-Perry Dell-X). Screen-
      play by Walt Davis, from a story by Charles Teitel. (W)

830. DEEP RED. (Mahler-1976-Dario Argento-R). Giuseppe Bas-
      san wrote the screenplay, from a story by Dario Argento and
      Bernardo Zapponi. (NYT, W)

831. THE DEER HUNTER. (Universal-1978-Michael Cimino-R).
      Deric Washburn wrote the screenplay, from a story by
      Michael Cimino, Deric Washburn, Louis Garfinkle, and Quinn
      K. Redeker; novelization by E. M. Corder; Jove, 1978, 189p.
      (HR, LACOPL, LAT, NYT, Q, V, W)

832. DEFIANCE. (Stu Segall Associates-1975-Armand Weston-X).
      Screenplay by Armand Weston. (W)

833. DEFIANCE. (American International Pictures-1980-John
      Flynn-PG). Thomas Michael Donnelly wrote the screenplay,
      based on a story by Thomas Michael Donnelly and Mark Tulin.
      (Q, V, W)

834. DELINQUENT SCHOOLGIRLS. (Rainbow-1975-Gregory
      Corarito-R). Screenplay credits not available. (W)

835. DELIRIUM. (Odyssey Pictures-1979-Peter Maris-R). Screen-
      play by Richard Yalem, from a story by Richard Yalem, Eddie
      Krell, and Jim Loew. (W)

836. DELIVER US FROM EVIL. (Dimension-1975-Robert McCahon-
      G). Screenplay by Robert McCahon. (W)

837. DELTA FOX. (Sebastian International-1979-Beverly Sebastian
      and Fred Sebastian-R). No screenplay credits available.
      (W)

838. THE DELUGE. (Polski-1975-Jerzy Hoffman-N/R). Screen-
      play by Wojciech Zukrowski, Adam Kerseten, and Jerzy Hoff-
      man, based on a novel by Henryk Sienkiewicz; Little Brown,
      1891. (W)

839. DELUSION. (New Line-1981-Alan Beattie-N/R). Screenplay
      by Jack Viertel. (W)

840. DELUSION OF GRANDEUR. (Joseph Green-1975-Gerard
      Oury-N/R). Screenplay by Gerard Oury, Marcel Julian, and
      Daniele Thompson. (NYT, W)

841. THE DEMISE OF HERMAN DURER. (Virginia Films B.V.-
      1980-Rene Seegers-N/R). Screenplay by Rene Seegers, Jean
      van de Velde, and Leon de Winter, based on a novel by Leon
      de Winter. (V)

842. DEMON. (New World Pictures-1977-Larry Cohen-R). An
      original screenplay written by Larry Cohen. (W)

843. THE DEMON OF THE ISLE. (AMLF-1983-Francis Leroi-N/R).
      Screenplay by Francis Leroi and Owen T. Rozmann. (V)

844. DEMON POND. (Shochiku Co. Ltd.-1980-Masahiro Shinoda-
      N/R). Screenplay by Haruhiko Minura and Takeshi Tamura,
      based on a story by Kyoka Izumi. (V)

845. DEMON SEED. (United Artists-1977-Donald Cammell-R).
      Screenplay by Robert Jaffe and Roger O. Hirson, based on a
      novel by Dean R. Koontz; Bantam Books, 1973, 182p.
      (LACOPL, NYT, Q, W)

846. DEMON WITCH CHILD. (Coliseum-1976-Armando Ossorio-R).
      Screenplay credits not available. (W)

847. DEMONOID. (American Panorama-1981-Alfred Zacharias-R).
      Screenplay by David Lee Fein, Alfred Zacharias, and E.
      Amos Powell, based on a story by Alfred Zacharias. (LAT,
      V)

848. DEMONS OF THE MIND. (Cinemation-1976-Peter Sykes-R).
      Screenplay by Christopher Wicking, from a story by Frank
      Goodwin and Christopher Wicking. (W)

LE DERNIER METRO see THE LAST METRO

LES DERNIERES ANNEES DE JEAN JACQUES ROUSSEAU see THE ROADS OF EXILE

849. DERSU UZALA. (New World-1977-Akira Kurosawa-N/R). Akira Kurosawa and Yuri Nagibin wrote the screenplay, based on a story by Vladimir Arseniev. (NYT, W)

850. THE DESERT OF THE TARTARS. (Gaumont-1976-Valerio Zurlini-N/R). Screenplay by Andre Brunelin and Jean-Louis Bertucelli, from the book by Dino Buzzate. (V)

851. DESIRE. (Hemisphere Pictures-1983-Eddie Romero-N/R). Screenplay by Eddie Romero. (LAT, V)

852. DESPAIR. (New Line-1978-Rainer Werner Fassbinder-N/R). Screenplay by Tom Stoppard, based on a novel by Vladimir Nabokov; Putnam, 1966. (LACOPL, W)

853. DESTINY. (BFI-1978-Mike Newell-N/R). Screenplay by David Edgar, based on his own play. (BFI)

854. THE DESTROYERS. (World Northal-1982-Chang Cheh-R). Screenplay by Yi Huang and Chang Cheh. (W)

855. THE DESTROYING ANGEL. (Hand-in-Hand-1976-Peter DeRome-X). No screenplay credits available. (W)

856. THE DESTRUCTORS. (American International-1975-Robert Parrish-PG). An original screenplay by Judd Bernard. (NYT, W)

857. THE DEVIL AND MAX DEVLIN. (Buena Vista-1981-Steven Hilliard Stern-PG). Screenplay by Mary Rodgers, from a story by Mary Rodgers and Jimmy Sangster. (Q, V, W)

858. THE DEVIL AND MR. JONES. (Stolen Moments-1975-David Davidson-X). Screenplay by Kiki Young. (W)

859. THE DEVIL IS A WOMAN. (20th Century-Fox-1975-Damiano Damiani-R). Screenplay by Damiano Damiani, Fabruzio Onofri, and Audrey Nohra, from a screen story by Damiano Damiani. (NYT, W)

860. DEVIL WITHIN HER. (American International-1976-Peter Sasdy-R). Screenplay by Stanley Price. (W)

861. THE DEVIL'S CLEAVAGE. (Kuchar-1975-George Kuchar-N/R). Screenplay written by George Kuchar. (NYT, W)

67 Devil's

862. THE DEVIL'S PLAYGROUND. (Entertainment Marketing-1979-Fred Schepisi-N/R). Screenplay by Fred Schepisi. (W)

863. THE DEVIL'S RAIN. (Bryanston-1975-Robert Fuest-PG). An original screenplay by Gabe Essoe, James Ashton, and Gerald Hopman. (NYT, W)

864. DEVILS THREE. (Aquarius-1980-Bobby A. Suarez-R). Screenplay by J. Zucherro and D. Adair. (W)

865. THE DEVONSVILLE TERROR. (Motion Picture Marketing-1983-Ulli Lomel-N/R). Screenplay by Ulli Lomel and George T. Lindsey, and Suzanna Love. (V)

866. DIAMONDS. (AVCO Embassy-1975-Menahem Golan-PG). Screenplay by David Paulsen, Menahem Golan, from an original story by Menahem Golan. (NYT, Q, W)

867. DIARY OF A CLOISTERED NUN. (Cineglobe-1975-Domenico Paolella-R). Screenplay by Tonino Cervi and Domenico Paolella. (W)

868. DIARY OF A LOVER. (Provobis/O. A, Kress-1977-Sohrab Shahid Saless-N/R). Screenplay by Sohrab Shahid Saless and Helga Houzer. (V)

869. DICK DEADEYE. (Intercontinental-1976-Bill Melendez-G). Screenplay by Leo Rost and Robin Miller. (W)

870. DIE LAUGHING. (Orion/Warner Bros.-1980-Jeff Werner-PG). Screenplay by Jerry Segal, Robby Benson, and Scott Parker, based on an original story by Scott Parker. (Q, V, W)

871. DIE SISTER, DIE! (Cinema Shares International-1978-Randall Hood-PG). Screenplay by Tony Sawyer. (W)

872. A DIFFERENT IMAGE. (Alile Sharon Larkin-1982-Alile Sharon Larkin-N/R). An original screenplay by Alile Sharon Larkin. (V)

873. A DIFFERENT STORY. (AVCO Embassy-1978-Paul Aaron-PG). An original screenplay by Henry Olek. (HR, LAT, NYT, Q, V, W)

DIKAIA OKHOTA KOROLIA STAKHA see WILD HUNTING OF KING STAKH

UN DIMANCHE A LA CAMPAGNE see A SUNDAY IN THE COUNTRY

874. DINER. (MGM/UA-1982-Barry Levinson-R). Screenplay written by Barry Levinson. (Q, V)

875. DINNER FOR ADELE. (New Yorker/Dimension-1980-Oldrich Lipsky-N/R). Screenplay by Jiri Brdecka. (W)

876. DIRT. (American Cinema-1979-Eric Karson and Cal Naylor-PG). Screenplay by S. S. Schweitzer, Bud Freidgen, Tom Madigan, and R. R. Young. (W)

877. DIRTY HANDS. (New Line-1976-Claude Chabrol-R). Screenplay by Claude Chabrol, based on a book by Richard Neely. (NYT, W)

878. DIRTY KNIGHTS' WORK. (Gamma III-1976-Kevin Connor-PG). An original screenplay by Julian Bond, Steven Rossen, and Mitchell Smith, from a story by Fred Weintraub and Paul Heller. (W)

879. THE DIRTY MIND OF YOUNG SALLY. (Boxoffice International-1975-Bethel G. Buckalew-N/R). Screenplay credits not available. (W)

880. DIRTY MONEY. (Allied Artists-1979-Jean-Pierre Melville-N/R). Screenplay written by Jean-Pierre Melville. (W)

881. DIRTY TRICKS. (AVCO Embassy-1981-Alvin Rakoff-PG). A screenplay by William Norton Sr., Eleanor Elias Norton, Thomas Gifford, and Camille Gifford, from a novel by Thomas Gifford. (LAT, Q, V)

882. A DIRTY WESTERN. (Cricket-1975-David Fleetwood-X). Screenplay by David Fleetwood. (W)

883. DISCIPLES OF DEATH. (Artists International-1975-Frank Q. Bobbs-PG). No screenplay credits available. (W)

884. DISCO FEVER. (Group 1-1978-Lamar Card-R). Screenplay written by John Arnoldy, from a story by George Barris. (W)

885. DISCO GODFATHER. (Transvue-1980-R). No production credits available. (W)

886. THE DISENCHANTED. (Elias Querejeta-1976-Jaime Chavarri-N/R). No screenplay credits available. (V)

887. DISTANCE. (Cine Bright-1975-Anthony Lover-N/R). Screenplay written by Jay Castle. (NYT, W)

888. A DISTANT CRY FROM SPRING. (Shochiku Films of America-1982-Yoji Yamada-N/R). Screenplay by Yoji Yamada and Yoshitaka Asama, from a story by Yoji Yamada. (W)

889. DISTANT THUNDER. (Cinema 5-1975-Satyajit Ray-N/R).
      Screenplay by Satyajit Ray, based on the novel by Bibhuti
      Bhusan Bannerji. (NYT, W)

890. DISTURBANCE. (Gruzia Film Studios-1976-Lana Gogoberidze-
      N/R). Screenplay by Lana Gogoberidze and Zaura Arsenasch-
      vili. (V)

891. DIVERSIONS. (Artemis-1976-Derek Ford-X). Screenplay
      written by Derek Ford. (W)

892. THE DIVINE EMMA. (Ambassador-1979-Jiri Krejcik-N/R).
      Screenplay by Zdenek Mahler, Jiri Krejcik, from a story by
      Zdenek Mahler. (BFI)

893. DIVINE MADNESS. (Ladd Co./Warner Bros./1980-Michael
      Ritchie-R). Screenplay written by Jerry Blatt, Bette Midler,
      and Bruce Vilanch. (Q, V, W)

894. THE DIVINE NYMPH. (Analaysis Films-1979-Giuseppe Patroni
      Griffi-N/R). Screenplay by Giuseppe Patroni Griffi and A.
      Valdarnini, based on the novel La Divina Fanciulla by
      Luciano Zuccoli. (W)

895. THE DIVINE OBSESSION. (Melody Films-1976-Louis Su-X).
      Screenplay credits not available. (W)

896. DIXIE. (Steve Brown-1976-Steve Brown-X). No screenplay
      credits available. (W)

897. DIXIE DYNAMITE. (Dimension-1976-Lee Frost-PG). Screen-
      play written by Lee Frost and Wes Bishop. (W)

898. DOC SAVAGE THE MAN OF BRONZE. (Warner Bros.-1975-
      Michael Anderson-G). Screenplay by George Pal and Joe
      Morhaim, based on the novel by Kenneth Robeson; Bantam
      Books, 1975, 170p. (LACOPL, W)

899. DR. BLACK MR. HYDE. (Dimension-1976-William Crain-R).
      Screenplay written by Larry LeBron. (W)

900. DR. BUTCHER M.D. (Aquarius-1982-Frank Martin-R).
      Original screenplay written by Frank Martin. (V, W)

901. DOCTOR DETROIT. (Universal-1983-Michael Pressman-R).
      A screenplay by Carl Gottlieb, Robert Boris, and Bruce Jay
      Friedman; story by Bruce Jay Friedman, based on his novel
      Detroit Abe. (LAT, V)

902. DOCTOR FEELGOOD. (Monarch-1975-X). No production
      credits available. (W)

903. DR. HECKYL & MR. HYPE. (Cannon-1980-Charles B.
      Griffith-R). An original screenplay by Charles B. Griffith.
      (V, W)

904. DR. JEKYLL'S DUNGEON OF DEATH. (New American Films-
      1982-James Wood-R). Screenplay written by James Mathers.
      (V, W)

905. DR. MINX. (Dimension-1975-Hikmet Avedis-R). Screenplay
      written by Hikmet Avedis. (W)

906. DR. TARR'S TORTURE DUNGEON. (Group 1-1976-Juan L.
      Moctezuma-R). Screenplay written by Charles Illescas, based
      on Edgar Allan Poe's The System of Dr. Tarr and Prof.
      Feather. (W)

907. DOCUMENTEUR: AN EMOTION PICTURE. (Cine-Tamaris-
      1982-Agnes Varda-N/R). Agnes Varda wrote the screenplay
      for this film. (W)

908. THE DOG. (Deva Cinematografica-1977-Antonio Isasi-N/R).
      Juan Antonio Porto, Antonio Isasi, and Alberto Vazquez
      Figueroa wrote the screenplay, based on the novel Como un
      Perro Rabioso by Alberto Vazquez Figueroa; Plaza y Janes,
      1975, 124p. (LACOPL, V)

909. DOG DAY. (UGC-1984-Yves Boisset-N/R). Screenplay writ-
      ten by Yves Boisset, Michel Audiard, Dominique Roulet, Serge
      Korber, and Jean Herman, from the novel by Jean Vautrin
      (aka Jean Herman). (V)

910. DOG DAY AFTERNOON. (Warner Bros.-1975-Sidney Lumet-
      R). An original screenplay by Frank Pierson. (NYT, W)

911. THE DOGS OF WAR. (United Artists-1981-John Irvin-R).
      Gary DeVore and George Malko, based on the novel by
      Frederick Forsyth. (Q, V, W)

912. DOLEMITE. (Dimension-1975-R). No production credits
      available. (W)

913. DOMINATION BLUE. (1976-Joe Davian-X). No screenplay
      credits available. (W)

914. DOMINATRIX WITHOUT MERCY. (1976-X). No production
      credits available. (W)

915. THE DOMINO PRINCIPLE. (AVCO Embassy-1977-Stanley
      Kramer-R). Screenplay by Adam Kennedy, based on his
      novel. (NYT, Q, V,)

DON CHISCIOTTE see DON QUIXOTE

916. DON GIOVANNI. (Gaumont-1979-Joseph Losey-N/R). Patricia
      and Joseph Losey adapted the screenplay from an opera by
      W. A. Mozart and Lorenzo Da Ponte. (V, W)

917. DON QUIXOTE. (Sacis-1984-Maurizio Scaparro-N/R). Raphael
      Azcona, Tullio Kezich and Maurizio Scaparro wrote the screen-
      play, from the novel by Miguel de Cervantes. (V)

918. DONA FLOR AND HER TWO HUSBANDS. (New Yorker-1978-
      Bruno Barreto-R). A screenplay by Bruno Barreto, based on
      a novel by Jorge Amado. (NYT, W)

919. DONKEY SKIN. (Janus Films-1975-Jacques Demy-N/R).
      Jacques Demy wrote the screenplay, from a story by Charles
      Perrault. (NYT, W)

920. DON'S PARTY. (Satori-1982-Bruce Beresford-N/R). Screen-
      play by David Williamson. (LAT, W)

921. DON'T ANSWER THE PHONE! (Crown International-1980-
      Robert Hammer-R). Robert Hammer and Michael Castle wrote
      the screenplay. (V, W)

922. DON'T CRY, IT'S ONLY THUNDER. (Sanrio Communications-
      1982-Peter Werner-PG). Screenplay by Paul Hensler. (LAT,
      V, W)

923. DON'T CRY WITH YOUR MOUTH FULL. (New Yorker-1975-
      Pascal Thomas-N/R). Screenplay by Pascal Thomas, Roland
      Duval, and Suzanne Schiffman. (NYT, W)

924. DON'T GO IN THE HOUSE. (Film Ventures International-1980-
      Joseph Ellison-R). Screenplay by Joseph Ellison, Ellen Ham-
      mill, and Joseph Masefield. (V, W)

925. DON'T GO IN THE WOODS ALONE. (Seymour Borde & Asso-
      ciates-1983-James Bryan-R). A screenplay by Garth Eliassen.
      (V, W)

926. DON'T OPEN THE WINDOW. (Newport-1976-Jorge Grau-R).
      Screenplay by Sandro Continenza, Marcello Coscia, and Jorge
      Grau. (W)

      DOOMED LOVE see AMOR DE PERDICAO

927. DOOMWATCH. (AVCO Embassy-1976-Peter Sasdy-N/R).
      Screenplay by Clive Exton, from a story by Dr. Kit Pedler
      and Gerry Davis. (W)

928. DOOR TO DOOR. (Shapiro Entertainment-1984-Patrick Bailey-
N/R). Peter Baloff and Dave Wollert wrote this screenplay.
(V)

929. THE DORM THAT DRIPPED BLOOD. (New Image Releasing-
1984-Jeffrey Obrow & Stephen Carpenter-R). An original
screenplay by Jeffrey Obrow, Stephen Carpenter, and Stacey
Giachino. (LAT, V)

LOS DOS MUNDOS DE ANGELITA see THE TWO WORLDS OF
ANGELITA

930. DOSSIER 51. (Gaumont/New Yorker-1978-Michel Deville-N/R).
Screenplay by Michel Deville and Gilles Perrault, adapted
from the novel by Gilles Perrault. (NYT, W)

931. THE DOUBLE. (Toho/20th Century-Fox-1980-Akira Kurosawa-
N/R). A screenplay by Akira Kurosawa and Masato Ide. (V)

932. DOUBLE DEAL. (Samuel Goldwyn Co.-1983-Brian Kavanagh-
N/R). An original screenplay written by Brian Kavanagh.
(V)

933. THE DOUBLE EXPOSURE OF HOLLY. (Scope Pictures-1976-
Bob Gill-X). Screenplay by Ronan O'Casey. (V, W)

934. DOUBLE FEATURE. (Nickel Odeon-1984-Jose Luis Garci-
N/R). A screenplay by Horacio Valcarcel and Jose Luis
Garci. (V)

935. DOUBLE IDENTITY. (Joseph Green-1980-Franz Peter Wirth-
PG). Screenplay by Oliver Storz, Karl Heinz Willcheri, and
Wilfried Schroder. (W)

936. THE DOUBLE MCGUFFIN. (Mulberry Square-1979-Joe Camp-
N/R). Joe Camp wrote the screenplay, from a story by Joe
Camp and Richard Baker. (V, W)

937. DOUBLE NEGATIVE. (Quadrant Films-1980-George Bloomfield-
N/R). Screenplay written by Thomas Hedley Jr., Charles
Dennis, and Janis Allen, based on The Three Roads by Ross
MacDonald. (V)

938. DOUBLE NICKELS. (Smokey Prods.-1977-Jack Vacek-PG).
Screenplay by Jack Vacek and Patrice Schubert. (V, W)

939. DOUBLE SUICIDE OF SONEZAKI. (Kodasha-Kimura-ATG-
1978-Yasuzo Masumura-N/R). Screenplay by Yoshio Shirasaka
and Yasuzo Masumura, based on a story by Chikamatsu Monzaemon. (V)

940. DOUBLES. (Cinema World-1978-Bruce Wilson-N/R). Screen-
      play by Bruce Wilson. (W)

941. DOWN AND DIRTY. (New Line Cinema-1979-Ettore Scola-
      N/R). Screenplay and story by Ruggero Maccari and Ettore
      Scola.

942. DOWN THE ANCIENT STAIRS. (20th Century-Fox-1975-
      Mauro Bolognini-N/R). Screenplay by Raffaele Andreassi,
      Mario Arosio, Tullio, Bernardino Zapponi, based on novel by
      Mario Tobino. (NYT, W)

943. THE DOZENS. (First Run Features/Calliope Film Resources-
      1981-Christine Dall & Randall Conrad-N/R). An original
      screenplay by Marian Taylor, Christine Dall, and Randall
      Conrad. (LAT, W)

944. DRACULA. (Universal-1979-John Badham-R). W. D. Richter
      wrote the screenplay, based on the stage play by Hamilton
      Deane and John L. Balderston, from the novel by Bram Stoker;
      Doubleday, 1973, 655p. (LACOPL, Q, V, W)

945. DRACULA AND SON. (Gaumont-1979-Edouard Molinaro-N/R).
      Screenplay by Edouard Molinaro, Jean-Marie Poire, and Alain
      Godard, from the book by Claude Klotz. (W)

946. DRACULA BLOWS HIS COOL. (Martin Films-1983-Carlo
      Ombra-R). Screenplay by Grunbach and Rosenthal. (V)

947. DRACULA SUCKS. (Kodiak Films-1980-Philip Marshak-R).
      Screenplay by Darryl A. Marshak and David J. Kern. (W)

948. DRACULA'S DOG. (Crown International-1978-Albert Band-
      N/R). An original screenplay by Frank Ray Perilli. (V, W)

949. DRACULA'S LAST RITES. (Cannon-1980-Domonic Paris-R).
      Screenplay by Ben Donnelly and Domonic Paris. (W)

950. THE DRAGON DIES HARD. (Allied Artists-1975-Kong Kung-
      PG). No screenplay credits available. (W)

951. THE DRAGON FLIES. (20th Century-Fox-1975-Brian Tren-
      chard Smith-R). An original screenplay by Brian Trenchard
      Smith. (W)

952. DRAGON LADY. (Joseph Green-1975-Joel M. Reed-R). No
      screenplay credits available. (W)

953. THE DRAGON LIVES. (Film Ventures-1978-Singloy Wang-R).
      Singloy Wang and Yi Kwan wrote the screenplay. (W)

954. THE DRAGON ON FIRE. (Joseph Kong-N/R). An original
      screenplay by Szeto On. (MFB)

955. DRAGON SISTER. (Cinema Shares International-1978-Ho
      Chang-R). No screenplay credits available. (W)

956. DRAGON SQUAD. (In-Frame Films-1975-Wang Yu-R).
      Screenplay written by Yi Kwan. (W)

      DRAGONFLY see ONE SUMMER LOVE

957. DRAGONS NEVER DIE. (JMG-1976-Charlie Chen-R). No
      screenplay credits available. (W)

958. DRAGONSLAYER. (Paramount-1981-Matthew Robbins-PG).
      Screenplay written by Hal Barwood and Matthew Robbins;
      novelization by Wayland Drew; Ballantine, 1981, 218p.
      (LACOPL, LAT, Q, V, W)

959. THE DRAUGHTSMAN'S CONTRACT. (BFI-1982-Peter Green-
      away-N/R). Written by Peter Greenaway. (LAT, V)

960. DREAM LIFE. (New Line-1975-Mireille Dansereau-R). No
      screenplay credits available. (W)

961. A DREAM OF PASSION. (AVCO Embassy-1978-Jules Dassin-
      R). Screenplay written by Jules Dassin. (NYT, W)

962. DREAM ON. (The Magic Cinema-1981-Ed Harker-N/R).
      Screenplay by Ed Harker. (LAT, V)

963. DREAMER. (20th Century-Fox-1979-Noel Nosseck-PG).
      James Proctor and Larry Bischof wrote the screenplay. (Q,
      V, W)

964. DREAMLAND. (First Run Features-1983-Oz Scott, Nancy
      Baker & Joel Schulman-N/R). Screenplay written by Nancy
      Baker and Richard Lourie. (V)

965. DREAMSCAPE. (20th Century-Fox-Joe Ruben-R). David
      Loughery, Chuck Russel, and Joe Ruben wrote this original
      screenplay. (V)

      DREAMWORLD see COVERGIRL

966. DRESSED TO KILL. (Filmways-1980-Brian De Palma-R).
      Screenplay written by Brian De Palma. (HR, LAT, Q, V, W)

967. THE DRESSER. (Columbia-1983-Peter Yates-PG). Screenplay
      written by Ronald Harwood. (LAT, V)

968. DRIFTER. (European Film Exchange-1975-Pat Rocco-R).
      Screenplay written by Edward Middleton. (W)

969. DRILLER KILLER. (Rochelle Films-1979-Abel Ferrara-N/R).
      Nicholas St. John wrote this original screenplay. (V, W)

970. DRIVE-IN. (Columbia-1976-Rod Amateau-PG). Screenplay by
      Bob Peete. (NYT, W)

971. DRIVE-IN MASSACRE. (New American Films-1982-Stuart
      Segall-R). John Goff and Buck Flower wrote the screenplay.
      (V, W)

972. THE DRIVER. (20th Century-Fox-1978-Walter Hill-R). An
      original screenplay by Walter Hill. (HR, LAT, NYT, Q, V,
      W)

973. THE DRIVER'S SEAT. (AVCO Embassy-1975-Giuseppe Patroni
      Griffi-R). Giuseppe Patroni Griffi and Raffaele La Capria
      wrote the screenplay, based on a novel by Muriel Spark. (Q,
      W)

974. LA DROLESSE. (Gaumont/New Yorker-1981-Jacques Doillon-
      N/R). An original screenplay by Jacques Doillon and Denis
      Ferraris. (W)

975. DROPOUT! (Scotia American-1975-Tinto Brass-R). No
      screenplay credits available. (W)

976. THE DROWNING POOL. (Warner Bros.-1975-Stuart Rosenberg-
      PG). Tracy Keenan Wynn, Lorenzo Semple Jr., and Walter
      Hill wrote the screenplay, based on the novel by Ross Mac-
      Donald; J. Curley & Associates, 1979, 413p. (HR, LACOPL,
      NYT, V, W)

977. DRUM. (United Artists-1976-Steve Carver-R). Screenplay
      by Norman Wexler, based on a novel by Kyle Onstott. (NYT,
      W)

978. DUBEAT-E-O. (H-Z-H-1984-Alan Sacks-N/R). Screenplay
      by Mark Sheffler, based on an idea by Alan Sacks. (V)

979. THE DUCHESS AND THE DIRTWATER FOX. (20th Century-
      Fox-1976-Melvin Frank-PG). Screenplay by Melvin Frank,
      Barry Sandler, and Jack Rose, from an original story by
      Barry Sandler. (NYT, Q, W)

980. DUEL IN THE TIGER DEN. (Tower-1976-Yu Ming Ho-R).
      No screenplay credits available. (W)

981. DUEL OF THE TOUGH. (Godfrey Ho-N/R). Screenplay
      written by Richard Hung. (BFI)

982. THE DUELLISTS. (CIC-1977-Ridley Scott-N/R). Screenplay
     written by Gerold Vaughan-Hughes, from a story by Joseph
     Conrad. (HR, LAT, NYT, Q, V, W)

983. DUNE. (Universal-1984-David Lynch-R). Screenplay by
     David Lynch, from the novel by Frank Herbert; Chilton, 1965.
     (FD, HR, LAT, LACOPL, NYT)

984. THE DYNAMITE TRIO. (Danny Cheung-1982-N/R). An original
     screenplay by Danny Cheung and Judy Hwang. (BFI)

985. DYNASTY. (Cinema Shares International-1977-Mei Chung
     Chang-R). No screenplay credits available. (V)

986. DYRYGENT. (Film Polski-Unite X-1980-Andrzej Wajda-N/R).
     An original screenplay by Andrzej Kijowski. (V)

     E LA NAVE VA see AND THE SHIP SAILS ON

986a. E. T. THE EXTRA-TERRESTRIAL. (Universal-1982-Steven
     Spielberg-PG). Screenplay written by Melissa Mathison;
     novelization by William Kotzwinkle; Putnam, 1982, 246p. (HR,
     LAT, Q, LACOPL, V, W)

987. EACH OTHER. (Franklin Media-1979-Michal Bat-Adam-R).
     Original story and screenplay written by Michal Bat-Adam.
     (W)

988. THE EAGLE HAS LANDED. (Columbia-1976-John Sturges-PG).
     Tom Mankiewicz wrote the screenplay, from a novel by Jack
     Higgins; Holt, 1975, 352p. (LACOPL, LAT, NYT, Q, V, W)

989. EAGLE VERSUS SILVER FOX. (Almi-1983-Godfrey Ho-R).
     No screenplay credits available. (W)

990. EAGLE'S CLAWS. (1978-Lee Tso-Nan-R). No screenplay
     credits available. (W)

991. THE EAGLE'S SHADOW. (Cinematic-1982-Yuen Woo Ping-PG).
     Screenplay by Ng See Yuen. (W)

992. EAGLE'S WING. (Rank-1979-Anthony Harvey-N/R). Screen-
     play by John Briley, based on an original story by Michael
     Syson. (V, W)

993. THE EARTH IS A SINFUL SONG. (Seaberg-1975-Rauni
     Mollberg-N/R). Screenplay by Rauni Mollberg, Pirjo Honkas-
     alo, and Panu Rajala, from the novel by Timo K. Mukka.
     (NYT, W)

994. EARTHBOUND. (Taft International-1981-James Conway-PG).
     Michael Fisher wrote the original screenplay. (V, W)

995. THE EARTHLING. (Filmways-1981-Peter Collinson-PG).
      Lanny Cotler wrote the screenplay. (Q, W)

996. EAST END HUSTLE. (Troma-1979-Frank Vitale-R). A
      screenplay by Frank Vitale and Allan Bozo Moyle. (W)

997. EASY ALICE. (California Continental Cinema-1979-Tom
      Hoffman-X). No screenplay credits available. (W)

998. EASY MONEY. (IFEX/Sovexportfilm-1982-Evgeny Mateev-
      N/R). Screenplay by Evgeny Mateev. (W)

999. EASY MONEY. (Orion-1983-James Signorelli-R). Screen-
      play by Rodney Dangerfield, Michael Endler, P. J. O'Rourke,
      and Dennis Blair. (HR, LAT, NYT, V, W)

1000. EAT MY DUST! (New World-1976-Charles B. Giffith-PG).
      Screenplay by Charles B. Griffith. (HR, LAT, NYT, W)

1001. EATING RAOUL. (20th Century-Fox International Classics/
      Quartet Films-1982-Paul Bartel-R). An original screenplay
      by Richard Blackburn and Paul Bartel. (LAT, NYT, V, W)

      EBOLI see CHRIST STOPPED AT EBOLI

1002. ECHOES. (Continental Distributing-1983-Arthur Allan
      Seidelman-R). Screenplay written by Richard J. Anthony.
      (LAT, V, W)

1003. ECHOES OF A SUMMER. (Cine Artists-1976-Don Taylor-PG).
      Robert L. Joseph wrote the original screenplay. (NYT, W)

1004. ECSTASY OF THE MACUMBA. (Hollywood International-1975-
      X). Screenplay credits not available. (W)

1005. EDDIE AND THE CRUISERS. (Embassy-1983-Martin Davidson-
      PG). Screenplay by Martin Davidson and Arlene Davidson,
      from a novel by P. F. Kluge. (W)

1006. EDDIE MACON'S RUN. (Universal-1983-Jeff Kanew-PG). A
      screenplay written by Jeff Kanew, based on a novel by
      James McLendon; Viking Press, 1980, 296p. (HR, LACOPL,
      LAT, V, W)

1007. EDGE OF FURY. (Mid-Broadway Releasing-1981-George Ho-
      R). No screenplay credits available. (W)

1008. EDITH AND MARCEL. (Parafrance-1983-Claude Lelouch-
      N/R). Screenplay by Claude Lelouch, with the collaboration
      of Gilles Durieux and Pierre Uytterhoeven. (V)

1009.   EDUCATING RITA. (Columbia-1983-Lewis Gilbert-PG).
        Screenplay by Willy Russell. (HR, LAT, V)

1010.   EDVARD MUNCH. (New Yorker-1976-Peter Watkins-N/R).
        Peter Watkins wrote the screenplay. (NYT, W)

1011.   EFFECTS. (Image Works-1979-Dusty Nelson-N/R). Dusty
        Nelson wrote the screenplay, based on a novel by William H.
        Mooney. (V, W)

1012.   EFFI BRIEST. (New Yorker-1977-Rainer Werner Fassbinder-
        N/R). Rainer Werner Fassbinder wrote the screenplay.
        (NYT, W)

1013.   EGON SCHIELE--EXCESS AND PUNISHMENT. (Gamma-1981-
        Herbert Vesely-N/R). Screenplay by Herbert Vesely and
        Leo Tichat. (V)

1014.   THE EIGER SANCTION. (Universal-1975-Clint Eastwood-R).
        Hal Dresner, Warren B. Murphy, and Rod Whitaker wrote
        the screenplay, based on a novel by Trevanian; Crown,
        1972, 316p. (HR, LACOPL, LAT, NYT, Q, V, W)

1015.   EIJANAIKA. (Shochiku-1982-Shohei Imamura-N/R). Screen-
        play by Shohei Imamura and Ken Miuamoto, from a story by
        Shohei Imamura. (W)

1016.   EL PASO WRECKING CORP. (Joe Gage Films-1978-Joe Gage-
        X). An original screenplay by Joe Gage. (V)

1017.   ELECTIVE AFFINITIES. (RAI-Istituto Luce-1978-Gianni
        Amico-N/R). Gianni Amico, Marco Melani, and I. Alighiero
        Chiusano wrote the screenplay, from the novel by Johann
        Wolfgang von Goethe. (V)

1018.   ELECTRIC DREAMS. (MGM/UA-1984-Steve Barron-PG).
        Screenplay by Rusty Lemorande. (V)

1019.   THE ELECTRIC HORSEMAN. (Columbia-1979-Sydney Pollack-
        PG). Screenplay by Robert Garland, from a story by Paul
        Gaer and Robert Garland, based on a story by Shelly Bur-
        ton; novelization by H. B. Gilmour; Pocket Books, 1979,
        224p. (HR, LACOPL, LAT, Q, V, W)

1020.   THE ELEMENT OF CRIME. (Per Holst-1984-Lars von Trier-
        N/R). Original story and screenplay by Lars von Trier and
        Niels Voersel; English translation by Steven Wakelam and
        William Quarshie. (V)

1021.   THE ELEPHANT MAN. (Paramount-1980-David Lynch-PG).
        Screenplay by Christopher DeVore, Eric Bergren, David

Lynch, based on "The Elephant Man and Other Reminiscences"
by Sir Frederick Treves, and in part on "The Elephant Man:
A Study in Human Dignity" by Ashley Montagu. (HR, LAT,
Q, V, W)

1022. THE ELEVATOR. (Tuschinski-1983-Dick Maas-N/R). Dick
Maas is credited with the original screenplay. (V)

1023. ELISA, MY LOVE. (Elias Querejeta-1977-Carlos Saura-N/R).
Screenplay by Carlos Saura. (V)

1024. ELIZA FRASER. (Roadshow-1976-Tim Burstall-N/R).
Screenplay written by Dave Williamson. (V)

1025. ELVIS. (Dick Clark-1979-John Carpenter-N/R). Screenplay written by Tony Lawrence. (W)

1026. EMBERS. (Sippy Films-United Producers-1977-Ramesh
Sippy-N/R). Screenplay written by Salim-Javed. (V)

1027. EMBRYO. (Cine Artists-1976-Ralph Nelson-PG). Screenplay by Anita Doohan and Jack W. Thomas, from a story by
Jack W. Thomas. (NYT, Q, W)

1028. EMILIENNE & NICOLE. (Joseph Green-1976-Guy Casaril-X).
No screenplay credits given; adapted from the novel by
Claude des Olbes. (W)

1029. EMILY. (An Emily Production-1976-Henry Herbert-N/R).
Screenplay written by Anthony Morris. (V)

1030. EMMA MAE. (PRO International-1976-Jamac Fanaka-R).
Screenplay written by Jamac Fanaka. (V)

1031. EMMANUELLE AROUND THE WORLD. (Jerry Gross-1980-
Joe D'Amato-R). Screenplay written by Maria Pia Fusco and
Gianfranco Clerici. (W)

1032. EMMANUELLE 4. (AAA/Sedpa-1984-Francis Leroy and Iris
Letans-N/R). Screenplay co-authored by Francis Leroy and
Iris Letans, from a story by Emmanuelle Arsan. (V)

1033. EMMANUELLE--THE JOYS OF A WOMAN. (Paramount-1976-
Francis Giacobetti-X). Screenplay written by Francis
Giacobetti and Bob Elia, from the book by Emmanuelle Arsan;
Grove Press, 1974. (LACOPL, NYT, W)

1034. EMPIRE OF PASSION. (Barbary Coast-1980-Nagisa Oshima-
N/R). Screenplay by Nagisa Oshima, based on the book by
Itoko Nakamura. (W)

1035.   EMPIRE OF THE ANTS. (American International Pictures-
        1977-Bert I. Gordon-PG). Screenplay by Jack Turley, from
        a screen story by Bert I. Gordon and a story by H. G.
        Wells. (HR, LAT, NYT, Q, V, W)

1036.   THE EMPIRE STRIKES BACK. (20th Century-Fox-1980-
        Irvin Kershner-PG). Screenplay by Leigh Brackett and
        Lawrence Kasdan, based on a story by George Lucas. (HR,
        LAT, NYT, Q, V, W)

1037.   THE EMPRESS DOWAGER. (Shaw Bros.-1975-Li Han-Hsiang-
        N/R). Screenplay credits not available. (W)

1038.   ENCOUNTER WITH THE UNKNOWN. (Libert-1975-Harry
        Thomason-PG). No screenplay credits given. (W)

1039.   THE END. (United Artists-1978-Burt Reynolds-R). Screen-
        play written by Jerry Belson; novelization by Carol Sturm
        Smith; Avon, 1978, 171p. (HR, LACOPL, NYT, W)

1040.   THE END OF AUGUST. (Quartet-1982-Bob Graham-PG).
        Screenplay by Eula Seaton, Leon Heller, Anna Thomas, and
        Gregory Nava, based on the novel The Awakening by Kate
        Chopin. (W)

1041.   END OF THE GAME. (20th Century-Fox-1976-Maximilian
        Schell-PG). Screenplay by Maximilian Schell, Bo Goldmann,
        and Friedrich Duerrenmatt; based on Durrenmatt's The Judge
        and His Hangman. (NYT, Q, W)

1042.   THE END OF THE WORLD IN OUR USUAL BED ON A NIGHT
        FULL OF RAIN. (Warner Bros.-1978-Lina Wertmuller-N/R).
        Screenplay written by Lina Wertmuller. (NYT, Q, V, W)

1043.   ENDANGERED SPECIES. (MGM/UA-1982-Alan Rudolph-R).
        Screenplay written by Alan Rudolph and John Binder,
        based on a story by Judson Klinger and Richard Woods.
        (V, W)

1044.   ENDLESS LOVE. (Universal-1981-Franco Zeffirelli-R).
        Screenplay by Judith Rascoe, based on the novel by Scott
        Spencer. (LACOPL, LAT, Q, V, W)

1045.   AN ENEMY OF THE PEOPLE. (Warner Bros.-1978-George
        Schaefer-G). Alexander Jacobs wrote the screenplay,
        based on an adaptation of the Henrik Ibsen play by Arthur
        Miller. (LAT, V, W)

1046.   THE ENFORCER. (Warner Bros.-1976-James Fargo-R).
        Screenplay by Stirling Silliphant and Dean Reisner, from a
        story by Gail Morgan Hickman and S. W. Schurr, based on

characters created by Harry Julian Fink and R. M. Fink.
(NYT, Q, V)

1047. THE ENFORCER FROM DEATH ROW. (Dinero-1978-R). No
       production credits available. (W)

1048. ENIGMA. (Embassy-1982-Jeannot Szwarc-PG). Screenplay
       by John Briley, based on the novel by Michael Barak; Mor-
       row, 1978, 240p. (LACOPL, V)

1049. ENTER THE NINJA. (Cannon Films-1982-Menahem Golan-R).
       Screenplay written by Dick Desmond. (V)

1050. ENTIRE DAYS IN THE TREES. (Theatre D'Orsay-Duras-
       1976-Marguerite Duras-N/R). Screenplay by Marguerite
       Duras, from her own play. (V)

1051. THE ENTITY. (20th Century-Fox-1982-Sidney J. Furie-R).
       Screenplay by Frank DeFelitta, based on his novel; Putnam,
       1978, 432p. (LACOPL, V)

1052. EQUINOX FLOWER. (New Yorker-1977-Yasujiro Ozu-N/R).
       Screenplay by Yasujiro Ozu and Kogo Noda, based on a
       novel by Ton Satomi. (NYT, W)

1053. EQUUS. (United Artists-1977-Sidney Lumet-R). Screenplay
       by Peter Shaffer, from his play. (NYT, Q, W)

1054. ERASERHEAD. (American Film Institute-1977-David Lynch-
       N/R). Screenplay by David Lynch. (V)

1055. EROTICA. (Brent Walker-1981-Brian Smedley Aston-N/R).
       Screenplay by Brian Smedley Aston. (V)

1056. THE ESCAPE. (CCC Kunstfilm-1980-Edwin Zbonek-N/R).
       Screenplay by Sigmund Bendkover and Al Bronsowy, based
       on an idea by Robert Azderball. (V)

1057. THE ESCAPE ARTIST. (Orion-1982-Caleb Deschanel-PG).
       Screenplay by Melissa Mathison and Stephen Zito, based on
       the novel by David Wagoner; Farrar, Straus & Giroux, 1965.
       (LACOPL, Q, V)

1058. ESCAPE FROM ALCATRAZ. (Paramount-1979-Donald Siegel-
       PG). Screenplay by Richard Tuggle, based on the book by
       J. Campbell Bruce; McGraw-Hill, 1963, 248p. (LACOPL, Q,
       V, W)

1059. ESCAPE FROM ANGOLA. (Doty-Dayton-1976-Leslie
       Martinson-G). Screenplay by Barry Clark, from a story
       by George Gale. (W)

1060. ESCAPE FROM NEW YORK. (AVCO Embassy-1981-John Carpenter-R). An original screenplay by John Carpenter and Nick Castle. (LAT, Q, V, W)

1061. ESCAPE TO ATHENA. (Associated Film Distributors-1979-George P. Cosmatos-N/R). Screenplay by Richard S. Lochte and Edward Anhalt, based on an original story by Richard S. Lochte and George P. Cosmatos. (Q, V, W)

1062- ESCAPE TO WITCH MOUNTAIN. (Buena Vista-1975-John
63. Hough-G). Screenplay by Robert Malcolm Young, based on book by Alexander Key; Westminster Press, 1968. (LACOPL, NYT, Q, W)

1064. EUGENE ATGET PHOTOGRAPHER. (1982-Peter Wyeth-N/R). Screenplay by Peter Wyeth. (BFI)

1065. EUREKA. (UA Classics-1983-Nicolas Roeg-N/R). Screenplay by Paul Mayersberg, based on a novel by Marshall Houts. (V)

1066. THE EUROPEANS. (Levitt-Pickman-1979-James Ivory-G). Screenplay by Ruth Prawer Jhabvala, from the novel by Henry James; Penguin, 1985, 208p. (LACOPL, V, W)

1067. EVENTS. (Alfred/Baker Films-1980-Fred Baker-R). Screenplay written by Fred Baker. (W)

1068. EVERY INCH A LADY. (Mature-1975-John and Len Amero-X). Screenplay written by John and Len Amero. (W)

1069. EVERY MAN FOR HIMSELF. (Zoetrope/New Yorker-1980-Jean-Luc Godard-N/R). Screenplay by Jean-Claude Carriere and Anne Marie Mieville. (W)

1070. EVERY WHICH WAY BUT LOOSE. (Warner Bros.-1978-James Fargo-R). Screenplay by Jeremy Joe Kronsberg; novelization by Jeremy Joe Kronsberg; Warner, 1979, 220p. (HR, LACOPL, LAT, NYT, Q, V, W)

1071. EVERYDAY. (American Films-1976-George B. Britton-R). Screenplay by Aaron Mann, Murray Kalis, and Rebecca Hillman. (W)

1072. THE EVICTORS. (American International-1979-Charles B. Pierce-PG). Screenplay by Charles B. Pierce, Garry Rusoff, and Paul Fisk. (V, W)

1073. THE EVIL. (New World Pictures-1978-Gus Trikonis-R). Screenplay written by Donald G. Thompson. (V, W)

1074. THE EVIL DEAD. (New Line Cinema-1983-Sam M. Raimi-
       N/R). Screenplay by Sam M. Raimi. (LAT, V)

1075. EVIL FINGERS. (Scotia American-1975-Luigi Bazzoni-N/R).
       Screenplay credits not available. (W)

1076. EVIL IN THE DEEP. (Golden-1976-Virginia Stone-PG). No
       screenplay credits available. (W)

1077. THE EVIL THAT MEN DO. (ITC Film Distributors-1984-J.
       Lee Thompson-N/R). Screenplay by David Lee Henry,
       based on a novel by R. Lance Hill; Times Books, 1978,
       309p. (LACOPL, V)

1078. EVIL UNDER THE SUN. (Universal-1982-Guy Hamilton-PG).
       Screenplay by Anthony Shaffer, based on a novel by Agatha
       Christie; Dodd, Mead, 1941, 260p. (HR, LACOPL, LAT, Q,
       V)

1079. EVILSPEAK. (Morena Co.-1982-Eric Weston-R). Screenplay
       by Joseph Garofalo and Eric Weston. (LAT, V, W)

1080. EXCALIBUR. (Orion-Warner Bros.-1981-John Boorman-R).
       Screenplay by Rospo Pallenberg and John Boorman, adapted
       from Malory's Le Morte d'Arthur by Rospo Pallenberg. (LAT,
       Q, V, W)

1081. THE EXECUTIONER. (Trans Continental-1978-Turno Ishii-
       R). Screenplay written by George Gonneau. (W)

1082. THE EXECUTIONER PART II. (21st Century Distribution-
       1984-James Bryant-R). Screenplay credits not available.
       (V)

1083. EXIT THE DRAGON ENTER THE TIGER. (Dimension
       Pictures-1976-Lee Tse Nam-R). Screenplay by Chang Shun
       Yee, adaptation by Hugo Grimaldi. (W)

1084. EXORCIST II: THE HERETIC. (Warner Bros.-1977-John
       Boorman-R). Screenplay by William Goodhart. (NYT, Q, V)

1085. EXPERIENCE PREFERRED BUT NOT ESSENTIAL. (Enigma-
       1982-Peter Duffel-N/R). Screenplay by June Roberts.
       (LAT, V)

1086. EXPOSE MY LOVELY. (Mature-1976-Armand Weston-X).
       Screenplay written by Armand Weston. (W)

1087. EXPOSED. (MGM/UA-1983-James Toback-R). Screenplay
       written by James Toback. (BFI, LAT, V)

EXTERIOR NUIT see NIGHT EXTERIOR

1088. THE EXTERMINATOR. (AVCO Embassy-1980-James Glicken-
       haus-R). Screenplay by James Glickenhaus. (V, W)

1089. EXTERMINATOR 2. (Cannon Releasing-1984-Mark Buntzman-
       R). Screenplay by Mark Buntzman. (V)

1090. AN EYE FOR AN EYE. (Brentwood-1975-Larry Brown-PG).
       Screenplay by Walter C. Dallenbach. (W)

1091. AN EYE FOR AN EYE. (AVCO Embassy-1981-Steve Carver-
       R). William Gray and James Bruner wrote the screenplay,
       from an original story by James Bruner. (LAT, Q, V, W)

1092. EYE OF THE NEEDLE. (United Artists-1981-Richard
       Marquand-R). Stanley Mann wrote the screenplay, based on
       the novel by Ken Follett. (LAT, Q, V, W)

1093. EYEBALL. (Joseph Brenner-1978-Umberto Lenzi-R). Screen-
       play credits not available. (V, W)

1094. EYES OF A STRANGER. (Warner Bros.-1981-Ken Wiederhorn-
       R). Screenplay by Mark Jackson and Eric L. Bloom. (LAT,
       Q, V, W)

1095. EYES OF FIRE. (Elysian Pictures-1984-Avery Crounse-N/R).
       Screenplay by Avery Crounse. (V)

1096. EYES OF LAURA MARS. (Columbia-1978-Irvin Kershner-
       R). Screenplay by John Carpenter and David Zelag
       Goodman, from a story by John Carpenter. (HR, NYT, Q,
       V, W)

1097. EYES OF THE BIRDS. (Channel 4 London-1983-Gabriel
       Auer-N/R). Screenplay by Carlos Andreu and Gabriel Auer.
       (V)

1098. EYES OF THE DRAGONS. (Cinematic-1981-Joseph Kong &
       Godfrey Ho-R). No screenplay credits available. (W)

1099. THE EYES, THE MOUTH. (Gaumont-1982-Marco Bellocchio-
       N/R). Screenplay by Marco Bellochio and Vincenzo Cerami.
       (V)

1100. EYEWITNESS. (20th Century-Fox-1981-Peter Yates-R).
       Screenplay by Steve Tesich; novelization by John Minahan;
       Avon, 1981, 176p. (LACOPL, LAT, Q, V, W)

1101. F.I.S.T. (United Artists-1978-Norman Jewison-PG). Screen-
       play by Joe Eszterhas and Sylvester Stallone, from a story

by Joe Eszterhas; novelization by Joe Eszterhas; Dell, 1978.
(LACOPL, NYT, W)

1102. FABIAN. (United Artists Classics-1982-Wolf Gremm-R).   No
screenplay credit; based on a novel by Erich Kastner.
(LAT, W)

1103. FACE TO FACE. (Paramount-1976-Ingmar Bergman-R).
Screenplay written by Ingmar Bergman; Pantheon, 1976,
118p. (LACOPL, NYT, Q, W)

1104. FACES OF LOVE. (Gaumont/New Yorker-1978-Michel Soutter-
N/R). Screenplay by Michel Soutter. (NYT, W)

1105. FADE TO BLACK. (American Cinema-1980-Vernon Zimmerman-
R). Vernon Zimmerman wrote the original screenplay. (Q,
V, W)

1106. FAIRY TALES. (Fairy Tales Distributors-1979-Harry Tampa-
R). Screenplay by Frank Ray Perilli and Franne Schacht.
(W)

1107. FAKE-OUT. (M. Riklis-1982-Matt Cimber-N/R). Screenplay
written by Matt Cimber and John Goff, from their original
screen story. (V)

1108. THE FAKING OF THE PRESIDENT. (Spencer-1976-Jeanne
and Alan Abel-N/R). Written by Jeanne and Alan Abel.
(W)

1109. THE FALL OF THE HOUSE OF USHER. (Sunn Classic-1979-
James L. Conway-PG). Screenplay written by Stephen Lord,
based on a story by Edgar Allan Poe. (W)

1110. FALLING IN LOVE. (Paramount-1984-Ulu Grosbard-PG-13).
Michael Cristofer wrote the original screenplay. (LAT, V)

1111. FALLING IN LOVE AGAIN. (International Picture Show-
1980-Steven Paul-PG). Screenplay written by Steven Paul,
Ted Allan, and Susannah York. (V, W)

FALSE FACE see SCALPEL

1112. FAME. (United Artists/MGM-1980-Alan Parker-R). Christopher Gore wrote this original screenplay. (Q, V, W)

1113. THE FAMILY. (Public-1982-Karei Naru Ichikozo-N/R).
Screenplay written by Satsuo Yamamoto and Nabuo Yamada,
based on the novel by Toyoko Yamazaki. (NYT, W)

1114. FAMILY ENFORCER. (First American-1978-Ralph DeVito-R).
Screenplay by Ralph DeVito. (W)

1115. FAMILY KILLER. (Cannon-1975-Vittorio Schiraldi-R).
       Screenplay written by Vittorio Schiraldi. (W)

1116. FAMILY PLOT. (Universal-1976-Alfred Hitchcock-PG).
       Ernest Lehman wrote the screenplay, from the novel Rain-
       bird Pattern by Victor Canning. (NYT, Q, W)

1117. THE FAN. (Paramount-1981-Edward Bianchi-R). Screen-
       play by Priscilla Chapman and John Hartwell, based on the
       novel by Bob Randall. (LAT, Q, V, W)

       THE FANATIC see THE LAST HORROR FILM

1118. FANNY AND ALEXANDER. (Embassy-1982-Ingmar Bergman-
       R). Screenplay written by Ingmar Bergman. (HR, LAT,
       NYT, V, W)

1119. FANNY HILL. (Brent Walker-n.d.-Gerry O'Hara-N/R).
       Screenplay by Stephen Chesley. (V)

1120. FANTASEX. (Command Cinema-1976-Howard Winters and
       Robert Norman-X). Screenplay written by Howard Winters
       and Robert Norman. (W)

1121. FANTASIES. (Joseph Brenner-1981-John Derek-R). Screen-
       play by John Derek. (LAT, V, W)

1122. FANTASTICA. (Gaumont-1980-Gilles Carle-N/R). Screen-
       play by Gilles Carle. (V)

1123. FANTASY IN BLUE. (Manson-1975-Roger Kramer-X).
       Screenplay by Roger Kramer. (W)

1124. FANTOZZI AGAINST THE WORLD. (Titanus-1980-Paolo
       Villaggio and Neri Parenti-N/R). Screenplay by Leo Ben-
       venuti, Piero De Bernardi, Paolo Villaggio, and Neri Parenti.
       (V)

1125. FAR AWAY AND CLOSE. (Swedish Film Institute-1976-
       Marianne Ahrne-N/R). Screenplay written by Marianne
       Ahrne and Bertrand Hurault. (V)

1126. FAR FROM POLAND. (Jill Godmilow-1984-Jill Godmilow-N/R).
       Screenplay credits not given. (V)

1127. THE FAR SHORE. (Bauer International-1978-Joyce Wieland-
       N/R). Screenplay by Bryan Barney, from a story by Joyce
       Wieland. (W)

1128. THE FAREWELL. (Scandinavia Today-1982-Tuija-Maija
       Nislanen-N/R). Screenplay by Eija-Elina Bergholm and
       Vivica Bandler. (W)

1129. FAREWELL, MY LOVELY. (AVCO Embassy-1975-Dick
       Richards-R). Screenplay by David Zelag Goodman, based
       on the novel by Raymond Chandler; Modern Library, 1967,
       438p. (FD, LACOPL, NYT, Q, V, W)

1130. FAREWELL SCARLET. (Command-1975-Chuck Vincent-X).
       Screenplay by J. Vidos, Howard Winters, and Chuck Vin-
       cent. (W)

1131. THE FARMER. (Columbia-1977-David Berlatsky-R). Screen-
       play by George Fargo, Janice Colson-Dodge, Patrick Regan,
       and John Carmody. (NYT, Q, V)

1132. FAST BREAK. (Columbia-1979-Jack Smight-PG). Screen-
       play by Sandor Stern, based on a story by Marc Kaplan;
       novelization by Paul B. Ross; Ballantine Books, 1979, 183p.
       (LACOPL, Q, V, W)

1133. FAST CHARLIE ... THE MOONBEAM RIDER. (Universal-
       1979-Steve Carver-PG). Screenplay by Michael Gleason,
       based on a story by Ed Spielman and Howard Friedlander.
       (V, W)

1134. FAST COMPANY. (Topar Films-1979-David Cronenberg-PG).
       Screenplay credit not given; from a story by Alan Treen.
       (W)

1135. FAST TIMES AT RIDGEMONT HIGH. (Universal-1982-Amy
       Heckerling-R). Screenplay by Cameron Crowe, based on
       his book of the same title; Simon & Schuster, 1982.
       (LACOPL, Q, V)

1136. FAST-WALKING. (Pickman Films-1982-James B. Harris-R).
       Screenplay written by James B. Harris. (V, W)

1137. FAT CHANCE. (Summit Features-1982-M. Summer-N/R).
       Screenplay credits not available. (W)

1138. FATAL GAMES. (Impact Films-1984-Michael Elliot-N/R).
       Screenplay by Christopher Mankiewicz, Rafael Bunuel, and
       Michael Elliot. (V)

1139. FATHER SERGIUS. (Corinth Films-1982-Igor Talankin-N/R).
       Screenplay written by Igor Talankin, based on a novel by
       Leo Tolstoy. (W)

1140. FATSO. (20th Century-Fox-1980-Anne Bancroft-PG).
       Screenplay by Anne Bancroft; novelization by Anne Ban-
       croft; Ballantine, 1980. (LACOPL, Q, V, W)

1141. FEAR CITY. (Zupnik-Curtis Enterprises-1984-Abel Ferrara-
       N/R). Screenplay by Nicholas St. John. (V)

1142. FEAR NO EVIL. (AVCO Embassy-1981-Frank LaLoggia-R).
       Screenplay by Frank LaLoggia. (LAT, Q, V, W)

1143. FEAR OF FEAR. (Westdeutscher Rundfunk-1976-Rainer
       Werner Fassbinder-N/R). Screenplay written by Rainer
       Werner Fassbinder. (NYT, V)

1144. FEAR OR FANTASY. (Bob Mason-1976-Bob Mason-X).
       Screenplay written by Bob Mason. (W)

1145. THE FEARLESS JACKAL. (Marvin-1982-Lei Chiu-R).
       Screenplay credits not given. (W)

1146. FEDORA. (United Artists-1978-Billy Wilder-PG). I. A. L.
       Diamond and Billy Wilder wrote the screenplay, from the
       book by Tom Tryon, Crowned Heads; Knopf, 1976, 340p.
       (LACOPL, Q, V, W)

1147. FEEDBACK. (Feedback Company-1979-Bill Doukas-N/R).
       Screenplay written by Bill Doukas. (V)

1148. FEELIN' UP. (Troma-1983-David Secter-R). Screenplay by
       David Secter. (W)

1149. FEELINGS. (Kemal Enterprises-1977-Kemal Horulu-X).
       Screenplay written by Jack Parro. (V)

       FELLINI'S CASANOVA see CASANOVA

1150. FEMALE CHAUVINISTS. (Jay Jackson-1976-Jay Jackson-X).
       Screenplay by Jack Holtzman. (W)

1151. FEMALE TROUBLE. (New Line Cinema-1975-John Waters-X).
       Screenplay written by John Waters. (NYT, W)

1152. FEMALES FOR HIRE. (Independent International-1976-Rolf
       Olsen-R). No screenplay credits given. (W)

       LA FEMME D'A COTE see THE WOMAN NEXT DOOR

1153. FEMMES DE SADE. (Variety-1976-Alex de Renzy-X).
       Screenplay by Alex de Renzy. (W)

1154. FFOLKES. (Universal-1980-Andrew V. McLaglen-PG). Jack
       Davies wrote the screenplay, based on his novel Esther,
       Ruth and Jennifer. (LACOPL, Q, V, W)

1155. FIEND. (Cinema Enterprises-1980-Don Dohler-N/R). Screen-
       play written by Don Dohler. (W)

1156. THE FIENDISH PLOT OF DR. FU MANCHU. (Orion/Warner

Bros.-1980-Piers Haggard-PG). Jim Moloney and Rudy
Dochtermann wrote the screenplay, based on characters
from the Sax Rohmer novels. (Q, V, W)

1157. THE FIFTH FLOOR. (Film Ventures International-1980-
Howard Avedis-R). Screenplay by Meyer Dolinsky, from a
story by Howard Avedis. (W)

1158. THE FIFTH MUSKETEER. (Columbia-1979-Ken Annakin-PG).
Screenplay by David Ambros, based upon the novel by
Alexandre Dumas and a screenplay by George Bruce. (HR,
LAT, V, W)

1159. THE $50,000 CLIMAX SHOW. (Artimes-1975-Anonymous-X).
Screenplay by J. P. Paradine. (W)

1160. FIGHTING BACK. (Paramount Pictures-1982-Lewis Teague-
R). Screenplay by Tom Hedley and David Z. Goodman.
(HR, LAT, Q, V, W)

1161. FIGHTING DRAGONS VS. THE DEADLY TIGER. (Fury
Films-1982-Pang Nim-R). Screenplay credits not available.
(W)

1162. FIGHTING MAD. (20th Century-Fox-1976-Jonathan Demme-
R). Screenplay written by Jonathan Demme. (NYT, W)

1163. FINAL ASSIGNMENT. (Almi Cinema 5-1982-Paul Almond-PG).
Screenplay by Marc Rosen. (W)

1164. FINAL CHAPTER--WALKING TALL. (American International-
1977-Jack Starrett-R). Screenplay by Howard B. Kreitsek
and Samuel A. Peeples, based on a story by Howard B.
Kreitsek. (NYT, V)

1165. THE FINAL CONFLICT. (20th Century-Fox-1981-Graham
Baker-R). Screenplay by Andrew Birkin, based on characters created by David Seltzer. (LAT, Q, V, W)

1166. THE FINAL COUNTDOWN. (United Artists-1980-Don Taylor-
PG). Screenplay by David Ambrose, Gerry Davis, Thomas
Hunter and Peter Powell, from a story by Thomas Hunter,
Peter Powell, and David Ambrose. (Q, V, W)

1167. FINAL EXAM. (Bedford Entertainment Group-1981-Jimmy
Huston-R). Screenplay written by Jimmy Huston. (LAT,
V, W)

1168. THE FINAL OPTION. (MGM/UA-1983-Ian Sharp-R). Screenplay written by Reginald Rose, based on The Tiptoe Boys
by George Markstein. (W)

1169.   THE FINAL TERROR. (Com World-1984-Andrew Davis-R).
        Screenplay by Jon George, Neill Hicks, and Ronald Shusett.
        (V, W)

1170.   FINDERS KEEPERS. (CBS Theatrical/Warner Bros.-1984-
        Richard Lester-R). Screenplay by Ronny Graham, Terence
        Marsh, Charles Dennis, based on the novel The Next to Last
        Train Ride by Charles Dennis; St. Martin's Press, 1974,
        216p. (LACOPL, V)

1171.   FINGERS. (Brut-1978-James Toback-R). Screenplay by
        James Toback. (NYT, W)

1172.   FIONA. (Rochelle Films-1979-James Kenelm Clarke-R).
        Screenplay by Michael Robson. (W)

1173.   FIRE AND ICE. (20th Century-Fox-1983-Ralph Bakshi-PG).
        Screenplay by Roy Thomas and Gerry Conway. (LAT, V,
        W)

1174.   FIRE SALE. (20th Century-Fox-1977-Alan Arkin-PG).
        Screenplay written by Robert Klane, based on his novel.
        (V)

1175.   FIRECRACKER. (New World-1981-Cirio Santiago-R). Screen-
        play by Ken Metcalfe and Cirio Santiago. (V, W)

1176.   FIREFOX. (Warner Bros.-1982-Clint Eastwood-PG). Screen-
        play written by Alex Lasker and Wendell Wellman, based on
        the novel by Craig Thomas; G. K. Hall, 1978, 529p.
        (LACOPL, Q, V)

1177.   FIREPOWER. (Associated Film Distribution-1979-Michael
        Winner-R). Gerald Wilson wrote the screenplay. (Q, V, W)

1178.   FIRESTARTER. (Universal-1984-Mark Lester-R). Screen-
        play by Stanley Mann, based on the book by Stephen King;
        Signet, 1980, 401p. (LACOPL, V)

1179.   FIRST BLOOD. (Orion-1982-Ted Kotcheff-R). Screenplay
        by Michael Kozoll, William Sackheim, Sylvester Stallone; based
        on a novel by David Morrell; Lippincott, 1972, 252p. (HR,
        LACOPL, V, W)

1180.   THE FIRST DEADLY SIN. (Filmways-1980-Brian G. Hutton-
        R). Screenplay by Mann Rubin, based on the novel by
        Lawrence Sanders. (Q, V, W)

1181.   FIRST FAMILY. (Warner Bros.-1980-Buck Henry-R).
        Screenplay by Buck Henry. (Q, V, W)

1182. FIRST LOVE. (Paramount-1977-Joan Darling-R). Jane
       Stanton Hitchcock and David Freeman wrote the screenplay,
       based on the story "Sentimental Education" by Harold Brod-
       key. (NYT, Q, W)

1183. FIRST MONDAY IN OCTOBER. (Paramount-1981-Ronald
       Neame-R). Screenplay written by Jerome Lawrence and
       Robert E. Lee, based on their play. (LAT, Q, V, W)

1184. THE FIRST NUDIE MUSICAL. (Paramount-1976-Mark Haggard
       and Bruce Kimmel-R). Screenplay written by Bruce Kimmel.
       (NYT, W)

1185. THE FIRST SWALLOW. (Corinth-1982-Nana Mchedlidze-N/R).
       Screenplay written by Levan Tchelidze and Nana Mchedlidze.
       (NYT, W)

1186. THE FIRST TIME. (EDP-1976-Claude Berri-N/R). Screen-
       play written by Claude Berri. (NYT, V, W)

1187. THE FIRST TIME. (New Line Cinema-1983-Charlie Loventhal-
       R). Screenplay written by Charlie Loventhal, Susan Weiser-
       Finley, and William Franklin Finley. (V, W)

1188. THE FIRST TURN-ON! (Troma-1984-Michael Herz & "Samuel
       Weil"-R). Screenplay written by Stuart Strutin. (V, W)

1189. FIRSTBORN. (Paramount-1984-Michael Apted-PG-13).
       Screenplay written by Ron Koslow. (V)

1190. FISH HAWK. (AVCO Embassy-1981-Donal Shebib-G).
       Screenplay by Blanche Hanalis, based on the novel by
       Mitchell Jayne. (W)

1191. THE FISH THAT SAVED PITTSBURGH. (United Artists-
       1979-Gilbert Moses-PG). Screenplay by Jaison Starkes,
       Edmond Stevens, from a story by Gary Stromberg and
       David Dashev. (Q, V, W)

1192. FIST OF FEAR TOUCH OF DEATH. (Aquarius-1980-Matthew
       Mallinson-R). Screenplay by Ron Harvey, based on an
       original story by Ron Harvey and Matthew Mallinson. (V)

1193. FIST OF GOLDEN MONEY. (Almi-1983-Godfrey Ho-R). No
       screenplay credits given. (W)

       A FISTFUL OF CHOPSTICKS see THEY CALL ME BRUCE?

1194. A FISTFUL OF TALONS. (Transmedia-1983-Sun Chung-R).
       Screenplay by Wong Ping Yiu. (W)

1195.   FISTS OF BRUCE LEE. (Cinema Shares International-1978-Bruce Li-R). No screenplay credits given. (W)

1196.   FISTS OF FURY PART 2. (21st Century-1980-Jimmy Shaw-R). No screenplay credits given. (W)

1197.   FITZCARRALDO. (Werner Herzog-1982-Werner Herzog-N/R). Screenplay by Werner Herzog. (V)

1198.   THE FIVE AT THE FUNERAL. (Gamalex-1975-Sergei Goncharoff-PG). Screenplay by Tony Crechales and E. A. Charles. (W)

1199.   FIVE DAYS FROM HOME. (Universal-1978-George Peppard-N/R). Screenplay written by William Moore. (BFI, W)

1200.   FIVE EVENINGS. (International Film Exchange/Satra Film Corp/Sovexportfilm-1979-Nikita Mikhalkov-N/R). Based on a play by Alexander Volodin. (W)

1201.   FIVE LOOSE WOMEN. (S.C.A.-1975-A. C. Stephen-R). No screenplay credits given. (W)

1202.   FIVE SEXY KITTENS. (Lurco-1975-Roger Fellous-R). Screenplay credits not given. (W)

1203.   THE FLAMINGO KID. (20th Century-Fox-1984-Garry Marshall-PG-13). Screenplay by Neal Marshall and Garry Marshall, from a story by Neal Marshall. (V)

1204.   FLASH AND THE FIRECAT. (Sebastian-1976-Ferd and Beverly Sebastian-PG). Screenplay written by Ferd and Beverly Sebastian. (W)

1205.   FLASH GORDON. (Universal-1980-Mike Hodges-PG). Screenplay by Lorenzo Semple Jr., adapted by Michael Allin, from characters created by Alex Raymond. (Q, V, W)

1206.   A FLASH OF GREEN. (Richard Jordan-1984-Victor Nunez-N/R). Screenplay written by Victor Nunez, from a novel by John D. MacDonald. (V)

1207.   FLASHDANCE. (Paramount-1983-Adrian Lyne-R). Screenplay written by Tom Hedley and Joe Eszterhas, story by Tom Hedley. (LAT, V)

1208.   FLASHPOINT. (Tri-Star Pictures-1984-William Tannen-R). Screenplay by Dennis Shryack and Michael Butler, based on the book by George La Fountaine. (V)

1209.   FLAT OUT. (Variety-1978-R). No production credits available. (W)

1210. FLATFOOT. (S. J. International-1975-Steno-PG). Screen-
       play written by Lucio DeCaro. (W)

1211. FLESHBURN. (Crown International-1984-George Gage-R).
       Screenplay written by Beth and George Gage, from the novel
       Fear in a Handful of Dust by Brian Garfield. (V)

1212. FLIGHTS OF FANCY. (IFEX-1983-Roman Balayan-N/R).
       Screenplay by Victor Merezhko. (W)

1213. FLIP CHICKS. (1975-X). No production credits given. (W)

1214. FLOATING CLOUD. (Corinth-1980-Akira Kurosawa-N/R).
       Screenplay written by Akira Kurosawa. (W)

1215. FLOSSIE. (Sunshine Unlimited-1975-Bert Torn-X). No
       screenplay credits given. (W)

1216. THE FLOWER WITH THE DEADLY STING. (P.A.B.-1976-
       Gianfranco Piccioli-R). Screenplay credits not given. (W)

       DIE FLUCHT see THE ESCAPE

1217. FM. (Universal-1978-John A. Alonzo-PG). Screenplay by
       Ezra Sacks. (NYT, W)

1218. THE FOG. (AVCO Embassy-1980-John Carpenter-R).
       Screenplay written by John Carpenter and Debra Hill.
       (LAT, Q, V, W)

1219. FOND MEMORIES. (National Film Board of Canada-1982-
       Francis Mankiewicz-N/R). Screenplay written by Rejean
       Ducharme. (V)

1220. THE FOOD OF THE GODS. (American International-1976-
       Bert I. Gordon-PG). Screenplay by Bert I. Gordon, based
       on a novel by H. G. Wells. (NYT, Q, W)

1221. FOOLIN' AROUND. (Columbia-1980-Richard T. Heffron-PG).
       Screenplay by Mike Kane, David Swift, based on a story
       by David Swift. (Q, V, W)

1222. FOOTLOOSE. (Paramount-1984-Herbert Ross-PG). Screen-
       play by Dean Pitchford. (V)

1223. FOR THE LOVE OF BENJI. (Mulberry Square-1977-Joe
       Camp-G). Screenplay written by Joe Camp, from an origi-
       nal story by Ben Vaughn and Joe Camp. (NYT, V, W)

1224. FOR THOSE I LOVED. (CIC-1983-Robert Enrico-N/R).
       Screenplay written by Roberto Enrico and Tony Sheer, from
       the book by Martin Gray and Max Gallo. (V)

1225. FOR YOUR EYES ONLY. (United Artists-1981-John Glen-
       PG). Screenplay by Richard Maibaum and Michael G. Wil-
       son. (HR, LAT, Q, V, W)

1226. FOR YOUR LOVE ONLY. (1982-Wolfgang Petersen-N/R).
       An original screenplay by Herbert Lichtenfeld and Wolfgang
       Petersen. (BFI)

1227. THE FORBIDDEN ACT. (Lima-1982-Tatsumi Kumashiro-N/R).
       Screenplay written by Tatsumi Kumashiro. (W)

1228. FORBIDDEN WORLD. (New World Pictures-1982-Allan Holzman-
       R). Screenplay by Tim Curnen, from a story by Jim Wynor-
       ski and R. J. Robertson. (V, W)

1229. FORBIDDEN ZONE. (Carl Borack-1980-Richard Elfman-N/R).
       Screenplay by Richard Elfman, M. Bright, Martin W. Nichol-
       son, and Nick Jones. (V, W)

       FORBRYDELSENS ELEMENT see THE ELEMENT OF CRIME

1230. FORCE: FIVE. (American Cinema-1981-Robert Clouse-R).
       Screenplay written by Robert Clouse, based on a screenplay
       by Emil Farkas and George Goldsmith. (LAT, V, W)

1231. FORCE FOUR. (Howard Mahler-1975-Michael Fink-R).
       Screenplay credits not available. (W)

1232. A FORCE OF ONE. (American Cinema Releasing-1979-Paul
       Aaron-R). Ernest Tidyman wrote the screenplay from a
       story by Pat Johnson and Ernest Tidyman. (V, W)

1233. FORCE 10 FROM NAVARONE. (American International-1978-
       Guy Hamilton-PG). Robin Chapman wrote the screenplay,
       based on a screen story by Carl Foreman, and the novel by
       Alistair MacLean; Doubleday, 1968, 274p. (LACOPL, NYT,
       Q, V, W)

1234. FORCED VENGEANCE. (MGM/UA-1982-James Fargo-R).
       Screenplay by Franklin Thompson. (W)

1235. THE FOREIGNER. (Amos Poe Visions-1978-Amos Poe-N/R).
       Amos Poe and Eric Mitchell wrote this original screenplay.
       (NYT, V)

1236. FOREPLAY. (Cinema National-1975-Robert J. McCarty,
       Bruce Malmuth, and John G. Avildsen-R). Screenplay
       written by Dan Greenberg, Jack Richardson, and David
       Odell. (W)

1237. THE FOREST. (Fury Films Distribution Ltd.-1983-Don
       Jones-R). Screenplay written by Evan Jones. (V, W)

1238.   FOREVER EMMANUELLE. (Movies For Cable-1982-Emmanuelle
        Arsan-R). Screenplay by Emmanuelle Arsan and Sonia
        Molteni. (V)

1239.   FOREVER YOUNG. (20th Century-Fox-1984-David Drury-
        N/R). Screenplay written by Ray Connolly. (V)

1240.   FOREVER YOUNG, FOREVER FREE. (Universal-1976-Ashley
        Lazarus-G). Screenplay written by Ashley Lazarus, from a
        story by Andre Pieterse. (V)

1241.   THE FORMULA. (MGM-1980-John G. Avildsen-R). Screen-
        play by Steve Shagan, from his novel. (HR, Q, V, W)

1242.   FORT APACHE, THE BRONX. (20th Century Fox-1981-
        Daniel Petrie-R). Screenplay by Heywood Gould, suggested
        by the experiences of Thomas Mulhearn and Pete Tessitore;
        novelization by Heywood Gould; Warner Books, 1981, 330p.
        (LACOPL, Q, V, W)

1243.   FORT SAGANNE. (A.A.A. Release-1984-Alain Corneua-N/R).
        Alain Corneau, Henri de Turenne, and Louis Gardel wrote
        the screenplay, based on a novel by Louis Gardel. (V)

1244.   FORTRESS IN THE SUN. (Independent-1978-George Rowe-
        R). No screenplay credits given. (W)

1245.   THE FORTUNE. (Columbia-1975-Mike Nichols-PG). Screen-
        play written by Adrien Joyce aka Carol Eastman. (HR,
        NYT, Q, V, W)

1246.   FORTY DEUCE. (Island Film-1982-Paul Morrissey-N/R).
        Screenplay by Alan Browne, based on his stage play. (V)

1247.   48 HRS. (Paramount-1982-Walter Hill-R). Screenplay by
        Roger Spottiswoode, Walter Hill, Larry Gross, and Steven E.
        de Souza. (HR, LAT, V, W)

1248.   FOUL PLAY. (Paramount-1978-Colin Higgins-PG). Colin
        Higgins wrote the original screenplay. (NYT, Q, V, W)

1249.   THE FOUR DEUCES. (AVCO Embassy-1976-William H. Bush-
        ness Jr.-R). Screenplay by C. Lester Franklin, from an
        original story by Don Martin. (W)

1250.   FOUR FRIENDS. (Filmways Pictures-1981-Arthur Penn-R).
        Steven Tesich wrote this original screenplay. (LAT, Q, V,
        W)

1251.   THE FOUR MUSKETEERS. (20th Century-Fox-1975-Richard
        Lester-PG). George MacDonald Fraser wrote the screenplay

based on Alexandre Dumas' novel The Three Musketeers. (NYT, Q, V, W)

1252. THE FOUR SEASONS. (Universal-1981-Alan Alda-PG). This original screenplay was written by Alan Alda. (HR, LAT, Q, V, W)

1253. FOUR TIMES THAT NIGHT. (Cinevision-1975-Mario Bava-N/R). No screenplay credits available. (W)

1254. FOURTEEN AND UNDER. (ATLAS-1976-Ernst Hofbauer-X). No screenplay credits given. (W)

1255. THE FOURTH MAN. (Verenigde Nederlandse Filmcompagnie-1983-Paul Verhoeven-N/R). Screenplay by Gerald Soeteman, based on the novel by Gerard Reve. (V)

1256. THE FOX AFFAIR. (Ruff-1978-Fereidun G. Jorjani-R). Screenplay written by Barry Victor. (W)

1257. FOX AND HIS FRIENDS. (New Yorker-1976-Rainer Werner Fassbinder-N/R). Screenplay written by Rainer Werner Fassbinder and Christian Hohoff. (NYT, W)

1258. THE FOX AND THE HOUND. (Buena Vista-1981-Art Stevens, Ted Berman, and Richard Rich-G). Story and screenplay by Larry Clemmons, Ted Berman, Peter Young, Steve Hulett, David Michener, Burny Mattinson, Earl Kress, and Vance Gerry, from the book by Daniel P. Mannix. (HR, LAT, Q, V, W)

1259. FOX STYLE KILLER. (Aquarius-1982-Clyde Houston-R). Screenplay by Clyde Houston and Michael Fox. (W)

1260. FOXES. (United Artists-1980-Adrian Lyne-R). Screenplay by Gerald Ayres. (HR, LAT, Q, V, W)

1261. THE FRAGRANCE OF WILD FLOWERS. (New Yorker-1979-Srdjan Karanovic-N/R). Screenplay by Rajko Grlic and Srdjan Karanovic. (W)

1262. FRAMED. (Paramount-1975-Phil Karlson-R). Screenplay by Mort Briskin, from the novel by Art Powers and Mike Misenheimer. (W)

1263. FRANCES. (Universal-1982-Graeme Clifford-R). Screenplay by Eric Bergren, Christopher Devore, and Nicholas Kazan. (V)

1264. FRANKENSTEIN'S CASTLE OF FREAKS. (Aquarius-1975-Robert Oliver-PG). Screenplay credits not available. (W)

1265. FRANKIE AND JOHNNY WERE LOVERS. (LCB-1975-Alan C. Colberg-X). Alan C. Colberg wrote the screenplay. (W)

1266. FRATERNITY ROW. (Paramount-1977-Thomas J. Tobin-PG). Screenplay by Charles Gary Allison. (NYT, Q, W)

1267. FREAKY FRIDAY. (Buena Vista-1976-Gary Nelson-G). Screenplay by Mary Rodgers, based on her book. (NYT, Q, V)

1268. FREE SPIRIT. (Joseph Brenner-1978-James Hill-N/R). Screenplay by James Hill, based on novel The Ballad of the Belstone Fox by David Rook. (W)

1269. FREEWHEELIN'. (Turtle-1976-Scott Dittrich-G). Screenplay credits not given. (V, W)

1270. FREEZE BOMB. (Movietime Films-1980-Al Adamson-R). Screenplay credits not available. (W)

1271. FRENCH CONNECTION II. (20th Century-Fox-1975-John Frankenheimer-R). Screenplay written by Alexander Jacobs, Robert Dillon, Lauri Dillon, from a story by Robert Dillon and Lauri Dillon. (NYT, Q, W)

1272. THE FRENCH DETECTIVE. (Quartet Films-1979-Pierre Granier-Deferre-N/R). Screenplay by Francis Veber. (W)

1273. FRENCH HEAT. (Cine Paris-1976-X). No production credits available. (W)

1274. THE FRENCH LIEUTENANT'S WOMAN. (United Artists-1981-Karel Reisz-R). Screenplay by Harold Pinter, based on the novel by John Fowles; Little, Brown, 1969, 467p. (HR, LACOPL, LAT, Q, V, W)

1275. FRENCH POSTCARDS. (Paramount-1979-Willard Huyck-PG). Screenplay written by Willard Huyck and Gloria Katz. (Q, V, W)

1276. FRENCH PROVINCIAL. (New Yorker-1976-Andre Techine-N/R). Andre Techine and Marilyn Goldin wrote this original screenplay. (NYT, W)

1277. FRENCH QUARTER. (Crown International-1978-Dennis Kane-R). Screenplay written by Barney Cohen and Dennis Kane. (W)

1278. FRENCH SHAMPOO. (Philip T. Drexler-1975-X). No production credits available. (W)

1279. THE FRENCH WAY. (Peppercorn-Wormser-1975-Michel
       Deville-R). Screenplay by Christopher Frank, based on
       the novel by Roger Blondel. (NYT, W)

1280. THE FRENCH WOMAN. (Monarch-1979-Just Jaeckin-N/R).
       Screenplay by Andre G. Brunelin, from the book Allo by
       Jacques Quoirez. (W)

1281. FRIDAY FOSTER. (American International-1975-Arthur
       Marks-R). Screenplay by Orville Hapton, from a story by
       Arthur Marks, based on the comic strip "Friday Foster."
       (NYT, W)

1282. FRIDAY THE 13TH. (Paramount-1980-Sean S. Cunningham-
       R). Screenplay by Victor Miller. (V, W)

1283. FRIDAY THE 13TH, PART 2. (Paramount-1981-Steve Miner-
       R). Screenplay by Ron Kurz, based on characters created
       by Victor Miller. (LAT, Q, V, W)

1284. FRIDAY THE 13TH, PART III. (Paramount-1982-Steve
       Miner-R). Screenplay by Martin Kitrosser and Carol Watson.
       (V)

1285. FRIDAY THE 13TH--THE FINAL CHAPTER. (Paramount-
       1984-Joseph Zito-R). Screenplay written by Barney Cohen,
       based on a story by Bruce Hidemi Sakow. (V)

1286. FRIDAY THE 14TH. (New World-1981-Howard R. Cohen-PG).
       Screenplay by Howard R. Cohen. (W)

1287. FRIENDS AND HUSBANDS. (Bioskop-Film/Les Films du
       Losange-1982-Margarethe von Trotta-N/R). Screenplay by
       Margarethe von Trotta and Patrick Delabriere. (BFI)

1288. FRIGHTMARE. (Eliman Enterprises-1975-Pete Walker-R).
       Screenplay by David McGillivray. (W)

1289. FRIGHTMARE. (Saturn International-1983-Norman Thaddeus
       Vane-R). Screenplay by Norman Thaddeus Vane. (LAT, V,
       W)

1290. THE FRISCO KID. (Warner Bros.-1979-Robert Aldrich-PG).
       Screenplay by Michael Elias and Frank Shaw; novelization by
       Robert Grossbach; Warner, 1979, 254p. (BFI, LACOPL, Q,
       V, W)

1291. FROM BEYOND THE GRAVE. (Howard Mahler-1975-Kevin
       Connor-PG). Screenplay by Raymond Christodoulou and
       Robin Clarke, based on stories by R. Chetwynd-Hayes.
       (NYT, W)

1292.   FROM HELL TO VICTORY. (New Film-1979-Hank Milestone-
        N/R). Screenplay by Umberto Lenzi, Jose Luis Martinez
        Molla, and Gianfranco Clerici. (V)

1293.   FROM NOON TILL THREE. (United Artists-1976-Frank D.
        Gilroy-PG). Screenplay by Frank D. Gilroy, based on his
        novel; Doubleday, 1973, 116p. (HR, LACOPL, LAT, NYT,
        Q, W)

1294.   FROM THE LIFE OF THE MARIONETTES. (Associated Film
        Distribution-1980-Ingmar Bergman-R). Screenplay by Ing-
        mar Bergman; Pantheon, 1980. (LACOPL, V, W)

1295.   THE FRONT. (Columbia-1976-Martin Ritt-PG). Walter Bern-
        stein wrote the screenplay; novelization by Robert Alley;
        Pocket Books, 1976, 158p. (LACOPL, NYT, Q, W)

1296.   THE FRUIT IS RIPE. (Espana-1978-Siggi Goetz-R). Screen-
        play credits not available. (W)

1297.   FRUITS OF PASSION. (Summit-1982-Shuji Terayama-N/R).
        Screenplay by Shuji Terayama, based on the novel Return to
        the Chateau by Pauline Reage. (W)

1298.   FUGITIVE KILLER. (Boxoffice International-1975-Emile A.
        Harvard-R). No screenplay credits available. (W)

        FUKUSHU SURUWA WARE NI ARI see VENGEANCE IS MINE

        FULL CIRCLE see THE HAUNTING OF JULIA

1299.   FULL MOON IN PARIS. (Orion Classics-1984-Eric Rohmer-
        R). Screenplay written by Eric Rohmer. (V)

1300.   FUN WITH DICK AND JANE. (Columbia-1977-Ted Kotcheff-
        PG). Screenplay by David Giler, Jerry Belson, Mordecai
        Richler, based on a story by Gerald Gaiser. (NYT, Q, V)

1301.   FUNERAL HOME. (MPM-1982-William Fruet-R). Screenplay
        by Ida Nelson. (W)

1302.   THE FUNHOUSE. (Universal-1981-Tobe Hooper-R). Screen-
        play written by Larry Block. (V, W)

1303.   FUNK. (Independent-1976-Julian Marsh-X). No screenplay
        credits available. (W)

1304.   THE FUNNY FARM. (New World-Mutual-1983-Ron Clark-
        N/R). Screenplay written by Ron Clark. (W)

1305.   FUNNY LADY. (Columbia-1975-Herbert Ross-PG). Screenplay

by Jay Presson Allen and Arnold Schulman, from a story by
Arnold Schulman. (NYT, Q, W)

1306.   FUNNY MONEY. (Cannon Film Distributors-1983-James Ken-
        elm Clarke-N/R). Screenplay by James Kenelm Clarke. (V)

1307.   THE FURIOUS MONK FROM SHAO-LIN. (Cinema Shares In-
        ternational-1978-Hu Chang-R). No screenplay credits avail-
        able. (W)

1308.   FURTHER ADVENTURES OF THE WILDERNESS FAMILY,
        PART II. (Pacific International Enterprises-1978-Frank
        Zuniga-G). Screenplay credited by Arthur Dubs. (NYT,
        V)

1309.   FURTIVOS. (Empresa-1978-Jose Luis Borau-N/R). Screen-
        play by Manuel Gutierrez and Jose Luis Borau. (NYT, W)

1310.   THE FURY. (20th Century-Fox-1978-Brian De Palma-R).
        Screenplay by John Farris, based on his novel; Playboy
        Press, 1976, 341p. (HR, LACOPL, LAT, NYT, Q, V, W)

1311.   FUTUREWORLD. (American International-1976-Richard T.
        Heffron-PG). Screenplay by Mayo Simon and George
        Schenck. (NYT, Q, W)

1312.   FYRE. (Compass International-1979-Richard Grand-N/R).
        Screenplay written by Richard Grand and Ted Zephro. (W)

1313.   GABLE AND LOMBARD. (Universal-1976-Sidney J. Furie-R).
        Screenplay by Barry Sandler. (NYT, W)

1314.   GABRIELA. (UA Classics-1983-Bruno Barreto-N/R).
        Screenplay by Leopoldo Serran and Bruno Barreto, from the
        novel Gabriela, clavo y canela by Jorge Amado; Knopf, 1962.
        (LACOPL, V)

1315.   GAL YOUNG UN. (Nunez Films-1979-Victor Nunez-N/R).
        Screenplay by Victor Nunez, based on a Marjorie Kinnan
        Rawlings short story. (LAT, V, W)

1316.   GALAXINA. (Crown International-1980-William Sachs-R).
        An original screenplay by William Sachs. (V, W)

1317.   GALAXY EXPRESS 999. (New World-1982-Taro Rin-PG).
        Screenplay by Shiro Ishimori and Paul Grogan, based on TV
        series of Leji Matsumoto. (W)

1318.   GALAXY OF TERROR. (New World-1981-Bruce Clark-PG).
        Screenplay by Marc Siegler and Bruce Clark. (V, W)

1319. GALILEO. (American Film Theatre-1975-Joseph Losey-PG).
       Screenplay by Barbara Bray and Joseph Losey, from Charles
       Laughton's English version of the German play by Bertolt
       Brecht; Methuen, 1963, 122p. (LACOPL, NYT, Q, W)

1320. GALLIPOLI. (Paramount-1981-Peter Weir-PG). Screenplay
       by David Williamson, from a story by Peter Weir. (LAT, Q,
       V, W)

1321. THE GAMBLER. (Corinth-1982-Alexei Batalov-N/R). Screen-
       play by M. Olshevsky, from the novella by Fyodor Dostoyev-
       sky; Norton, 1981, 192p. (LACOPL, W)

1322. GAME FOR VULTURES. (New Line Cinema-1980-James Fargo-
       R). Screenplay by Phillip Baird from the book by Michael
       Hartmann. (W)

1323. GAME OF DEATH. (Columbia-1979-Robert Clouse-R).
       Screenplay by Jan Spears. (V, W)

1324. THE GAMEKEEPER. (ATV Network-1980-Kenneth Loach-
       N/R). Screenplay by Kenneth Loach, adapted from the
       novel by Barry Hines. (V)

1325. THE GAMES GIRLS PLAY. (General Film-1975-Jack Arnold-
       R). Jameson Brewer and Peer J. Oppenheimer wrote this
       screenplay. (W)

       GAMMA 693 see NIGHT OF THE ZOMBIES

1326. GANDHI. (Columbia-1982-Richard Attenborough-PG).
       Screenplay by John Briley; Grove Press, 1983, 181p. (BFI,
       HR, LACOPL, LAT, V, W)

1327. GARAGE SALE. (Independent-1976-Norman Yonemoto-X).
       Screenplay by Norman Yonemoto. (V, W)

1328. GARBO TALKS. (MGM/UA-1984-Sidney Lumet-PG-13).
       Screenplay written by Larry Grusin. (LAT, V)

1329. GARCON! (AMLF-1983-Claude Sautet-N/R). Screenplay by
       Claude Sautet and Jean-Loup Dabadie. (V)

1330. THE GARDEN OF TORTURE. (Parafrance-1976-Christian
       Gion-N/R). Screenplay by Pascal Laine from the book by
       Octave Mirbeau. (V)

1331. THE GARDENER. (United Marketing/KKI-1975-James H.
       Kay III-R). Screenplay by James H. Kay III. (W)

1332. GAS. (Paramount-1981-Les Rose-R). Screenplay by Richard
       Wolf. (LAT, Q, V)

1333. GAS PUMP GIRLS. (Cannon-1979-Joel Bender-R). Screenplay written by David A. Davies, Joel Bender, and Isaac
Blech. (V, W)

1334. GASP! (Avala Films-1977-Vlatko Gilic-N/R). Screenplay
written by Vlatko Gilic. (V)

1335. THE GATES OF HELL. (Motion Picture Marketing-1983-
Lucio Fulci-X). Screenplay written by Lucio Fulci and
Dardano Sacchetti. (V)

1336. GATOR. (United Artists-1976-Burt Reynolds-PG). Screenplay written by William Norton. (NYT, Q, W)

1337. 'GATOR BAIT. (Sebastian Films Ltd.-1983-Ferd and Beverly
Sebastian-R). Screenplay written by Beverly Sebastian.
(V)

1338. THE GAUNTLET. (Warner Bros.-1977-Clint Eastwood-R).
Screenplay by Michael Butler and Dennis Shryack; novelization by Michael Butler and Dennis Shryack; Warner Books,
1972. (HR, LACOPL, LAT, NYT, Q, V, W)

1339. GAYANE. (Special Event Entertainment-1979-Horace King-
N/R). No screenplay credits given; ballet created by Aram
Khachaturian. (W)

1340. GEEK MAGGOT BINGO. (Weirdo Films-1983-Nick Zedd-N/R).
Screenplay by Nick Zedd, from a story idea by Robert Kirkpatrick and Nick Zedd. (V, W)

1341. A GEISHA. (New Yorker-1978-Kenji Mozoguchi-N/R).
Screenplay by Yoshikata Yoda, from a story by Matsutaro
Kawaguchi. (NYT, W)

1342. GEMINI AFFAIR. (Moonstone-1975-Matt Cimber-X). No
screenplay credits available. (V, W)

1343. GET CRAZY. (Embassy-1983-Allan Arkush-R). Screenplay
by Danny Opatoshu, Henry Rosenbaum, and David Taylor.
(W)

1344. GET MEAN. (Cee Note-1976-Ferdinando Baldi-PG). Screenplay by Lloyd Battista and Wolf Lowenthal. (W)

1345. GET OUT YOUR HANDKERCHIEFS. (New Line Cinema-1978-
Bertrand Blier-N/R). Screenplay written by Bertrand Blier.
(NYT, W)

1346. GET ROLLIN'. (Get Rollin' Group-1980-J. Terrance Mitchell-
N/R). Screenplay written by J. Terrance Mitchell. (W)

1347. GETTING EVEN. (Quantum Films-1981-Mark Feldberg-N/R).
       Screenplay written by Mark Feldberg. (V)

1348. GETTING IT ON. (Comworld Pictures-1983-William Olsen-R).
       Screenplay written by William Olsen. (LAT, V, W)

1349. THE GETTING OF WISDOM. (Atlantic-1980-Bruce Beresford-
       N/R). Eleanor Witcombe wrote the screenplay, based on a
       novel by Henry Handel Richardson; screenplay published by
       Heinemann Eds., 1978. (LACOPL, W)

1350. GETTING OVER. (Continental-1981-Bernie Rollins-PG).
       Screenplay written by Bernie Rollins from a story by John R.
       Daniels and Bernie Rollins. (LAT, V, W)

1351. GETTING TOGETHER. (Total Impact-1976-David Secter-N/R).
       David Secter wrote the screenplay. (V, W)

       GHARE BAIRE see THE HOME AND THE WORLD

1352. GHOST STORY. (Universal-1981-John Irvin-R). Screenplay
       by Lawrence D. Cohen, based on the novel by Peter Straub;
       Pocket Books, 1981. (BFI, HR, LACOPL, LAT, W)

1353. GHOSTBUSTERS. (Columbia-1984-Ivan Reitman-PG). Screen-
       play by Dan Aykroyd and Harold Ramis. (HR, LAT, NYT,
       V)

1354. THE GIANT SPIDER INVASION. (Group I-1975-Bill Rebane-
       PG). Screenplay credits not available. (W)

1355. THE GIFT. (United Artists-1982-Michel Lang-N/R). Screen-
       play by Michel Lang, based on the play Anche i Bancari
       Hanno un Anima by Vaime and Terzoli. (V)

1356. GIFT OF AN EAGLE. (C. B. Bartell-1975-Rex Fleming-G).
       Screenplay by Dale Myers from the book by Kent Durden;
       Simon & Schuster, 1972, 160p. (LACOPL, W)

1357. GILDA LIVE. (Warner Bros.-1980-Mike Nichols-R). Screen-
       play by Anne Beatts, Lorne Michaels, Marilyn Suzanne Miller,
       Don Novello, Michael O'Donoghue, Gilda Radner, Paul Shaffer,
       Rosie Shuster, Alan Zeibel, from the original Broadway pro-
       duction. (Q, V)

1358. GIMME AN "F." (20th Century-Fox-1984-Paul Justman-R).
       Screenplay written by Jim Hart. (V)

1359. GIOVANNI. (Studio Nieuwe Gronden-1982-Annette Apon-
       N/R). Screenplay written by Annette Apon. (V)

1360. THE GIRL FROM LORRAINE. (New Yorker-1983-Claude
       Goretta-N/R). Screenplay written by Claude Goretta,
       Jacques Kirsner, and Rosine Rochette. (W)

1361. THE GIRL FROM THE RED CABARET. (Independent
       International-1976-Eugenia Martin-PG). Screenplay credits
       not available. (W)

1362. THE GIRL FROM TRIESTE. (Faso Film-1983-Pasquale Festa
       Campanile-N/R). Screenplay written by Ottavio Jemma,
       based on the novel by Pasquale Festa Campanile. (BFI)

1363. THE GIRL IN THE TRUNK. (Gaumont Goldstone-1975-
       Georges Lautner-N/R). Screenplay by Francis Veber. (W)

1364. A GIRL NAMED POO LOM. (Chokchai Mahasombat-1977-
       Choomphorn Tepitak-N/R). Screenplay by Lom Maniya. (V)

1365. GIRL WITH A SEASHELL. (International Film Exchange-
       1983-Jiri Svoboda-N/R). Miloslav Vydra wrote the screen-
       play, from a story by Jaromira Kolarova. (W)

1366. THE GIRL WITH THE RED HAIR. (United Artists Classics-
       1983-Ben Verbong-PG). Screenplay by Ben Verbong and
       Pieter de Vos, based on a novel by Theun De Vries. (W)

1367. GIRLFRIENDS. (Warner Bros.-1978-Claudia Weill-PG).
       Screenplay by Vicki Polon, from a story by Claudia Weill
       and Vicki Polon. (NYT, W)

1368. GIRLS AND THE LOVE GAMES. (Atlas-1976-F. G. Gottlieb-
       X). No screenplay credits given. (W)

1369. GIRLS IN TROUBLE. (Group One-1976-E. Schroder-R). No
       screenplay credits available. (W)

1370. THE GIRLS NEXT DOOR. (Columbus America-1979-James
       Hong-R). Screenplay credits not available. (W)

1371. GIRLS NITE OUT. (Aries International Releasing-1984-
       Robert Deubel-R). Screenplay written by Gil Spencer Jr.,
       Joe Bolster, Kevin Kurgis, and Anthony N. Gurvis. (V)

1372. GIRO CITY. (Silvarealm-1983-Karl Francis-N/R). Screen-
       play by Karl Francis. (V)

1373. GISELLE. (International TV Trading-1978-Hugo Niebeling-
       N/R). Based on the ballet by Adolphe Adam. (W)

1374. GISELLE. (21st Century Distribution-1982-Victor DiMello-
       R). Written by Victor DiMello. (V, W)

1375. GIVE 'EM HELL, HARRY! (Theatre Television-1975-Steve
       Binder-N/R). Screenplay by Samuel Gallu based on his
       play; Avon, 1983. (LACOPL, NYT, W)

1376. GIVE MY REGARDS TO BROAD STREET. (20th Century-
       Fox-1984-Peter Webb-PG). Screenplay by Paul McCartney.
       (HR, LAT, NYT, V)

1377. GIZMO! (New Line Cinema-1980-Howard Smith-G). Screen-
       play by Kathleen Cox and Nicholas Hollander and Clark
       Whelton. (W)

1378. GLADYS AND HER ALL GIRL BAND. (1975-X). No pro-
       duction credits available. (W)

1379. GLORIA. (Columbia-1980-John Cassavetes-R). Screenplay
       written by John Cassavetes. (Q, V, W)

1380. THE GLOVE. (Pro International-1981-Ross Hagen-R).
       Screenplay by Hubert Smith and Julian Roffman. (V, W)

1381. GO FOR IT. (World Entertainment-1976-Paul Rapp-PG).
       Screenplay by Nell Rapp. (W)

1382. GO TELL IT ON THE MOUNTAIN. (Learning in Focus-1984-
       Stan Lathan-N/R). Screenplay written by Gus Edwards and
       Leslie Lee, based on the novel by James Baldwin; Dial
       Press, 1963, 253p. (LACOPL, V)

1383. GO TELL THE SPARTANS. (Avco Embassy-1978-Ted Post-
       R). Screenplay written by Wendell Mayes, based on Incident
       at Muc Wa by Daniel Ford; Doubleday, 1967, (HR, LACOPL,
       NYT, Q, V, W)

1384. GOD TOLD ME TO. (New World-1976-Larry Cohen-R).
       Screenplay by Larry Cohen. (R)

1385. THE GODFATHER SQUAD. (Cannon-1976-M. Cardinal-R).
       No writing credits given. (W)

1386. GOD'S BLOODY ACRE. (Omni-1975-Harry E. Kerwin-R).
       Screenplay by Robert Woodburn and Wayne Crawford. (W)

1387. GOD'S GUN. (Irwin Yablans-1978-Frank Kramer-R). Screen-
       play credits not available. (W)

1388. THE GODS MUST BE CRAZY. (TLC-1984-Jamie Uys-PG).
       Screenplay by Jamie Uys. (LAT, V)

1389. GODS OF THE PLAGUE. (New Yorker-1977-Rainer Werner
       Fassbinder-N/R). Screenplay written by Rainer Werner
       Fassbinder. (NYT, W)

1390. THE GODSEND. (Cannon-1980-Gabrielle Beaumont-R).
       Screenplay by Olaf Pooley, based on the novel by Bernard
       Taylor; St. Martin's Press, 1976, 184p. (LACOPL, V, W)

1391. THE GODSON. (Boxoffice International-1975-William Rotsler-
       N/R). Screenplay written by William Rotsler. (W)

1392. GODZILLA VS. MEGALON. (Cinema Shares International-
       1976-Jun Fukuda-G). Screenplay written by Jun Fukuda.
       (W)

1393. GOIN' ALL THE WAY. (Saturn International-1982-Robert
       Freedman-R). Screenplay by Roger Stone and Jack Cooper.
       (V, W)

1394. GOIN' COCONUTS. (Osmond Distribution Co-1978-Howard
       Morris-PG). Screenplay by Raymond Harvey; novelization
       by Vic Crume; Dell, 1978, 108p. (LACOPL, V, W)

1395. GOIN' HOME. (Prentiss-1976-Chris Prentiss-G). Screen-
       play by Chris Prentiss. (W)

1396. GOIN' SOUTH. (Paramount-1978-Jack Nicholson-PG).
       Screenplay written by John Herman Shaner, Al Ramrus,
       Charles Shyer, and Alan Mandel; novelization by Madeline
       Shaner; Jove, 1978. (LACOPL, NYT, Q, V, W)

1397. GOING APE! (Paramount-1981-Jeremy Joe Kronsberg-PG).
       Screenplay by Jeremy Joe Kronsberg. (LAT, Q, V, W)

1398. GOING BERSERK. (Universal-1983-David Steinberg-R).
       Screenplay by Dana Olsen and David Steinberg. (V, W)

1399. [No entry]

1400. GOING FOR BROKE. (Merry Film-1977-Gabriel Axel-N/R).
       Screenplay by Gabriel Axel, Ole Boje, based on Jean Halain
       and Jacques Besnard's Trinacra production of "C'est pas,
       parce qu'on a rien a dire qu'il faut fermer sa gueule."
       (V)

1401. GOING IN STYLE. (Warner Bros.-1979-Martin Brest-PG).
       Screenplay by Martin Brest; novelization by Robert Gross-
       bach; Warner, 1979, 238p. (LACOPL, Q, V, W)

1402. THE GOLDCABBAGE FAMILY BREAKS THE BANK. (A/S
       Panorama-1976-Fabriel Axel-N/R). Screenplay by Poul-
       Henrik Trampe. (V)

1403. GOLDEN GIRL. (Avco Embassy-1979-Joseph Sargent-PG).

Screenplay by John Kohn, based on a novel by Peter Lear;
Doubleday, 1977, 332p. (LACOPL, Q, V, W)

1404. THE GOLDEN LADY. (Target International-1979-Jose
       Larraz-N/R). Screenplay by Joshua Sinclair. (V)

1405. THE GOLDEN SEAL. (Samuel Goldwyn Company-1983-Frank
       Zuniga-PG). Screenplay by John Groves, based on the
       novel A River Ran out of Eden by James Vance Marshall;
       Morrow, 1962. (LACOPL, LAT, V, W)

1406. GOLIATHON. (World Northal-1980-Homer Gaugh-PG).
       Screenplay credits not available. (W)

1407. GONE WITH THE WEST. (International Cinefilm-1975-
       Bernard Girard-R). Screenplay credits not listed. (W)

1408. THE GONG SHOW MOVIE. (Universal-1980-Chuck Barris-R).
       Screenplay written by Chuck Barris and Robert Downey.
       (Q, V, W)

1409. GOOD GUYS WEAR BLACK. (American Cinema Releasing-
       1978-Ted Post-R). Screenplay by Bruce Cohn and Mark
       Medoff, from a story by Joseph Fraley; novelization by Max
       Franklin; New American Library, 1978. (HR, LACOPL, LAT,
       V, W)

1410. GOOD LUCK, MISS WYCKOFF. (Bel-Air/Gradison-1979-
       Marvin J. Chomsky-R). Screenplay by Polly Platt, based
       on the novel by William Inge; Little Brown, 1970, 179p.
       (LACOPL, V, W)

       GOOD RIDDANCE see LES BONS DEBARRAS

1411. THE GOOD, THE BAD AND THE BEAUTIFUL. (Orrin-1975-
       R). Production credits not given. (W)

1412. GOODBYE BRUCE LEE: HIS LAST GAME OF DEATH.
       (Aquarius-1976-R). No production credits listed. (W)

1413. GOODBYE CRUEL WORLD. (Sharp Features-1983-David
       Irving-R). Screenplay by Nicholas Niciphor and Dick Shawn.
       (W)

1414. GOODBYE EMMANUELLE. (Miramax-1980-Francois Leterrier-
       R). Screenplay written by Francois Leterrier, based on
       characters created by Emmanuelle Astier. (LAT, W)

1415. GOODBYE, FLICKMANIA. (Nippon Herald-1979-Masato
       Harada-N/R). Screenplay by Masato Harada. (V, W)

1416. GOODBYE FRANKLIN HIGH. (Cal-Am-1978-Mike MacFarland-PG). Screenplay written by Stu Krieger. (W)

1417. THE GOODBYE GIRL. (Warner Bros.-1977-Herbert Ross-PG). Screenplay by Neil Simon; novelization by Robert Grossbach; Warner Books, 1977, 221p. (HR, LACOPL, LAT, NYT, Q, W)

1418. GOODBYE, NORMA JEAN. (Stirling Gold-1976-Larry Buchanan-R). Screenplay by Lynn Hubert and Larry Buchanan. (NYT, W)

1419. THE GOODBYE PEOPLE. (Embassy Pictures-1984-Herb Gardner-PG). Screenplay by Herb Gardner, based on his stage play; Farrar, 1974, 167p. (LACOPL, V)

1420. GOODNIGHT, LADIES AND GENTLEMEN. (Titanus-1976). Age and Scarpelli, Leo Benvenuti, Luigi Comencini, Piero De Bernardi, Nanni Loy, Ruggero Maccari, Luigi Magni, Mario Monicelli, Ugo Pirro and Ettore Scola wrote this original screenplay. (V)

1421. THE GORILLA GANG. (Hampton International-1975-Alfred Vohrer-R). Screenplay by Freddy Gregor. (W)

1422. GORKY PARK. (Orion-1983-Michael Apted-R). Screenplay by Dennis Potter, based on a novel by Martin Cruz Smith; Random House, 1981, 365p. (BFI, HR, LACOPL, LAT, V)

1423. GORP. (American International/Filmways-1980-Joseph Ruben-R). Screenplay by Jeffrey Konvitz, based on a story by Jeffrey Konvitz and Martin Zweiback. (V)

1424. GOTTA RUN. (Scandinavia Today-1982-Mikkjo Niskanen-N/R). Screenplay by Matti Ijas and Mikkjo Niskanen. (W)

1425. GRADUATE FIRST. (New Yorker-1982-Maurice Pialat-N/R). Screenplay by Maurice Pialat. (LAT, W)

1426. GRADUATION DAY. (IFI/Scope III-1981-Herb Freed-R). Screenplay by Anne Marisse and Herb Freed. (LAT, V)

GRAF DRACULA (BEISST JETZT) IN OBERBAYERN see DRACULA BLOWS HIS COOL

1427. GRAND THEFT AUTO. (New World-1977-Ron Howard-PG). Screenplay by Ranse Howard, Ron Howard. (NYT, V)

1428. LA GRANDE BOURGEOISE. (Atlantic-Buckley Bros.-1977-Mauro Bolognini-N/R). Screenplay credits not given. (W)

1429. GRANDVIEW, U.S.A. (Warner Bros.-1984-Randal Kleiser-R).
       Screenplay by Ken Hixon. (V)

1430. GRAY LADY DOWN. (Universal-1978-David Greene-PG).
       Screenplay by James Whittaker and Howard Sackler, based
       on the novel Event 1000 by David Lavallee, with adaptation
       by Frank P. Rosenberg; Holt, 1971, 279p. (HR, LACOPL,
       LAT, NYT, Q, V, W)

1431. GREASE. (Paramount-1978-Randal Kleiser-PG). Screenplay
       by Bronte Woodard, from the musical by Jim Jacobs and
       Warren Casey, as adapted by Allan Carr; Winter House,
       1972, 99p. (BFI, HR, LACOPL, LAT, NYT, Q, V, W)

1432. GREASE 2. (Paramount-1982-Patricia Birch-PG). Screen-
       play by Ken Finkleman; novelization by William Rotsler;
       Wanderer Books, 1982, 192p. (HR, LACOPL, Q)

1433. GREASED LIGHTNING. (Warner Bros.-1977-Michael Schultz-
       PG). Screenplay by Kenneth Vose, Lawrence DuKore, Mel-
       vin Van Peebles, and Leon Capetanos; novelization by Ken-
       neth Vose and Lawrence DuKore; Warner Books, 1977.
       (LACOPL, NYT, Q, V)

1434. THE GREAT BANK HOAX. (Warner Bros.-1979-Joseph
       Jacoby-PG). Screenplay by Joseph Jacoby. (W)

1435. THE GREAT BRAIN. (Osmond-1978-Sidney Levin-G).
       Screenplay by Alan Cassidy, based on a book by John D.
       Fitzgerald; Dial Press, 1967. (LACOPL, W)

1436. THE GREAT GEORGIA BANK HOAX. (Warner Bros.-1978-
       Joseph Jacoby-N/R). Screenplay by Joseph Jacoby. (W)

1437. THE GREAT GUNDOWN. (Sun Prods.-1977-Paul Hunt-PG).
       Screenplay by Steve Fisher, from a story by Robert Padilla
       and Paul Hunt. (V)

       THE GREAT LESTER BOGGS see THE HARD HEADS

1438. THE GREAT MCGONAGALL. (Scotia American-1975-Joseph
       McGrath-N/R). Screenplay by Joseph McGrath, Spike Milli-
       gan. (NYT, W)

1439. THE GREAT MASSAGE PARLOR BUST. (Hollywood Interna-
       tional-1975-Eddy Karek-Las-N/R). Screen story by John
       Harris and Marvin Rothman. (W)

1440. THE GREAT MUPPET CAPER. (Universal Associated Film
       Distribution-1981-Jim Henson-G). Screenplay by Tom

Patchett, Jay Tarses, Jerry Juhl and Jack Rose. (HR, LAT, Q, V, W)

1441.   THE GREAT ROCK 'N' ROLL SWINDLE. (Kendon-1980-Julian Temple-N/R). Screenplay written by Julian Temple. (V)

1442.   THE GREAT SANTINI. (Orion-1979-Lewis John Carlino-PG). Screenplay by Lewis John Carlino, based on a novel by Pat Conroy; Houghton Mifflin, 1976, 536p. (HR, LACOPL, LAT, Q, V, W)

1443.   THE GREAT SCOUT AND CATHOUSE THURSDAY. (American International-1976-Don Taylor-PG). Screenplay by Richard Shapiro. (HR, LAT, NYT, W)

1444.   THE GREAT SMOKEY ROADBLOCK. (Dimension-1978-John Leone-PG). Screenplay by John Leone. (HR, LAT, W)

1445.   THE GREAT TEXAS DYNAMITE CHASE. (New World-1976-Michael Pressman-R). Screenplay by David Kirkpatrick, based on story by Mark Rosin. (LAT, NYT, W)

1446.   THE GREAT TRAIN ROBBERY. (United Artists-1979-Michael Crichton-PG). Screenplay by Michael Crichton, based on his novel; Knopf, 1975, 266p. (HR, LACOPL, LAT, Q, V, W)

1447.   THE GREAT WALDO PEPPER. (Universal-1975-George Roy Hill-PG). Screenplay by William Goldman, from a story by George Roy Hill. (HR, LAT, NYT, Q, W)

1448.   THE GREAT WHITE. (Film Ventures International-1982-Enzo G. Castellari-PG). Screenplay by Mark Princi. (LAT, V, W)

1449.   THE GREATEST. (Columbia-1977-Tom Gries-PG). Screenplay by Ring Lardner Jr., based on The Greatest: My Own Story by Muhammad Ali, Herbert Muhammad, and Richard Durham; Random House, 1975, 415p. (LACOPL, NYT, Q, V)

1450.   THE GREEK TYCOON. (Universal-1978-J. Lee Thompson-R). Screenplay by Mort Fine, from a story by Nico Mastorakis, Win Wells, and Mort Fine. (HR, LAT, NYT, W)

1451.   GREEN ICE. (Lou Grade-1981-Ernest Day-N/R). Screenplay by Edward Anhalt, Ray Hassett, Anthony Simmons, and Robert de Laurentis, based on a book by Gerald Browne; Delacorte Press, 1978. (LACOPL, V)

1452.   THE GREEN JACKET. (Arturo La Pegna/CEP-1979-Franco Giraldi-N/R). Screenplay by Franco Giraldi, Lucio Battistrada, Sandra Onofri, and Cesare Garboli. (V)

1453.   THE GREEN ROOM. (New World-1979-Francois Truffaut-PG).
        Screenplay by Francois Truffaut and Jean Gruault, based on
        Henry James' writings. (W)

1454.   GREGORY'S GIRL. (Samuel Goldwyn Co.-1982-Bill Forsyth-
        PG). Screenplay written by Bill Forsyth. (V)

1455.   GREMLINS. (Warner Bros.-1984-Joe Dante-PG). Screenplay
        by Chris Columbus; novelization by George Gipe; Avon,
        1984. (HR, LACOPL, LAT, V)

1456.   GRENDEL, GRENDEL, GRENDEL. (Victoria Film Corp.-1981-
        Alexander Stitt-N/R). Screenplay written by Alexander
        Stitt. (V, W)

1457.   GREYSTOKE: THE LEGEND OF TARZAN, LORD OF THE
        APES. (Warner Bros.-1984-Hugh Hudson-PG). Screenplay
        by P. H. Vazak and Michael Austin, based on the story
        "Tarzan of the Apes" by Edgar Rice Burroughs; Grosset,
        1914. (BFI, HR, LACOPL, LAT, NYT, V)

1458.   GRIMACES. (Hungarofilm-1980-Ferenc Kardos and Janos
        Rozsa-N/R). Screenplay by Ferenc Kardos and Janos Rozsa.
        (V)

1459.   THE GRIM REAPER. (Film Ventures International-1981-Joe
        D'Amato-R). Screenplay by Aristide Massaccesi and Lewis
        Montefiore. (V)

1460.   GRIZZLY. (Film Ventures International-1976-William Girdler-
        PG). Screenplay by David Sheldon and Harvey Flaxman.
        (NYT, W)

1461.   GROUP PORTRAIT WITH LADY. (Public Cinema-1980-
        Aleksandar Petrovic-N/R). Screenplay by Aleksandar
        Petrovic and Heinrich Boll. (W)

1462.   GROWING PAINS. (New World-1984-Bobby Houston-R).
        Screenplay by Bobby Houston and Joseph Kwong. (V)

1463.   GUARDIAN OF THE WILDERNESS. (Sunn Classics Pictures-
        1976-David O'Malley-G). Screenplay by Casey Conlon, from
        a story by Charles E. Sellier Jr., based on the book Galen
        Clark, Yosemite Guardian; Sierra Club, 1964, 176p.
        (LACOPL, V, W)

1464.   GUERNICA. (New Line Cinema-1976-Fernando Arrabal-N/R).
        Screenplay by Fernando Arrabal. (W)

        LA GUERRE DU FEU see QUEST FOR FIRE

1465. THE GUEST AT STEENKAMPSKRAAL. (Guest Productions Ltd.-1977-Ross Devenish-N/R). Screenplay by Athol Fugard. (V)

       GUI XIN SHI JIAN see ANXIOUS TO RETURN

1466. GULLIVER'S TRAVELS. (Sunn Classic Pictures-1981-Peter Hunt-G). Screenplay by Don Black. (W)

1467. THE GUMBALL RALLY. (Warner Bros.-1976-Chuck Bail-PG). Screenplay by Leon Capetanos, from a story by Chuck Bail. (NYT, W)

1468. GUMS. (Masada-1976-Robert J. Kaplan-N/R). Screenplay by Robert J. Kaplan. (W)

1469. THE GUNS AND THE FURY. (1981-Tony Zarindast-N/R). Screenplay by Donald Fredette, Tony Zarindast, additional dialogue by M. B. France, and Michael Dale Brown. (BFI)

1470. GUS. (Buena Vista-1976-Vincent McEveety-G). Screenplay by Arthur Alsberg, Don Nelson, based on a story by Ted Key. (HR, LAT, NYT, Q, W)

1471. GUYANA CULT OF THE DAMNED. (Universal-1980-Rene Cardona Jr.-R). Screenplay by Carlos Valdemar and Rene Cardona Jr. (W)

1472. GWENDOLINE. (Samuel Goldwyn Co.-1984-Just Jaeckin-R). Screenplay written by Just Jaeckin, inspired by the comic strip by John Wilie. (HR, LAT, V)

1473. H.O.T.S. (Derio Prods.-1979-Gerald Sindell-R). Screenplay by Cheri Caffaro and Joan Buchanan. (V, W)

1474. HABANERA. (Cuban Institute of Cinematographic Art & Industry-1984-Pastor Vega-N/R). Screenplay by Ambrosio Fornet, story by Pastor Vega and Ambrosio Fornet. (V)

1475. HADLEY'S REBELLION. (ADI Marketing-1984-Fred Walton-PG). Screenplay written by Fred Walton. (V)

1476. HAIR. (United Artists-1979-Milos Forman-PG). Screenplay by Michael Weller, based on the musical play, book and lyrics by Gerome Ragni and James Rado; Pocket Books, 1969, 205p. (HR, LACOPL, LAT, V, W)

1477. HALF A HOUSE. (First American Films-1979-Brice Mack-PG). Screenplay by Lois Hire from a story by Joe Connelly and Lois Hire. (W)

1478. HALLOWEEN. (Compass International-1978-John Carpenter-
       R). Screenplay by John Carpenter and Debra Hill; noveli-
       zation by Curtis Richards; Bantam Books, 1981, 176p. (HR,
       LACOPL, LAT, V, W)

1479. HALLOWEEN II. (Universal-1981-Rick Rosenthal-R). Screen-
       play by John Carpenter and Debra Hill; novelization by Jack
       Martin; Zebra Press, 1981. (BFI, HR, LACOPL, LAT, Q, V,
       W)

1480. HALLOWEEN III: SEASON OF THE WITCH. (Universal-1982-
       Tommy Lee Wallace-R). Screenplay by Tommy Lee Wallace;
       novelization by Jack Martin; Jove, 1982, 240p. (HR,
       LACOPL, LAT, V, W)

1481. HAMLET. (Royal College of Art-1976-Celestino Coronado-
       N/R). Screenplay by Celestino Coronado, based on the play
       by William Shakespeare in The Riverside Shakespeare; Hough-
       ton Mifflin, 1974, pp. 1135-1197. (LACOPL, V)

1482. HAMMETT. (Orion-1982-Wim Wenders-N/R). Screenplay by
       Ross Thomas and Dennis O'Flaherty, adaptation by Thomas
       Pope, based on a book by Joe Gores; Putnam, 1975, 251p.
       (HR, LACOPL, LAT, V, W)

1483. THE HAND. (Orion-1981-Oliver Stone-R). Screenplay by
       Oliver Stone, based on the book The Lizard's Tail by Marc
       Brandel; Simon & Schuster, 1979, 286p. (LACOPL, LAT, Q,
       V, W)

1484. HANDGUN. (Warner Bros.-1983-Tony Garnett-N/R). Screen-
       play by Tony Garnett. (V)

       HANDLE WITH CARE see BREAKER BREAKER

1485. HANDS OF LIGHTNING. (Almi-1982-R). No production
       credits available. (W)

1486. HANGAR 18. (Sunn Classic-1980-James L. Conway-PG).
       Screenplay by Steven Thornley, based on a story by Tom
       Chapman and James L. Conway. (V, W)

1487. THE HANGING WOMAN. (International Artists-1975-R). No
       production credits available. (W)

1488. HANK WILLIAMS: THE SHOW HE NEVER GAVE. (Simcom-
       1982-David Acomba-N/R). Screenplay by Maynard Collins,
       based on his original stage play. (V)

1489. HANKY PANKY. (Columbia-1982-Sidney Poitier-PG). Screen-
       play by Henry Rosenbaum and David Taylor. (Q, V)

1490. HANNAH K. (Universal-1983-Constantine Costa-Gavras-R).
       Screenplay by Costa-Gavras and Franco Solinas. (LAT, V)

1491. HANOVER STREET. (Columbia-1979-Peter Hyams-PG).
       Screenplay by Peter Hyams; novelization by Maureen Greg-
       son; Bantam, 1979, 214p. (LACOPL, Q, V, W)

1492. HAPPY BIRTHDAY, GEMINI. (United Artists-1980-Richard
       Benner-R). Screenplay by Richard Benner, based on the
       play Gemini by Albert Innaurato. (Q, V, W)

1493. HAPPY BIRTHDAY TO ME. (Columbia-1981-J. Lee Thompson-
       R). Screenplay by John Saxton, Peter Jobin, and Timothy
       Bond, from a story by John Saxton. (LAT, Q, V, W)

1494. THE HAPPY HOOKER. (Cannon-1975-Nicholas Sgarro-N/R).
       Screenplay by William Richert, based on the book by
       Xaviera Hollander, Robin Moore, and Yvonne Dunleavy.
       (NYT, W)

1495. THE HAPPY HOOKER. (Cannon Group-1980-Alan Roberts-R).
       Screenplay by Devin Goldenberg. (W)

1496. THE HAPPY HOOKER GOES TO HOLLYWOOD. (Cannon-
       1980-Alan Roberts-R). Screenplay by Devin Goldenberg.
       (V)

1497. THE HAPPY HOOKER GOES TO WASHINGTON. (Cannon-
       1977-William A. Levey-R). Screenplay written by Robert
       Kaufman. (NYT, V)

1498. HARD CANDY. (Debonair-1976-Norm De Plume-X). Screen-
       play by Mark Thunderbuns and Ann Onymous. (W)

1499. HARD COUNTRY. (Associated Film Distribution-1981-David
       Greene-PG). Screenplay by Michael Kane, from a story by
       Michael Kane and Michael Martin Murphey. (LAT, V, W)

1500. THE HARD HEADS. (K-TEL-1975-PG). No production
       credits given. (W)

1501. HARD TIMES. (Columbia-1975-Walter Hill-PG). Screenplay
       by Walter Hill, Bryan Gindorff, and Bruce Henstell, from a
       story by Bryan Gindorff and Bruce Henstell. (NYT, Q, W)

       HARD TO HANDLE see BREAKER BREAKER

1502. HARD TO HOLD. (Universal-1984-Larry Peerce-PG).
       Screenplay by Tom Hendley, based on a story by Tom Hend-
       ley and Richard Rothstein. (HR, LAT, V)

1503. A HARD WAY TO DIE. (Transmedia-1980-R). No production credits available. (W)

1504. HARDBODIES. (Columbia-1984-Mark Griffiths-R). Steve Greene, Eric Alter, and Mark Griffiths wrote the screenplay, from a story by Steve Greene and Eric Alter. (HR, LAT, V)

1505. HARDCORE. (Columbia-1979-Paul Schrader-R). Screenplay by Paul Schrader; novelization by Leonard Schrader; Warner Books, 1979, 174p. (LACOPL, Q, V, W)

1506. HARDCORE WOMAN. (Dog Eat Dog Films-1975-Abe Snake aka Peter Locke-X). Screenplay by Abe Snake (aka Peter Locke). (W)

1507. HARDLY WORKING. (20th Century-Fox-1981-Jerry Lewis-PG). Screenplay by Michael Janover and Jerry Lewis, story by Michael Janover. (Q, V, W)

1508. THE HARDY GIRLS. (Gold-1975-Allen Ruskin-X). No screenplay credits available. (W)

1509. HARLEQUIN. (New Image-1983-Simon Wincer-N/R). Screenplay written by Everett De Roche. (W)

1510. HARPER VALLEY PTA. (April Fools-1978-Richard Bennett-PG). Screenplay by George Edwards and Barry Schneider, from a story by George Edwards. (BFI, V, W)

1511. HARRY AND SON. (Orion-1984-Paul Newman-PG). Screenplay by Paul Newman and Ronald L. Buck, suggested by the novel A Lost King by Raymond DeCapite; McKay, 1961. (HR, LACOPL, LAT, NYT, V)

1512. HARRY AND THE HOOKERS. (Joseph Brenner-1975-Lindsey Shonteff-R). Screenplay credits not available. (W)

1513. HARRY AND WALTER GO TO NEW YORK. (Columbia-1976-Mark Rydell-PG). Screenplay by John Byrum and Robert Kaufman, story by Don Devlin and John Byrum. (NYT, Q, W)

1514. HARRY TRACY. (QFI/Quartet-1983-PG). Screenplay written by David Lee Henry. (W)

1515. HARRY'S WAR. (Taft International-1981-Keith Merrill-G). Screenplay by Keith Merrill. (V, W)

THE HATCHET MURDERS see DEEP RED

1516. THE HATTER'S GHOSTS. (Gaumont-1982-Claude Chabrol-
       N/R). Screenplay by Claude Chabrol, from the novel by
       Georges Simenon. (V)

1517. THE HAUNTING OF JULIA. (Discovery-1981-Richard Lon-
       craine-R). Screenplay by Dave Humphries, based on the
       novel Julia by Peter Straub and adapted by Harry Bromley
       Davenport; Coward, McCann & Geoghegan, 1975, 287p.
       (LACOPL, LAT, W)

1518. THE HAUNTING OF M. (Nu-Image-1981-Anna Thomas-R).
       Screenplay by Anna Thomas. (V, W)

1519. HAUNTS. (Intercontinental-1977-Herb Freed-PG). Anne
       Marisse and Herb Freed wrote the screenplay. (V)

1520. HAWK THE SLAYER. (ITC-1980-Terry Marcel-N/R).
       Screenplay by Terry Marcel and Harry Robertson. (V)

1521. HAWMPS. (Mulberry Square-1976-Joe Camp-G). William
       Bickley wrote the screenplay, from a story by William
       Bickley, Michael Warren, and Joe Camp. (HR, NYT, W)

1522. THE HAZING. (Miraleste Company-1978-Douglas Curtis).
       Screenplay by Bruce Shelly and David Ketchum, based on
       idea by Bruce Shelly. (V, W)

1523. HE IS MY BROTHER. (Atlantic-1976-Edward Dmytryk-G).
       Screenplay credits not available. (W)

1524. HE KNOWS YOU'RE ALONE. (MGM/United Artists-1980-
       Armand Mastroianni-R). Scott Parker wrote the screenplay.
       (Q, V, W)

1525. HEAD OVER HEELS. (United Artists-1979-Joan Micklin
       Silver-PG). Screenplay by Joan Micklin Silver, based on
       the novel Chilly Scenes of Winter by Ann Beattie; Double-
       day, 1976, 280p. (LACOPL, LAT, Q, V, W)

1526. HEADIN' FOR BROADWAY. (20th Century-Fox-1980-Joseph
       Brooks-PG). Joseph Brooks, Hilary Henkin, and Larry
       Gross wrote the screenplay. (V)

1527. THE HEADLESS EYES. (J.E.R. Pictures-1983-Kent Bateman-
       X). Screenplay by Kent Bateman. (V, W)

1528. HEADMASTER. (Jason Russell-1976-X). Screenplay credits
       not available. (W)

1529. HEADS OR TAILS. (Castle Hill-1983-Robert Enrico-N/R).
       Screenplay by Michel Audiard, adapted by Marcel Julian,

Robert Enrico, and Michel Audiard from the novel <u>Follow the</u>
<u>Widower</u> by Alfred Harris. (W)

1530. HEALTH. (20th Century-Fox-1980-Robert Altman-PG).
Screenplay by Frank Barhydt, Paul Dooley, and Robert
Altman. (HR, LAT, V, W)

1531. THE HEARSE. (Crown International-1980-George Bowers-
PG). Screenplay by Bill Bleich, from an idea by Mark
Tenser. (LAT, V, W)

1532. HEART BEAT. (Orion/Warner Bros.-1979-John Byrum-R).
Screenplay written by John Byrum. (HR, Q, V, W)

1533. HEART LIKE A WHEEL. (20th Century-Fox-1983-Jonathan
Kaplan-PG). Screenplay written by Ken Friedman. (HR,
LAT, V)

1534. HEART OF THE STAG. (New World-1984-Michael Firth-
N/R). Screenplay by Neil Illingworth, from a story by
Michael Firth. (V)

1535. HEART TO HEART. (New Yorker-1981-Pascal Thomas-N/R).
Screenplay by Jacques Lourcelles and Pascal Thomas. (LAT,
W)

1536. HEARTACHES. (Rising Star-1981-Donald Shebib-N/R).
Screenplay by Terence Heffernan. (V, W)

1537. HEARTBEEPS. (Universal-1981-Allan Arkush-PG). John
Hill wrote the screenplay. (LAT, Q, V, W)

1538. HEARTBREAKER. (Monorex-1983-Frank Zuniga-R). Screenplay by Vicente Gutierrez. (V, W)

1539. HEARTBREAKERS. (Orion-1984-Bobby Roth-R). Screenplay written by Bobby Roth. (V)

1540. HEARTLAND. (Filmhaus-1979-Richard Pearce-N/R).
Screenplay by Beth Ferris. (LAT, W)

1541. HEARTS OF THE WEST. (United Artists-1975-Howard
Zieff-PG). Screenplay by Bob Thompson. (NYT, Q, W)

1542. HEAT AND DUST. (Curzon Films-1983-James Ivory-R).
Screenplay written by Ruth Prawer Jhabvala, based on her
novel; Harper & Row, 1976, 181p. (BFI, HR, LACOPL,
LAT, V)

1543. HEATWAVE. (New Line Cinema-1983-Phillip Noyce-R).
Screenplay by Marc Rosenberg and Phillip Noyce, based

on an original screenplay by Mark Stiles and Tim Gooding. (V, W)

1544. HEAVEN CAN WAIT. (Paramount-1978-Warren Beatty and Buck Henry-PG). Screenplay by Warren Beatty and Elaine May, based on the play by Harry Segall. (HR, LAT, NYT, Q, V, W)

1545. HEAVEN'S GATE. (United Artists-1980-Michael Cimino-R). Screenplay by Michael Cimino. (LAT, NYT, Q, V, W)

1546. HEAVY LOAD. (AIC-1975-Mark Ubell-X). No screenplay credits given. (W)

1547. HEDDA. (Brut-1975-Trevor Nunn-PG). Screenplay by Trevor Nunn, based on the play Hedda Gabler by Henrik Ibsen; Scribner's, 1912, 365p. (LACOPL, NYT, Q, W)

1548. HEIDI'S SONG. (Paramount-1982-Robert Taylor-G). Screenplay by Joseph Barbera, Robert Taylor and Jameson Brewer, based on the novel by Johanna Spyri; Macmillan, 1912. (LACOPL, V, W)

1549. THE HEIST. (First American Films-1979-Sergio Goffi-R). Screenplay by Sergio Goffi. (W)

1550. HELENA. (Euram-1976-Alain Maury-X). Screenplay credits not given. (W)

1551. HELL HOUSE GIRLS. (American International-1975-Robert Hartford-Davis-R). Screenplay credits not given. (W)

1552. HELL NIGHT. (Aquarius-1981-Tom Desimone-R). Screenplay by Randolph Feldman. (LAT, V, W)

1553. HELL RIVER. (1978-Stole Jankovic-N/R). Screenplay by Howard Berk and Stole Jankovic. (W)

1554. HELP ME ... I'M POSSESSED. (Riviera-1976-Charles Nizet-PG). Screenplay credits not available. (W)

1555. HENNESSY. (American International-1975-Don Sharp-PG). Screenplay by John Gay, from a story by Richard Jonson. (NYT, Q, W)

1556. HER FAMILY JEWELS. (M. Shuffey-1976-Martin Campbell-X). Screenplay credits not given. (W)

1557. HERBIE GOES BANANAS. (Buena Vista-1980-Vincent McEveety-G). Screenplay by Don Tait, based on characters created by Gordon Buford. (V, W)

1558. HERBIE GOES TO MONTE CARLO. (Buena Vista-1977-Vincent McEveety-G). Screenplay by Arthur Alsberg and Don Nelson, based on characters created by Gordon Buford; novelization by Vic Crume; Scholastic, 1974. (LACOPL, NYT, Q, V)

1559. HERCULES. (MGM/UA-1983-Lewis Coates aka Luigi Cozzi-PG). Screenplay written by Lewis Coates aka Luigi Cozzi. (LAT, V, W)

1560. HERE COME THE TIGERS. (American International-1978-Sean S. Cunningham-PG). Screenplay written by Arch McCoy. (NYT, W)

1561. HERO. (Maya Films/Channel Four-1982-Barney Platts Mills-N/R). Screenplay by Barney Platts Mills, from a book by J. F. Campbell. (V)

1562. A HERO AIN'T NOTHING BUT A SANDWICH. (New World-1978-Ralph Nelson-PG). Screenplay by Alice Childress, based on her novel; Avon, 1982, 128p. (LACOPL, NYT)

1563. HERO AT LARGE. (MGM-1980-Martin Davidson-PG). Screenplay by A. J. Carothers; novelization by A. J. Carothers; Ballantine Books, 1980. (LACOPL, Q, V, W)

1564. THE HEROES. (United Artists-1975-Duccio Tessari-PG). Screenplay written by Luciano Vincenzoni and Sergio Donati; novelization by James Carabestos; Berkley, 1975. (LACOPL, NYT, W)

1565. HESTER STREET. (Midwest-1975-Joan Micklin Silver-PG). Screenplay by Joan Micklin Silver, adapted from Yekl by Abraham Cahan. (NYT, Q, W)

1566. HEY BABE! (Rafal-1984-Rafal Zielinski-N/R). Screenplay by Edith Rey, from an original story by Edith Rey and Rafal Zielinski. (V)

1567. HEY, GOOD LOOKIN'. (Warner Bros.-1982-Ralph Bakshi-R). Screenplay by Ralph Bakshi. (V, W)

1568. HI-RIDERS. (Dimension-1978-Greydon Clark-R). Screenplay by Greydon Clark. (W)

1569. HIDE IN PLAIN SIGHT. (United Artists/MGM-1980-James Caan-PG). Screenplay by Spencer Eastman, based on a book by Leslie Walter; Delacorte Press, 1976. (LACOPL, Q, V, W)

1570. THE HIDING PLACE. (World Wide-1975-James F. Collier-PG).

Screenplay by Allan Sloane, Lawrence Holben, based on a
book by Corrie ten Boom and John and Elizabeth Sherrill;
Chosen Books, 1972, 219p. (LACOPL, NYT, Q, W)

1571. HIGH ANXIETY. (20th Century-Fox-1977-Mel Brooks-PG).
Screenplay by Mel Brooks, Ron Clark, Rudy DeLuca, and
Barry Levinson; novelization by Robert H. Pilpel; Ace Books,
1977. (HR, LACOPL, NYT, Q, W)

1572. HIGH-BALLIN'. (American International-1978-Peter Carter-
PG). Screenplay by Paul Edwards, from a story by Richard
Robinson and Stephen Schneck. (Q, V, W)

1573. THE HIGH COUNTRY. (Crown International-1981-Harvey
Hart-PG). Screenplay by Bud Townsend. (LAT, V)

1574. HIGH ICE. (1979-Eugene S. Jones-N/R). Screenplay by
Sy Gomberg and Jack Turley, story by Natalie R. Jones
and Eugene S. Jones. (BFI)

1575. HIGH RISK. (American Cinema-1981-Stewart Raffill-R).
Screenplay by Stewart Raffill. (LAT, V, W)

1576. HIGH ROAD TO CHINA. (Warner Bros.-1983-Brian G.
Hutton-PG). Screenplay by Sandra Weintraub Roland and
S. Lee Pogostin, based on the book by Jon Cleary; Morrow,
1977, 276p. (HR, LACOPL, LAT, V)

1577. HIGH ROLLING IN A HOT CORVETTE. (Martin-1978-Igor
Auzins-PG). Screenplay by Forest Redlich. (W)

1578. HIGH SCHOOL FANTASIES. (Freeway-1975-Morris Deal-X).
Screenplay by Morris Deal. (W)

1579. HIGH SCHOOL HONIES. (Beehive-1976-Tom Gordon-X).
Screenplay written by Lem Lary. (W)

1580. HIGH VELOCITY. (Turtle-1976-Remi Kramer-PG). Screenplay by Remi Kramer and Michael J. Parson. (W)

1581. HIGHPOINT. (New World-1984-Peter Carter-N/R). Screenplay by Richard Guttman and Ian Sutherland. (V)

1582. HIGHWAY HOOKERS. (Hudson-1976-Carter Stevens-X). No
screenplay credits available. (W)

1583. HILARY'S BLUES. (Golden Union-1984-Peter Jensen-R).
Screenplay by Elmer Kline. (W)

1584. THE HILLS HAVE EYES. (Vanguard-1978-Wes Craven-R).
Screenplay by Wes Craven. (W)

1585. THE HINDENBURG. (Universal-1975-Robert Wise-PG).
       Screenplay by Nelson Gidding, story by Richard Levinson,
       and William Link, based on the book by Michael M. Mooney;
       Dodd, 1972, 278p. (LACOPL, NYT, W)

1586. HINOTORI. (Toho International Co.-1980-Ken Ichikawa-N/R).
       Screenplay by Shuntaro Tanikawa, original story by Osamu
       Tezuka. (V)

1587. HISTORY OF THE WORLD PART I. (20th Century-Fox-1981-
       Mel Brooks-R). Screenplay by Mel Brooks, novelization by
       Mel Brooks. (LACOPL, LAT, Q, V, W)

1588. HIT AND RUN. (Comworld-1982-Charles Braverman-N/R).
       Screenplay by Don Enright, based on the novel 80 Dollars
       to Stamford. (V)

1589. HITCHHIKE TO HELL. (Boxoffice International-1978-Irv
       Berwick-R). Screenplay by John Buckley. (W)

1590. THE HITTER. (Peppercorn-Wormser-1979-Christopher
       Leitch-R). Screenplay by Ben Harris. (W)

1591. HOG WILD. (Avco Embassy-1980-Les Rose-PG). Screen-
       play by Andrew Peter Marin. (V, W)

1592. THE HOLES. (Burbank International-1976-PG). No screen-
       play credits available. (NYT, W)

1593. HOLIDAY HOOKERS. (M & M-1979-Armando Nannuzzi-R).
       No screenplay credits available. (W)

1594. HOLLYWOOD HIGH. (Peter Perry-1976-Patrick Wright-R).
       Screenplay credits not available. (W)

1595. HOLLYWOOD HIGH PART II. (Lone Star Pictures-1984-Lee
       Thornburg-R). Screenplay by Lee Thornburg, Caruth C.
       Byrd, Cotton Whittington, and Colleen Meeker. (V)

1596. HOLLYWOOD KNIGHT. (First American Films-1979-David
       Worth-PG). Screenplay by Michael Christian. (W)

1597. THE HOLLYWOOD KNIGHTS. (Columbia-1980-Floyd Mutrux-
       R). Screenplay by Floyd Mutrux, based on a story by
       Floyd Mutrux, Richard Lederer, and William Tennant. (Q,
       V, W)

       HOLY TERROR see ALICE, SWEET ALICE

1598. THE HOME AND THE WORLD. (National Film Development
       Corporation of India-1984-Satyajit Ray-N/R). Screenplay by
       Satyajit Ray, from a novel by Rabindranath Tagore. (V)

1599. A HOME FOR GENTLE SOULS. (Bulgaria Film Production-
       1981-Evgeni Mihailov-N/R). Screenplay by Bojan Papasov.
       (V)

1600. HOME MOVIES. (SLC Films-1979-Brian De Palma-N/R).
       Screenplay by Robert Harders, Gloria Norris, Kim Ambler,
       Dana Edelman, Stephen Le May, Charles Loventhal, from a
       story by Brian De Palma. (NYT, V, W)

1601. HOME SWEET HOME. (Libra-1981-Benoit Lamy-N/R).
       Screenplay by Rudolph Pauli and Benoit Lamy. (W)

1602. HOMETOWN U.S.A. (Film Ventures International-1979-Max
       Baer-R). Screenplay by Jesse Vint, from his original story.
       (V, W)

1603. HOMEWORK. (Jensen Farley-1982-James Beshears-R).
       Screenplay written by Maurice Peterson and Don Safran.
       (V, W)

       L'HOMME QUI AMAIT LES FEMMES see THE MAN WHO
       LOVED WOMEN (1977)

1604. HOMO EROTICUS. (Universal-1975-Marco Vicario-R).
       Screenplay and story by Piero Chiara and Marco Vicario.
       (NYT, W)

1605. HONEYPIE. (Ded Films-1976-Hans Johnson-X). Screenplay
       credits not available. (W)

1606. HONEYSUCKLE ROSE. (Warner Bros.-1980-Jerry Schatzberg-
       PG). Screenplay by Carol Sobieski, William D. Wittliff, and
       John Binder; novelization by Robert Alley; Bantam Books,
       1980. (LACOPL, Q, V, W)

1607. HONG KONG STRONGMAN. (Cinema Shares-1978-R). No
       production credits available. (W)

1608. HONKY TONK FREEWAY. (Universal-Associated Film
       Distribution-1981-John Schlesinger-R). Screenplay by Ed-
       ward Clinton. (LAT, Q, V, W)

1609. HONKYTONK MAN. (Warner Bros.-1982-Clint Eastwood-PG).
       Clancy Carlile wrote the screenplay, based on his novel;
       Simon & Schuster, 1980, 345p. (LACOPL, V)

1610. HOODWINK. (C.B. Films-1981-Chad Whatham-N/R). Screen-
       play by Ken Quinnell. (V)

1611. HOOPER. (Warner Bros.-1978-Hal Needham-PG). Screenplay
       by Thomas Rickman and Bill Kerby, from a story by Walt

Green and Walter S. Herndon; novelization by Walt Green;
Warner Books, 1978. (HR, LACOPL, LAT, NYT, Q, V, W)

1612. HOPSCOTCH. (Avco Embassy-1980-Ronald Neame-R).
Screenplay by Brian Garfield and Bryan Forbes, based on a
novel by Brian Garfield; Evans, 1975, 284p. (LACOPL, V,
W)

1613. HORROR HOSPITAL. (Hallmark-1975-Anthony Balch-PG).
Screenplay by Anthony Balch and Alan Watson. (W)

1614. HORROR PLANET. (Almi-1982-Norman J. Warren-R).
Screenplay by Nick Maley and Gloria Maley. (V, W)

1615. HORROR RISES FROM THE TOMB. (Avco Embassy-1976-
Carlos Aured-R). No screenplay credits given. (W)

1616. HORSE OF PRIDE. (Planfilm-1980-Claude Chabrol-N/R).
Screenplay by Claude Chabrol and Daniel Boulanger, from
the book by Pierre-Jakez Helias. (V)

1617. HOSPITAL MASSACRE. (Cannon-1983-Boaz Davidson-R).
Screenplay by Marc Behm. (V, W)

1618. HOT AND DEADLY. (Arist-1984-Elliot Hong-R). Screenplay written by Larry Stamper. (V)

1619. HOT DALLAS NIGHTS. (Miracle Films-1981-Tony Kendrick-
N/R). Screenplay by Robert Oakwood and Tony Kendrick.
(W)

1620. HOT DOG ... THE MOVIE. (MGM/UA-1983-Peter Markle-R).
Screenplay by Mike Marvin. (V)

1621. HOT LEAD AND COLD FEET. (Buena Vista-1978-Robert
Butler-G). Screenplay by Joe McEveety, Arthur Alsberg,
and Don Nelson. (V, W)

1622. HOT MOVES. (Cardinal-1984-Jim Sotos-R). Screenplay by
Larry Anderson and Peter Foldy. (V)

1623. HOT NASTIES. (Troma-1976-Alexander Newman-X). No
screenplay credits available. (W)

1624. HOT OVEN. (Smith & Jones-1975-Carter Stevens-X). No
screenplay credits available. (W)

1625. HOT POTATO. (Warner Bros.-1976-Oscar Williams-PG).
Screenplay written by Oscar Williams. (W)

1626. HOT STUFF. (Columbia-1979-Dom DeLuise-PG). Screenplay
by Michael Kane and Donald E. Westlake. (NYT, V, W)

1627.   HOT SUMMER IN THE CITY.   (Imperial-1976-The Hare-X).
        Screenplay by P. James Write.   (W)

1628.   HOT T-SHIRTS.   (Cannon-1980-Chuck Vincent-R).   Screen-
        play written by Chuck Vincent and Bill Slobodian.   (W)

1629.   HOT TOMORROWS.   (American Film Institute-1978-Martin
        Brest-N/R).   Screenplay written by Martin Brest.   (NYT, W)

1630.   THE HOTEL NEW HAMPSHIRE.   (Orion-1984-Tony Richardson-
        R).   Screenplay by Tony Richardson, based on the novel by
        John Irving.   (V)

1631.   HOTHEAD.   (Quartet Films-1980-Jean-Jacques Annaud-N/R).
        Screenplay by Francis Veber, Jean-Jacques Annaud, from an
        original idea by Alain Godard.   (W)

1632.   THE HOUND OF THE BASKERVILLES.   (Hemdale International-
        1978-Paul Morrissey-N/R).   Screenplay by Peter Cook, Dud-
        ley Moore, and Paul Morrissey.   (NYT, V, W)

1633.   THE HOUND OF THE BASKERVILLES.   (Mapleton Films-
        1982-Douglas Hickox-N/R).   Screenplay by Charles Pogue,
        from the Sherlock Holmes tale by Sir Arthur Conan Doyle;
        Dodd, 1968, 204p.   (LACOPL, LAT, V)

1634.   THE HOUSE BY THE CEMETERY.   (Almi-1984-Lucio Fulci-X).
        Screenplay by Lucio Fulci, Dardano Sacchetti, and Giorgio
        Mariuzzo, from a story by Elisa Livia Briganti.   (V)

1635.   THE HOUSE BY THE LAKE.   (American International-1977-
        William Fruet-R).   Screenplay by William Fruet.   (NYT, Q,
        V)

1636.   HOUSE CALLS.   (Universal-1978-Howard Zieff-PG).   Screen-
        play by Max Shulman, Julius J. Epstein, Alan Mandel, and
        Charles Shyer, from a story by Max Shulman and Julius J.
        Epstein.   (NYT, W)

        HOUSE OF EVIL see THE HOUSE ON SORORITY ROW

1637.   HOUSE OF EXORCISM.   (Peppercorn-Wormser-1976-Mickey
        Lion aka Mario Bava-R).   Screenplay by Alberto Cittini and
        Alfred Leone.   (W)

1638.   THE HOUSE OF GOD.   (United Artists-1984-Donald Wrye-
        N/R).   Screenplay by Donald Wrye, based on the novel by
        Samuel Shem; R. Marek, 1978, 382p.   (LACOPL, V)

1639.   THE HOUSE OF LONG SHADOWS.   (Cannon-1983-Pete Walker-
        N/R).   Screenplay by Michael Armstrong.   (V)

1640. HOUSE OF PSYCHOTIC WOMEN. (Independent International-1976-Carlos Aured-R). No screenplay credits available. (W)

HOUSE OF TERROR see THE FIRE AT THE FUNERAL

1641. THE HOUSE OF WHIPCORD. (American International-1975-Pete Walker-R). Screenplay by David McGillivray. (W)

1642. THE HOUSE ON SORORITY ROW. (Artists Releasing Co.-1983-Mark Rosman-R). Screenplay by Mark Rosman, with additional dialogue by Bobby Fine. (BFI, V, W)

1643. THE HOUSE WHERE DEATH LIVES. (New American Films-1984-Alan Beattie-R). Screenplay written by Jack Viertel, from a story by Alan Beattie. (V, W)

1644. THE HOUSE WHERE EVIL DWELLS. (MGM/UA-1982-Kevin Connor-R). Screenplay by Robert Suhosky, based on the novel by James Hardiman. (Q, V, W)

1645. HOW COME NOBODY'S ON OUR SIDE? (American Films Ltd.-1975-Richard Michaels-PG). Screenplay by Leigh Chapman. (W)

1646. HOW TO BEAT THE HIGH COST OF LIVING. (American International/Filmways-1980-Robert Scheerer-PG). Screenplay by Robert Kaufman, from a story by Leonora Thuna. (Q, V, W)

1647. HOW TO DROWN DR. MRACEK. (IFEX-1983-Vaclav Vorlicek-N/R). Screenplay by Milos Macourek and Petr Markov, and V. Vorlicek, from a story by Petr Markov. (W)

1648. HOW TO SCORE WITH GIRLS. (NMD-1980-Ogden Lowell-R). Screenplay by Ogden Lowell. (W)

1649. HOW'D YOU GET IN? DIDN'T SEE YOU LEAVE. (Gaumont-1984-Philippe Clair-N/R). Screenplay by Philippe Clair, Daniel Saint-Hamon, and Bruno Tardon. (V)

1650. THE HOWLING. (Avco Embassy-1981-Joe Dante-R). Screenplay by John Sayles, Terence H. Winkless, based on a novel by Gary Brandner; Fawcett, 1979. (LACOPL, LAT, Q, V, W)

1651. HUGHES AND HARLOW: ANGELS IN HELL. (PRO International-1978-Larry Buchanan-R). Screenplay by Lynn Shubert and Larry Buchanan. (W)

1652. HUGO THE HIPPO. (20th Century-Fox-1976-Bill Feigenbaum-G). Screenplay by Tom Baum. (V)

1653. HULLABALOO OVER GEORGIE AND BONNIE'S PICTURES.
       (Contemporary Films-1979-James Ivory-N/R). Screenplay by
       Ruth Prawer Jhabvala. (V, W)

1654. HUMAN EXPERIMENTS. (Essex-1980-Gregory Goodell-R).
       Screenplay by Richard Rothstein. (W)

1655. HUMAN FACTOR. (Bryanston-1975-Edward Dmytryk-R).
       Screenplay by Tom Hunter and Peter Powell. (Q, W)

1656. THE HUMAN FACTOR. (MGM/UA-1979-Otto Preminger-R).
       Screenplay by Tom Stoppard, based on the novel by Graham
       Greene; Simon & Schuster, 1978, 347p. (LACOPL, Q, V, W)

1657. HUMAN HIGHWAY. (Shakey Pictures-1982-Bernard Shakey
       with Dean Stockwell-N/R). Screenplay by Bernard Shakey,
       Jeanne Fields, Dean Stockwell, Russ Tamblyn, and James
       Beshears. (V, W)

1658. THE HUMAN TORNADO. (Dimension-1976-Cliff Roquemore-R).
       Screenplay by Jerry Jones. (W)

1659. HUMANOIDS FROM THE DEEP. (New World-1980-Barbara
       Peeters-R). Screenplay by Frederick James, based on a
       story by Frank Arnold and Martin B. Cohen. (V, W)

1660. HUMONGOUS. (Embassy-1982-Paul Lynch-R). Screenplay
       by William Gray. (BFI, Q, V, W)

1661. THE HUNCHBACK OF THE MORGUE. (Janus-1975-Javier
       Aguirre-R). Screenplay credits not available. (W)

1662. HUNGARIANS. (IFEX-1981-Zoltan Fabri-N/R). Screenplay
       by Zoltan Fabri, based on a novel by Jozsef Balasz. (W)

1663. THE HUNGER. (MGM/UA-1983-Tony Scott-R). Screenplay
       by Ivan Davis and Michael Thomas, based on the novel by
       Whitley Strieber; Morrow, 1981, 320p. (LACOPL, LAT, V)

1664- THE HUNTED. (Atlas-1976-PG). No screenplay credits
  65. available. (W)

1666. THE HUNTER. (Paramount-1980-Buzz Kulik-PG). Screen-
       play by Ted Leighton, Peter Hyams, based on the book by
       Christopher Keane and the life of Ralph Thorson; Dutton,
       1976, 289p. (LACOPL, Q, V, W)

       HUNTER OF THE APOCALYPSE see THE LAST HUNTER

1667. THE HUNTER WILL GET YOU! (Joseph Green-1980-Philippe
       Labro-PG). Screenplay by Philippe Labro. (W)

1668. THE HUNTERS OF THE GOLDEN COBRA. (World Northal-
1984-Anthony M. Dawson aka Antonio Margheriti-N/R).
Screenplay by Tito Carpi, from a story by Gianfranco
Couyoumdjian. (V)

1669. HUNTING FLIES. (1981-Andrzej Wajda-N/R). Screenplay
by Janusz Glowacki. (W)

1670. HURRICANE. (Paramount-1979-Jan Troell-PG). Screenplay
by Lorenzo Semple Jr., based on the novel by Charles Nord-
hoff and James Norman Hall; Little, Brown, 1936. (LACOPL,
Q, V, W)

1671. HUSSY. (Kendon-1980-Matthew Chapman-N/R). Matthew
Chapman wrote this original screenplay. (V)

1672. HUSTLE. (Paramount-1975-Robert Aldrich-R). Screenplay
by Steve Shagan, from his novel City of Angels; Putnam,
1975, 255p. (LACOPL, NYT, Q, W)

1673. HUSTLER SQUAD. (Crown International-1976-Cesar Gallardo-
R). Screenplay credits not available. (W)

1674. HYPNOROTICA. (Savage Enterprises-1975-Armond Peters-
X). Screenplay written by Armond Peters. (W)

1675. HYSTERICAL. (Embassy-1983-Chris Bearde-PG). Screenplay by William Hudson, Mark Hudson, Brett Hudson, and
Trace Johnston. (W)

1676. I, A WOMAN PART III. (Orrin-1975-Mac Ahlberg-R).
Screenplay written by Peer Guldbrandsen. (W)

1677. I, A WOMAN PART II. (Chevron-1975-Mac Ahlberg-R).
Screenplay by Peer Guldbrandsen. (W)

1678. I AM A CAT. (Toho-1982-Ken Ichikawa-N/R). Toshio
Yasumi wrote the screenplay from a novel by Soseki Natsume.
(W)

1679. I AM CURIOUS TAHITI. (Hollywood International-1975-
Carlos Tobalina-X). No screenplay credits given. (W)

1680. I AM THE CHEESE. (Almi-1983-Robert Jiras-PG). Screen-
play by David Lange and Robert Jiras, from a novel by
Robert Cormier; Pantheon, 1977, 224p. (HR, LACOPL, LAT,
V, W)

1681. I DISMEMBER MAMA. (Valiant International-1983-Paul Leder-
R). William Norton wrote this original screenplay. (V)

1682.   I LOVE YOU. (Atlantic-1982-Arnaldo Jabor-N/R). Screenplay written by Arnaldo Jabor. (W)

1683.   I MARRIED A DEAD MAN. (AMLF-1983-Robin Davis-N/R).
Screenplay by Robin Davis and Patrick Laurent, based on
William Irish's novel. (V)

1684.   I NEVER PROMISED YOU A ROSE GARDEN. (New World-
1977-Anthony Page-R). Screenplay by Lewis John Carlino
and Gavin Lambert, based on the Joanne Greenberg novel of
the same title; Holt, 1964. (HR, LACOPL, NYT, V)

1685.   I OUGHT TO BE IN PICTURES. (20th Century-Fox-1982-
Herbert Ross-PG). Screenplay by Neil Simon, based on his
play; Random House, 1981, 96p. (HR, LACOPL, V, W)

1686.   I REMEMBER LOVE. (Lone Star Pictures-1981-Norbert
Meisel-R). Screenplay written by Norbert Meisel. (W)

1687.   I SENT A LETTER TO MY LOVE. (Atlantic-1981-Moshe
Mizrahi-PG). Screenplay by Moshe Mizrahi and Gerard
Brach, from a novel by Bernice Rubens. (W)

I SPIT ON YOUR GRAVE see DAY OF THE WOMAN

1688.   I, THE JURY. (20th Century-Fox-1982-Richard T. Heffron-
R). Screenplay by Larry Cohen, based on a novel by
Mickey Spillane; NAL, 1972. (BFI, LACOPL, V, W)

1689.   I WANNA HOLD YOUR HAND. (Universal-1978-Robert
Zemeckis-PG). Screenplay by Robert Zemeckis and Bob
Gale. (HR, LAT, NYT, Q, V, W)

1690.   I WILL, I WILL ... FOR NOW. (20th Century-Fox-1976-
Norman Panama-R). Screenplay by Norman Panama and
Albert E. Lewin. (NYT, W)

1691.   ICE CASTLES. (Columbia-1979-Donald Wrye-PG). Screenplay by Donald Wrye and Gary L. Baim, based on a true
story by Gary L. Baim; novelization by Leonore Fleischer;
Fawcett Books, 1978, 220p. (HR, LACOPL, LAT, Q, V, W)

1692.   THE ICE PIRATES. (MGM/UA-1984-Stewart Raffill-PG).
Screenplay written by Stewart Raffill and Stanford Sherman.
(HR, LAT, V)

1693.   ICEMAN. (Universal-1984-Fred Schepisi-PG). Screenplay by
Chip Proser and John Drimmer. (LAT, V)

1694.   ICY BREASTS. (Joseph Green-1975-Georges Lautner-N/R).
Screenplay by Georges Lautner, from a novel by Richard
Matheson. (NYT, W)

1695. IDAHO TRANSFER. (Cinemation Industries-1975-Peter Fonda-N/R). Screenplay by Thomas Matthiesen. (W)

1696. THE IDOLMAKER. (United Artists-1980-Taylor Hackford-PG). Screenplay by Edward Di Lorenzo. (HR, LAT, NYT,Q, V, W)

1697. IF EVER I SEE YOU AGAIN. (Columbia-1978-Joe Brooks-PG). Screenplay by Joe Brooks and Martin Davidson. (NYT, W)

1698. IF MUSIC BE THE FOOD OF LOVE. (Norsk Film-1980-Hans Lindgren-N/R). Screenplay by Hans Lindgren. (V)

1699. IF YOU COULD SEE WHAT I HEAR. (Jensen Farley Pictures-1982-Eric Till-PG). Screenplay by Stuart Gillard, from the book by Tom Sullivan; Harper & Row, 1979, 313p. (LACOPL, Q, V, W)

1700. I'LL DIE FOR MAMA. (Trimurti Films-1979-Yash Chopra-N/R). Screenplay and story by Salim-Javed. (W)

       THE ILLEGAL see ALAMBRISTA!

1701. ILLUMINATION. (Bauer International-1978-Krzystof Zanussi-N/R). No screenplay credits given. (W)

1702. ILSA, HAREM KEEPER OF THE OIL SHEIKS. (Cambist-1976-Don Edmonds-R). Screenplay by Langton Stafford. (W)

1703. ILSA, SHE WOLF OF THE SS. (Cambist-1975-Don Edmonds-N/R). Screenplay credits not available. (NYT, W)

1704. I'M DANCING AS FAST AS I CAN. (Paramount-1982-Jack Hofsiss-R). Screenplay by David Rabe, based on the book by Barbara Gordon; Harper & Row, 1979, 313p. (LACOPL, LAT, Q, V)

1705. I'M GOING TO BE FAMOUS. (L.T. Prods. Ltd.-1983-Paul Leder-N/R). Screenplay written by Paul Leder, from his original screen story. (V)

1706. THE IMAGE. (Audubon-1976-Radley Metzger-X). Screenplay written by Jake Barnes. (W)

1707. IMMORAL TALES. (New Line Cinema-1976-Walerian Borowczyk-X). Screenplay by Walerian Borowczyk. (NYT, W)

1708. THE IMMORTAL BACHELOR. (S.J. International-1980-Marcello Fondato-PG). Screenplay by Marcello Fondato and Francesco Scardamaglia. (W)

1709. IMPERATIVE. (Telefilm Saar-1982-Krzysztof Zanussi-N/R).
       Screenplay by Krzysztof Zanussi. (V)

1710. IMPOSTERS. (First Run Features-1981-Mark Rappaport-
       N/R). Screenplay by Mark Rappaport. (W)

1711. IMPROPER CONDUCT. (Promovision International-1984-
       Nestor Almendros and Orlando Jimenez-Leal-N/R). Screen-
       play written by Nestor Almendros and Orlando Jimenez-Leal.
       (V)

1712. THE IMPUDENT GIRL. (AMLF-1979-Jacques Doillon-N/R).
       Screenplay by Jacques Doillon. (V)

1713. IMPULSE. (Camelot Entertainment-1975-William Grefe-PG).
       Screenplay by Tony Crechales. (W)

1714. IMPULSE. (20th Century-Fox-1984-Graham Baker-R).
       Screenplay by Bart Davis and Don Carlos Dunaway. (V)

1715. IN A YEAR OF THIRTEEN MOONS. (New Yorker-1980-
       Rainer Werner Fassbinder-N/R). Screenplay written by
       Rainer Werner Fassbinder. (W)

1716. IN CELEBRATION. (American Film Theatre-1975-Lindsay
       Anderson-PG). Screenplay by David Story. (NYT, Q, W)

1717. IN FOR TREATMENT. (Het Werkteatre-1980-Erik van
       Zuylen and Marja Kok-N/R). Screenplay by Het Werk-
       teatre. (V, W)

1718. IN GOD WE TRUST. (Universal-1980-Marty Feldman-PG).
       Screenplay by Marty Feldman and Chris Allen. (HR, LAT,
       Q, V, W)

1719. THE IN-LAWS. (Warner Bros.-1979-Arthur Hiller-PG).
       Screenplay by Andrew Bergman; novelization by David
       Rogers; Ballantine, 1977, 408p. (LACOPL, Q, V, W)

1720. THE IN-LAWS. (Shanghai Film Studio-1983-Zhao Huanzhang-
       N/R). Screenplay by Xin Xianling. (V)

1721. IN LOVE. (Platinum-1983-Chuck Vincent-R). Screenplay by
       Rick Marx and Chuck Vincent, from a story by Henri Pachard.
       (W)

1722. IN PRAISE OF OLDER WOMEN. (Avco Embassy-1979-George
       Kaczender-R). Screenplay by Paul Gottlieb, from the novel
       by Stephen Vizinczey; Trident Press, 1965. (LACOPL, W)

1723. IN SARAH'S EYES. (MSW-1975-Carter Stevens-X). Screen-
       play by Katya Kiss. (W)

1724. IN SEARCH OF HISTORIC JESUS. (Schick Sunn Classics-
       1980-Henning Schellerup-G). Screenplay by Marvin Wald
       and Jack Jacobs, based on the novel by Lee Roddy and
       Charles E. Sellier Jr. (HR, LAT, V, W)

1725. IN SEARCH OF NOAH'S ARK. (Schick Sunn Classics-1977-
       James L. Conway-G). Screenplay by James L. Conway and
       Charles E. Sellier Jr.; Sunn Classic Books, 1976, 218p.
       (LACOPL, V)

1726. IN THE KING OF PRUSSIA. (1982-Emile De Antonio-N/R).
       Screenplay by Emile De Antonio. (BFI, LAT)

1727. IN THE WHITE CITY. (Contemporary-1983-Alain Tanner-
       N/R). Screenplay by Alain Tanner. (BFI)

1728. INCHON. (One Way Productions-1981-Terence Young-N/R).
       Screenplay by Robin Moore and Laird Koenig, story by
       Robin Moore and Paul Savage. (V, W)

1729. INCOMING FRESHMEN. (Cannon-1979-Eric Lewald & Glenn
       Morgan-R). Screenplay by Eric Lewald and Glenn Morgan.
       (W)

1730. INCORRIGIBLE. (EDP Films-1980-Philippe DeBroca-N/R).
       Screenplay by Michel Audiard. (W)

1731. THE INCREDIBLE SARAH. (Reader's Digest-1976-Richard
       Fleischer-PG). Ruth Wolff wrote the original screenplay.
       (NYT, W)

1732. THE INCREDIBLE SHRINKING WOMAN. (Universal-1981-
       Joel Schumacher-PG). Screenplay by Jane Wagner. (HR,
       LAT, Q, V, W)

       THE INCREDIBLE TORTURE SHOW see BLOODSUCKING
       FREAKS

1733. THE INCUBUS. (Artists Releasing Corp-1982-John Hough-
       R). Screenplay by George Franklin, from the novel by Ray
       Russell; Morrow, 1976, 286p. (LACOPL, V, W)

1734. INDEPENDENCE DAY. (Unifilm-1981-Bobby Roth-N/R).
       Screenplay by Bobby Roth. (NYT, W)

1735. INDEPENDENCE DAY. (Warner Bros.-1983-Robert Mandel-R).
       Screenplay by Alice Hoffman. (V)

1736. INDIAN SUMMER. (Analysis-1978-Valerio Zurlini-R).
       Screenplay by Enrico Medioli and Valerio Zurlino. (W)

1737. INDIANA JONES AND THE TEMPLE OF DOOM. (Paramount-

1984-Steven Spielberg-PG). Screenplay written by Willard Huyck and Gloria Katz, from a story by George Lucas; novelization by James Kahn; Ballantine Books, 1984, 216p. (HR, LACOPL, LAT, V)

1738. THE INFIDEL. (Freeway-1976-Charles Bodine-X). Screenplay by Charles Bodine. (W)

1739. THE INHERITANCE. (S. J. International-1978-Mauro Bolognini-R). Screenplay by Ugo Pirro and Sergio Bazzini. (W)

1740. THE INNOCENCE OF VALERIE. (Brown-1975-Steve Brown-X). Screenplay written by Steve Brown. (W)

1741. THE INNOCENT. (Analysis Films-1979-Luchino Visconti-N/R). Screenplay written by Suso Cecchi D'Amico, Enrico Medioli, and Luchino Visconti, freely based on Gabriele D'Annunzio's novel L'Innocente. (W)

INSEMINOID see HORROR PLANET

1742. INSERTS. (United Artists-1976-John Byrum-X). Screenplay written by John Byrum. (NYT, V, W)

1743. INSIDE AMY. (Adpix-1975-Ron Garcia-R). Screenplay by Helene Arthur. (W)

1744. INSIDE JENNIFER WELLES. (Evart Releasing-1977-Jennifer Welles-X). Screenplay credits not available; based on The Memoirs of Jennifer Welles. (V)

1745. INSIDE MOVES. (Associated Film Distribution-1980-Richard Donner-PG). Screenplay by Valerie Curtin and Barry Levinson, based on the novel by Todd Walton; NAL, 1983. (LACOPL, Q, V, W)

1746. INSIDE OUT. (Warner Bros.-1976-Peter Duffell-N/R). Screenplay by Judd Bernard and Stephen Schneck. (W)

1747. INSTANT PICTURES. (Public Cinema-1981-George Schouten-N/R). Screenplay by George Schouten and Bernard Roeters. (W)

1748. THE INSTRUCTOR. (American Eagle Film International-1983-Don Bendell-N/R). Screenplay by Don Bendell. (V, W)

1749. INSTRUCTORS OF DEATH. (World Northal-1982-Liu Chia-Liang-R). No screenplay credits available. (W)

1750. INTENSIVE CARE. (1975-X). No production credits available. (W)

1751. INTERIORS. (United Artists-1978-Woody Allen-R). Screenplay by Woody Allen. (HR, NYT, V, W)

1752. INTERNATIONAL VELVET. (United Artists-1978-Bryan Forbes-PG). Screenplay by Bryan Forbes, adapted from the novel National Velvet by Enid Bagnold; novelization by Bryan Forbes; Bantam Books, 1978, 167p. (LACOPL, NYT, Q, V, W)

1753. INTIMATE FRIENDS: AN HISTORIC LEGEND. (Peking Film Studio-1982-Xie Tieli, Chen Huaiai and Ba Hong-N/R). Screenplay by Hua Ershi. (V)

1754. THE INTIMATE TEENAGERS. (William Mishkin-1975-Walter Boos-X). No screenplay credits given. (W)

1755. INVASION OF THE BLOOD FARMERS. (NMD-1976-Ed Adlum-PG). Screenplay by Ed Kelleher and Ed Adlum. (W)

1756. INVASION OF THE BODY SNATCHERS. (United Artists-1978-Philip Kaufman-PG). Screenplay by W. D. Richter, based on the novel by Jack Finney. (HR, LAT, NYT, Q, W, V)

1757. INVISIBLE ADVERSARIES. (Public Cinema-1980-Valie Export-N/R). Screenplay written by Peter Weibel and Valie Export. (W)

1758. INVISIBLE STRANGLER. (Seymour Borde-1984-John Florea-N/R). An original screenplay by Arthur C. Pierce, from a story by Jordan Lyon. (V)

1759. THE INVITATION. (Janus-1975-Claude Goretta-N/R). Screenplay by Claude Goretta and Michel Viala. (NYT, W)

1760. IPHIGENIA. (Cinema 5-1977-Michael Cacoyannis-N/R). Screenplay by Michael Cacoyannis, based on Iphigenia in Aulis by Euripides; Oxford University Press, 1973, 88p. (LACOPL, NYT, W)

1761. IRACEMA. (Embrafilme-1982-Jorge Bodanzky-N/R). Screenplay by Orlando Senna. (W)

1762. IRRECONCILABLE DIFFERENCES. (Hemdale-1984-Charles Shyer-N/R). Nancy Meyers and Charles Shyer wrote the screenplay. (V)

1763. THE ISLAND. (MBC Prods.-1979-Alejandro Doria-N/R). Screenplay by Aida Bortnik. (V)

1764.   THE ISLAND. (Universal-1980-Michael Ritchie-R). Screen-
        play by Peter Benchley, based on his novel; Doubleday,
        1979, 302p. (LACOPL, Q, V, W)

1765.   THE ISLAND OF DR. MOREAU. (American International-
        1977-Don Taylor-PG). Screenplay by John Herman Shaner
        and Al Ramrus, from the novel by H. G. Wells; Berkley,
        1973, 128p. (LACOPL, LAT, NYT, Q, V)

1766.   ISLAND OF LOST GIRLS. (Hampton International-1975-R).
        No screenplay credits available. (W)

1767.   THE ISLAND OF THE DAMNED. (American International-
        1978-Narciso Ibanez Serrador-R). Screenplay by Luis Pena-
        fiel, based on the novel El Juego by J. J. Plans. (W)

1768.   ISLANDS IN THE STREAM. (Paramount-1977-Franklin J.
        Schaffner-PG). Screenplay written by Denne Bart Petit-
        clerc, based on the novel by Ernest Hemingway; Scribner's,
        1970, 466p. (LACOPL, NYT, Q, V)

1769.   IT CAME FROM HOLLYWOOD. (Paramount-1982-Andrew Solt
        & Malcolm Leo-PG). Screenplay written by Dana Olsen.
        (V, W)

1770.   IT LIVES AGAIN. (Warner Bros.-1978-Larry Cohen-R).
        Screenplay written by Larry Cohen, based on characters
        created in the film It's Alive. (NYT, W)

1771.   IT SEEMED LIKE A GOOD IDEA AT THE TIME. (Selective
        Cinema-1976-John Trent-PG). Screenplay by David Main
        and John Trent, from a story by Claude Harz. (W)

        IT SHOULDN'T HAPPEN TO A VET see ALL THINGS
        BRIGHT AND BEAUTIFUL

1772.   IT WAS NIGHT IN ROME. (Joseph Papp-1982-Roberto
        Rossellini-N/R). Screenplay by Roberto Rossellini, Sergio
        Amidei, Diego Fabri, and Brunello Rondi. (W)

1773.   IT'S A LONG TIME I'VE LOVED YOU. (Films de la Tour-
        1979-Jean-Charles Tacchella-N/R). Screenplay written by
        Jean-Charles Tacchella. (V)

1774.   IT'S MY TURN. (Columbia-1980-Claudia Weill-R). Screen-
        play by Eleanor Bergstein. (Q, V, W)

1775.   IT'S NICE TO MEET YOU. (Morena Productores de Art/
        Embrafilme-1982-David Neves-N/R). Screenplay by David
        Neves and Joaquim V. Carvalho. (V)

1776. IT'S NOT THE SIZE THAT COUNTS! (Joseph Brenner-1979-
       Ralph Thomas-R). Screenplay by Sid Colin, from a story
       by Harry Corbett, with additional dialog by Ian La Frenais.
       (V, W)

1777. IVAN THE TERRIBLE. (Corinth-1979-L. Ohrimenko-N/R).
       Screenplay written by Vadim Derbenev and Yuri Grigorovich.
       (W)

1778. J.D.'S REVENGE. (American International-1976-Arthur
       Marks-R). Screenplay by Jaison Starkes. (NYT, W)

1779. JABBERWOCKY. (Cinema 5-1977-Terry Gilliam-N/R).
       Screenplay by Terry Gilliam and Charles Alverson, based
       on a poem by Lewis Carroll. (NYT, V)

1780. JACKSON COUNTY JAIL. (New World-1976-Michael Miller-
       R). Screenplay by Donald Stewart. (NYT, W)

1781. JACOB THE LIAR. (MacMillan Films-1977-Frank Beyer-N/R).
       Screenplay by Jurek Becker, from his novel; Harcourt,
       Brace, Jovanovich, 1975, 266p. (LACOPL, NYT, W)

1782. JACOB TWO-TWO MEETS THE HOODED FANG. (Cinema
       Shares International-1978-Theodore J. Flicker-G). Screen-
       play by Theodore J. Flicker, based on the novel by Mordecai
       Richler. (W)

1783. JACQUELINE SUSANN'S ONCE IS NOT ENOUGH. (Paramount-
       1975-Guy Green-R). Screenplay by Julius J. Epstein, based
       on a novel by Jacqueline Susann; Morrow, 1973, 467p.
       (LACOPL, NYT, Q, V, W)

1784. JACQUES BREL IS ALIVE AND WELL AND LIVING IN PARIS.
       (American Film Theatre-1975-Denis Heroux-G). Screenplay
       by Eric Blau; Dutton, 1971, 191p. (LACOPL, NYT, Q, W)

1785. JAGUAR LIVES! (American International-1979-Ernest Pintoff-
       PG). Screenplay by Yabo Yablonsky. (V, W)

1786. JAIL BAIT. (New Yorker-1977-Rainer Werner Fassbinder-
       N/R). Screenplay by Rainer Werner Fassbinder, based on
       the play by Franz Eymesz. (NYT, W)

1787. JANE AUSTEN IN MANHATTAN. (Contemporary Films-1980-
       James Ivory-N/R). Screenplay by Ruth Prawer Jhabvala.
       (V)

1788. JAWS. (Universal-1975-Steven Spielberg-PG). Screenplay
       by Peter Benchley and Carl Gottlieb, based on the novel

by Peter Benchley; Doubleday, 1974, 311p. (HR, LAT, LACOPL, NYT, Q, V, W)

1789.   THE JAWS OF DEATH. (Cannon-1976-William Grefe-PG). Screenplay by Robert Madaris. (W)

1790.   JAWS OF SATAN. (United Artists-1984-Bob Claver-R). Screenplay by Gerry Holland, from a story by James Callaway. (V)

1791.   JAWS 3-D. (Universal-1983-Joe Alves-PG). Screenplay by Richard Matheson and Carl Gottlieb, story by Guerdon Trueblood, suggested by the novel Jaws by Peter Benchley. (BFI, HR, LAT, V, W)

1792.   JAWS 2. (Universal-1978-Jeannot Szwarc-PG). Screenplay by Carl Gottlieb and Howard Sackler, based on characters created by Peter Benchley; novelization by Hank Searles; Bantam Books, 1978. (HR, LACOPL, LAT, NYT, Q, V, W)

1793.   THE JAZZ SINGER. (AFD-1980-Richard Fleischer-PG). Screenplay by Herbert Baker, adaptation by Stephen H. Foreman, based on the play by Samson Raphaelson; novelization by Richard Woodley; Bantam, 192p. (HR, LACOPL, LAT, Q, V, W)

1794.   JEANNE DIELMAN, 23 QUAI DU COMMERCE, 1080 BRUXELLES. (New Yorker-1983-Chantal Akerman-N/R). Screenplay by Chantal Akerman. (W)

1795.   JEKYLL AND HYDE TOGETHER AGAIN. (Paramount-1982-Jerry Belson-R). Screenplay by Monica Johnson, Harvey Miller, Jerry Belson, and Michael Lesson, inspired by the novel of Robert Louis Stevenson; Arco, 1964. (LACOPL, W)

1796.   JENNIFER. (American International-1978-Brice Mack-PG). Screenplay by Kay Cousins Johnson, from a story by Steve Krantz. (NYT, W)

1797.   THE JERK. (Universal-1979-Carl Reiner-R). Steve Martin, Carl Gottlieb, and Michael Elias wrote the screenplay from a story by Steve Martin and Carl Gottlieb. (HR, LAT, Q, V, W)

1798.   JESSIE'S GIRLS. (Manson-1976-Al Adamson-R). Screenplay by Budd Donnelly. (W)

1799.   JESUS. (Warner Bros.-1979-Peter Sykes and John Kirsh-G). Screenplay by Barnet Fishbein, based on the Gospel of Luke. (BFI, Q, V, W)

1800. JETLAG. (Wieland Schulz-Keil/Figaro Films S.A.-1981-
       Gonzalo Herralde and Aldo Vigliarolo-N/R). Screenplay by
       Gonzalo Herralde and Aldo Vigliarolo. (V)

1801. THE JEWISH GAUCHOS. (Julio Tanjeloff-1976-Juan Jose
       Jusid-PG). Screenplay by Juan Jose Jusid, Oscar Viale,
       and Alejandro Saderman, based on Alberto Gerchunoff's
       novel. (W)

       THE JEZEBELLES see SWITCHBLADE SISTERS

1802. THE JIGSAW MAN. (Ben Fisz-1984-Terence Young).
       Screenplay by Joe Eisinger, based on the novel by Dorothea
       Bennet; Coward, McCann, Geoghegan, 1976, 256p. (LACOPL,
       V)

1803. JIM--THE WORLD'S GREATEST. (Universal-1976-Don
       Coscarelli & Craig Mitchell-PG). Screenplay by Don Cos-
       carelli and Craig Mitchell. (W)

1804. JIMMY THE KID. (New World-1982-Gary Nelson-PG).
       Screenplay by Sam Bobrick, based on a novel by Donald E.
       Westlake; Evans, 1974, 191p. (FD, LACOPL, W)

1805. JINXED! (MGM/UA-1982-Don Siegel-R). Screenplay by
       Bert Blessing and David Newman, from a story by Bert
       Blessing. (FD, HR, LAT, V, W)

1806. JIVE TURKEY. (Goldstone-1976-Bill Brame-R). No screen-
       play credits given. (W)

1807. JOANNA FRANCESA. (Joseph Papp-1981-Carlos Diegues-
       N/R). Screenplay by Carlos Diegues. (W)

1808. "JOCK" PETERSEN. (Avco Embassy-1975-Tim Burstall-R).
       Screenplay by David Williamson. (W)

1809. JOE AND MAXI. (Cohen & Gold-1980-Joel Gold & Maxi
       Cohen-N/R). Screenplay credits not given. (W)

1810. JOE PANTHER. (Artist Creation-1976-Paul Krasny-G).
       Screenplay by Dale Eunson, from a novel by Zachary Ball.
       (FD, V, W)

1811. JOE'S BED-STUY BARBERSHOP: WE CUT HEADS. (First
       Run Features-1983-Spike Lee-N/R). Screenplay written by
       Spike Lee. (V, W)

1812. JOHNNY DANGEROUSLY. (20th Century-Fox-1984-Amy
       Heckerling-PG-13). Screenplay by Norman Steinberg,

Bernie Kukoff, Harry Colomby, and Jeff Harris. (HR, LAT, V)

1813. JOHNNY FIRECLOUD. (Entertainment Ventures-1975-William Allen Castleman-R). Screenplay by Wilston Denmark. (W)

1814. JOHN'S WIFE. (French Embassy-1979-Yannick Bellon-N/R). Screenplay by Yannick Bellon. (W)

1815. JOM. (New Yorker-1983-Ababacar Samb-N/R). Screenplay by Ababacar Samb and Babacar Sine. (W)

1816. JONI. (World Wide Pictures-1980-James F. Collier-G). James F. Collier wrote the screenplay, based on the book by Joni Eareckson; Zondervan, 1976, 228p. (FD, LACOPL, V, W)

1817. JOSEPH ANDREWS. (Paramount-1977-Tony Richardson-R). Screenplay by Allan Scott and Chris Bryant, from a screen story by Tony Richardson, based on the novel by Henry Fielding; Oxford University Press, 1973, 379p. (FD, LACOPL, NYT, V)

1818. JOSEPHA. (Triumph-1982-Christopher Frank-R). Screenplay by Christopher Frank, based on his novel. (W)

1819. JOSHUA. (Po-boy Release-1976-Larry Spangler-R). Screenplay written by Fred Williamson. (FD, V, W)

DES JOURNEES ENTIERES DANS LES ARBRES see ENTIRE DAYS IN THE TREES

1820. THE JOURNEY OF O. (Inner Films-1975-X). No screenplay credits available. (W)

1821. JOY. (UGC-1983-Serge Bergon-N/R). Screenplay by Marie-Francoise Hans and Christian Charriere and Serge Bergon, based on the book by Joy Laurey. (V)

1822. THE JOY OF LETTING GO. (Summer Brown-1976-John Gregory-X). Screenplay by Cynthia Holm. (W)

1823. JOY OF SEX. (Paramount-1984-Martha Coolidge-R). Screenplay by Kathleen Rowell and J. J. Salter. (V)

1824. JOYRIDE. (American International-1977-Joseph Ruben-R). Screenplay written by Joseph Ruben and Peter Rainer. (FD, Q, V)

1825. JOYSTICKS. (Jensen Farley-1983-Greydon Clark-R). Screenplay by Al Gomez, Mickey Epps, and Curtis Burch. (FD, V, W)

1826. JUBILEE. (Cinegate-1979-Derek Jarman-N/R). No screenplay credits available. (V, W)

1827. THE JUDGE AND THE ASSASSIN. (Libra-1982-Bertrand
Tavernier-N/R). Screenplay by Bertrand Tavernier and
Jean Aurenche. (FD, W)

1828. JUDGE FAYARD CALLED THE SHERIFF. (CCFC Release-
1977-Yves Boisset-N/R). Screenplay by Yves Boisset and
Claude Veillot. (V)

1829. JUDGEMENT DAY. (Playtime-1976-Jon Cutaia-X). No
screenplay credit available. (W)

LE JUGE FAYARD DIT LE SHERIFF see JUDGE FAYARD
CALLED THE SHERIFF

1830. JULIA. (20th Century-Fox-1977-Fred Zinnemann-PG).
Screenplay by Alvin Sargent, based on the story by Lillian
Hellman in Pentimento; Little, Brown, 1973, 297p. (FD, HR,
LACOPL, LAT, NYT, Q, V, W)

1831. JULIA: INNOCENCE ONCE REMOVED. (Cine-Media-1976-
Sigi Rothemund-R). Screenplay by Wolfgang Bauer. (W)

1832. JULIE DARLING. (TAT and Cinequity-1982-Paul Nicolas-
N/R). Screenplay by Paul Nicolas and Maurice Smith. (FD,
V)

LE JUMEAU see THE TWIN

1833. JUN. (New Yorker-1980-Hiroto Yokoyama-N/R). Screenplay
by Hiroto Yokoyama. (W)

1834. THE JUNKMAN. (H.B. Halicki International-1982-H. B.
Halicki-PG). Screenplay by H. B. Halicki. (FD, V, W)

1835. JURY OF ONE. (Avco Embassy-1975-Andre Cayatte-R).
Screenplay by Andre Cayatte, Henri Coupon, Pierre Dumayet,
and Paul Andreota. (Q, W)

1836. JUST A GIGOLO. (United Artists Classics-1979-David
Hemmings-R). Screenplay by Joshua Sinclair and Ennio de
Concini. (FD, LAT, V, W)

1837. JUST BEFORE DAWN. (Picturemedia Limited-1982-Jeff
Lieberman-R). Screenplay by Mark L. Arywitz and Gregg
Irving, based on a story by Joseph Middleton. (FD, W)

1838. JUST BEFORE NIGHTFALL. (Libra-1975-Claude Chabrol-PG).
Screenplay by Claude Chabrol, based on the novel The Thin
Line by Edouard Atiyah. (FD, Q, W)

1839. JUST LIKE AT HOME. (New Yorker-1978-Marta Meszaros-
       N/R). Screenplay by Ildiko Korody. (V, W)

1840. JUST TELL ME WHAT YOU WANT. (Warner Bros.-1980-
       Sidney Lumet-R). Screenplay by Jay Presson Allen from
       her own novel; Dutton, 1975, 344p. (FD, LACOPL, LAT,
       Q, V, W)

1841. JUST THE TWO OF US. (Boxoffice International-1975-
       Barbara Peeters-R). Screenplay credits not given. (W)

1842. JUST THE WAY YOU ARE. (MGM/UA-1984-Edouard
       Molinaro-PG). Screenplay written by Allan Burns. (V)

1843. JUST YOU AND ME, KID. (Columbia-1979-Leonard Stern-
       PG). Screenplay written by Oliver Hailey and Leonard
       Stern, from a story by Tom Lazarus. (FD, HR, LAT, Q,
       V, W)

1844. JUSTICE OF THE DRAGON. (Almi-1982-R). Production
       credits not given. (W)

1845. KAGEMUSHA, THE SHADOW WARRIOR. (20th Century-Fox-
       1980-Akira Kurosawa-PG). Screenplay by Akira Kurosawa
       and Masato Ide. (LAT, W)

1846. KAHUNA! (Oakwood-1981-Frank Sillman-R). Screenplay
       credit not given, based on a novel by Allan Silliphant. (W)

1847. KAMOURASKA. (New Line Cinema-1975-Claude Jutra-R).
       Screenplay by Claude Jutra and Anne Hebert. (NYT, W)

1848. KANSAS CITY TRUCKING CO. (Joe Gage Films-1976-Joe
       Gage-X). Screenplay by Joe Gage. (V)

1849. THE KARATE KID. (Columbia-1984-John G. Avildsen-PG).
       Screenplay by Robert Mark Kamen, novelization by B. B.
       Hiller; Scholastic, 1984, 144p. (HR, LACOPL, LAT, V)

1850. KARATE WARRIORS. (Silverstein Films-1981-Kazuhiko
       Yamaguchi-R). Screenplay by Tatsuhiko Kamoi. (W)

1851. KASEKI. (New Yorker-1976-Masaki Kobayashi-N/R). Screen-
       play by Shun Inagaki. (W)

1852. KATZELMACHER. (New Yorker-1977-Rainer Werner
       Fassbinder-N/R). Screenplay by Rainer Werner Fassbinder.
       (NYT, W)

1853. THE KEEP. (Paramount-1983-Michael Mann-R). Screenplay
       by Michael Mann, from the novel by Paul Wilson; Morrow,
       1981. (FD, HR, LACOPL, LAT, V, W)

1854. KEEP IT UP, JACK! (Topar-1975-Tom Parker-R). No
screenplay credits available. (W)

1855. KEEP OFF! KEEP OFF! (Gamalex-1975-Shelley Berman-PG).
Screenplay by Austin and Irma Kalish. (W)

1856. KEETJE TIPPEL. (Cinema National-1976-Paul Verhoeven-
N/R). Screenplay by Gerard Goetman. (W)

1857. KENNY & CO. (20th Century-Fox-1976-Don Coscarelli-PG).
Screenplay by Don Coscarelli. (FD, V, W)

1858. THE KENTUCKY FRIED MOVIE. (United Film Distribution-
1977-John Landis-R). Screenplay by David Zucker, Jim
Abrahams, and Jerry Zucker. (FD, NYT, Q, V)

1859. THE KEY THAT SHOULD NOT BE HANDED ON. (Lenfilm-
1976-Diana Assanova-N/R). Screenplay by Georgi Pononski.
(V)

1860. KID VENGEANCE. (Irwin Yablans-1977-Joe Manduke-N/R).
Screenplay by Bud Robbins, Jay Telfer, Ken Globus, from
a story by Ken Globus. (BFI, FD)

1861. KIDCO. (20th Century-Fox-1984-Ronald F. Maxwell-N/R).
Screenplay by Bennett Tramer. (V)

1862. THE KIDNAP OF MARY LOU. (Joseph Brenner-1975-
Umberto Lenzi-R). Screenplay credits not available. (W)

1863. KIDNAPPED CO-ED. (Boxoffice International-1978-Frederick
R. Friedel-R). Screenplay by Frederick R. Friedel. (W)

1864. THE KIDNAPPING OF THE PRESIDENT. (Crown International-
1980-George Mendeluk-R). Screenplay by Richard Murphy,
from the novel by Charles Templeton; Simon & Schuster,
1974, 284p. (FD, LACOPL, V, W)

1865. KILL AND GO HIDE. (New American Films-1983-Robert
Voskanian-R). Screenplay by Ralph Lucas. (V, W)

1866. KILL AND KILL AGAIN. (Film Ventures International-1981-
Ivan Hall-PG). Screenplay by John Crowther. (LAT, V, W)

1867. KILL OR BE KILLED. (Film Ventures International-1980-
Ivan Hall-PG). Screenplay by C. F. Beyers-Boshoff. (V,
W)

1868. KILL SQUAD. (Summa Vista-1982-Patrick G. Donahue-R).
Screenplay by Patrick G. Donahue. (LAT, V, W)

1869. KILL THE GOLDEN GOOSE. (Lone Star-1979-Elliot Hong-R). Screenplay credits not available. (W)

1870. THE KILLER ELITE. (United Artists-1975-Sam Peckinpah-PG). Screenplay by Stirling Silliphant, based on a novel by Robert Rostand. (LACOPL, NYT, Q, W)

1871. KILLER FISH. (Associated Film Distribution-1979-Anthony M. Dawson-PG). Screenplay by Michael Rogers. (V, W)

1872. KILLER FORCE. (American International-1975-Val Guest-R). Screenplay by Michael Winder. (NYT, W)

1873. THE KILLER INSIDE ME. (Warner Bros.-1976-Burt Kennedy-R). Screenplay by Edward Mann and Robert Chamblee, from the novel by Jim Thompson. (FD, V, W)

1874. KILLER OF SHEEP. (1977-Charles Burnett-N/R). Screenplay by Charles Burnett. (BFI, NYT)

1875. KILLER SNAKES. (Howard Mahler-1975-R). Screenplay credits not available. (W)

1876. KILLER'S DELIGHT. (Intercontinental-1978-Jeremy Hoenack-R). Screenplay by Maralyn Thoma. (W)

1877. THE KILLING FIELDS. (Warner Bros.-1984-Roland Joffe-R). Screenplay by Bruce Robinson, based on the article "The Death and Life of Dith Pran" by Sydney Schanberg; novelization by Christopher Hudson; Dell, 1984. (BFI, FD, HR, LACOPL, LAT, NYT, V)

1878. THE KILLING MACHINE. (Cinema Shares International-1976-Noribumi Suzuki-R). Screenplay by Isao Matsumoto. (W)

1879. THE KILLING OF A CHINESE BOOKIE. (Faces-1976-John Cassavetes-R). Screenplay by John Cassavetes. (FD, NYT, W)

1880. THE KILLING OF ANGEL STREET. (Satori-1983-Donald Crombie-PG). Screenplay by Evan Jones, Michael Craig, and Cecil Holmes, from an original story by Michael Craig. (FD, W)

1881. KILLPOINT. (Crown International-1984-Frank Harris-R). Screenplay by Frank Harris. (V)

1882. THE KING AND THE MOCKINGBIRD. (Gaumont-1980-Paul Grimault-N/R). Screenplay by Paul Grimault and Jacques Prevert. (V)

1883. KING BLANK. (King Blank-1980-Michael Oblowitz-N/R).
       Screenplay by Michael Oblowitz and Rosemary Hochschild,
       with additional dialogue by Barbara Kruger. (BFI)

       KING COBRA see JAWS OF SATAN

1884. KING FRAT. (Mad Makers-1979-Ken Wiederhorn-R).
       Screenplay credits not given. (FD, W)

1885. KING KONG. (Paramount-1976-John Guillermin-PG).
       Screenplay by Lorenzo Semple Jr., based on a script by
       James Creelman and Ruth Rose, from a concept of Merian C.
       Cooper and Edgar Wallace. (FD, HR, LAT, NYT, Q, V, W)

1886. KING LEAR. (Artkino-1975-Grigory Kozintsev-N/R).
       Screenplay by Grigory Kozintsev, based on the play by
       William Shakespeare. (NYT, W)

1887. THE KING OF COMEDY. (20th Century-Fox-1983-Martin
       Scorsese-PG). Screenplay by Paul D. Zimmerman. (FD,
       HR, LAT, V)

1888. KING OF KUNG FU. (Cinematic-1980-Joseph Velasco-R).
       No screenplay credits available. (W)

1889. KING OF THE GYPSIES. (Paramount-1978-Frank Pierson-R).
       Screenplay by Frank Pierson, suggested by King of the
       Gypsies by Peter Maas; Viking Press, 1975, 171p. (FD, HR,
       LACOPL, LAT, NYT, Q, V, W)

1890. KING OF THE HILL. (Lone Star-1978-PG). No production
       credits available. (W)

1891. KING OF THE JOROPO. (Balumba Films C. A.-1980-Carlos
       Rebolledo and Thaelman Urguelles-N/R). Screenplay by
       Carlos Rebolledo and Thaelman Urguelles, based upon the
       book Los Cuentos de Alfredo Alvarado, "El Rey del Joropo"
       by Edmundo Aray. (V)

1892. KING OF THE MOUNTAIN. (Universal-1981-Noel Nosseck-
       PG). Screenplay by H. R. Christian, inspired by an article
       by David Barry; novelization by David Barry. (FD, LACOPL,
       LAT, Q, V, W)

1893. THE KINGFISH CAPER. (Cinema Shares International-1976-
       Dirk DeVilliers-PG). Screenplay adapted by Roy Boulting,
       based on the novel by Wilbur Smith. (W)

1894. THE KINKY COACHES AND THE POM-POM PUSSYCATS.
       (Summa Vista-1981-Mark Warren-R). Screenplay by Doughlas
       Ditonto, Richard Sauer, and Bruce Calman. (FD, LAT, V)

1895.   KIPPERBANG. (United Artists Classics-1984-Michael Apted-
        PG). Screenplay by Jack Rosenthal. (V)

1896.   THE KIRLIAN WITNESS. (Sarno-1981-Jonathan Sarno-PG).
        Screenplay by Jonathan Sarno, Lamar Sanders, from a story
        by Jonathan Sarno. (W)

1897.   KISS ME GOODBYE. (20th Century-Fox-1982-Robert
        Mulligan-PG). Screenplay by Charlie Peters. (FD, HR,
        LAT, W)

1898.   KISS ME MONSTER. (Joseph Green-1975-Jesus Franco-R).
        Screenplay by Luis Revenga and Jesus Franco. (W)

1899.   KISS OF THE TARANTULA. (Omni-1976-Chris Munger-PG).
        Screenplay by Warren Hamilton Jr., from a story by Daniel
        B. Cady. (W)

1900.   KITTY AND THE BAGMAN. (Quartet-1983-Donald Crombie-
        R). Screenplay by John Burney and Phillip Cornford. (FD,
        W)

1901.   KITTY CAN'T HELP IT. (Mammoth-1975-Peter Locke-R).
        Screenplay credits not available. (W)

        KLUJCH BEZ PRAVA PEREDACHI see THE KEY THAT
        SHOULD NOT BE HANDED ON

1902.   KNIFE IN THE HEAD. (New Yorker-1980-Reinhard Hauff-
        N/R). Screenplay by Peter Schneider. (W)

1903.   THE KNIGHT. (Zespoly Filmowe-1983-Lech Majewski-N/R).
        Screenplay by Lech Majewski. (FD, W)

1904.   KNIGHTRIDERS. (United Film Distribution-1981-George A.
        Romero-R). Screenplay by George A. Romero. (FD, LAT,
        Q, V, W)

1905.   THE KOWLOON CONNECTION. (1975-X). No production
        credits available. (W)

1906.   KRAMER VS. KRAMER. (Columbia-1979-Robert Benton-PG).
        Screenplay by Robert Benton, from the novel by Avery
        Corman; Random House, 1977. (FD, HR, LACOPL, LAT,
        NYT, Q, V, W)

1907.   KRULL. (Columbia-1983-Peter Yates-PG). Screenplay by
        Stanford Sherman; novelization by Alan Dean Foster; Warner,
        1983, 237p. (BFI, FD, HR, LACOPL, LAT, NYT, V)

1908.   KUNG FU GOLD. (Cinema Shares International-1975-R).
        Production credits not available. (W)

1909. KUNG FU-RY. (Joseph Green-1975-Shaw Fung James-R).
Screenplay credits not given. (W)

1910. KUNG FU WARLORDS. (World Northal-1983-R). No production credits available. (W)

1911. KUNG-FU WARLORDS PART II. (World Northal-1983-Chang
Chen-R). No screenplay credits available. (W)

1912. THE LACEMAKER. (New Yorker-1977-Claude Goretta & Pas-
cal Laine-N/R). Screenplay by Claude Goretta and Pascal
Laine, from the novel by Pascal Laine; Gallimard, 1974, 176p.
(FD, LACOPL, NYT, W)

1913. LACEY BODINE. (De Neuve Sisters-1976-X). No production
credits available. (W)

1914. LADIES AND GENTLEMEN THE FABULOUS STAINS. (Para-
mount-1982-Lou Adler-R). Screenplay by Rob Morton. (V,
W)

1915. IL LADRONE. (1981-Pasquale Festa Campanile-N/R). Screenplay by Ottavio Jemma, Stefano Ubezio, and Santino Sparta.
(W)

1916. LADY CHATTERLEY'S LOVER. (Prodis-1981-Just Jaeckin-
N/R). Screenplay by Christopher Wicking and Just Jaeckin,
adaptation by Marc Behm, based on the novel by D. H.
Lawrence; Knopf, 1932, 327p. (FD, LACOPL, V, W)

1917. LADY COCOA. (Dimension-1975-Matt Cimber-R). Screenplay by George Theakos. (FD, W)

1918. LADY GREY. (Maverick Pictures International-1980-Worth
Keeter-N/R). Screenplay by Tom McIntyre. (V)

1919. THE LADY IN RED. (New World Pictures-1979-Lewis Teague-
R). Screenplay by John Sayles. (FD, V, W)

1920. THE LADY ON THE BUS. (Atlantic-1982-Neville d'Almeida-
R). Screenplay by Nelson Rodriguez. (W)

1921. LADY ON THE COUCH. (Beattie-1975-X). No production
credits available. (W)

1922. THE LADY VANISHES. (Rank Organization-1979-Anthony
Page). Screenplay by George Axelrod, based on novel by
Ethel Lina White; Collins, 1940, 286p. (FD, LACOPL, V,
W)

1923. THE LADY WITHOUT CAMELIAS. (Italtoons-1981-Michelangelo

Antonioni-N/R). Screenplay by Suso Cecchi d'Amico, Francesco Maselli, P. M. Pasinetti, and Michelangelo Antonioni. (W)

1924. LANCELOT OF THE LAKE. (New Yorker-1975-Robert Bresson-N/R). Screenplay written by Robert Bresson. (FD, NYT, W)

1925. THE LAND OF NO RETURN. (International Picture Show-1978-Kent Bateman-PG). Screenplay by Kent Bateman and Frank Ray Perilli. (V, W)

1926. THE LAND THAT TIME FORGOT. (American International-1975-Kevin Connor-PG). Screenplay by James Cawthorn and Michael Moorcock, based on a book by Edgar Rice Burroughs; Funk, 1937, 274p. (FD, LACOPL, NYT, Q, W)

1927. LANDSCAPE AFTER BATTLE. (New Yorker-1978-Andrzej Wajda-N/R). Screenplay by Andrzej Wajda and Andrzej Brzozowski, based on stories by Tadeusz Borowski. (FD, NYT, W)

DER LANDVOGT VON GRIEFENSEE see THE BAILIFF OF GRIEFENSEE

LANGT BORTA OCH NAERA see FAR AWAY AND CLOSE

1928. LAS VEGAS LADY. (Crown International-1976-Noel Nosseck-PG). Screenplay by Walter Dallenbach. (FD, W)

1929. LASERBLAST. (Irwin Yablans-1978-Michael Rae-PG). Screenplay by Franne Schacht and Frank Ray Perilli. (BFI, FD, NYT, V, W)

1930. LASSITER. (Warner Bros.-1983-Roger Young-R). Screenplay by David Taylor. (FD, V)

1931. THE LAST AFFAIR. (Chelex-1976-Henri Charbakshi-R). Screenplay by Henri Charbakshi. (W)

1932. LAST AMERICAN VIRGIN. (Cannon-1982-Boaz Davidson-R). Screenplay by Boaz Davidson. (V, W)

THE LAST CASTLE see ECHOES OF A SUMMER

1933. THE LAST CHALLENGE OF THE DRAGON. (Cine World-1978-Steve Chan-R). Screenplay written by Steve Chan and Kung Ming. (W)

1934. THE LAST CHASE. (Crown International-1981-Martyn Burke-PG). Screenplay by C. R. O'Christopher, Taylor Sutherland, and Martyn Burke. (FD, LAT, V, W)

1935. LAST EMBRACE. (United Artists-1979-Jonathan Demme-R). Screenplay by David Shaber, based on the novel The Thirteenth Man by Murray Teigh Bloom; Macmillan, 1977, 232p. (FD, LACOPL, Q, V, W)

1936. THE LAST FIGHT. (Best Film & Video-1983-Fred Williamson-R). Screenplay by Fred Williamson, from a story by Jerry Masucci. (FD, LAT, V, W)

1937. THE LAST FLIGHT OF NOAH'S ARK. (Buena Vista-1980-Charles Jarrot-G). Screenplay by Steven W. Carabatsos, Sandy Glass, George Arthur Bloom, based on a story by Ernest K. Gann. (FD, Q, V, W)

1938. THE LAST HARD MEN. (20th Century-Fox-1976-Andrew V. McLaglen-R). Screenplay by Guerdon Trueblood, from a novel Gun Down by Brian Garfield. (FD, LACOPL, NYT, Q, W)

1939. THE LAST HOLE. (Herbert Achternbusch-1982-Herbert Achternbusch-N/R). No screenplay credits available. (V)

1940. THE LAST HORROR FILM. (Twin Continental Films-1984-David Winters-R). Screenplay by Judd Hamilton, Tom Classen, and David Winters. (V)

1941. THE LAST HUNTER. (World Northal-1984-Anthony M. Dawson aka Antonio Margheriti-N/R). Screenplay by Dardano Sacchetti, from a story by Gianfranco Couyoumdjian. (V)

1942. THE LAST MARRIED COUPLE IN AMERICA. (Universal-1980-Gilbert Cates-R). Screenplay by John Herman Shaner. (FD, Q, V, W)

1943. THE LAST METRO. (United Artists-1981-Francois Truffaut-R). Screenplay by Francois Truffaut, Suzanne Schiffman, and Jean-Claude Grumberg. (FD, LAT, V, W)

1944. LAST NIGHT AT THE ALAMO. (Alamo Films-1983-Eagle Pennell-N/R). Screenplay by Kim Henkel. (V)

1945. THE LAST OF THE COWBOYS. (Mar Vista-1977-John Leone-N/R). Screenplay by John Leone. (FD, V)

1946. THE LAST OF THE KNUCKLEMEN. (Hexagon-1981-Tim Burstall-N/R). Screenplay by Tim Burstall, based on the play by John Powers. (LAT, V)

1947. LAST PLANE OUT. (Jack Cox-1983-David Nelson-N/R). Screenplay written by Ernest Tidyman. (FD, V, W)

1948. THE LAST REMAKE OF BEAU GESTE. (Universal-1977-

Marty Feldman-PG). Screenplay by Marty Feldman and Chris
Allen, from a story by Marty Feldman and Sam Bobrick.
(NYT, Q, V)

1949. LAST RITES. (Cannon-1980-Domonic Paris-R). Screenplay
by Ben Donnelly and Domonic Paris. (V)

1950. THE LAST ROMANTIC LOVER. (New Line Cinema-1979-Just
Jaeckin-R). Screenplay by Just Jaeckin and Ennio De Concini. (FD, HR, LAT, W)

1951. THE LAST STARFIGHTER. (Universal-1984-Nick Castle-PG).
Screenplay by Jonathan Betuel; novelization by Alan Dean
Foster; Berkley Books, 1984, 218p. (FD, HR, LACOPL,
LAT, NYT, V)

1952. LAST STOP ON THE NIGHT TRAIN. (Bryanston-1976-Evans
Isle-R). Screenplay credits not available. (W)

1953. THE LAST SUPPER. (Tricontinental-1978-Tomas Gutierrez
Alea-N/R). Screenplay by Tomas Gonzalez, Maria Eugenia
Haya, and Tomas Gutierrez Alea. (NYT, W)

1954. THE LAST SURVIVOR. (American International-1978-Ruggero
Deodato-R). Screenplay by Tito Cardi, Gianfranco Clerici,
and Renzo Genta. (FD, NYT, V, W)

1955. THE LAST TANGO IN ACAPULCO. (Hollywood International-
1975-Carlos Tobalina-X). Screenplay by Carlos Tobalina.
(W)

1956. THE LAST TYCOON. (Paramount-1976-Elia Kazan-PG).
Screenplay by Harold Pinter, based on the unfinished novel
by F. Scott Fitzgerald; Scribner's, 1941. (FD, LACOPL,
NYT, Q, V)

1957. THE LAST UNICORN. (Jensen Farley-1982-Arthur Rankin
Jr. & Jules Bass-G). Screenplay by Peter S. Beagle, based
on his novel; Ballantine, 1968, 248p. (FD, LACOPL, V, W)

1958. THE LAST WAVE. (World Northal-1978-Peter Weir-PG).
Screenplay by Peter Weir, Tony Morphett, and Peter Popescu,
from an original idea by Peter Weir. (FD, W)

1959. THE LAST WOMAN. (Columbia-1976-Marco Ferreri-X).
Screenplay by Rafael Azcona, Dante Matelli, and Marco
Ferreri. (FD, NYT, W)

1960. THE LAST WORD. (Variety International-1979-Roy Boulting-
N/R). Screenplay by Michael Varhol, Greg Smith, L. M. Kit
Carson, based on a story by Horatius Haeberle. (FD, NYT,
V, W)

1961. THE LATE GREAT PLANET EARTH. (Pacific International-
       1979-Robert Amram-PG). Screenplay by Robert Amram,
       based on the book by Hal Lindsey with C. C. Carlson;
       biblical sequences written and directed by Rolf Forsberg;
       Zondervan, 1970, 192p. (LACOPL, V)

1962. THE LATE SHOW. (Warner Bros.-1977-Robert Benton-PG).
       Screenplay written by Robert Benton. (BFI, FD, HR, LAT,
       NYT, Q, V, W)

1963. LAUGHTER HOUSE. (Film Four International-1984-Richard
       Eyre-N/R). Screenplay by Brian Glover. (V)

1964. LEADBELLY. (Paramount-1976-Gordon Parks-PG). Screen-
       play by Ernest Kinoy. (FD, NYT, Q, W)

1965. LEAP INTO THE VOID. (Summit-1982-Marco Bellocchio-
       N/R). Screenplay by Marco Bellocchio, Piero Natoli, and
       Vincenzo Cerami, from a story by Marco Bellocchio. (FD, W)

1966. LED BY THE NOSE. (Parafrance-1984-Gerard Lauzier-N/R).
       Screenplay written by Gerard Lauzier and Edouard Molinaro.
       (V)

1967. THE LEFT-HANDED WOMAN. (New Yorker-1978-Peter Handke-
       N/R). Screenplay by Peter Handke. (HR, LAT, W)

1968. LEGACY. (Kino International-1976-Karen Arthur-R). Screen-
       play by Joan Hotchkis. (W)

1969. THE LEGACY. (Universal-1979-Richard Marquand-R). Jimmy
       Sangster, Patrick Tilley, and Paul Wheeler wrote the screen-
       play from a story by Jimmy Sangster. (FD, LAT, NYT, Q,
       V, W)

1970. THE LEGEND OF BIGFOOT. (Palladium Pictures-1976-Harry
       S. Winer-G). Screenplay by Harry S. Winer and Paula
       Labrot. (W)

1971. THE LEGEND OF BLOOD CASTLE. (Film Ventures Interna-
       tional-1975-Jorge Grau-R). Screenplay credits not available.
       (W)

1972. THE LEGEND OF COUGAR CANYON. (First American Films-
       1980-James T. Flicker-G). Screenplay credits not available.
       (W)

1973. THE LEGEND OF EARL DURAND. (Howco International-
       1975-John D. Patterson-PG). Screenplay written by J.
       Frank James. (W)

1974. THE LEGEND OF SEA WOLF. (Cougar-1978-Joseph Green-

PG). Screenplay credits not available; based on the novel by Jack London; Macmillan, 1975, 366p. (LACOPL, W)

1975. LEGEND OF SLEEPY HOLLOW. (Sunn Classics-1979-Henning Schellerup-PG). Screenplay by Marvin Wald, Jack Jacobs, Tom Chapman, based on a story by Washington Irving; Watts, 1966. (FD, LACOPL, W)

1976. THE LEGEND OF SPIDER FOREST. (New Line-1975-Peter Sykes-PG). Screenplay credits not available. (FD, W)

1977. THE LEGEND OF THE LONE RANGER. (Universal/Associated Film Distribution-1981-William A. Fraker-PG). Screenplay by Ivan Goff, Ben Roberts, Michael Kane, and William Roberts, adapted by Jerry Derloshon. (FD, LAT, Q, V, W)

1978. LEGEND OF THE WILD. (Jensen Farley-1981-G). Screenplay written by Charles E. Sellier Jr. and Brian Russell. (W)

1979. THE LEGENDARY CURSE OF LEMORA. (Media Cinema-1975-Richard Blackburn-PG). Screenplay credits not available. (W)

1980. LEO AND LOREE. (United Artists-1980-Jerry Paris-PG). Screenplay by James Ritz. (FD, V)

1981. LEOPARD IN THE SNOW. (New World-1979-Gerry O'Hara-PG). Screenplay by Ann Mather and Jill Hyem. (FD, W)

1982. LEPKE. (Warner Bros.-1975-Menahem Golan-R). Screenplay by Wesley Lau and Tamar Hoffs. (FD, W)

1983. LET IT BE SUNDAY. (Roissy Films-1983-Francois Truffaut-N/R). Screenplay by Francois Truffaut and Suzanne Schiffman and Jean Aurel, based on The Long Saturday Night by Charles Williams; Penguin, 1983. (LACOPL, V)

1984. LET'S DO IT AGAIN. (Warner Bros.-1975-Sidney Poitier-PG). Screenplay by Richard Wesley from a story by Timothy March. (FD, NYT, Q, W)

1985. LET'S FACE IT, C'EST LA VIE. (KSP Entertainment-1978-Samy Paval-N/R). Screenplay written by Samy Paval. (NYT, W)

1986. LET'S TALK ABOUT MEN. (Allied Artists-1976-Lina Wertmuller-PG). Screenplay by Lina Wertmuller. (FD, NYT, W)

DAS LETZTE LOCH see THE LAST HOLE

1987. LIANNA. (United Artists Classics-1983-John Sayles-R).
       Screenplay written by John Sayles. (FD, V)

1988. LIAR'S DICE. (Butros Makdissy and Ed Eubanks-1980-
       Issam B. Makdissy-N/R). Screenplay written by Terry
       Eubanks Makdissy. (W)

1989. LIAR'S MOON. (Crown International-1982-David Fisher-PG).
       Screenplay by David Fisher, based on a story by Janice
       Thompson and Billy Hanna. (FD, V, W)

1990. LIBERTY. (Thomas Lynch Jr.-1976-James Wilson-X).
       Screenplay written by Jacob Hart. (W)

       LIEBE DAS LEBEN-LEBE DAS LIEBEN see LOVE LIVING,
       LIVE LOVING

       EINE LIEBE IN DEUTSCHLAND see A LOVE IN GERMANY

1991. LIEBELEI. (Elite Tonfilm-1983-Max Ophuls-N/R). Screen-
       play by Hans Wilhelm and Curt Alexander, from the play by
       Arthur Schnitzler. (W)

1992. LIES MY FATHER TOLD ME. (Columbia-1975-Jan Kadar-PG).
       Screenplay by Ted Allan, from an original screen story by
       Ted Allan. (FD, NYT, Q, W)

1993. LIFE AND TIMES OF GRIZZLY ADAMS. (1976-Richard
       Friedenberg-G). No screenplay credits available. (FD)

1994. LIFE SIZE. (Dimension-1976-Luis Berlanga-X). Screenplay
       by Rafael Azcona and Luis Berlanga. (W)

1995. LIFE TRIUMPHS. (International Film Exchange/Satra Film
       Corp./Sovexportfilm-1979-Genrikh Malyan-N/R). No screen-
       play credits available. (W)

1996. LIFEGUARD. (Paramount-1976-Daniel Petrie-PG). Screen-
       play by Ron Koslow, novelization by Thom Racima; Warner
       Books, 1976, 157p. (FD, LACOPL, LAT, NYT, Q, W)

1997. THE LIGHT AHEAD. (Carmel-1982-Edgar G. Ulmer-N/R).
       Screenplay by Chaver Pahver, based on a story by Mendele
       Mocher S'forim. (W)

1998. LIGHT YEARS AWAY. (New Yorker-1983-Alain Tanner-N/R).
       Screenplay by Alain Tanner, based on the novel La Voie
       Sauvage by Daniel Odier. (FD, W)

1999. LIGHTNING KUNG FU. (East-West-1982-R). No production
       credits available.

2000. LIKE A TURTLE ON ITS BACK. (New Line Cinema-1981-
Luc Beraud-N/R). Screenplay by Luc Beraud and Claude
Miller. (W)

2001. LILI MARLEEN. (United Artists Classics-1981-Rainer Werner
Fassbinder-N/R). Screenplay by Manfred Purzer and Joshua
Sinclair, based on the novel by Lale Andersen. (LAT, V,
W)

2002. LIN TSE-HSU: THE OPIUM WAR. (Sino-American-1978-Chen
Chun-li-N/R). Screenplay credits not available. (W)

2003. LINDA. (Lanir-1976-Rick Deconinck-X). No screenplay
credits available. (W)

2004. LINDA LOVELACE FOR PRESIDENT. (General Film-1975-
Claudio Guzman-R). No screenplay credits available.
(W)

2005. LINDA LOVELACE MEETS MISS JONES. (LMMJ-1975-Angelo
Spaveni-X). No screenplay credits available. (W)

2006. L'INGORGO. (Silvio Clementilli-1981-Luigi Comencini-N/R).
Screenplay by Luigi Comencini, Ruggero Maccari, Bernardino
Zapponi, from a story by Luigi Comencini. (W)

2007. LINUS AND THE MYSTERIOUS RED BRICK HOUSE. (Svenska
Filminstutet-1979-Vilgot Sjoman-N/R). Screenplay by Vilgot
Sjoman, from his own book. (FD, V)

2008. LION OF THE DESERT. (United Film Distribution-1981-
Moustapha Akkad-PG). Screenplay by H. A. L. Craig.
(FD, LAT, Q, V, W)

2009. LIPSTICK. (Paramount-1976-Lamont Johnson-R). Screen-
play by David Rayfiel; novelization by Leonore Fleischer;
Pocket Books, 1976, 159p. (FD, LACOPL, LAT, NYT, Q,
V, W)

2010. LIQUID LIPS. (Freeway-1976-Bob Chinn-X). Screenplay by
Robert Mathews. (W)

2011. LIQUID SKY. (Cinevista-1983-Slava Tsukerman-R). Screenplay by Slava Tsukerman, Anne Carlisle, and Nina V.
Kerova. (BFI, FD, LAT, V, W)

2012. LISTEN TO THE CITY. (International Spectrafilm-1984-Ron
Mann-N/R). Screenplay by Ron Mann and Bill Schroeder,
from an original story by Bill Schroeder. (V)

2013. LISZTOMANIA. (Warner Bros.-1975-Ken Russell-R). Screenplay by Ken Russell. (FD, LAT, NYT, V, W)

2014. LE LIT ... ZE BAWDY BED. (Joseph Green-1975-Jacques
      Lem-N/R). Screenplay by Jacques Lem, adaptation and dia-
      logue by Jacques Lem, Rita Krauss, and Robert Thomas.
      (W)

2015. A LITTLE AFFAIR. (B. R. Films-1977-Basu Chatterji-N/R).
      Screenplay written by Basu Chatterji. (V)

2016. LITTLE ANGEL PUSS. (DeNeuve Sisters-1976-Danielle De
      Neuve-X). Screenplay credits not available. (W)

2017. LITTLE DARLINGS. (Paramount-1980-Ronald F. Maxwell-R).
      Screenplay by Kimi Peck and Dalene Young; novelization by
      Sonia Pilcer; Ballantine Books, 1980. (FD, HR, LACOPL,
      LAT, Q, V, W)

2018. THE LITTLE DRAGONS. (Aurora Film Corp.-1980-Curtis
      Hanson-PG). Screenplay by Harvey Applebaum, Louis G.
      Atlee,Rudolph Borchert, and Alan Ormsby. (FD, V, W)

2019. THE LITTLE DRUMMER GIRL. (Warner Bros.-1984-George
      Roy Hill-R). Screenplay by Loring Mandel, based on the
      novel by John le Carre; Knopf, 1983, 430p. (FD, LACOPL,
      LAT, V)

2020. LITTLE ESCAPES. (New Yorker-1980-Yves Yersin-N/R).
      Screenplay written by Yves Yersin and Claude Muret.
      (LAT, W)

2021. THE LITTLE GIRL WHO LIVES DOWN THE LANE. (American
      International Pictures-1977-Nicolas Gessner-R). Screenplay
      written by Laird Koenig, based on his novel; Coward, 1974,
      254p. (FD, LACOPL, NYT, Q, V)

2022. LITTLE GIRLS BLUE. (New Day-1978-Joanna Williams-X).
      Screenplay by William Dancer and Joanna Williams. (W)

2023. LITTLE JERK. (Gaumont-1984-Gerard Lauzier-N/R). Screen-
      play by Gerard Lauzier. (V)

2024. LITTLE JOSEPH. (Gaumont-1982-Jean-Michel Barjol-N/R).
      Screenplay by Jean-Michel Barjol and Chris Donner, from
      the novel by Chris Donner. (V)

2025. LITTLE MISS MARKER. (Universal-1980-Walter Bernstein-
      PG). Screenplay by Walter Bernstein, based on a story by
      Damon Runyon. (FD, LAT, Q, V, W)

2026. A LITTLE NIGHT MUSIC. (Sashca Wien/Elliott Kastner-1977-
      Herold Prince). Screenplay by Hugh Wheeler, based on the
      film Smiles of a Summer Night by Ingmar Bergman, and the
      musical by Stephen Sondheim. (FD, LAT, NYT, V, W)

2027. A LITTLE ROMANCE. (Orion-1979-George Roy Hill-PG). Screenplay by Allan Burns; novelization by Patrick Cauvin; Dell, 1979. (FD, LACOPL, Q, V, W)

2028. A LITTLE SEX. (Universal-1982-Bruce Paltrow-R). Screenplay written by Robert DeLaurentis. (FD, Q, V)

2029. THE LITTLEST HORSE THIEVES. (Buena Vista-1977-Charles Jarrott-G). Screenplay by Rosemary Anne Sisson, from a story by Rosemary Anne Sisson and Burt Kennedy. (FD, NYT, Q, W)

2030. LIVES. (Animatografo-Producao de Filmes Lda.-1984-Antonio da Cunha Telles-N/R). Screenplay by Antonio da Cunha Telles and Jose Sebag. (V)

2031. LIVING LEGEND. (Maverick-1980-Worth Keeter-PG). Screenplay by Tom McIntyre. (V, W)

2032. LIZ. (Group I-1979-Paul Gerber-N/R). Screenplay by Arthur Dent. (V)

2033. LIZA. (Horizon-1976-Marco Ferreri-N/R). Screenplay by Marco Ferreri and Jean-Claude Carriere, from the book by Ennio Flaiano. (FD, W)

2034. LOBSTER FOR BREAKFAST. (Quartet-1983-Giorgio Capitani-R). Screenplay credits not available. (W)

2035. LOCAL HERO. (Warner Bros.-1983-Bill Forsyth-PG). Screenplay by Bill Forsyth; novel by David Benedictus; Penguin, 1983, 144p. (LACOPL, LAT, V)

2036. LOGAN'S RUN. (United Artists-1976-Michael Anderson-PG). Screenplay by David Zelag Goodman, based on a novel by William F. Nolan and George Clayton Johnson; Dial Press, 1967. (FD, HR, LACOPL, NYT, Q, W)

2037. LOLA. (Rialto Film/Trio Film-1981-Rainer Werner Fassbinder-N/R). Screenplay by Peter Marthesheimer, Pia Frohlich, and Rainer Werner Fassbinder. (BFI, V)

2038. THE LOLLIPOP GIRLS IN HARD CANDY. (Debonair Films-1976-Norm De Plume-X). Screenplay written by Mark Thunderbuns and Ann Onymous. (V)

2039. LOLLIPOP PALACE. (Lollipix-1976-Kirdy Stevens-X). Screenplay credits not available. (W)

2040. LONE WOLF MCQUADE. (Orion-1983-Steve Carver-PG). Screenplay by B. J. Nelson, story by H. Kaye Dyal and B. J. Nelson. (BFI, LAT, V, W)

2041. THE LONELY GUY. (Universal-1984-Arthur Hiller-R).
       Screenplay by Ed Weinberger and Stan Daniels, adaptation
       by Neil Simon, based on the book The Lonely Guy's Book of
       Life by Bruce Jay Friedman. (FD, V)

2042. LONELY HEART. (Toho-1982-Kon Ichikawa-N/R). Screen-
       play by Masaya Hidaka, Ikuko Oya and Kon Ichikawa, based
       on Ed McBain's Lady, Lady, I Did It! (W)

2043. THE LONELY LADY. (Universal-1983-Peter Sasdy-R).
       Screenplay by John Kershaw and Shawn Randall, based on
       the novel by Harold Robbins. (BFI, FD, HR, LAT, V, W)

       THE LONER see RUCKUS

2044. THE LONG GOOD FRIDAY. (Embassy-1982-John Mackenzie-
       R). Screenplay by Barrie Keeffe. (FD, Q, V, W)

2045. THE LONG NIGHT. (Howard Mahler-1976-Woodie King-PG).
       Screenplay by Julian Mayfield and Woodie King, based on a
       novel by Julian Mayfield. (NYT, W)

2046. THE LONG RIDERS. (United Artists-1980-Walter Hill-R).
       Screenplay by Bill Bryden, Steven Phillip Smith, Stacy
       Keach, and James Keach; novelization by Steven Smith;
       Avon, 1980. (FD, LACOPL, Q, V, W)

2047. LONG SHOT. (Mithras-1981-Maurice Hatton-PG). Screen-
       play by Eoin McCann and The Players from a yarn spun by
       Maurice Hatton. (V, W)

2048. LOOKER. (Ladd Co./Warner Bros.-1981-Michael Crichton-
       PG). Screenplay by Michael Crichton. (FD, LAT, Q, V, W)

2049. LOOKING FOR MR. GOODBAR. (Paramount-1977-Richard
       Brooks-R). Screenplay by Richard Brooks, based on a
       novel by Judith Rossner; Simon & Schuster, 1975, 249p.
       (LACOPL, NYT, Q, W)

2050. LOOKING UP. (Levitt-Pickman-1977-Linda Yellen-PG).
       Screenplay written by Jonathan Platnick. (FD, NYT, Q, V)

2051. LOONEY LOONEY LOONEY BUGS BUNNY MOVIE. (Warner
       Bros.-1981-Friz Freleng-G). Screenplay by David Dunn,
       David Detiege, Friz Freleng. (HR, LAT, V)

2052. LOOPHOLE. (Brent Walker-1981-John Quested-N/R).
       Screenplay by Jonathan Hales, based on a novel by Robert
       Pollock. (FD, V)

2053. LOOSE ENDS. (American Eagel/Fat Chance-1975-David

Burton Morris-N/R). Screenplay by Victoria Vozniak and
David Burton Morris. (NYT, W)

2054. LOOSE SHOES. (Atlantic Films-1980-Ira Miller-N/R).
Screenplay by Ira Miller, Varley Smith, Ian Paiser, and
Royce Applegate. (V, W)

2055. LORD OF THE RINGS. (United Artists-1978-Ralph Bakshi-
PG). Screenplay by Chris Conkling, Peter S. Beagle, based
on the novels of J. R. R. Tolkien. (FD, NYT, Q, V, W)

2056. LORD SHANGO. (Bryanston-1975-Raymond Marsh-R).
Screenplay by Paul Carter Harrison. (W)

2057. THE LORDS OF DISCIPLINE. (Paramount-1983-Franc Roddam-
R). Screenplay by Thomas Pope and Lloyd Fonvielle, based
on the novel by Pat Conroy; Houghton Mifflin, 1980, 499p.
(BFI, FD, HR, LACOPL, LAT, NYT, V)

2058. LOSIN' IT. (Embassy-1983-Curtis Hanson-R). Screenplay
by B. W. L. Norton. (FD, HR, LAT, V, W)

2059. LOST AND FOUND. (Columbia-1979-Melvin Frank-PG).
Screenplay by Melvin Frank and Jack Rose; novelization by
Melvin Frank and Jack Rose; Ballantine, 1979, 153p. (FD,
LACOPL, NYT, Q, V, W)

2060. THE LOST HONOR OF KATHARINA BLUM. (New World-
1975-Volker Schlondorff-R). Volker Schlondorff and Margarethe von Trotta wrote the screenplay, based on a novel
by Heinrich Boll; McGraw-Hill, 1975, 140p. (FD, LACOPL,
NYT, W)

2061. LOUISIANA. (Parafrance-1984-Philippe de Broca-N/R).
Screenplay by Dominique Fabre, Etienne Perier, and Chuck
Israel, freely adapted from Louisiane and Fausse-Riviere
by Maurice Denuziere. (FD, V)

2062. LOULOU. (New Yorker-1980-Maurice Pialat-N/R). Screenplay by Arlette Langmann and Maurice Pialat, from a story
by Arlette Langmann. (W)

2063. LOVE. (Barry Levinson and Velvet Films-1982-Mai Zetter-
ling, Liv Ullmann, Nancy Dowd, Annette Cohen-N/R).
Screenplay by Nancy Dowd, Gael Greene, Joni Mitchell,
Edna O'Brien, Liv Ullmann, and Mai Zetterling. (FD, V)

2064. LOVE AND BULLETS. (AFD-1979-Stuart Rosenberg-PG).
Screenplay by Wendell Mayes and John Melson. (FD, V, W)

2065. LOVE AND DEATH. (United Artists-1975-Woody Allen-PG).
Screenplay by Woody Allen. (FD, NYT, Q, W)

2066. LOVE AND FAITH OF OGIN. (Toho-1982-Kei Kumal-N/R).
       Screenplay by Yoshitaka Yorita, from a story by Toko Kan.
       (W)

2067. LOVE AND LIES. (International Film Exchange-1982-Ilva
       Frez-N/R). Screenplay and story by G. Scherbakova and
       Ilva Frez. (V, W)

2068. LOVE AND MONEY. (Paramount-1982-James Toback-R).
       Screenplay by James Toback. (FD, LAT, Q, V)

2069. LOVE AND THE MIDNIGHT AUTO SUPPLY. (Producers
       Capital Corporation-1978-James Polakof). Screenplay by
       James Polakof. (V, W)

2070. LOVE AT FIRST BITE. (American International-1979-Stan
       Dragoti-PG). Screenplay by Robert Kaufman. (FD, Q, V,
       W)

2071. LOVE AT FIRST SIGHT. (Movietime-1978-Rex Bromfield-
       PG). Screenplay by Rex Bromfield. (FD, W)

       LOVE AT THE TOP see THE FRENCH WAY

2072. THE LOVE BUTCHER. (Manson-1982-Mikel Angel and Don
       Jones-R). Screenplay by Don Jones and James Evergreen.
       (V, W)

       LOVE BY APPOINTMENT see HOLIDAY HOOKERS

2073. LOVE CHILD. (Ladd Co./Warner Bros.-1982-Larry Peerce-
       R). Screenplay by Anne Gerard and Katherine Specktor,
       from a story by Anne Gerard. (FD, V, W)

       LOVE DOLL see LIFE SIZE

2074. LOVE GIRLS REPORT. (New Line-1975-Stanley Long-X).
       Screenplay by Suzanne Mercer and Stanley Long. (W)

2075. LOVE IN A TAXI. (Davey Co.-1980-Robert Sickinger-N/R).
       Screenplay by Michael Kortchmar. (V)

2076. A LOVE IN GERMANY. (CCC-Filmkunst/Gaumont-1983-
       Andrzej Wajda-N/R). Screenplay by Boleslaw Michalek,
       Agnieszka Holland, and Andrzej Wajda, based on Rolf Hoch-
       huth's novel of the same title; Little, Brown, 1980, 269p.
       (LACOPL, V)

2077. LOVE IN STRANGE PLACES. (Pendulus-1976-Robert D.
       Walters-X). Screenplay by Robert D. Walters. (W)

2078. LOVE LETTERS. (New World-1983-Amy Jones-R). Screenplay by Amy Jones. (W)

2079. LOVE LIVING, LIVE LOVING. (Lutz Eisholz Film Production-1977-N/R). Screenplay credits not available. (V)

2080. LOVE, LUST AND VIOLENCE. (M & R-1975-Norbert Meisel-X). Screenplay by Stan Kamber. (W)

2081. THE LOVE MATES. (New Line Cinema-1976-Roger Kahane-N/R). Screenplay credits not available. (W)

2082. LOVE ME STRANGELY. (Sunset International-1976-Sergio Gobbi-R). Based on the novel by Dominique Fabre. (W)

2083. LOVE ON THE GROUND. (Spectrafilm-1984-Jacques Rivette-N/R). Screenplay by Jacques Rivette, Pascal Bonitzer, Marilu Parolini, Suzanne Schiffman. (V)

2084. LOVE ON THE RUN. (AMLF-1979-Francois Truffaut-N/R). Screenplay by Francois Truffaut, Marie-France Pisier, Jean Aurel, and Suzanne Schiffman; in The Adventures of Antoine Doinel; Simon & Schuster, 1971, 320p. (FD, LACOPL, V, W)

2085. LOVE SLAVES. (Savant-1976-Robert Husong-X). Screenplay credits not available. (W)

2086. LOVE STREAMS. (MGM/UA-1984-John Cassavetes-N/R). Screenplay by John Cassavetes. (FD, V)

2087. THE LOVE SUICIDES AT SONEZAKI. (Kurisaki-1982-Midori Kurisaki-N/R). Screenplay written by Chikamatsu Monzaemon. (V, W)

2088. LOVE SWINDLERS. (Shaw Bros.-1976-Li Han-hsiang-N/R). Screenplay by Li Han-hsiang. (V)

2089. LOVE UNTO DEATH. (Philippe Dussart/Les Films Ariane-1984-Alain Resnais-N/R). Screenplay by Jean Gruault. (V)

2090. LOVELINES. (Tri-Star-1984-Rod Amateau-R). Screenplay by Chip Hand and William Hillman, from a story by Chip Hand, Michael Lloyd, and William Hillman. (V)

2091. LOVELY BUT DEADLY. (Juniper Releasing Co.-1983-David Sheldon-R). Screenplay by David Sheldon and Patricia Joyce, from a story by Lawrence D. Foldes. (V, W)

2092. LOVERS AND LIARS. (Levitt-Pickman-1981-Mario Monicelli-R). Screenplay by Paul Zimmerman and Mario Monicelli. (FD, LAT, V, W)

2093. LOVERS AND OTHER RELATIVES. (Crystal-1976-Salvatore Samperi-R). Screenplay by Allessandro Parenzo and Ottavio Jemma. (W)

2094. THE LOVES AND TIMES OF SCARAMOUCHE. (Avco Embassy-1976-Enzo G. Castellari-PG). Screenplay by Tito Carpi and Enzo Castellari. (W)

2095. THE LOVES OF LISZT. (Ellman-1975-Marton Keleti-N/R). Screenplay credits not available. (W)

2096. LOVESICK. (Ladd Co./Warner Bros.-1983-Marshall Brickman-PG). Screenplay by Marshall Brickman. (FD, V, W)

2097. LOVING COUPLES. (20th Century-Fox-1980-Jack Smight-PG). Screenplay by Martin Donovan. (FD, Q, V, W)

2098. LOVING COUSINS. (Independent International-1976-Sergio Martino-R). Screenplay by Sergio Martino, Savro Scavocini, and Fernando Poli. (NYT, W)

2099. LOWLAND. (Janus Films-1981-Leni Riefenstahl-N/R). Screenplay credits not available; based on the opera by Eugen D'Albert. (V)

2100. LUCIE SUR SEINE. (Nicole Jouve Interama-1983-Jean-Louis Bertucelli-N/R). Screenplay by S. Majerowitcz, adapted by Jean-Louis Bertucelli. (V, W)

2101. LUCIFER'S WOMEN. (Constellation-1978-Paul Aratow-R). Screenplay credits not available. (W)

2102. LUCIO FLAVIO. (Embrafilme/Unifilm-1981-Hector Babenco-N/R). Screenplay by Jose Louzeiro, Hector Babenco, and Jorge Duran. (V)

2103. LUCKY LADY. (20th Century-Fox-1975-Stanley Donen-PG). Screenplay by Willard Huyck and Gloria Katz. (FD, LAT, NYT, Q, W)

2104. LUCKY PIERRE. (Seaberg-1975-Claude Ziti-PG). Screenplay credits not available. (W)

2105. THE LUCKY STAR. (Tele-Metropole International-1980-Max Fischer-N/R). Screenplay by Max Fischer and Jack Rosenthal, from an original idea by Roland Topor. (V, W)

2106. LUDWIG. (American Zoetrope-1980-Hans-Jurgen Syberberg-N/R). Screenplay by Hans-Jurgen Syberberg. (FD, W)

2107. LUGGAGE OF THE GODS. (General Pictures-1983-Jeff Folmsbee-N/R). Screenplay credits not available. (W)

2108. LULU THE TOOL. (New Line Cinema-1975-Elio Petri-N/R).
Screenplay by Ugo Pirro and Elio Petri. (NYT, W)

2109. LUMIERE. (New World-1976-Jeanne Moreau-R). Screenplay
by Jeanne Moreau. (FD, NYT, W)

2110. LUNA. (20th Century-Fox-1979-Bernardo Bertolucci-R).
Screenplay by Giuseppe Bertolucci, Clare Peploe, Bernardo
Bertolucci, from an original story by Franco Arcalli, Ber-
nardo Bertolucci, and Giuseppe Bertolucci. (FD, Q, V, W)

2111. LUNCH WAGON. (Seymour Borde-1981-Ernest Pintoff-R).
Screenplay by Leon Phillips, Marshall Harvey, and Terrie
Frankie. (FD, LAT, V, W)

2112. LUST IN THE DUST. (Fox Run-1984-Paul Bartel-R).
Screenplay by Philip Taylor. (V)

2113. M3: THE GEMINI STRAIN. (Group 1-1980-Ed Hunt-PG).
Written by Ed Hunt. (W)

2114. M*A*S*H*D. (Hudson-1976-Emton Smith-X). Screenplay by
Emton Smith. (W)

2115. MACARTHUR. (Universal-1977-Joseph Sargent-PG). Screenplay written by Hal Barwood and Matthew Robbins. (FD,
HR, LAT, Q, V, W)

2116. MACKINTOSH & T.J. (Penland-1975-Marvin J. Chomsky-PG).
Screenplay written by Paul Savage. (FD, W)

2117. MCVICAR. (Crown International-1982-Tom Clegg-N/R).
Screenplay by John McVicar and Tom Clegg. (LAT, V, W)

2118. MAD DOG. (Cinema Shares International-1976-Philippe Mora-
R). Screenplay by Philippe Mora, based on Morgan and Bold
Bushranger by Margaret Carnegie. (FD, NYT, W)

2119. MAD MAX. (American International/Filmways-1980-George
Miller-R). Screenplay by James McCausland and George
Miller. (FD, HR, LAT, NYT, W)

2120. MAD MEMORIES OF A LIFEGUARD. (Globe-1975-Sergio
Casstner-N/R). Screenplay written by Heinrich von Trep-
tow. (W)

2121. MADAM KITTY. (American International Pictures-1977-Tinto
Brass-X). Screenplay by Ennio De Concini, Maria Pia Fusco,
and Tinto Brass; English dialog by Louise Vincent. (V)

MADAME CLAUDE see THE FRENCH WOMAN

2122. MADE. (International C-Production-1975-John Mackenzie-
       N/R). Screenplay by Howard Barker, based on his play No
       One Was Saved. (FD, W)

2123. MADMAN. (Jensen Farley Pictures-1982-Joe Giannone-R).
       Screenplay written by Joe Giannone. (LAT, V, W)

2124. MADO. (Joseph Green-1978-Claude Sautet-N/R). Screen-
       play written by Claude Sautet and Claude Neron. (FD, W)

2125. THE MAFU CAGE. (Clouds-1979-Karen Arthur-R). Screen-
       play by Don Chastain from a French play by Eric Westpha.
       (FD, W)

2126. MAG WHEELS. (Peter Perry-1978-Bethel Buckalew-R).
       Screenplay written by Bethel Buckalew. (W)

2127. MAGIC. (20th Century-Fox-1978-Richard Attenborough-R).
       Screenplay written by William Goldman, based on his novel;
       Delacorte Press, 1976. (FD, LACOPL, Q, V, W)

2128. THE MAGIC FLUTE. (Surrogate-1975-Ingmar Bergman-G).
       Screenplay by Ingmar Bergman, based on Wolfgang Amadeus
       Mozart's opera; libretto by Emanuel Schikaneder; Oxford
       University Press, 1937, 48p. (FD, LACOPL, NYT, Q, W)

2129. THE MAGIC OF LASSIE. (International Picture Show-1978-
       Don Chaffey-N/R). Screenplay by Jean Holloway, Robert B.
       Sherman, and Richard M. Sherman. (FD, V)

2130. THE MAGICIAN OF LUBLIN. (Cannon-1979-Menahem Golan-
       R). Screenplay by Irving S. White and Menahem Golan,
       based on the novel by Isaac Bashevis Singer; Noonday Press,
       1960. (FD, HR, LACOPL, V, W)

2131. LE MAGNIFIQUE. (Cine III-1976-Philippe De Broca-N/R).
       Screenplay written by Philippe De Broca. (NYT, W)

2132. MAHLER. (Mayfair-1975-Ken Russell-PG). Screenplay writ-
       ten by Ken Russell. (FD, NYT, W)

2133. MAHOGANY. (Paramount-1975-Berry Gordy-PG). Screen-
       play by John Byrum, based on a story by Toni Amber;
       novelization by Burton Wohl; Bantam Books, 1975. (FD,
       LACOPL, NYT, W)

2134. THE MAIDS. (American Film Theatre-1975-Christopher Miles-
       PG). Screenplay by Robert Enders and Christopher Miles,
       based on the play by Jean Genet; Grove Press, 1954, 102p.
       (FD, LACOPL, NYT, Q, W)

2135. THE MAIN EVENT. (Warner Bros.-1979-Howard Zieff-PG).
       Gail Parent, Andrew Smith wrote the screenplay; noveliza-
       tion by Andrew Smith and Gail Parent; Bantam Books, 1979,
       215p. (FD, LACOPL, Q, V, W)

2136. MAKE ROOM FOR TOMORROW. (Robert A. McNeil-1980-
       Peter Klassovitz-N/R). Screenplay by Peter Klassovitz and
       E. Pressman. (W)

2137. MAKE THEM DIE SLOWLY. (Aquarius Film Releasing-1983-
       Umberto Lenzi-X). Screenplay written by Umberto Lenzi.
       (V, W)

2138. MAKING LOVE. (20th Century-Fox-1982-Arthur Hiller-R).
       Screenplay by Barry Sandler, from a story by A. Scott
       Berg; novelization by Leonore Fleischer; Ballantine Books,
       1982. (FD, HR, LACOPL, LAT, Q, V, W)

2139. THE MAKING OF A LADY. (Sunset International-1976-
       Christian Jacque-R). Jameson Brewer and Christian Jacque
       wrote the screenplay, from a novel by Alexandre Dumas.
       (W)

2140. MAKING OUT. (SRC Films-1983-Walter Boos-R). Screenplay
       by Gunther Heeler. (LAT, V, W)

2141. MAKING THE GRADE. (MGM/UA-1984-Dorian Walker-R).
       Screenplay written by Gene Quintano from a story by Gene
       Quintano and Charles Gale. (V)

2142. MALE OF THE CENTURY. (Joseph Green-1976-Claude Berri-
       N/R). Screenplay written by Claude Berri, from an idea by
       Milos Forman. (FD, NYT, W)

2143. MALEVIL. (UGC-1981-Christian de Chalonge-N/R). Screen-
       play by Christian de Chalonge and Pierre Dumayet, based on
       the novel Malevil by Robert Merle; Simon & Schuster, 1973,
       575p. (LACOPL, V)

2144. MALIBU BEACH. (Crown International-1978-Robert J.
       Rosenthal-R). Screenplay by Celia Susan Cotelo and Robert
       J. Rosenthal. (FD, W)

2145. MALIBU HIGH. (Crown International-1979-Irv Berwick-R).
       Screenplay written by John Buckley and Tom Singer, from
       an original story by John Buckley. (FD, V, W)

2146. MALIZIA. (Paramount-1979-Salvatore Samperi-R). Screen-
       play by Ottavio Jemma, Salvatore Samperi, and Alessandro
       Parenzo. (W)

2147.   MALOU. (Cinegate-1980-Jeanine Meerapfel-N/R). Screenplay by Jeanine Meerapfel, with the collaboration by Grischa
Huber and Michael Juncker. (BFI)

2148.   A MAN, A WOMAN, AND A BANK. (Avco Embassy-1979-Noel
Black-PG). Screenplay by Raynold Gideon, Bruce A. Evans,
and Stuart Margolin, from a story by Raynold Gideon, and
Bruce A. Evans. (FD, W)

2149.   A MAN, A WOMAN AND A KILLER. (Schmidt-1975-Richard
R. Schmidt and Wayne Wang-N/R). Screenplay by Richard
A. Richardson, Richard R. Schmidt, and Wayne Wang. (FD,
NYT, W)

2150.   MAN AT THE TOP. (Anglo EMI-1975-Mike Vardy-R).
Screenplay by Hugh Whitemore, with additional material by
John Junkin, based on characters created by John Braine.
(W)

2151.   MAN FRIDAY. (Avco Embassy-1975-Jack Gold-PG). Screenplay by Adrian Mitchell, based on Daniel Defoe's Robinson
Crusoe; Macmillan, 1962, 348p. (FD, LACOPL, NYT, W)

2152.   THE MAN FROM S.E.X. (Group 1-1983-Lindsay Shonteff-R).
Screenplay written by Jeremy Lee Francis. (V)

2153.   THE MAN IN THE GLASS BOOTH. (American Film Theatre-
1975-Arthur Hiller-PG). Screenplay by Edward Anhalt,
from the play by Robert Shaw; Grove Press, 1968, 74p.
(FD, LACOPL, NYT, W)

2154.   THE MAN IN THE TRUNK. (Gaumont International-1975-
Georges Lautner-PG). Screenplay by Francis Veber. (NYT,
W)

2155.   MAN OF IRON. (United Artists Classics-1981-Andrzej Wajda-
PG). Screenplay by Aleksander Scibor-Rylski. (FD, LAT,
V, W)

2156.   MAN OF MARBLE. (New Yorker-1981-Andrzej Wajda-N/R).
Screenplay by Aleksander Scibor-Rylski. (FD, LAT, W)

2157.   MAN ON THE ROOF. (Cinema 5-1977-Bo Widerberg-R).
Screenplay by Bo Widerberg, based on the novel The Abomi-
nable Man by Maj Sjowall and Per Wahloo; Pantheon, 1972,
214p. (FD, LACOPL, Q, W)

2158.   THE MAN WHO FELL TO EARTH. (British Lion-1976-Nicolas
Roeg-R). Screenplay by Paul Mayersberg, from the novel
by Walter Tevis; Avon, 1976, 189p. (FD, LACOPL, NYT,
V, W)

2159. THE MAN WHO LOVED WOMEN. (United Artists-1977-
Francois Truffaut-N/R). Screenplay by Francois Truffaut,
Michel Fernand, and Suzanne Schiffman. (V)

2160. THE MAN WHO LOVED WOMEN. (Columbia-1983-Blake
Edwards-R). Screenplay written by Blake Edwards, Milton
Wexler, and Geoffrey Edwards. (FD, LAT, V)

2161. THE MAN WHO SAW TOMORROW. (Warner Bros.-1981-Robert
Guenette-PG). Screenplay by Robert Guenette and Alan
Hopgood. (FD, V, W)

2162. THE MAN WHO STOLE THE SUN. (Kitty-1982-Kazuhiko
Hasegawa-N/R). Screenplay by Leonard Schrader and
Kazuhiko Hasegawa. (LAT, W)

2163. THE MAN WHO WASN'T THERE--3D. (Paramount-1983-Bruce
Malmuth-R). Screenplay by Stanford Sherman. (FD, V, W)

2164. THE MAN WHO WOULD BE KING. (Allied Artists-1975-John
Huston-PG). Screenplay by John Huston and Gladys Hill.
(FD, NYT, W)

2165. THE MAN WHO WOULD NOT DIE. (Centaur-1975-Robert
Arkless-PG). Screenplay written by George Chesbro,
Stephen Taylor, and Robert Arkless, based on the novel
The Sailcloth Shroud by Charles Williams; Viking, 1960.
(LACOPL, W)

2166. THE MAN WITH BOGART'S FACE. (20th Century-Fox-1980-
Robert Day-N/R). Screenplay by Andrew J. Fenady, based
on his novel; H. Regnery Co., 1977, 186p. (FD, HR,
LACOPL, V)

2167. THE MAN WITH TWO BRAINS. (Warner Bros.-1983-Carl
Reiner-R). Screenplay written by Carl Reiner, Steve Martin, and George Gipe. (FD, LAT, V)

2168. MAN, WOMAN AND CHILD. (Paramount-1983-Dick Richards-
PG). Screenplay written by Erich Segal and David Z. Good-
man, based on a novel by Erich Segal; Harper & Row, 1980.
(BFI, FD, LACOPL, LAT, V)

2169. THE MANCHU EAGLE MURDER CAPER MYSTERY. (United
Artists-1975-Dean Hargrove-PG). Screenplay by Dean Har-
grove and Gabriel Dell. (FD, W)

2170. MANDINGO. (Paramount-1975-Richard Fleischer-R). Screenplay by Norman Wexler, based on a novel by Kyle Onstott
and a play by Jack Kirkland; Fawcett, 1978. (FD, LACOPL,
NYT, Q, W)

2171. THE MANGO TREE. (Satori-1982-Kevin Dobson-N/R).
       Screenplay by Michael Pate. (FD, W)

2172. THE MANHANDLERS. (Premiere-1975-Lee Madden-R).
       Screenplay written by Gil Lasky. (W)

2173. MANHATTAN. (United Artists-1979-Woody Allen-R).
       Screenplay by Woody Allen and Marshall Brickman. (FD,
       HR, LAT, NYT, Q, V, W)

2174. MANIAC. (Analysis Film Corp-1981-William Lustig-X).
       Screenplay by C. A. Rosenberg and Joe Spinell, from a
       story by Joe Spinell. (FD, Q, V, W)

2175. THE MANITOU. (Avco Embassy-1978-William Girdler).
       Screenplay by William Girdler, Jon Cedar, and Tom Pope,
       based on a novel by Graham Masterton; Pinnacle Books,
       1976, 216p. (LACOPL, Q, V, W)

2176. MANNEQUIN. (Joseph Brenner-1976-Alain Van Damme, Alex
       Nubarr, and Gerard Kikoine-X). Screenplay by Alain Van
       Damme. (W)

2177. MANSION OF THE DOOMED. (Group 1-1976-Michael Pataki-
       R). Screenplay by Frank Ray Perilli. (W)

2178. THE MANSON MASSACRE. (Newport-1976-Kentucky Jones-
       R). No screenplay credits available. (W)

2179. MANTHAN. (The Churning-1980-Shyam Benegal-N/R). No
       screenplay credits available. (W)

       MAR DE ROSAS see SEA OF ROSES

2180. MARATHON MAN. (Paramount-1976-John Schlesinger-R).
       Screenplay by William Goldman, from his novel; Delacorte
       Press, 1974, 309p. (FD, LACOPL, NYT, W)

2181. MARCH OR DIE. (Columbia-1977-Dick Richards-PG).
       Screenplay by David Zelag Goodman, from a story by David
       Zelag Goodman and Dick Richards; novelization by Robert
       Weverka; Bantam Books, 1977. (FD, LACOPL, V)

2182. MARDI GRAS MASSACRE. (Omni Capital-1984-Jack Weis-
       N/R). Screenplay by Jack Weis. (V)

       MARIA DE MI CORAZON see MARY MY DEAREST

       MARIANNE see MIRRORS

2183. MARIA'S LOVERS. (MGM/UA-1984-Andrei Konchalovsky-

N/R). Screenplay by Gerard Brach, Andrei Konchalovsky, Paul Zindel, and Marjorie David. (FD, V)

2184. MARIKEN. (Joseph Green-1975-Jos Stelling-N/R). Screenplay by Jos Stelling. (W)

2185. MARILYN AND THE SENATOR. (Hollywood International-1975-Carlos Tobalina-X). Screenplay written by Carlos Tobalina. (W)

2186. MARK OF THE DEVIL PART 2. (Hallmark-1975-Adrian Hoven-R). Screenplay credits not available. (W)

2187. MARK OF THE WITCH. (Lone Star-1982-Tom Moore-R). Screenplay by Mary Davis and Martha Peters. (W)

2188. MARK TWAIN, AMERICAN. (Emerson-1976-Robert Wilbor-G). Screenplay adapted by Ed Trostle. (W)

2189. THE MARQUISE OF O. (New Line Cinema-1976-Eric Rohmer-PG). Screenplay by Eric Rohmer, from a story by Heinrich Von Kleist. (NYT, W)

2190. A MARRIAGE. (Cinecom International-1983-Sandy Tung-N/R). Screenplay by Sandy Tung. (FD, V)

2191. MARRIAGE AND OTHER FOUR LETTER WORDS. (Robert Raymond-1976-Rick Jr.-X). Screenplay by J. W. Mitchel. (W)

2192. THE MARRIAGE OF MARIA BRAUN. (New Yorker-1979-Rainer Werner Fassbinder-R). Screenplay written by Peter Marthesheimer, Pia Frohlich, and Rainer Werner Fassbinder. (W)

2193. THE MARRIED PRIEST. (Matterhorn-1975-Marco Vicario-R). Screenplay by Marco Vicario. (W)

2194. MARTIN. (Libra Films-1978-George A. Romero-R). Screenplay by George A. Romero. (FD, V, W)

2195. THE MARTYR. (Joseph Green-1976-Aleksander Ford-N/R). Screenplay by Josef Gross, based on a scenario by Alexander Ramati. (NYT, W)

2196. MARVIN AND TIGE. (Major Films-1983-Eric Weston-PG). Screenplay by Wanda Dell and Eric Weston, based on the novel by Franckina Glass; St. Martin's Press, 1977, 232p. (FD, LACOPL, LAT, V)

2197. MARY, MARY, BLOODY MARY. (Translor-1975-Juan Lopez

Moctezuma-R). Screenplay by Malcolm Marmorstein, from a
story by Don Rico and Don Henderson. (W)

2198. MARY MY DEAREST. (Azteca-1984-Jaime Humberto
Hermosillo-N/R). Screenplay by Gabriel Garcia Marquez
and Jaime Humberto Hermosillo. (V)

2199. MASOCH. (Difilm S.R.L.-Franco Brogi Taviani-N/R).
Screenplay by Franco Brogi Taviani. (V)

2200. MASS APPEAL. (Universal-1984-Glenn Jordan-PG). Screenplay by Bill C. Davis, based on his stage play; Avon, 1981,
80p. (FD, LACOPL, V)

2201. MASSACRE AT CENTRAL HIGH. (Brian-1976-Renee Daalder-
R). Screenplay by Renee Daalder. (V, W)

MASSACRE MANSION see THE TERROR OF DR. CHANEY

2202. MASSAGE PARLOR WIFE. (Boxoffice International-1976-
Barry Spinello-N/R). Screenplay by Barry Spinello. (W)

2203. THE MASTER AND MARGARITA. (Public Cinema-1980-
Aleksandar Petrovic-N/R). Based on the novel by Mikhail
Bulgakov; Grove Press, 1967. (LACOPL, W)

2204. THE MASTER GUNFIGHTER. (Taylor-Laughlin-1975-Frank
Laughlin-PG). Screenplay written by Harold Lapland. (FD,
LAT, NYT, Q, V, W)

2205. MASTER KILLER. (World Northal-1979-Liu Chia-liang-R).
Screenplay credits not available. (W)

2206. MATER AMATISIMA. (Imatco S.A.-1980-J. A. Salgot-N/R).
Screenplay by J. A. Salgot, based on a story by Bigas Luna.
(V)

2207. MATILDA. (American International-1978-Daniel Mann-G).
Screenplay by Albert S. Ruddy and Timothy Galfas, based
on the book by Paul Gallico; Coward, 1970, 313p. (FD,
LACOPL, Q, V, W)

2208. A MATTER OF LOVE. (William Mishkin-1979-Chuck Vincent-
R). Screenplay by James Vidos and Chuck Vincent, based
on a novel by Sharon Mason. (V)

2209. A MATTER OF TIME. (American International-1976-Vincente
Minnelli-PG). Screenplay by John Gay, based on the novel
Film of Memory by Maurice Druon; Scribner, 1955. (FD,
LACOPL, NYT, V, W)

2210. MAUSOLEUM. (Motion Picture Marketing-1983-Michael Dugan-
       R). Screenplay by Robert Barich and Robert Madero, from
       an original screenplay and story by Katherine Rosenwink.
       (FD, W)

       MAUVAISE CONDUITE see IMPROPER CONDUCT

2211. MAX DUGAN RETURNS. (20th Century-Fox-1983-Herbert
       Ross-PG). Screenplay by Neil Simon. (FD, LAT, V, W)

2212. MAX HAVELAAR. (Atlantic Releasing Corp-1979-Fons
       Rademakers-N/R). Screenplay by Gerard Soeteman, based
       on the novel Multatuli by Peter King; Twayne, 1972, 185p.
       (LACOPL, W)

2213. MAYA. (Claridge Pictures-1982-Agust Agustsson-N/R).
       Screenplay by Berta Dominguez and Joseph D. Rosevich.
       (V, W)

2214. THE MEAL. (Ambassador-1975-R. John Hugh-R). Screen-
       play by R. John Hugh. (W)

2215. MEAN DOG BLUES. (American International-1978-Mel Stuart).
       Screenplay by George Lefferts. (V, W)

2216. MEAN FRANK AND CRAZY TONY. (Aquarius-1976-Michele
       Lupo-R). Screenplay credits not given. (W)

2217. MEAN JOHNNY BARROWS. (Atlas-1976-Fred Williamson-R).
       Screenplay credits not available. (W)

2218. MEAT. (Pentagramma Film-1979-Rainer Erler-N/R). Screen-
       play by Rainer Erler. (V)

2219. MEATBALLS. (Paramount-1979-Ivan Reitman-PG). Screen-
       play by Len Blum, Dan Goldberg, Janis Allen, and Harold
       Ramis. (FD, Q, V, W)

2220. MEATBALLS PART II. (Tri-Star Pictures-1984-Ken
       Wiederhorn-PG). Screenplay by Bruce Singer, from a story
       by Martin Kitrosser and Carol Watson. (V)

2221. THE MEDUSA TOUCH. (Elan Films-1978-Jack Gold-R).
       Screenplay by John Briley, Jack Gold, from a novel by
       Peter Van Greenaway; Stein & Day, 1973, 255p. (FD,
       LACOPL, Q, V, W)

2222. MEETINGS WITH REMARKABLE MEN. (Libra-1978-Peter
       Brook-G). Screenplay by Jeanne De Salzmann and Peter
       Brook, adapted from the book by G. I. Gurdjieff; Dutton,
       1963. (FD, LACOPL, W)

2223. MEGAFORCE. (20th Century-Fox-1982-Hal Needham-PG).
Screenplay by James Whittaker, Albert S. Ruddy, Hal
Needham, and Andre Morgan. (FD, Q, V, W)

O MEGALEXANDROS see ALEXANDER THE GREAT

2224. MELANIE. (Embassy-1982-Rex Bromfield-N/R). Screenplay
by Robert Guza Jr. and Richard Paluck, from a story by
Michael Green. (FD, V)

2225. THE MELON AFFAIR. (EMC-1979-Art Lieberman-R). No
screenplay credits given. (W)

2226. MELVIN AND HOWARD. (Universal-1980-Jonathan Demme-
R). Screenplay by Bo Goldman. (FD, Q, V, W)

2227. MEMOIRS OF A FRENCH WHORE. (Aidart-1982-Daniel Duval-
N/R). Screenplay by Daniel Duval, Christopher Frank, and
Jeanne Cordelier, based on The Life by Jeanne Cordelier;
Viking Press, 1978, 368p. (LACOPL, W)

2228. MEMORIES, MEMORIES. (Gaumont/A.J.O.-1984-Ariel Zeitoun-
N/R). Screenplay by Ariel Zeitoun and Daniel Saint-Hamon.
(V)

2229. THE MEN. (International Film Exchange/Satra Film Corp/
Sovexportfilm-1979-Edmond Keosayan-N/R). Screenplay
credits not available. (W)

2230. MEN PREFER FAT GIRLS. (GEF/CCFC-1981-Jean Marie
Poire-N/R). Screenplay by Josiane Balasko and Jean-Marie
Poire. (V)

2231. MENUDO. (Embassy-1983-Orestes A. Trucco-N/R). Screenplay credits not available. (W)

2232. MEPHISTO. (Analysis Films Releasing-1981-Istvan Szabo-R).
Screenplay by Istvan Szabo and Peter Dobai, based on a
novel by Klaus Mann; Random House, 1977. (FD, LACOPL,
LAT, Q, V, W)

2233. MERRY GO ROUND. (New Line-1976-Otto Schenk-R).
Screenplay credit not given; based on the play Reigan by
Arthur Schnitzler; Weidenfeld and Nicolson, 1953, 90p.
(LACOPL, NYT, W)

2234. MESSAGE FROM SPACE. (United Artists-1978-Kinji
Fukasaku-PG). Screenplay written by Hiroo Matsuda. (Q,
V, W)

2235. MESSIAH OF EVIL. (International Cinefilm-1975-Gloria Katz and Willard Huyck-R). Screenplay written by Gloria Katz and Willard Huyck. (FD, W)

2236. MESSIDOR. (New Yorker-1981-Alain Tanner-N/R). Screenplay by Alain Tanner. (FD, LAT, W)

2237. METALSTORM: THE DESTRUCTION OF JARED-SYN. (Universal-1983-Charles Band-PG). Screenplay written by Alan J. Adler. (FD, LAT, V, W)

2238. METEOR. (American International-1979-Ronald Neame-PG). Screenplay written by Stanley Mann and Edmund H. North, based on a story by Edmund H. North; novelization by Edmund H. North; Warner Books, 1979, 236p. (FD, HR, LACOPL, LAT, Q, V, W)

2239. MEXICO IN FLAMES. (Mosfilm/Conacitez/Vides International-1982-Sergei Bondarchuk-N/R). Screenplay written by Sergei Bondarchuk and V. Ezhov. (V)

2240. MICHAEL KOHLHAAS. (Horst Film GmbH.-1979-Wolf Vollmar-N/R). Screenplay written by Wolf Vollmar. (V)

2241. MICHAEL KOHLHAAS. (Columbia-1980-Volker Schlondorff-N/R). Screenplay written by Edward Bond, Clement Biddle-Wood, and Volker Schlondorff, based on a novella by Heinrich von Kleist; Blackie, 1967. (FD, LACOPL, W)

2242. MICKI & MAUDE. (Columbia-1984-Blake Edwards-PG-13). Screenplay written by Jonathan Reynolds. (V)

2243. MICROWAVE MASSACRE. (Reel Life Prods.-1983-Wayne Berwick-N/R). Screenplay written by Thomas Singer, from a story by Craig Muckler. (V)

2244. MIDDLE AGE CRAZY. (20th Century-Fox-1980-John Trent). Screenplay written by Carl Kleinschmidt. (FD, Q, V, W)

2245. MIDDLE OF THE WORLD. (New Yorker-1975-Alain Tanner-N/R). Screenplay by John Berger and Alain Tanner. (NYT, W)

2246. THE MIDDLEMAN. (Bauer International-1979-Satyajit Ray-N/R). Screenplay written by Satyajit Ray, based on a story by Shankar. (NYT, W)

2247. MIDNIGHT. (Independent-International-1983-John A. Russo-R). Screenplay written by John A. Russo, from his novel. (V, W)

2248. MIDNIGHT DESIRES. (Ambar-1976-Amanda Barton-X). Screenplay written by Amanda Barton. (W)

2249. MIDNIGHT EXPRESS. (Columbia-1978-Alan Parker-R).
Screenplay written by Oliver Stone, based on the book by
Billy Hayes and William Hoffer; Dutton, 1977, 280p. (HR,
LACOPL, LAT, V, W)

2250. MIDNIGHT MADNESS. (Buena Vista-1980-David Wechter and
Michael Nankin-PG). Screenplay written by David Wechter
and Michael Nankin. (Q, V, W)

2251. A MIDSUMMER NIGHT'S SEX COMEDY. (Orion-1982-Woody
Allen-PG). Screenplay written by Woody Allen. (Q, V)

2252. MIDWAY. (Universal-1976-Jack Smight-PG). Screenplay
by Donald S. Sanford. (NYT, W)

2253. MIKE'S MURDER. (Ladd Co-1984-James Bridges-R).
Screenplay written by James Bridges. (LAT, V)

2254. MIKEY AND NICKY. (Paramount-1976-Elaine May-R).
Screenplay written by Elaine May. (NYT, Q, V)

2255. MILESTONES. (Stone-1975-Robert Kramer & John Douglas-
N/R). Screenplay written by Robert Kramer and John
Douglas. (NYT, W)

2256. MIRACLE. (Experimental Cinema of the Philippines-1983-
Ishmael Bernal-N/R). Screenplay written by Ricardo Lee.
(NYT, V)

2257. MIRAGE D'AMOUR. (Command Cinema-1975-X). No production credits available. (W)

2258. THE MIRROR. (Mosfilm-1976-Andrei Tarkovsky-N/R).
Screenplay written by Andrei Tarkovsky. (NYT, V, W)

2259. THE MIRROR CRACK'D. (AFD-1980-Guy Hamilton-PG).
Screenplay written by Jonathan Hale and Barry Sandler,
from the novel The Mirror Crack'd from Side to Side by
Agatha Christie; Ulverscroft, 1966, 400p. (HR, LACOPL,
Q, V, W)

2260. MIRRORS. (First American Films-1978-Noel Black-PG).
Screenplay written by Sidney L. Stebel from a story by
Sidney L. Stebel and Noel Black. (V, W)

2261. LES MISERABLES. (C.C.F.C.-1982-Robert Hossein-N/R).
Screenplay by Robert Hossein and Alain Decaux, from the
novel by Victor Hugo; Dodd, Mead, 1979, 585p. (LACOPL,
V)

2262. THE MISLAID GENIE. (Cineclub 24-1976-Eric and Shelley

Haims-X). Screenplay written by Thomas Earl and Shelley
Haims. (W)

2263. MISS LESLIE'S DOLLS. (World Wide-1975-Joseph G. Prieto-
R). Screenplay credits not available. (W)

2264. MISSING. (Universal-1982-Costa-Gavras-PG). Screenplay
by Costa-Gavras and Donald Stewart, based on the book by
Thomas Hauser, Execution of Charles Horman: An American
Sacrifice; Harcourt Brace Jovanovich, 1978, 255p. (HR,
LACOPL, LAT, Q, V)

2265. MISSING IN ACTION. (Cannon-1984-Joseph Zito-R).
Screenplay written by James Bruner, based on a story by
John Crowther and Lance Hool. (V)

2266. THE MISSION. (New Film Group-1983-Parviz Sayyad-N/R).
Screenplay by Parviz Sayyad, from a story by Hesam
Kowsar. (W)

2267. THE MISSOURI BREAKS. (United Artists-1976-Arthur Penn-
PG). Screenplay written by Thomas McGuane. (NYT, W)

2268. MR. BILLION. (20th Century-Fox-1977-Jonathan Kaplan-PG).
Screenplay written by Friedman Kaplan. (Q, V)

2269. MR. KLEIN. (Quartet-1977-Joseph Losey-PG). Screenplay
written by Franco Solinas. (Q, W)

2270. MR. MIKE'S MONDO VIDEO. (New Line Cinema-1979-
Michael O'Donoghue-R). Screenplay by Michael O'Donoghue,
Mitchell Glazer, Emily Prager, and Dirk Wittenborn. (V, W)

2271. MR. PATMAN. (Film Consortium of Canada-1980-John
Guillermin-N/R). Screenplay written by Thomas Hedley.
(V)

2272. MR. QUILP. (Avco Embassy-1975-Michael Tuchner-G).
Screenplay by Louis and Irene Kamp, based on Charles
Dickens' novel The Old Curiosity Shop; Penguin Books,
1972, 720p. (LACOPL, NYT, W)

2273. MR. RICCO. (United Artists-1975-Paul Bogart-PG). Screenplay by Robert Hoban, story by Ed Harvey and Francis
Kiernan. (NYT, Q, W)

2274. MR. SYCAMORE. (Film Venture-1975-Pancho Kohner-N/R).
Screenplay by Ketti Frings and Pancho Kohner, from a
story by Robert Ayre and a play by Ketti Frings. (W)

2275. MRS. SOFFEL. (MGM/UA-1984-Gillian Armstrong-PG-13).
Screenplay by Ron Nyswaner. (HR, LAT, V)

2276. MISTY. (Cineworld-1976-Joe Sarno-X). Screenplay by Joe
Sarno. (W)

2277. MISUNDERSTOOD. (MGM/UA-1984-Jerry Schatzberg-PG).
Screenplay written by Barra Grant, based on the novel by
Florence Montgomery. (V)

2278. MITCHELL. (Allied Artists-1975-Andrew V. McLaglen-R).
Screenplay by Ian Kennedy Martin. (NYT, W)

2279. MIXED BLOOD. (Sara Films-1984-Paul Morrissey-N/R).
Screenplay written by Paul Morrissey. (V)

2280. MODERN DAY HOUDINI. (Mid America Promotions-1983-
Eddie Beverly Jr.-PG). Screenplay written by Steven
Meyers. (V, W)

2281. MODERN PROBLEMS. (20th Century-Fox-1981-Ken Shapiro-
PG). Screenplay by Ken Shapiro, Tom Sherohman, and
Arthur Sellers. (LAT, Q, V, W)

2282. MODERN ROMANCE. (Columbia-1981-Albert Brooks-R).
Screenplay by Albert Brooks and Monica Johnson. (Q, V,
W)

2283. THE MOELLEBY AFFAIR. (Nordisk Film Kompagni-1976-Tom
Hedegaard-N/R). Screenplay by Henning Bahs, Erik Balling,
and Tom Kedegaard, based on the novel by Morten Korch.
(V)

2284. MOHAMMAD, MESSENGER OF GOD. (Anthony Birley-Tarik
Films-1977-Moustapha Akkad-PG). Screenplay by H. A. L.
Craig. (Q, W)

2285. MOLIERE. (New Yorker-1980-Ariane Mnouchkine-N/R).
Screenplay written by Ariane Mnouchkine. (W)

2286. MOMENT BY MOMENT. (Universal-1978-Jane Wagner-R).
Screenplay written by Jane Wagner; novelization by Darcy
O'Brien; Ballantine Books, 1979, 246p. (HR, LACOPL, Q,
V, W)

2287. MOMENTS. (Rosa-1979-Michal Bat-Adam-N/R). Screenplay
by Michal Bat-Adam. (V)

2288. MOMMIE DEAREST. (Paramount-1981-Frank Perry-PG).
Screenplay by Frank Yablans, Frank Perry, Tracy Hotchner,
Robert Getchell, based on the book by Christina Crawford;
Morrow, 1978, 286p. (BFI, HR)

2289. MON ONCLE D'AMERIQUE. (New World-1980-Alain Resnais-
       PG). Screenplay by Jean Gruault. (W)

2290. THE MONEY. (Coliseum-1976-Carl Workman-R). Screenplay
       by Carl Workman. (W)

2291. MONEY. (AMLF-1983-Robert Bresson-N/R). Screenplay
       written by Robert Bresson, inspired by The Counterfeit
       Note by Leo Tolstoy. (V)

2292. MONKEY GRIP. (Cinecom International-1983-Ken Cameron-
       N/R). Screenplay by Ken Cameron and Helen Garner. (W)

2293. THE MONKEY HUSTLE. (American International Pictures-
       1976-Arthur Marks-PG). Screenplay by Charles Johnson,
       from a story by Odie Hawkins. (NYT, V, W)

2294. MONSIGNOR. (20th Century-Fox-1982-Frank Perry-R).
       Screenplay written by Abraham Polonsky and Wendell Mayes,
       based on the novel by Jack Alain Leger; Dell Books, 1982.
       (HR, LACOPL, V, W)

2295. THE MONSTER CLUB. (ITC Film Distributors-1981-Ray
       Ward Baker-N/R). Screenplay by Edward and Valerie
       Abraham, based on the novel by Ronald Chetwynd-Hayes.
       (V)

2296. MONSTER ISLAND. (Fort Films-1981-J. Piquer Simon-N/R).
       Screenplay written by J. Grau, J. Piquer, and R. Gantman,
       based on a Jules Verne story. (V)

2297. MONTY PYTHON AND THE HOLY GRAIL. (Cinema 5-1975-
       Terry Gilliam & Terry Jones-PG). Screenplay by Graham
       Chapman, John Cleese, Terry Gilliam, Eric Idle, Terry Jones,
       and Michael Palin. (NYT, Q, W)

2298. MONTY PYTHON MEETS BEYOND THE FRINGE. (New Line-
       1978-Roger Graef-N/R). Screenplay credits not available.
       (W)

2299. MONTY PYTHON'S LIFE OF BRIAN. (Warner Bros./Orion
       Pictures-1979-Terry Jones-R). Screenplay by Graham Chap-
       man, John Cleese, Terry Gilliam, Eric Idle, Terry Jones,
       and Michael Palin. (LAT, Q, V, W)

2300. MONTY PYTHON'S THE MEANING OF LIFE. (Universal-1983-
       Terry Jones-R). Screenplay written by Graham Chapman,
       John Cleese, Terry Gilliam, Eric Idle, Terry Jones, and
       Michael Palin. (LAT, V)

2301. THE MOON IN THE GUTTER. (Triumph-1983-Jean-Jacques

Beineix-N/R). Screenplay written by Jean-Jacques Beineix,
based on a novel by David Goodis. (LAT, V, W)

2302. MOONRAKER. (United Artists-1979-Lewis Gilbert-PG).
Screenplay by Christopher Wood; novelization by Christopher
Wood; Jove Books, 1979, 222p. (LACOPL, LAT, Q, V, W)

2303. MOONSHINE COUNTY EXPRESS. (New World Pictures-1977-
Gus Trikonis-PG). Screenplay written by Hubert Smith and
Daniel Ansley. (V)

MOORD IN EXTASE see MURDER IN ECSTASY

2304. MORE AMERICAN GRAFFITI. (Universal-1979-B. W. L.
Norton-PG). Screenplay by B. W. L. Norton, based on
characters created by George Lucas, Gloria Katz, and Willard Huyck. (Q, V, W)

2305. MORGIANA. (IFEX-1983-Juraj Herz-N/R). Screenplay by
Juraj Herz and Vladimir Bor, from the novel Jessie and
Morgiana by Alexander Grin. (W)

2306. MORTUARY. (Artists Releasing Corp.-1983-Howard Avedis-
R). Screenplay by Howard Avedis and Marlene Schmidt.
(LAT, V, W)

2307. MOSCOW ON THE HUDSON. (Columbia-1984-Paul Mazursky-
R). Screenplay by Paul Mazursky and Leon Capetanos. (V)

2308. MOSES. (AVCO Embassy-1976-Gianfranco de Bosio-PG).
Screenplay by Anthony Burgess, Vitorio Bonicelli, and
Gianfranco de Bosio. (NYT, W)

2309. MOSES AND AARON. (New Yorker-1975-Jean-Marie Straub
& Daniele Huillet-N/R). Screenplay by Jean-Marie Straub
and Daniele Huillet. (W)

2310. MOTEL HELL. (United Artists-1980-Kevin Connor-R).
Screenplay by Robert Jaffe and Steven-Charles Jaffe.
(V, W)

2311. MOTHER AND DAUGHTER. (1978-Giovanna Gagliardo-N/R).
Screenplay written by Giovanna Gagliardo. (W)

2312. MOTHER, JUGS AND SPEED. (20th Century-Fox-1976-Peter
Yates-PG). Screenplay by Tom Mankiewicz, from a story by
Stephen Manes and Tom Mankiewicz. (NYT, W)

2313. MOTHER KUSTERS GOES TO HEAVEN. (New Yorker-1977-
Rainer Werner Fassbinder-N/R). Screenplay by Rainer
Werner Fassbinder and Kurt Raab. (Q, W)

2314. MOTHER LODE. (Martin Shafter/Andrew Scheinman-1982-
       PG). Screenplay written by Fraser Clarke Heston and Peter
       Snell. (V, W)

2315. MOTHER'S DAY. (United Film Distribution-1980-Charles
       Kaufman-N/R). Screenplay by Charles Kaufman and Warren
       D. Leight. (V, W)

2316. THE MOUNT OF VENUS. (Classic-1975-Carter Stevens aka
       Malcolm Worob-X). Screenplay written by Merry Seaman.
       (W)

2317. MOUNTAIN FAMILY ROBINSON. (Pacific International
       Enterprises-1979-John Cotter-G). Screenplay by Arthur R.
       Dubbs. (V, W)

2318. THE MOUNTAIN MEN. (Columbia-1980-Richard Lang-R).
       Screenplay written by Fraser Clarke Heston. (Q, V, W)

2319. THE MOUSE AND HIS CHILD. (DeFaria-Lockhart-Sanrio-
       1977-Fred Wolf and Charles Swenson-N/R). Screenplay
       written by Carol Mon Pere, from the novel by Russell Hoban.
       (V)

2320. MOVIE, MOVIE. (Warner Bros.-1978-Stanley Donen-PG).
       Screenplay by Larry Gelbart and Sheldon Keller. (Q, V, W)

2321. MOVING VIOLATION. (20th Century-Fox-1976-Charles S.
       Dubin-PG). Screenplay by David R. Osterhout and William
       Norton, from a story by David R. Osterhout. (W)

2322. MOZART--A CHILD CHRONICLE. (1980-Klaus Kirschner-
       N/R). Screenplay by Klaus Kirschner. (W)

2323. MS. DON JUAN. (Scotia American-1976-Roger Vadim-R).
       Screenplay by Jean Cau and Roger Vadim. (W)

2324. MS. .45. (Navaron-1981-Abel Ferrara-R). Screenplay by
       Nicholas St. John. (LAT, V, W)

2325. THE MUCKER. (Stopfilm Ltd.-1980-Wolf Gauer and Jorge
       Dodanzky-N/R). Screenplay by Wolf Gauer. (V)

2326. MUDDY MAMA. (North American Films-1975-Bob Favorite-X).
       No screenplay credits available. (W)

2327. MUDDY RIVER. (Japan Film Center-1982-Kohei Oguri-N/R).
       Screenplay by Takako Shigemori, from the novel by Teru
       Miyamoto. (V, W)

       LA MUJER DE LA TEIRRA CALIENTE see WOMAN FROM
       THE TORRID LAND

UNA MUJER SIN AMOR see A WOMAN WITHOUT LOVE

2328. THE MUPPET MOVIE. (Associated Film Distribution-1979-James Frawley-G). Screenplay by Jerry Juhl and Jack Burns. (Q, V, W)

2329. THE MUPPETS TAKE MANHATTAN. (Tri-Star Pictures-1984-Frank Oz-G). Screenplay by Frank Oz, Tom Patchett, and Jay Tarses, from a story by Tom Patchett and Jay Tarses. (V)

2330. MURDER BY DEATH. (Columbia-1976-Robert Moore-PG). Screenplay by Neil Simon. (NYT, W)

2331. MURDER BY DECREE. (AVCO Embassy-1979-Bob Clark-PG). Screenplay written by John Hopkins; novelization by Robert Weverka. (LACOPL, Q, V, W)

2332. MURDER BY PHONE. (New World Pictures-1982-Michael Anderson-R). Screenplay by Michael Butler, Dennis Shryack, and John Kent Harrison. (V, W)

2333. MURDER IN ECSTASY. (Tuschinski Film Distribution-1984-Hans Scheepmaker-N/R). Screenplay by Felix Thijssen, based upon the novel by A. C. Baanater. (V)

2334. THE MURDER OF PEDRALBES. (1980-Gonzalo Herralde-N/R). Screenplay credits not available. (W)

THE MURRI AFFAIR see LA GRANDE BOURGEOISE

2335. THE MUSIC MACHINE. (Norfolk International Pictures-1979-Ian Sharp-N/R). Screenplay by John Kenelm Clarke. (V)

2336. MUSTANG COUNTRY. (Universal-1976-John Champion-G). Screenplay written by John Champion. (W)

2337. THE MUTHERS. (Dimension-1976-Cirio H. Santiago-R). Screenplay written by Cyril St. James, from a story by Leonard Hermes. (W)

2338. MY BLOODY VALENTINE. (Paramount-1981-George Mihalka-R). Screenplay by John Beaird, story by Stephen Miller. (Q, W)

2339. MY BODYGUARD. (20th Century-Fox-1980-Tony Bill-PG). Screenplay by Alan Ormsby. (Q, V, W)

2340. MY BREAKFAST WITH BLASSIE. (Bill Stern-Neal Wiener Amusement-1983-Johnny Legend and Linda Lautrec-N/R). Screenplay credits not available. (LAT, W, V)

2341.   MY BRILLIANT CAREER. (Analysis Films-1980-Gillian
        Armstrong-N/R). Screenplay by Eleanor Witcombe, adapted
        from a novel by Miles Franklin. (W)

2342.   MY DEATH SHOULD BE BLAMED ON KLAVA K. (IFEX/
        Sovexportfilm-1982-Nikolai Lebedev & Ernest Yasin-N/R).
        Screenplay by Mikhail Lvovsky. (W)

2343.   MY DINNER WITH ANDRE. (New Yorker-1981-Louis Malle-
        N/R). Screenplay by Wallace Shawn and Andre Gregory;
        screenplay published by Grove Press, 1981, 240p. (BFI,
        LACOPL, LAT, W)

2344.   MY EROTIC FANTASIES. (William Mishkin-1976-X). No
        production credits available. (W)

2345.   MY FAVORITE YEAR. (MGM/UA-1982-Richard Benjamin-PG).
        Screenplay written by Norman Steinberg and Dennis Palumbo,
        from a story by Dennis Palumbo. (V)

2346.   MY FRIENDS. (Allied Artists-1976-Mario Monicelli-N/R).
        Screenplay written by Pietro Germi, Piero de Barnardi,
        Leo Benvenuti, and Tullio Pinelli. (NYT, W)

2347.   MY FRIENDS NEED KILLING. (Nick Felix-1984-Paul Leder-
        R). Screenplay written by Paul Leder. (V)

2348.   MY LOVE HAS BEEN BURNING. (New Yorker-1979-Kenji
        Mizoguchi-N/R). Screenplay written by Yoshikata Yoda and
        Kaneto Shindo, from a story by Kogo Noda. (W)

2349.   MY LOVE LETTERS. (New World Pictures-1983-Amy Jones-
        R). Screenplay written by Amy Jones. (V)

2350.   MY MICHAEL. (Alfred Plaine-1976-Dan Wolman-N/R).
        Screenplay by Dan Wolman. (NYT, W)

2351.   MY NAME IS LEGEND. (SR-1976-Duke Kelly-G). Screen-
        play credits not available. (W)

2352.   MY NAME IS ROCCO PAPALEO. (Rumson-1979-Ettore Scola-
        N/R). Screenplay written by Ruggero Maccari and Ettore
        Scola. (W)

2353.   MY PLEASURE IS MY BUSINESS. (Brian-1975-Albert S.
        Waxman-R). Screenplay written by Alvin Boretz. (W)

2354.   MY TUTOR. (Crown International Pictures-1983-George
        Bowers-R). Screenplay written by Joe Roberts. (BFI,
        LAT, V, W)

2355. THE MYSTERIOUS CASTLE IN THE CARPATHIANS. (IFEX-
       1983-Oldrich Lipsky-N/R). Screenplay by Jiri Brdecka and
       Oldrich Lipsky, based on the novel of the same title by
       Jules Verne. (W)

2356. THE MYSTERIOUS HOUSE OF DR. C. (Samuel Bronston-
       1976-Ted Kneeland-N/R). Screenplay and story freely
       adapted and expanded from the ballet Copelia, by Jo-Anna
       Kneeland and Ted Kneeland. (V)

2357. THE MYSTERY OF KASPAR HAUSER. (Cinema 5-1975-
       Werner Herzog-N/R). Screenplay written by Werner Herzog.
       (W)

2358. NADIA. (Dave Bell/Tribune Entertainment-1984-Allan Cooke-
       N/R). Screenplay by James T. McGinn, from an original
       story. (V)

2359. NAKED AFTERNOON. (Westwood-1976-Alan B. Goldberg-
       X). Screenplay by Utah Green. (W)

2360. NAKED CAME THE STRANGER. (Catalyst-1975-Henry Paris
       aka Radley Metzger-X). Screenplay by Jake Barnes, based
       on the novel by Penelope Ashe. (W)

2361. NAKED EVIL. (Hampton International-1975-Stanley Goulder-
       PG). Screenplay credits not available, based on the play
       The Obi by Jon Manchip White. (W)

2362. THE NAKED FACE. (MGM/UA-1984-Bryan Forbes-N/R).
       Screenplay by Bryan Forbes, based on the novel by Sidney
       Sheldon; Morrow, 1970, 214p. (LACOPL, V)

2363. NANA. (Cannon Group-1983-Dan Wolman-N/R). Screenplay
       by Marc Behm. (V, W)

2364. THE NARK. (A.A.A.-1982-Bob Swain-N/R). Screenplay by
       Bob Swain and M. Fabiani. (V)

2365. NASHVILLE. (Paramount-1975-Robert Altman-R). Screen-
       play by Joan Tewkesbury. (Q, W)

2366. NASHVILLE GIRL. (New World-1976-Gus Trikonis-R).
       Screenplay written by Peer J. Oppenheimer. (W)

2367. NASTY HABITS. (Brut-1976-Michael Lindsay-Hogg-PG).
       Screenplay by Robert Enders, adapted from Muriel Spark's
       The Abbess of Crewe; Viking Press, 1974, 116p. (LACOPL,
       Q, V)

2368. NATE AND HAYES. (Paramount-1983-Ferdinand Fairfax-PG).

Screenplay by John Hughes and David Odell, from a screen
story by David Odell, based on a story by Lloyd Phillips.
(LAT, V, W)

2369. THE NATIONAL HEALTH OR NURSE NORTON'S AFFAIR.
       (Columbia-1979-Jack Gold-N/R). Screenplay written by
       Peter Nichols, from his play. (W)

2370. NATIONAL LAMPOON GOES TO THE MOVIES. (United
       Artists-1983-Bob Giraldi, Henry Jaglom-R). Screenplay by
       Tod Carroll, Shary Flenniken, Pat Mephitis, Gerald Sussman,
       and Ellis Weiner. (V)

2371. NATIONAL LAMPOON'S ANIMAL HOUSE. (Universal-1978-
       John Landis-R). Screenplay by Harold Ramis, Douglas
       Kenney, and Chris Miller. (Q, V, W)

2372. NATIONAL LAMPOON'S CLASS REUNION. (20th Century-
       Fox-1982-Michael Miller-R). Screenplay written by John
       Hughes. (V, W)

2373. NATIONAL LAMPOON'S VACATION. (Warner Bros.-1983-
       Harold Ramis-R). Screenplay by John Hughes. (LAT, V)

2374. THE NATURAL. (Tri-Star-1984-Barry Levinson-PG).
       Screenplay by Roger Towne and Phil Dusenberry, based
       on the novel by Bernard Malamud; Harcourt, 1952.
       (LACOPL, LAT, V)

2375. NATURAL ENEMIES. (Cinema 5-1979-Jeff Kanew-R).
       Screenplay by Jeff Kanew, based on a novel by Julius
       Horwitz; Holt, 1975, 215p. (LACOPL, Q, V, W)

2376. THE NAUGHTY ROOMMATES. (Hemisphere-1975-Franz Antel-
       R). Screenplay by Kurt Nachman. (W)

2377. NAUGHTY SCHOOL GIRLS. (NMD-1976-Jean Paul Scardino-
       R). Screenplay by Alonzo Pye. (W)

2378. THE NAUGHTY STEWARDESSES. (Independent International-
       1975-Al Adamson-R). Screenplay credits not available. (W)

2379. THE NAUGHTY VICTORIANS. (Hawthorne International-
       1975-Robert S. Kinger-X). Screenplay by Robert S. Kinger,
       from A Man with a Maid. (W)

2380. NEA: A NEW WOMAN. (Libra-1978-Nelly Kaplan-R). Screen-
       play written by Nelly Kaplan and Jean Chapot. (LACOPL, W)

2381. NEIGE. (Papp/Public-1983-Juliet Berto and Jean-Henri
       Roger-N/R). Screenplay by Marc Villard, from an idea by
       Juliet Berto. (W)

2382. NEIGHBORS. (Columbia-1981-John G. Avildsen-R). Screen-
       play by Larry Gelbart, based on the novel by Thomas Ber-
       ger; Dell, 1981, 288p. (BFI, HR, LACOPL, LAT, Q, V, W)

2383. NELLY'S VERSION. (Mithras Films-1983-Maurice Hatton-
       N/R). Screenplay by Maurice Hatton. (V)

       NEMO see DREAM ON

2384. THE NEST. (Quartet-1982-Jaime De Arminan-PG). Screen-
       play by Jaime De Arminan. (W)

2385. A NEST IN THE WIND. (IFEX-Sovexportfilm-1982-Olav
       Neuland-N/R). Screenplay by Izakas Fridbergas and
       Grigory Kanovicus. (W)

2386. NEST OF VIPERS. (Paramount-1979-Tonino Cervi-R).
       Screenplay by Tonino Cervi, Cesare Frugoni, Goffredo
       Parise, based on the short story "The Piano Teacher" by
       Roger Peyrefitte. (V, W)

2387. THE NESTING. (Feature Films-1981-Armand Weston-R).
       Screenplay by Daria Price and Armand Weston. (V, W)

2388. NETWORK. (United Artists-1976-Sidney Lumet-R). Screen-
       play written by Paddy Chayefsky; novelization by Sam Hed-
       rin; Pocket Books, 1976, 188p. (HR, LACOPL, LAT, NYT,
       Q, V, W)

2389. NEVER CRY WOLF. (Buena Vista-1984-Carroll Ballard-PG).
       Screenplay by Curtis Hanson, Sam Hamm and Richard Klet-
       ter, based on a book by Farley Mowat; Little, Brown, 1963,
       247p. (BFI, LACOPL, V)

2390. NEVER NEVER LAND. (Sharp Features-1982-Paul Annell-G).
       Screenplay written by Marjorie L. Sigley. (W)

2391. NEVER SAY NEVER AGAIN. (Warner Bros.-1983-Irvin
       Kershner-PG). Screenplay by Lorenzo Semple Jr., story by
       Kevin McClory, Jack Whittingham, and Ian Fleming. (BFI,
       HR, LAT, V, W)

2392. NEVER TOO YOUNG TO ROCK. (Libert International-1976-
       Dennis Abey-G). Screenplay by Ron Inkpen and Dennis
       Abey. (W)

2393. THE NEVERENDING STORY. (Warner Bros.-1984-Wolfgang
       Petersen-PG). Screenplay by Wolfgang Petersen and Herman
       Weigel, from a novel by Michael Ende; Doubleday, 1983,
       396p. (BFI, HR, LACOPL, LAT, V)

2394. NEVERMORE, FOREVER. (French Embassy-1979-Jacqueline
       Doye-N/R). Screenplay by Yannick Bellon. (W)

2395. THE NEW ADVENTURES OF SNOW WHITE. (NMD-1980-Rolf
       Thiel-R). Screenplay written by Tom Baum. (W)

2396. THE NEW BARBARIANS. (1983-Enzo G. Castellari). Screen-
       play by Tito Carpi, Enzo Girolami, from a story by Tito
       Carpi. (BFI)

2397. A NEW GIRL IN TOWN. (Stone-1975-Veronica Stone-X).
       Screenplay by Veronica Stone. (W)

2398. NEW HOUSE ON THE LEFT. (Central Park-1978-Evans
       Isle-R). Screenplay credits not available. (W)

2399. NEW YEAR'S EVIL. (Cannon-1981-Emmett Alston-R).
       Screenplay by Leonard Neubauer. (BFI, V, W)

2400. NEW YORK, NEW YORK. (United Artists-1977-Martin
       Scorsese-PG). Screenplay written by Earl Mac Rauch and
       Mardik Martin; novelization by Earl Mac Rauch; Pocket Books,
       1977, 224p. (HR, LACOPL, LAT, Q, V, W)

2401. NEW YORK NIGHTS. (Bedford Entertainment-1984-Simon
       Nuchtern-R). Screenplay by Romano Vanderbes, loosely
       based on Arthur Schnitzler's play Reigen. (V)

2402. NEWSFRONT. (New Yorker-1979-Phillip Noyce-PG). Screen-
       play by Phillip Noyce and Bob Ellis, from a concept by
       Phillipe Mora and David Elfick. (W)

2403. THE NEXT MAN. (Allied Artists-1976-Richard Sarafian-R).
       Screenplay by Mort Fine, Alan Trustman, David M. Wolf,
       and Richard Sarafian, based on a story by Martin Bregman
       and Alan Trustman; novelization by Michael Z. Lewin; War-
       ner, 1976, 221p. (LACOPL, Q, V)

2404. NEXT OF KIN. (Miracle-1982-Tony Williams-N/R). Screen-
       play by Michael Heath and Tony Williams. (BFI)

2405. THE NEXT ONE. (Allstar Prods.-1984-Nico Mastorakis-N/R).
       Screenplay written by Nico Mastorakis. (V)

2406. NEXT STOP, GREENWICH VILLAGE. (20th Century-Fox-
       1976-Paul Mazursky-R). Screenplay by Paul Mazursky. (W)

2407. NEXT YEAR IF ALL GOES WELL. (New World-1983-Jean-
       Loup Hubert-R). Screenplay by Jean-Loup Hubert, Josyane
       Balasko, and Gerard Zingg. (W)

2408. NICKELODEON. (Columbia-1976-Peter Bogdanovich-PG).
       Screenplay by W. D. Richter and Peter Bogdanovich. (Q,
       V)

       EL NIDO see THE NEST

2409. NIGHT CALLER. (Columbia-1975-Henri Verneuil-R).
       Screenplay adaptation by Henri Verneuil, Jean Laborde,
       Francois Veber, and Paulette Rubinstein. (W)

2410. NIGHT CALLER. (Essex-1976-Wes Brown-X). Screenplay
       by Dean Rogers. (W)

2411. NIGHT CHILD. (Film Ventures International-1976-Max
       Dallamano-R). Screenplay written by Max Dallamano. (W)

2412. NIGHT CREATURE. (Dimension-1979-Lee Madden-PG).
       Screenplay by Hubert Smith, based on a story by Lee Mad-
       den and Hubert Smith. (V)

2413. NIGHT CROSSING. (Buena Vista-1981-Delbert Mann-PG).
       Screenplay by John McGreevey. (LAT, Q, V)

2414. NIGHT EXTERIOR. (Les Films Noirs-1980-Jacques Bral-
       N/R). Screenplay by Jacques Bral, from an idea by Noel
       Burch. (V)

2415. NIGHT GAMES. (Avco Embassy-1980-Roger Vadim-R).
       Screenplay by Anton Diether, Clarke Reynolds, based on
       a story by Anton Diether and Barth Jules Sussman. (V, W)

2416. THE NIGHT GOD SCREAMED. (Cinemation-1975-Lee Madden-
       R). Screenplay by Gil Lasky. (W)

2417. A NIGHT IN HEAVEN. (20th Century-Fox-1983-John G.
       Avildsen-R). Screenplay written by Joan Tewkesbury.
       (HR, LAT, V, W)

2418. NIGHT MOVES. (Warner Bros.-1975-Arthur Penn-R).
       Screenplay written by Alan Sharp. (Q, W)

2419. THE NIGHT OF COUNTING THE YEARS. (New Yorker-
       1975-Shadi Abdelsalam-N/R). Screenplay written by Shadi
       Abdelsalam. (W)

2420. NIGHT OF THE ASKARI. (Topar-1978-Juergen Goslar-R).
       Screenplay by Juergen Goslar and Scot Finch, based on the
       novel by Daniel Carney. (W)

2421. NIGHT OF THE COMET. (Atlantic Releasing-1984-Thom
       Eberhardt-PG-13). Screenplay by Thom Eberhardt. (V)

2422. NIGHT OF THE JUGGLER. (Columbia-1980-Tobert Butler-R).
       Screenplay by Bill Norton Sr. and Rick Natkin, from a novel
       by William P. McGivern; Putnam, 1975, 310p. (LACOPL, V,
       W)

2423. THE NIGHT OF THE PROWLER. (International Harmony-
       1979-Jim Sharman-N/R). Screenplay written by Patrick
       White. (W)

2424. THE NIGHT OF THE SHOOTING STARS. (United Artists
       Classics-1982-Paolo and Vittorio Taviani-R). Screenplay
       written by Paolo and Vittorio Taviani, Giuliani G. DeNegri,
       and Tonino Guerra. (W)

2425. NIGHT OF THE STRANGLER. (Howco-1975-Joy N. Houck
       Jr.-R). Screenplay credits not available. (W)

2426. NIGHT OF THE ZOMBIES. (NMD-1981-Joel M. Reed-R).
       Screenplay by Joel M. Reed. (V, W)

2427. NIGHT OF THE ZOMBIES. (Motion Picture Marketing-1983-
       Vincent Dawn-N/R). Screenplay by Claudio Fragasso and
       J. M. Cunilles. (V)

2428. NIGHT PATROL. (New World Pictures-1984-Jackie Kong-R).
       Screenplay by Murray Langston, Bill Levy, Bill Osco, and
       Jackie Kong. (V)

2429. NIGHT PLEASURES. (San Fran-1976-Hans Christian-X).
       Screenplay credits not available. (W)

2430. NIGHT SCHOOL. (Lorimar/Paramount-1981-Kenneth Hughes-
       R). Screenplay by Ruth Avergon. (V, W)

2431. NIGHT SHADOWS. (Film Ventures International-1984-John
       Bud Cardos-R). Screenplay written by Peter Z. Orton,
       Michael Jones, John C. Kruize, from a story by Michael
       Jones and John C. Kruize. (V)

2432. NIGHT SHIFT. (Ladd Co.-Warner Bros.-1982-Ron Howard-
       R). Screenplay by Lowell Ganz and Babaloo Mandel. (Q,
       V, W)

2433. THE NIGHT THE LIGHTS WENT OUT IN GEORGIA. (Avco
       Embassy-1981-Ronald F. Maxwell-PG). Screenplay by Bob
       Bonney, based on the song by Bobby Russell. (LAT, Q,
       V, W)

2434. THE NIGHT THEY ROBBED BIG BERTHA'S. (Scotia Ameri-
       can-1975-Peter Kares-R). Screenplay based on a story by
       Albert T. Viola and Robert Vervoordt, from an idea by
       Robert N. Langworthy. (W)

2435. NIGHT WARNING. (Comworld Pictures-1983-William Asher-R).
       Screenplay written by Stephen Breimer, Alan Jay Glueckman,
       and Boon Collins, from a story by Alan Jay Glueckman and
       Boon Collins. (V, W)

2436. NIGHTBEAST. (Amazing Films-1982-Don Dohler-R). Screen-
       play written by Don Dohler. (W)

2437. NIGHTHAWKS. (Four Corner Films-1978-Ron Peck-N/R).
       Screenplay by Ron Peck and Paul Hallam. (V, W)

2438. NIGHTHAWKS. (Universal-1981-Bruce Malmuth-R). Screen-
       play by David Shaber, story by David Shaber and Paul
       Sylbert. (LAT, Q, W)

2439. NIGHTMARE. (21st Century Distribution-1981-Romano
       Scavolini-N/R). Screenplay by Romano Scavolini. (V, W)

       NIGHTMARE CITY see NIGHTMARE

2440. NIGHTMARE IN BLOOD. (PFE-1978-John Stanley-R).
       Screenplay by John Stanley and Kenn Davis. (BFI, W)

2441. A NIGHTMARE ON ELM STREET. (New Line Cinema-1984-
       Wes Craven-R). Screenplay by Wes Craven. (V)

2442. NIGHTMARES. (Universal-1983-Joseph Sargent-R). Screen-
       play written by Christopher Crowe and Jeffrey Bloom.
       (BFI, LAT, V, W)

2443. NIGHTS AT O'REAR'S. (American Film Institute-1981-Robert
       Mandel-N/R). Screenplay by Maurice Noel, from a story by
       Patricia Griffith. (V)

2444. NIGHTSONGS. (Thomas A. Fucci-1984-Marva Nabili-N/R).
       Screenplay by Marva Nabili. (V)

2445. NIGHTWING. (Columbia-1979-Arthur Hiller-PG). Screenplay
       by Steve Shagan, Bud Shrake, Martin Cruz Smith, based on
       a novel by Martin Cruz Smith; Jove, 1977, 255p. (LACOPL,
       Q, V, W)

2446. NIJINSKY. (Paramount-1980-Herbert Ross-R). Screenplay
       by Hugh Wheeler, based on Nijinsky by Romola Nijinsky--
       Simon & Schuster, 1934--and the Diary of Vaslav Nijinsky--
       Cape, 1963, 160p. (LACOPL, Q, V, W)

2447. NINE LIVES OF A WET PUSSYCAT. (Navaron-1976-Jimmy
       Laine-X). Screenplay written by Nicholas George. (W)

2448. NINE MONTHS. (New Yorker-1981-Marta Meszaros-N/R).

Screenplay by Gyula Hernadi, Ildiko Korody, and Marta Meszaros. (W)

2449. 9/30/55. (Universal-1977-James Bridges-PG). Screenplay by James Bridges; novelization by John Minahan; Avon, 1977. (LACOPL, V, W)

2450. NINE TO FIVE. (20th Century-Fox-1980-Colin Higgins-PG). Screenplay by Colin Higgins and Patricia Resnick, based on a story by Patricia Resnick; novelization by Thom Racima; Bantam Books, 1980. (LACOPL, Q, V, W)

2451. 1984. (Atlantic Releasing Organisation-1984-Michael Radford-R). Screenplay by Michael Radford, based on the book by George Orwell; Harcourt, 1949, 314p. (BFI, HR, LACOPL, LAT, NYT, V)

2452. 1941. (Universal-1979-Steven Spielberg-PG). Screenplay by Robert Zemeckis and Bob Gale, from a story by Robert Zemeckis, Bob Gale, and John Milius; novelization by Bob Gale; Ballantine Books, 1979. (HR, LACOPL, LAT, V, W)

2453. 1900. (Paramount-1977-Bernardo Bertolucci-N/R). Screenplay by Bernardo Bertolucci, Franco Arcalli, and Giuseppe Bertolucci. (Q, W)

2454. 1990: THE BRONX WARRIORS. (United Film Distribution-1983-Enzo G. Castellari-R). Screenplay by Dardano Sacchetti, Elisa Livia Briganti, and Enzo G. Castellari, from a story by Dardano Sacchetti. (LAT, V, W)

2455. 92 IN THE SHADE. (United Artists-1975-Thomas McGuane-R). Screenplay by Thomas McGuane. (W)

2456. NINJA III--THE DOMINATION. (MGM/UA-1984-Sam Firstenberg-N/R). Screenplay by James R. Silke, from his original story. (HAR, LAT, V)

2457. THE NINTH CONFIGURATION. (Warner Bros.-1980-William Peter Blatty-R). Screenplay by William Peter Blatty, from his novel; Harper, 1978, 135p. (LACOPL, V)

2458. THE NINTH HEART. (Ceskoslovensky Filmexport-1980-Juraj Herz-N/R). Screenplay by Juraj Herz, story by Josef Hanzlik. (V)

2459. NO DEPOSIT, NO RETURN. (Buena Vista-1976-Norman Tokar-G). Screenplay by Arthur Alsberg and Don Nelson, story by Joe McEveety. (W)

2460. NO LONGER ALONE. (World Wide Pictures-1978-Nicholas

Webster-N/R). Screenplay by Lawrence Holben, based on
an autobiography by Joan Winmill Brown. (V, W)

2461. THE NO MERCY MAN. (Cannon-1975-Daniel Vance-R).
Screenplay by Daniel Vance and Mike Nolin. (W)

2462. NO PLACE TO HIDE. (American Films Ltd.-1975-Robert
Allen Schnitzer-R). Screenplay by Robert Allen Schnitzer
and Larry Beinhart. (W)

2463. NO PROBLEM! (Cine III-1978-Georges Lautner-N/R).
Screenplay by Jean-Marie Poire. (W)

2464. NO REGRETS FOR OUR YOUTH. (Corinth-1980-Akira
Kurosawa-N/R). Screenplay credits not available. (W)

2465. NO SEX PLEASE--WE'RE BRITISH. (Columbia-1979-Cliff
Owen-N/R). Screenplay by Anthony Marriott, Johnnie
Mortimer, and Brian Cooke. (W)

2466. NO SMALL AFFAIR. (Columbia-1984-Jerry Schatzberg-R).
Screenplay by Charles Bolt and Terence Mulcahy, story by
Charles Bolt. (V)

2467. NO TIME FOR BREAKFAST. (Daniel Bourla-1980-Jean-
Louis Bertucelli-N/R). Screenplay written by Andre G.
Brunelin and M. Bertucelli, based on the book Un Cri by
Noelle Loriot; B. Grosset, 1976, 221p. (LACOPL, W)

2468. NO WAY BACK. (Atlas-1976-Fred Williamson-R). Screenplay written by Fred Williamson. (W)

2469. NO WAY OUT. (Cinema Shares International-1975-Duccia
Tessari-R). Screenplay credits not available. (W)

2470. NOBODY'S PERFEKT. (Columbia-1981-Peter Bonerz-PG).
Screenplay by Tony Kenrick, based on his novel Two for
the Price of One; Bobbs, 1974, 241p. (LACOPL, Q, V, W)

2471. NOCTURNA. (Compass International-1979-Harry Tampa aka
Harry Hurwitz-R). Screenplay by Harry Tampa (aka Harry
Hurwitz), based on a story by Nai Bonet. (V, W)

2472. NORMA RAE. (20th Century-Fox-1979-Martin Ritt-PG).
Screenplay by Irving Ravetch and Harriet Frank Jr. (Q,
V, W)

2473. NORMAN ... IS THAT YOU? (United Artists-1976-George
Schlatter-PG). Screenplay by Ron Clark, Sam Bobrick, and
George Schlatter, based on the play of the same title by Ron
Clark and Sam Bobrick. (Q, W)

2474. NORMAN LOVES ROSE. (Atlantic-1982-Henri Safran-R).
       Screenplay by Henri Safran. (W)

2475. NORMANDE. (Fred Baker Films-1979-Gilles Carle-PG).
       Screenplay by Gilles Carle and Ben Barzman. (W)

2476. THE NORSEMAN. (American International-1978-Charles B.
       Pierce-PG). Screenplay written by Charles B. Pierce. (W)

2477. THE NORTH AVENUE IRREGULARS. (Buena Vista-1979-
       Bruce Bilson-G). Screenplay by Don Tait, from the book
       by Rev. Albert Fay Hill; Cowles, 1968, 248p. (LACOPL,
       Q, V, W)

2478. NORTH DALLAS FORTY. (Paramount-1979-Ted Kotcheff-R).
       Screenplay by Frank Yablans, Ted Kotcheff, and Peter Gent,
       based on the novel by Peter Gent; Morrow, 1973, 314p.
       (LACOPL, Q, V, W)

2479. THE NORTH STAR. (Parafrance-1982-Pierre Granier-
       Deferre-N/R). Screenplay by Pierre Granier-Deferre, Jean
       Aurenche, and Michel Grisolia, based on Le Locataire by
       Georges Simenon. (V)

2480. NORTHERN LIGHTS. (Cine Manifest-1978-John Hanson and
       Rob Nilsson-N/R). Screenplay by John Hanson and Rob
       Nilsson. (V, W)

2481. THE NORTHVILLE CEMETERY MASSACRE. (Cannon-1976-
       William Dear and Thomas L. Dyke-R). Screenplay credits
       not available. (W)

2482. NOSFERATU THE VAMPYRE. (20th Century-Fox-1979-
       Werner Herzog-PG). Screenplay by Werner Herzog. (W)

       NOSTALGHIA see NOSTALGIA

2483. NOSTALGIA. (Grange Communication-1983-Andrei Tarkovsky-
       N/R). Screenplay by Andrei Tarkovsky and Jestore Bara-
       tella. (BFI, V, W)

2484. NOT FOR PUBLICATION. (Anne Kimmel-1984-Paul Bartel-
       N/R). Screenplay by John Meyer and Paul Bartel. (V)

2485. NOT MY DAUGHTER. (Carvel-1975-Jerry Schafer-R).
       Screenplay and story by Lawrence Holden. (W)

2486. NOT NOW DARLING. (Dimension-1975-David Croft and Ray
       Cooney-R). Screenplay by John Chapman. (W)

2487. NOTHING BUT THE NIGHT. (Cinema Systems-1975-Peter

Sasdy-PG). No screenplay credit given; based on the novel
by John Blackburn. (W)

2488. NOTHING BY CHANCE. (R. C. Riddle-1975-William H.
Barnett-G). Screenplay by Richard Bach, based on his
book of the same title; Morrow, 1969, 223p. (LACOPL, W)

2489. NOTHING LASTS FOREVER. (MGM/UA Classics-1984-Tom
Schiller-PG). Screenplay written by Tom Schiller. (V)

2490. NOTHING PERSONAL. (American International Pictures-
1980-George Bloomfield-PG). Screenplay by Robert Kaufman. (V, W)

2491. THE NOVICES. (Monarch-1976-Guy Casaril-R). Screenplay
credits not given. (W)

2492. NOW AND FOREVER. (Inter Planetary-1983-Adrian Carr-R).
Screenplay by Richard Cassidy, based on the novel by
Danielle Steel; Dell, 1978, 429p. (LACOPL, W)

2493. THE NUDE BOMB. (Universal-1980-Clive Donner-PG).
Screenplay by Arne Sultan, Bill Dana, and Leonard B.
Stern, based on characters created by Mel Brooks and Buck
Henry. (Q, V, W)

NUDO DI DONNA see PORTRAIT OF A WOMAN, NUDE

2494. LA NUIT DE VARENNES. (Triumph/Columbia-1982-Ettore
Scola-N/R). Screenplay by Ettore Scola and Sergio Amidei.
(FD, V)

LES NUITS DE LA PLEINE LUNE see FULL MOON IN PARIS

2495. NUNZIO. (Universal-1978-Paul Williams-PG). Screenplay by
James Andronica; novelization by John Minahan; Ballantine
Books, 1978. (LACOPL, W)

I NUOVI BARBARI see THE NEW BARBARIANS

2496. NURITH. (Cinemagic-1975-George Ovadia-PG). Screenplay
by Ada Ben Nachum. (W)

2497. NURSE SHERRI. (Independent International-1978-Al Adamson-
R). Screenplay by Michael Bockman and Gregg Tittinger.
(W)

2498. NUTCRACKER. (Jezzshaw Film-1982-Anwar Kawadri-N/R).
Screenplay by Raymond Christodoulou. (V)

2499. NUTCRACKER FANTASY. (Sanrio Films-1979-Takeo Nakamura-

G). Screenplay adaptation by Thomas Joachim and Eugene
Fournier, from a story by Shintaro Tsuji, based on "The
Nutcracker and the Mouseking" by E. T. A. Hoffman. (V,
W)

2500. NYMPH. (Jack H. Harris-1975-William Dear-R). Screenplay
credits not available. (W)

2501. LES NYMPHO TEENS. (Troma-1976-David Stitt-X). Screenplay credits not available. (W)

O MEGALEXANDROS see ALEXANDER THE GREAT

2502. THE OASIS. (Titan-1984-Sparky Greene-N/R). Screenplay
written by Tom Klassen, based on a story by Myron Meisel
and Sparky Greene. (V)

2503. OBLOMOV. (International Film Exchange-1981-Nikita Mikhal-
kov-N/R). Screenplay by Alexander Adabashyan, Nikita
Mikhalkov, based on the novel by Ivan Goncharov. (LAT,
W)

2504. THE OBSESSED ONE. (21st Century-1978-Ramdjan
Abdoelrahman-R). Screenplay by Ramdjan Abdoelrahman.
(W)

2505. OBSESSION. (Columbia-1976-Brian De Palma-PG). Screenplay written by Paul Schrader. (Q, W)

2506. THE OCTAGON. (American Cinema-1980-Eric Karson-R).
Screenplay by Leigh Chapman, from a story by Paul Aaron
and Leigh Chapman. (V, W)

2507. OCTOPUSSY. (MGM/UA-1983-John Glen-PG). Screenplay
and screen story by George MacDonald Fraser, Richard
Maibaum, and Michael G. Wilson, based on the stories "Octopussy" and "The Property of a Lady" by Ian Fleming.
(LAT, V)

2508. THE ODD JOB. (Columbia-1978-Peter Medak-N/R). Screenplay by Bernard McKenna and Graham Chapman. (V)

2509. ODE TO BILLY JOE. (Warner Bros.-1976-Max Baer-PG).
Screenplay by Herman Raucher, story by Herman Raucher
based on a song by Bobbie Gentry. (W)

2510. ODYSSEY. (ASOM Distributing-1977-Gerard Damiano-X).
Screenplay written by Gerard Damiano. (V)

2511. OF UNKNOWN ORIGIN. (Warner Bros.-1983-George Pan
Cosmatos-R). Screenplay by Brian Taggert, from the novel
The Visitor by Chauncey G. Parker III. (LAT, V, W)

2512. OFF THE WALL. (Jensen Farley-1983-Rick Friedberg-R).
       Screenplay by Ron Kurz, Dick Chudnow, and Rick Friedberg.
       (W)

2513. THE OFFENDERS. (B Movies-1980-Scott B and Beth B-N/R).
       Screenplay written by Scott B and Beth B. (W)

2514. AN OFFICER AND A GENTLEMAN. (Paramount-1982-Taylor
       Hackford-R). Screenplay written by Douglas Day Stewart;
       novelization by Stephen P. Smith; Avon, 1982. (HR,
       LACOPL, Q, V)

2515. OH! ALFIE. (Cinema National-1976-Ken Hughes-R).
       Screenplay by Ken Hughes, based on the novel Alfie Darling
       by Bill Naughton. (W)

       OH BROTHERHOOD see FRATERNITY ROW

2516. OH, GOD! (Warner Bros.-1977-Carl Reiner-PG). Screen-
       play by Larry Gelbart, based on a novel by Avery Corman;
       Simon & Schuster, 1971, 190p. (LACOPL, Q, W)

2517. OH, GOD! BOOK II. (Warner Bros.-1980-Gilbert Cates-
       PG). Screenplay by Josh Greenfeld, Hal Goldman, Fred S.
       Fox, Seaman Jacbos, and Melissa Miller, from a story by
       Josh Greenfeld. (Q, V, W)

2518. OH, GOD, YOU DEVIL. (Warner Bros.-1984-Paul Bogart-
       PG). Screenplay by Andrew Bergman. (V)

2519. OH HEAVENLY DOG. (20th Century-Fox-1980-Joe Camp-
       PG). Screenplay by Rod Browning and Joe Camp; noveliza-
       tion by Joe Camp; Scholastic, 1980. (LACOPL, Q, V, W)

2520. O'HARA'S WIFE. (Davis-Panzer-1982-William S. Bartman-
       N/R). Screenplay by James Nasella and William S. Bartman,
       based on a story by William S. Bartman and Joseph Scott
       Kierland. (V)

2521. OIL LAMPS. (Filmaco-1975-Juraj Herz-PG). Screenplay by
       Vaclav Sasek, Lubor Dohani, and Juraj Herz, from a novel
       by Jaroslav Havlicek. (W)

2522. OLD BOYFRIENDS. (Avco Embassy-1979-Joan Tewkesbury-
       R). Screenplay by Paul Schrader and Leonard Schrader;
       novelization by Susan Braudy; Jove, 1979, 192p. (HR,
       LACOPL, LAT, Q, V, W)

2523. OLD DRACULA. (American International-1975-Clive Donner-
       PG). Screenplay by Jeremy Lloyd. (W)

2524. OLD ENOUGH. (Orion Classics-1984-Marisa Silver-N/R). Screenplay by Maris Silver. (V)

2525. THE OLD GUN. (Surrogate-1976-Robert Enrico-N/R). Screenplay by Pascal Jardin, Robert Enrico, and Claude Veillot. (W)

2526. OLIVER'S STORY. (Paramount-1978-John Korty-PG). Screenplay by Erich Segal and John Korty, based on Erich Segal's novel; Harper & Row, 1977, 264p. (BFI, HR, LACOPL, LAT, Q, V, W)

2527. OLLY, OLLY, OXEN FREE. (Sanrio Film Distribution-1978-Richard A. Colla-G). Screenplay by Eugene Poinc, based on a story by Maria L. de Ossio, Eugene Poinc, and Richard A. Colla. (HR, V, W)

2528. THE OMEN. (20th Century-Fox-1976-Richard Donner-R). Screenplay by David Seltzer; novelization by David Seltzer; New American Library, 1976, 202p. (HR, LACOPL, LAT, NYT, Q, V, W)

ON AURA TOUT TU see THE BOTTOM LINE

2529. ON GOLDEN POND. (Universal-AFD-1981-Mark Rydell-PG). Screenplay by Ernest Thompson, based on his play. (HR, LAT, Q, V)

2530. ON THE AIR LIVE WITH CAPTAIN MIDNIGHT. (Sebastian International-1979-Beverly Sebastian and Ferd Sebastian-PG). Screenplay by Beverly Sebastian and Ferd Sebastian. (W)

2531. ON THE NICKEL. (Rose's Park-1980-Ralph Waite-N/R). Screenplay by Ralph Waite. (V, W)

2532. ON THE RIGHT TRACK. (20th Century-Fox-1981-Lee Philips-PG). Screenplay by Tina Pine, Avery Buddy, and Richard Moses. (LAT, V, W)

2533. ON THE RUN. (Cineworld-1983-Mende Brown-N/R). Screenplay by Michael Fisher. (V, W)

2534. ON THE YARD. (Midwest Films-1978-Raphael D. Silver-N/R). Screenplay by Malcolm Braly, from his novel of the same title; Little, Brown, 1967. (BFI, LACOPL, Q, V, W)

2535. ONCE IN PARIS. (Frank D. Gilroy-1978-Frank D. Gilroy-N/R). Screenplay by Frank D. Gilroy. (Q, V, W)

2536. ONCE UPON A GIRL. (PRO International-1976-Don Jurwich-X). Screenplay credits not given. (W)

2537. ONCE UPON A TIME. (Janus-1982-Girish Karnad-N/R).
Screenplay by Krishna Basrur and Girish Karnad; dialogue
by G. B. Joshi. (W)

2538. ONCE UPON A TIME IN AMERICA. (Ladd Co.-1984-Sergio
Leone-R). Screenplay by Leonardo Benvenuti, Piero DeBernardi, Enrico Medioli, Franco Arcalli, Franco Ferrini, and
Sergio Leone; additional dialogue by Stuart Kaminsky; based
on the novel The Hoods by Harry Grey. (V)

2539. ONCE UPON A TIME IN THE EAST. (SNC-1975-Andre Bras-
sard-N/R). Screenplay by Andre Brassard and Michel Trem-
blay. (W)

2540. ONE AND ONE. (New Line-1980-Erland Josephson-N/R).
Screenplay by Erland Josephson. (W)

2541. THE ONE AND ONLY. (Paramount-1978-Carl Reiner-PG).
Screenplay by Steve Gordon; novelization by Ron de Christofaro; Pocket Books, 1978. (LACOPL, Q, V, W)

2542. ONE-ARMED EXECUTIONER. (Super Pix-1983-Bobby A.
Suarez-R). Screenplay by Wray Hamilton. (W)

2543. ONE CHANCE TO WIN. (Pan American-1976-G). No screenplay credits available. (W)

2544. ONE DARK NIGHT. (ComWorld-1983-Tom McLoughlin-PG).
Screenplay by Tom McLoughlin and Michael Hawes. (V, W)

2545. ONE DEADLY SUMMER. (SNC-1983-Jean Becker-N/R).
Screenplay written by Sebastien Japrisot from his novel.
(V)

2546. ONE DOWN, TWO TO GO. (Almi Distribution Corp.-1982-
Fred Williamson-R). Screenplay by Jeff Williamson. (V, W)

2547. ONE FLEW OVER THE CUCKOO'S NEST. (United Artists-
1975-Milos Forman-R). Screenplay by Lawrence Hauben, Bo
Goldman, based on the novel of the same title by Ken Kesey;
Viking Press, 1962, 311p. (LACOPL, Q, W)

2548. ONE FROM THE HEART. (Zoetrope Studios-1982-Francis
Coppola-N/R). Screenplay by Armyan Bernstein and Francis
Coppola, based on a story by Armyan Bernstein. (LAT, Q,
V)

2549. ONE MAN. (Billy Baxter-1979-Robin Spry-PG). Screenplay
by Robin Spry, Peter Pearson, and Peter Madden. (W)

2550. ONE MAY JURY. (Cal-Am Artists-1978-Charles Martin-R).
Screenplay by Charles Martin. (W)

2551.   ONE MORE CHANCE. (Cannon-1983-Sam Firstenberg-N/R).
        Screenplay by Sam Firstenberg. (W)

2552.   ONE NIGHT STAND. (Janus-1982-Allan King-N/R). Screen-
        play by Carol Bolt. (W)

2553.   ONE OF A KIND. (Hollywood International-1976-Troy Benny-
        X). Screenplay written by Michelangelo Gianini. (W)

2554.   ONE OF OUR DINOSAURS IS MISSING. (Buena Vista-1975-
        Robert Stevenson-G). Screenplay by Bill Walsh, based on
        the novel The Great Dinosaur Robbery by David Forrest.
        (Q, W)

2555.   ONE ON ONE. (Warner Bros.-1977-Lamont Johnson-PG).
        Screenplay by Robby Benson and Jerry Segal; novelization
        by Jerry Segal; Warner Books, 1977, 202p. (LACOPL, V)

2556.   ONE OR THE OTHER. (Wolfgang Petersen-1978-Wolfgang
        Petersen-N/R). Screenplay written by Manfred Purzer, based
        on a thriller by Ky. (V)

2557.   ONE PAGE OF LOVE. (United Theatrical Amusement-1979-
        Ted Roter-R). Screenplay by Ted Roter. (W)

2558.   ONE PEOPLE. (Actuel-1976-Pim de la Parra-N/R). Screen-
        play by Pim de la Parra and Rudi F. Korss. (V)

2559.   ONE SUMMER LOVE. (American International-1976-Gilbert
        Cates-PG). Screenplay by N. Richard Nash. (W)

2560.   ONE-TRICK PONY. (Warner Bros.-1980-Robert M. Young-
        R). Screenplay by Paul Simon. (V, W)

2561.   ONE WILD MOMENT. (Quartet-1981-Claude Berri-N/R).
        Screenplay by Claude Berri. (LAT, W)

2562.   ONE WONDERFUL SUNDAY. (FDM-1982-Akira Kurosawa-
        N/R). Screenplay by Keinosuke Uekusa. (W)

2563.   ONIMASA. (Toei Co.-1983-Hideo Gosha-N/R). Screenplay
        by Koje Takata and Hideo Gosha. (V)

2564.   THE ONION FIELD. (Avco Embassy-1979-Harold Becker-R).
        Screenplay by Joseph Wambaugh, from his book; Delacorte
        Press, 1973, 427p. (LACOPL, Q, V, W)

2565.   ONLY WHEN I LAUGH. (Columbia-1981-Glenn Jordan-R).
        Screenplay by Neil Simon, based on his play The Ginger-
        bread Lady. (BFI, LAT, Q, V, W)

2566. OOPSIE POOPSIE. (Joseph Green-1980-Giorgio Capitani-PG).
       Screenplay by Ernesto Gastaldi. (W)

2567. OPENING NIGHT. (Faces-1979-John Cassavetes-N/R).
       Screenplay by John Cassavetes. (W)

2568. THE OPENING OF MISTY BEETHOVEN. (Catalyst-1976-
       Henry Paris aka Radley Metzger-X). Screenplay by Jake
       Barnes. (W)

2569. OPERATION DAYBREAK. (Warner Bros.-1975-Lewis Gilbert-
       N/R). Screenplay by Ronald Harwood, from the novel Seven
       Men at Daybreak by Alan Burgess. (W)

2570. OPERATION THUNDERBOLT. (Cinema Shares International-
       1978-Menahem Golan-PG). Screenplay by Clarke Reynolds.
       (W)

2571. THE OPIUM WAR. (Sino-American Corp.-1978-Chen Chun-li-
       N/R). Screenplay credits not available. (V)

2572. ORCA. (Paramount-1977-Michael Anderson-PG). Screenplay
       by Luciano Vencenzoni and Sergio Donati. (Q, V)

2573. ORCHESTRA REHEARSAL. (New Yorker-1979-Federico
       Fellini-N/R). Screenplay by Federico Fellini. (W)

2574. ORDEAL BY INNOCENCE. (MGM/UA-1984-Desmond Davis-
       N/R). Screenplay by Alexander Stuart, based on the novel
       by Agatha Christie; Dodd, 1958. (LACOPL, V)

2575. ORDER TO KILL (Joseph Green-1975-Jose Maesso-R).
       Screenplay by Santiago Moncada, Eugenio Martin, Massimo
       de Rita, and Jose Maesso. (W)

2576. ORDINARY PEOPLE. (Paramount-1980-Robert Redford-R).
       Screenplay by Alvin Sargent, based on the novel by Judith
       Guest; Viking Press, 1976, 263p. (HR, LACOPL, LAT, Q,
       V)

2577. ORGY AMERICAN STYLE. (Hollywood International-1975-X).
       Production credits not available. (W)

2578. ORIENTAL BLUE. (A & B-1975-Philip T. Drexler Jr.-X).
       Screenplay by V. Merania, based on the "Lady Fang" stories
       by Chio-Len Huk. (W)

2579. THE ORPHAN. (World Northal-1979-John Ballard-R).
       Screenplay by John Ballard. (W)

2580. THE ORPHANS. (International Film Exchange-1979-Nikolai
       Gubenko-N/R). Screenplay credits not available. (W)

2581. THE OSTERMAN WEEKEND. (20th Century-Fox-1983-Sam
       Peckinpah-R). Screenplay credits by Alan Sharp, adapta-
       tion by Ian Masters, based on the book by Robert Ludlum.
       (BFI, LAT, V, W)

2582. THE OTHER SIDE OF MIDNIGHT. (20th Century-Fox-1977-
       Charles Jarrott-R). Screenplay by Herman Raucher and
       Daniel Taradash, based on the novel by Sidney Sheldon;
       Morrow, 1973, 440p. (LACOPL, Q, V)

2583. THE OTHER SIDE OF THE MOUNTAIN. (Universal-1975-
       Larry Peerce-PG). Screenplay by David Seltzer, based on
       A Long Way Up by E. G. Valens. (Q, W)

2584. THE OTHER SIDE OF THE MOUNTAIN--PART 2. (Universal-
       1978-Larry Peerce). Screenplay by Douglas Day Stewart;
       novelization by E. G. Valens; Warner Books, 1978, 270p.
       (LACOPL, Q, V, W)

2585. THE OTHER SIDE OF THE UNDERNEATH. (Jack Bond-
       1976-Jane Arden-R). Screenplay by Jane Arden. (W)

2586. OUR HITLER. (Omni Zoetrope-1980-Hans-Jurgen Syberberg-
       N/R). Screenplay written by Hans-Jurgen Syberberg; Far-
       rar, Straus, Giroux, 1982, 268p. (LACOPL, W)

2587. OUR WINNING SEASON. (American International-1978-Joseph
       Ruben-PG). Screenplay written by Nick Niciphor. (W)

2588. OUT OF SEASON. (Athenaeum-1975-Alan Bridges-R).
       Screenplay written by Eric Bercovici and Reuben Bercovitch.
       (W)

2589. OUT OF THE BLUE. (Discovery-1982-Dennis Hopper-R).
       Screenplay by Leonard Yakir and Gary Jules Jouvenat.
       (V, W)

2590. OUT OF THE DARKNESS. (Dimension-1982-Lee Madden-PG).
       Screenplay by Hubert Smith. (W)

2591. OUTLAND. (Ladd Co./Warner Bros.-1981-Peter Hyams-R).
       Screenplay written by Peter Hyams; novelization by Alan
       Dean Foster. (LACOPL, LAT, Q, V, W)

2592. OUTLAW BLUES. (Warner Bros.-1977-Richard T. Heffron-
       PG). Screenplay written by B. W. L. Norton. (Q, V)

2593. THE OUTLAW JOSEY WALES. (Warner Bros.-1976-Clint
       Eastwood-PG). Screenplay by Phil Kaufman, Sonia Chernus,
       from the novel Gone to Texas by Forrest Carter; Delacorte
       Press, 1973, 206p. (LACOPL, Q, W)

2594. OUTLAW LOVE. (Analysis-1982-Bruno Barreto-N/R).
       Screenplay by Leopoldo Serran. (LAT, W)

2595. OUTRAGEOUS! (Cinema 5-1977-Richard Benner-N/R).
       Screenplay by Richard Benner, based on a story by Mar-
       garet Gibson, "Butterfly Ward"; Vanguard Press, 1980, 133p.
       (LACOPL, Q, W)

2596. OUTSIDE CHANCE. (New World Pictures-1978-Michael Miller).
       Screenplay by Michael Miller and Ralph Gaby Wilson. (V)

2597. THE OUTSIDER. (Paramount/CIC-1979-Tony Luraschi-N/R).
       Screenplay by Tony Luraschi, based on the novel The Heri-
       tage of Michael Flaherty by Colin Leinster. (V, W)

2598. OUTSIDER IN AMSTERDAM. (Venenigade Nederland Filmcom-
       pagnie-1983-Wim Verstappen-N/R). Screenplay by Wim Ver-
       stappen and Kees Holierhoek. (V)

2599. THE OUTSIDERS. (Warner Bros.-1983-Francis Coppola-PG).
       Screenplay by Kathleen Knutsen Rowell, based on the novel
       by S. E. Hinton; Viking Press, 1967, 188p. (BFI, LACOPL,
       LAT, V)

2600. OVER THE BROOKLYN BRIDGE. (MGM/UA-1984-Menahem
       Golan-R). Screenplay written by Arnold Somkin. (V)

2601. OVER THE EDGE. (Orion/Warner Bros.-1979-Jonathan Kaplan-
       PG). Screenplay by Charles Haas and Tim Hunter. (V, W)

       OVERVALLERS IN DE DIERENTUIN see ROBBERS IN THE
       ZOO

2602. OXFORD BLUES. (MGM/UA-1984-Robert Boris-PG). Screen-
       play by Robert Boris. (V)

2603. PACIFIC CHALLENGE. (Concord-1975-Robert Amram-G).
       Screenplay written by Robert Amram. (W)

2604. THE PACK. (Warner Bros.-1977-Robert Clouse-PG).
       Screenplay by Robert Clouse, from the novel by Dave Fisher;
       Putnam, 1976, 249p. (LACOPL, V, W)

2605. PACO. (Cinema National-1976-Robert Vincent O'Neil-N/R).
       Screenplay by Andre Marquis. (W)

2606. PACO THE INFALLIBLE. (Filmoblic-Lotus Films-1980-Didier
       Haudepin-N/R). Screenplay by Didier Haudepin and Nadie
       Feuz, dialog by Didier Haudepin and Jose M. Forque, based
       on the novel by Andras Naszlo. (V)

2607. PADRE PADRONE. (Cinema 5-1977-Paolo Taviani & Vittorio
       Taviani-N/R). Screenplay by Paolo Taviani and Vittorio
       Taviani, from the novel by Gavino Ledda. (W)

2608. A PAGE OF MADNESS. (New Line-1975-Teinosuke Kinugasa-
       N/R). No screenplay credits available. (W)

2609. A PAIN IN THE A.... (Corwin-Mahler-1975-Edouard Molinaro-
       PG). Screenplay by Francis Veber. (NYT, W)

2610. PALLET ON THE FLOOR. (Mirage Films-1984-Lynton Butler-
       N/R). Screenplay by Martyn Sanderson, Lynton Butler,
       and Robert Rising. (V)

2611. PANAMA RED. (American Films-1976-Robert C. Chinn-PG).
       Screenplay by Robert C. Chinn. (W)

2612. PANCHO VILLA. (Scotia International-1975-Eugenio Martin-
       PG). No screenplay credits available. (W)

2613. PANDEMONIUM. (MGM/UA-1982-Alfred Sole-PG). Screen-
       play by Richard Whitley and Jaime Klein. (W)

2614. PANHANDLE CALIBER 38. (Scotia American-1975-Tony
       Secchi-N/R). Screenplay credits not given. (W)

2615. PANORAMA BLUE. (Ellman Film Enterprises-1975-Alan
       Roberts-N/R). Screenplay by Steve Michaels. (W)

2616. PAPER TIGER. (Joseph E. Levine-1975-Ken Annakin-PG).
       Screenplay by Jack Davies. (W)

2617. PAPERBACK HERO. (Rumson-1975-Peter Pearson-R).
       Screenplay by Les Rose and Barry Pearson. (W)

2618. PARADISE. (Embassy-1982-Stuart Gillard-R). Screenplay
       by Stuart Gillard. (V, W)

2619. PARADISE ALLEY. (Universal-1978-Sylvester Stallone-PG).
       Sylvester Stallone wrote the screenplay, from his novel;
       Berkley Books, 1978. (LACOPL, Q, V, W)

2620. PARASITE. (Embassy-1982-Charles Band-R). Screenplay
       by Alan Adler, Michael Shoob, and Frank Levering. (V, W)

2621. PARIS, TEXAS. (20th Century-Fox-1984-Wim Wenders-R).
       Screenplay by Sam Shepard, story adaptation by L. M. Kit
       Carson. (V)

2622. PART 2, SOUNDER. (Gamma III-1976-William Graham-G).
       Screenplay by Lonne Elder III, based on the novel by
       William H. Armstrong; Harper, 1969, 116p. (LACOPL, V, W)

2623. PART 2, WALKING TALL. (American International-1975-Earl Bellamy-PG). Screenplay by Howard B. Kreitsek; novelization by Webster Carey; Bantam Books, 1975, 109p. (LACOPL, W)

PARTISANI see HELL RIVER

2624. PARTNERS. (Paramount-1982-James Burrows-R). Screenplay by Francis Veber. (Q, V)

2625. PARTS--THE CLONUS HORROR. (Group 1-1979-Robert S. Fiveson-R). Screenplay by Ron Smith, Bob Sullivan, based on a story by Bob Sullivan. (V)

2626. THE PASSAGE. (United Artists-1979-J. Lee Thompson-R). Screenplay by Bruce Nicolaysen, based on the novel Perilous Passage by Bruce Nicolaysen; Playboy Press, 1976, 245p. (LACOPL, Q, V, W)

2627. A PASSAGE TO INDIA. (Columbia-1984-David Lean-PG). Screenplay written by David Lean, based on the novel by E. M. Forster and the play by Santha Rama Rau; Harcourt, Brace & World, 1969, 322p. (BFI, HR, LACOPL, LAT, V)

2628. THE PASSENGER. (United Artists-1975-Michelangelo Antonioni-PG). Screenplay by Mark Peploe, Peter Wollen, and Michelangelo Antonioni; story by Mark Peploe. (LAT, Q, W)

2629. THE PASSIONS OF CAROL. (Ambar-1975-Amanda Barton-X). Screenplay by Amanda Barton, based on Charles Dickens' A Christmas Carol; St. Martin's Press, 1979, 78p. (LACOPL, W)

2630. THE PASSOVER PLOT. (Atlas Films-1976-Michael Campus-PG). Screenplay by Millard Cohan and Patricia Knop, from the book by Hugh J. Schonfield; Hutchinson, 1965, 287p. (LACOPL, NYT, V)

2631. PASTORAL HIDE AND SEEK. (Unifilm-1980-Shuji Terayama-N/R). Screenplay by Shuji Terayama. (W)

2632. PATERNITY. (Paramount-1981-David Steinberg-PG). Screenplay by Charlie Peters. (LAT, Q, V, W)

2633. PATRICK. (Monarch-Vanguard-1979-PG). Screenplay by Everett De Roche. (W)

2634. PATTY. (Trans World-1976-Robert L. Roberts-X). Screenplay written by Joyce Richards and Robert Roberts. (W)

2635. PAUL, LISA & CAROLINE. (Belladonna Films-1977-Peter

Balakoff-N/R). Screenplay by Peter and Belinda Balakoff.
(V)

PAULINE A LA PLAGE see PAULINE AT THE BEACH

2636.   PAULINE AT THE BEACH. (A.A.A.-1983-Eric Rohmer-N/R).
Screenplay by Eric Rohmer. (BFI, LAT, V)

2637.   PEEPER. (20th Century-Fox-1976-Peter Hyams-PG). Screenplay by W. D. Richter from the novel Deadfall by Keith
Laumer; Doubleday, 1971, 204p. (LACOPL, W)

2638.   PELVIS. (Funky Films-1977-R. T. Megginson-N/R). Screenplay by Straw Weisman from a story by Straw Weisman and
R. T. Megginson. (V)

2639.   PENITENTIARY. (Jerry Gross Organization-1979-Jamac
Fanaka-R). Screenplay by Jamac Fanaka. (Q, V, W)

2640.   PENITENTIARY II. (MGM/UA-1982-Jamac Fanaka-R).
Screenplay written by Jamac Fanaka. (Q, V, W)

2641.   PENNIES FROM HEAVEN. (MGM-1981-Herbert Ross-R).
Screenplay by Dennis Potter. (LAT, Q, V, W)

2642.   THE PEOPLE THAT TIME FORGOT. (American International-
1977-Kevin Connor-PG). Screenplay by Patrick Tilley,
based on a novel by Edgar Rice Burroughs; Ace Books,
1973, 125p. (LACOPL, Q, V)

2643.   PEPPERMINT SODA. (Gaumont/New Yorker-1979-Diane
Kurys-PG). Screenplay by Diane Kurys. (W)

2644.   PERCEVAL. (Gaumont/New Yorker-1978-Eric Rohmer-N/R).
Screenplay by Eric Rohmer, from the book by Chretien de
Troyes. (V, W)

2645.   A PERFECT COUPLE. (20th Century-Fox-1979-Robert
Altman-PG). Screenplay by Robert Altman and Allan Nicholls.
(LAT, Q, V, W)

2646.   THE PERFUMED NIGHTMARE. (Kidlat Tahimik-1980-Kidlat
Tahimik-N/R). Screenplay written by Kidlat Tahimik.
(LAT, W)

THE PERILS OF GWENDOLINE see GWENDOLINE

2647.   PERMANENT VACATION. (Gray City-1981-Jim Jarmusch-
N/R). Screenplay by Jim Jarmusch. (V, W)

2648.   PERMISSION TO KILL. (Avco Embassy-1975-Cyril Frankel-
PG). Screenplay by Robin Estridge from his novel. (W)

2649. PERMISSIVE. (Variety-1975-Lindsey Shonteff-X). Screenplay by Jeremy Craig Dryden. (W)

2650. PERSECUTION. (Blueberry Hill-1975-Don Chaffey-PG). Screenplay by Robert B. Hutton and Rosemary Wooten. (W)

2651. PERSONAL BEST. (Warner Bros.-1982-Robert Towne-R). Screenplay by Robert Towne. (Q, V)

2652. THE PERSONALS. (New World Pictures-1982-Peter Markle-PG). Screenplay by Peter Markle. (LAT, V, W)

2653. PETE'S DRAGON. (Buena Vista-1977-Don Chaffey-G). Screenplay by Malcolm Marmorstein, based on a story by Seton I. Miller and S. S. Field. (Q, W)

PETIT JOSEPH see LITTLE JOSEPH

LES PETITES FUGUES see LITTLE ESCAPES

2654. PETRIA'S WREATH. (New Yorker-1983-Srdjan Karanovic-N/R). Screenplay written by Srdjan Karanovic, based on a novel by Dragoslav Mihajlovic. (W)

2655. PHANTASM. (Avco Embassy-1979-Don Coscarelli-R). Screenplay by Don Coscarelli. (Q, V, W)

2656. PHAR LAP. (Hoyts Distribution-1983-Simon Wincer-N/R). Screenplay by David Williamson. (V)

2657. PHARAOH. (Hallmark-1976-Jerzy Kawalerowicz-R). Screenplay by Tadeusz Konwicki and Jerzy Kawalerowicz, based on a novel by Boleslaw Prus. (W)

2658. THE PHILADELPHIA EXPERIMENT. (New World Pictures-1984-Stewart Raffill-PG). Screenplay by William Gray and Michael Janover. (V)

2659. PHOBIA. (Spiegel-Bergman Films-1980-John Huston-N/R). Screenplay by Ronald Shusett, Gary Sherman, Lew Lehman, James Sangster, and Peter Bellwood. (LAT, V, W)

2660. PICK-UP. (Crown International-1975-Bernie Hirschenson-R). Screenplay credits not available. (W)

2661. PICK-UP SUMMER. (Film Ventures International-1981-George Mihalka-R). Screenplay by Richard Zelniker. (V, W)

2662. PICNIC AT HANGING ROCK. (Atlantic Releasing Corp-1979-Peter Weir-N/R). Screenplay written by Cliff Green, based on a novel by Joan Lindsay. (W)

2663. THE PICTURE SHOW MAN. (Cinema World-1979-John Power-PG). Screenplay written by Joan Long. (W)

2664. A PIECE OF PLEASURE. (Joseph Green-1976-Claude Chabrol-R). Screenplay written by Paul Gegauff. (W)

2665. A PIECE OF THE ACTION. (Warner Bros.-1977-Sidney Poitier-PG). Screenplay by Charles Blackwell, story by Timothy March. (Q, W)

2666. PIECES. (Artists Releasing Corp.-1983-Juan Piquer Simon-X). Screenplay by Dick Randall and John Shadow. (LAT, V, W)

2667. THE PIGKEEPER'S DAUGHTER. (Boxoffice International-1975-Bethel G. Buckalew-N/R). Screenplay credits not available. (W)

THE PIGS see DADDY'S DEADLY PICKUP

PINBALL PICKUP see PICK-UP SUMMER

PINBALL SUMMER see PICK-UP SUMMER

2668. PINK DREAMS. (Slovak State Film-1978-Dusan Hanak-N/R). Screenplay by Dusan Hanak. (V)

2669. PINK FLOYD--THE WALL. (MGM/UA-1982-Alan Parker-N/R). Screenplay by Roger Waters. (Q, V, W)

2670. PINK MOTEL. (New Image-1983-Mike MacFarland-R). Screenplay by M. James Kouf Jr. (V, W)

2671. THE PINK PANTHER STRIKES AGAIN. (United Artists-1976-Blake Edwards-PG). Screenplay by Frank Waldman and Blake Edwards. (Q, V)

2672. PINOCCHIO'S STORYBOOK ADVENTURES. (First American-1979-Ron Merk-G). Screenplay by Ron Merk. (W)

2673. PIPE DREAMS. (Avco Embassy-1976-Stephen Verona-PG). Screenplay by Stephen Verona. (Q, V)

2674. PIPPE GOES ON BOARD. (G.G. Communications-1975-Olle Hellblom-G). Screenplay credits not given, based on a book by Astrid Lindgren; Viking Press, 1957, 140p. (LACOPL, W)

2675. PIRANHA. (New World-1978-Joe Dante). Screenplay by John Sayles, based on a story by Richard Robinson and John Sayles. (LAT, V, W)

2676. PIRANHA II THE SPAWNING. (Saturn International Pictures-
1983-James Cameron-R). Screenplay by H. A. Milton. (W)

2677. THE PIRATE MOVIE. (20th Century-Fox-1983-Ken Annakin-
PG). Screenplay by Trevor Farrant, based on The Pirates
of Penzance by H. S. Gilbert and Arthur Sullivan; Stoddart,
1880. (LACOPL, Q, V, W)

2678. THE PIRATES OF PENZANCE. (Universal-1983-Wilford
Leach-G). Screenplay written by Wilford Leach, based on
the musical by H. S. Gilbert and Arthur Sullivan; Stoddart,
1880. (HR, LACOPL, LAT, V)

2679. PIROSMANI. (Gruzia Film Studio-1978-Georgy Shengelaya-
N/R). Screenplay by Georgy Shengelaya and Erlom
Ackvledlani. (W)

2680. PIXOTE. (Unifilm/Embrafilm-1981-Hector Babenco-N/R).
Screenplay by Hector Babenco and Jorge Duran, based on
the novel Infancia Dos Martos by Jose Louzeiro. (LAT, W)

2681. PLACES IN THE HEART. (Tri-Star Pictures-1984-Robert
Benton-PG). An original screenplay by Robert Benton.
(HR, LAT, V)

2682. PLAGUE. (Group I-1979-PG). Ed Hunt and Barry Pearson
wrote this original screenplay. (W)

2683. THE PLAGUE DOGS. (United International Pictures-1982-
Martin Rosen-N/R). Screenplay by Martin Rosen, based on
a novel by Richard Adams; Collings, 1977, 461p. (LACOPL,
V)

PLANET OF HORRORS see GALAXY OF TERROR

2684. PLATANOV. (Mosfilm-1976-Nikita Mikhalkov-N/R). Screenplay based on the play by Anton Chekhov; Hill, 1964, 195p.
(LACOPL, V)

2685. PLAYERS. (Paramount-1979-Anthony Harvey-PG). Screenplay written by Arnold Schulman. (HR, LAT, NYT, Q, V,
W)

2686. PLEASURE MASTERS. (Good Time-1975-Alex De Renzy-X).
Screenplay written by Alex De Renzy. (W)

2687. PLEASURE PARTY. (1975-Claude Chabrol-N/R). Paul
Gegauff wrote the screenplay. (W)

2688. THE PLOUGHMAN'S LUNCH. (Goldcrest & Michael White-

1983-Richard Eyre-N/R). An original screenplay by Ian
McEwan. (V)

2689.   THE PLUMBER. (South Australian Film Corp.-1980-Peter
        Weir-N/R). Screenplay by Peter Weir. (V)

2690.   POLAR. (Les Films Noirs-1984-Jacques Bral-N/R). Screen-
        play by Jacques Bral, Jean-Paul Leca, and Julien Levi,
        based on the novel Morgue Pleine by Jean Patrick Manchette.
        (V)

2691.   POLICE ACADEMY. (Ladd Co./Warner Bros.-1984-Hugh
        Wilson-R). Screenplay by Neal Israel, Pat Proft, and Hugh
        Wilson, from a story by Neal Israel and Pat Proft. (V)

2692.   POLTERGEIST. (MGM/UA-1982-Tobe Hooper-PG). Screen-
        play by Steven Spielberg, Michael Grais, and Mark Victor;
        novelization by James Kahn; Warner Books, 1982, 301p.
        (HR, LACOPL, LAT, NYT, Q, V, W)

2693.   POLYESTER. (New Line Cinema-1981-John Waters-R).
        Screenplay by John Waters. (BFI, LAT, V, W)

2694.   THE POM POM GIRLS. (Crown International-1976-Joseph
        Ruben-PG). Screenplay by Joseph Ruben. (W)

        POMOCNIK see THE ASSISTANT

2695.   PONY EXPRESS RIDER. (Doty Dayton-1976-Hal Harrison
        Jr.-G). Screenplay by Lyman Dayton, Dan Greer, Hal
        Harrison Jr., and Robert Totten. (W)

2696.   POOPSIE. (Cougar-1978-Georgio Capitani-R). Screenplay
        by Ernesto Gastaldi. (W)

        POOR ALBERT AND LITTLE ANNIE see I DISMEMBER MAMA

2697.   POOR IDA. (Scandinavia Today-1982-Lalla Mikkelsen-N/R).
        Screenplay by Marit Paulsen, from her novel Liten Ida, in
        collaboration with Lalla Mikkelsen. (W)

2698.   POOR PRETTY EDDIE. (Westamerican Films-1975-Richard
        Robinson-R). Screenplay by B. W. Sandefur. (W)

2699.   POOR WHITE TRASH, PART 2. (Dimension-1976-S. F.
        Brownrigg-R). Screenplay by Mary Davis and Gene Ross.
        (W)

2700.   THE POPE OF GREENWICH VILLAGE. (MGM/UA-1984-Stuart
        Rosenberg-R). Screenplay by Vincent Patrick, based on his
        novel; Harper & Row, 1979, 280p. (HR, LACOPL, LAT, NYT,
        V)

2701. POPEYE. (Paramount-1980-Robert Altman-PG). Screenplay
by Jules Feiffer, based on cartoon characters created by
E. C. Segar. (LAT, Q, V, W)

2702. PORKY'S. (20th Century-Fox-1981-Bob Clark-R). Screenplay written by Bob Clark; novelization by Ron Renaud;
Pocket Books, 1983. (HR, LACOPL, LAT, NYT, Q, V, W)

2703. PORKY'S II: THE NEXT DAY. (20th Century-Fox-1983-
Bob Clark-R). Screenplay by Roger E. Swaybill, Alan Ormsby, and Bob Clark. (BFI, HR, LACOPL, LAT, V, W)

2704. PORN FLAKES. (RFD-1977-Chuck Vincent-X). Screenplay
by Chuck Vincent and Christopher Covino. (V)

2705. PORRIDGE. (ITC Film Distributors-1979-Dick Clement-N/R).
Screenplay by Dick Clement and Ian La Frenais. (V)

PORTRAIT OF A FEMALE DRUNKARD see TICKET OF NO
RETURN

2706. PORTRAIT OF A WOMAN, NUDE. (Horizon Films-1983-Nino
Manfredi-PG). Screenplay by Agenore Incrocci, Ruggero
Maccari, Nino Manfredi, Furio Scarpelli, and Silvana Buzzo;
story by Nino Manfredi and Paolo Levi. (W)

2707. PORTRAIT OF TERESA. (Unifilm-1980-Pastor Vega-N/R).
Screenplay and story by Pastor Vega and Ambrosio Fornet.
(W)

2708. A PORTRAIT OF THE ARTIST AS A YOUNG MAN. (Howard
Mahler-1979-Joseph Strick-N/R). Screenplay by Judith Ras-
coe, based on the novel by James Joyce; Viking Press, 1964,
253p. (LACOPL, V, W)

2709. PORTRAIT OF THE ARTIST'S WIFE. (IFEX/Sovexportfilm-
1982-Aleksandr Pankratov-N/R). Screenplay by Natalya
Ryazantzeva. (W)

2710. POSSE. (Paramount-1975-Kirk Douglas-PG). Screenplay by
William Roberts, Christopher Knopf, from a story by
Christopher Knopf. (W)

2711. POSSE FROM HEAVEN. (P.M.-1976-Phillip Pine-R). Screenplay by Ward Wood and Phillip Pine. (W)

2712. POSSESSION. (Limelight International-1981-Andrzej Zulawski-
N/R). Screenplay written by Andrzej Zulawski, with dialogue
by Frederic Tuten. (LAT, V, W)

2713. THE POSTMAN ALWAYS RINGS TWICE. (Paramount-1981-Bob
Rafelson-R). Screenplay by David Mamet, based on the

novel by James M. Cain, in Cain X 3; Knopf, 1969, 465p.
(HR, LACOPL, LAT, NYT, Q, V, W)

2714. POT! PARENTS! POLICE! (Hampton International-1975-
        Phillip Pine-PG). Phillip Pine wrote this original screenplay.
        (W)

        POURQUOI PAS! see WHY NOT!

2715. THE POWER. (Artists Releasing Corp.-1984-Jeffrey Obrow-
        R). Screenplay by Stephen Carpenter and Jeffrey Obrow, from
        a story by Jeffrey Obrow, Stephen Carpenter, John Penney,
        and John Hopkins. (V)

2716. POWER KILL. (Aquarius-1975-Michele Lupo-R). Screenplay
        credits not available. (W)

2717. THE POWER OF MEN IS THE PATIENCE OF WOMEN. (Isis-
        1982-Cristina Perincioli-N/R). Screenplay by Cristina Perin-
        cioli. (W)

2718. POWER PLAY. (Robert Cooper-1978-Martyn Burke-N/R).
        Screenplay by Martyn Burke. (V)

2719. POWERFORCE. (Bedford Entertainment-1983-Michael King-R).
        Screenplay by Terry Chalmers and Dennis Thompsett. (W)

2720. PRACTICE MAKES PERFECT. (Quartet Films-1980-Philippe
        de Broca-N/R). Screenplay written by Philippe de Broca
        and Michel Audiard. (W)

2721. PRANKS. (New Image-1982-Jeffrey Obrow and Stephen
        Carpenter-R). Screenplay by Stephen Carpenter, Jeffrey
        Obrow, and Stacey Giachino. (W)

2722. PRAYING MANTIS. (Portman-1982-Jack Gold-N/R). Screen-
        play authored by Philip Mackie. (V)

2723. THE PREMONITION. (Avco Embassy-1976-Robert Allen
        Schnitzer-PG). Screenplay by Anthony Mahon, Robert A.
        Schnitzer, and Louis Pastore. (W)

2724. PREPPIES. (Platinum Pictures-1984-Chuck Vincent-R).
        Screenplay by Rick Marx and Chuck Vincent, from a story
        by Todd Kessler. (V)

2725. THE PRESIDENTIAL PEEPERS. (Independent-1976-X). No
        production credits available. (W)

2726. THE PRESIDENT'S WOMEN. (Trona-1981-John Avildsen-R).
        Screenplay by David Odell, Jack Richardson, and Dan Green-
        berg. (W)

2727. PRESSURE. (British Film Institute-1976-Horace Ove-N/R).
       Screenplay written by Horace Ove and Samuel Selvon. (V)

2728. PRETTY BABY. (Paramount-1978-Louis Malle-R). Polly
       Platt wrote the screenplay, based on a story by Polly Platt
       and Louis Malle, from material in Storyville by Al Rose;
       novelization by William Harrison; Bantam Books, 1978.
       (BFI. HR, LACOPL, LAT, Q, V, W)

2729. THE PREY. (New World Pictures-1984-Edwin Scott Brown-R).
       Screenplay by Edwin Scott Brown and Summer Brown. (V)

2730. PRIEST OF LOVE. (Filmways-1981-Christopher Miles-R).
       Screenplay by Alan Plater, based on Harry T. Moore's book
       and the writing and letters of D. H. Lawrence; Farrar, 1974,
       550p. (BFI, LACOPL, Q, V, W)

2731. PRIMAL FEAR. (Nu-Image Film-1980-Anne Claire Poirier-
       N/R). Screenplay by Marthe Blackburn and Anne Claire
       Poirier, from a story by Andree Major. (LAT, V, W)

2732. PRINCE JACK. (LMF Production-1984-Bert Lovitt-N/R).
       Screenplay by Bert Lovitt. (V)

2733. PRINCE OF THE CITY. (Orion/Warner Bros.-1981-Sidney
       Lumet-R). Screenplay by Jay Presson Allen and Sidney
       Lumet, based on the book by Robert Daley; Houghton Mif-
       flin, 1978, 311p. (HR, LACOPL, LAT, NYT, Q, V, W)

2734. THE PRISONER OF SECOND AVENUE. (Warner Bros.-1975-
       Melvin Frank-PG). Screenplay by Neil Simon, based on his
       play of the same name; Random House, 1972, 87p. (LACOPL,
       Q, V, W)

2735. THE PRISONER OF ZENDA. (Universal-1979-Richard Quine-
       PG). Screenplay by Anthony Hope, as dramatized by Ed-
       ward Rose; Heritage Press, 1966, 188p. (LACOPL, Q, V, W)

2736. PRISONERS. (American Films Ltd.-1975-William H. Bushness
       Jr.-R). Screenplay by William H. Bushness Jr. and John
       Marley, based on the novel The Prisoners of Quai Dong by
       Victor Kolpacoff; New American Library, 1967. (LACOPL, W)

2737. PRISONERS OF THE LOST UNIVERSE. (Marcel/Robertson
       Productions Ltd.-1984-Terry Marcel-N/R). Screenplay by
       Terry Marcel and Harry Robertson. (V)

2738. THE PRIVATE AFTERNOONS OF PAMELA MANN. (Hudson
       Valley-1975-Henry Paris-X). Screenplay credits not avail-
       able. (W)

2739. PRIVATE BENJAMIN. (Warner Bros.-1980-Howard Zieff-R).

Screenplay by Nancy Meyers, Charles Shyer, and Harvey Miller. (HR, LAT, Q, V, W)

2740. THE PRIVATE EYES. (Raymond Chow-Golden Harvest-1977-Michael Hui-N/R). Screenplay written by Michael Hui. (V)

2741. THE PRIVATE EYES. (New World-1981-Lang Elliott-PG). Screenplay by Tim Conway and John Myhers. (V, W)

2742. THE PRIVATE FILES OF J. EDGAR HOOVER. (American International-1978-Larry Cohen-PG). Larry Cohen wrote this original screenplay. (LAT, W)

2743. PRIVATE LESSONS. (Jensen Farley-1981-Alan Myerson-R). Screenplay by Dan Greenberg, from his novel Philly; Simon & Schuster, 1969, 158p. (BFI, LACOPL, LAT, V, W)

2744. PRIVATE SCHOOL. (Universal-1983-Noel Black-R). Screenplay by Dan Greenberg and Suzanne O'Malley. (LAT, V, W)

2745. PRIVATES ON PARADE. (Hand Made Films-1982-Michael Blakemore-N/R). Screenplay by Peter Nichols, based on his play. (V, W)

2746. PRIVILEGED. (New Yorker-1983-Michael Hoffman-N/R). Screenplay written by Michael Hoffman, David Woolcombe, and Rupert Walters. (V, W)

2747. THE PRIZE FIGHTER. (New World-1979-Michael Preece-PG). Tim Conway and John Myhers wrote this screenplay. (V, W)

2748. PROJECT: KILL. (Stirling Gold-1976-William Girdler-R). A screenplay by Donald G. Thompson, from a story by David Sheldon and Donald G. Thompson. (W)

2749. PROM NIGHT. (Avco Embassy-1980-Paul Lynch-R). Screenplay by William Gray, from a story by Robert Guza Jr. (V, W)

2750. THE PROMISE. (Universal-1978-Gilbert Cates-PG). Screenplay by Garry Michael White; novelization by Danielle Steel; Dell, 1978, 288p. (HR, LACOPL, LAT, NYT, Q, V, W)

2751. PROMISES IN THE DARK. (Orion-1979-Jerome Hellman-PG). Loring Mandel wrote this screenplay; novelization by Hillary James. (LACOPL, Q, V, W)

2752. PROPHECY. (Paramount-1979-John Frankenheimer-PG). Screenplay by David Seltzer; novelization by David Seltzer; Ballantine, 1979. (HR, LACOPL, V, W)

2753. PROSTITUTE. (Kestral Films-1980-Tony Garnett-N/R). Tony Garnett wrote this original screenplay. (V)

2754. PROTOCOL. (Warner Bros.-1984-Herbert Ross-PG). An original screenplay by Buck Henry. (V)

2755. PROVIDENCE. (Cinema 5-1977-Alain Resnais-R). Screenplay by David Mercer. (Q, V, W)

2756. PROVINCIAL ACTORS. (New Yorker-1983-Agnieszka Holland-N/R). Screenplay by Agnieszka Holland and Witold Zatorski. (W)

2757. THE PROWLER. (Sandhurst Corp.-1981-Joseph Zito-N/R). Screenplay by Glen Leopold and Neil Barbera. (BFI, LAT, V)

2758. THE PSYCHIC. (Group I-1979-Lucio Fulci-R). No screenplay credits available. (V, W)

2759. THE PSYCHIC KILLER. (Avco Embassy-1975-Raymond Danton-PG). Greydon Clark, Mike Angel, and Raymond Danton wrote this original screenplay. (W)

2760. PSYCHO FROM TEXAS. (New American Films-1982-Jim Feazell-R). Screenplay by Jim Feazell. (V, W)

2761. PSYCHO II. (Universal-1983-Richard Franklin-R). Screenplay by Tom Holland, based on characters created by Robert Bloch; novelization by Robert Bloch; Warner Books, 1982, 317p. (BFI, HR, LACOPL, LAT, V, W)

2762. THE PSYCHOTRONIC MAN. (International Harmony-1980-Jack M. Sell-PG). Screenplay by Peter Spelson and Jack M. Sell, based on an original story by Peter Spelson. (V, W)

P'TIT CON see LITTLE JERK

2763. PUBERTY BLUES. (Universal Classics-1983-Bruce Beresford-R). Screenplay by Margaret Kelly. (W)

2764. PURPLE HAZE. (Thomas Fucci-1982-David Burton Morris-N/R). Screenplay by Victoria Wozniak, based on a story by Tom Kelsey, Victoria Wozniak and David Burton Morris. (LAT, V, W)

2765. PURPLE HEARTS. (Ladd Co./Warner Bros.-1984-Sidney J. Furie-R). Screenplay by Rick Natkin and Sidney J. Furie. (HR, LAT, V)

2766. PURPLE RAIN. (Warner Bros.-1984-Albert Magnoli-R).

Screenplay by Albert Magnoli and William Blinn. (HR, LAT, NYT, V)

2767. THE PURPLE TAXI. (Parafrance-1977-Yves Boisset-N/R). Screenplay by Michel Deon and Yves Boisset. (V, W)

2768. PURSUIT. (Key International-1975-Thomas Quillen-R). Screenplay credits not available. (W)

2769. THE PURSUIT OF D. B. COOPER. (Universal-1981-Roger Spottiswoode-PG). Screenplay by Jeffrey Alan Fiskin, based on the book Free Fall by J. D. Reed; Delacorte Press, 1980, 212p. (HR, LACOPL, LAT, NYT, Q, V, W)

2770. PUSSY TALK. (Catalyst-1975-Frederic Lansac-X). Screenplay credits not available. (W)

2771. Q: QUETZALCOATL. (UFD-1982-Larry Cohen-R). Screenplay written by Larry Cohen. (V)

2772. QUADROPHENIA. (Curbishley-Baird-1979-Franc Roddam). Screenplay by Dave Humphries, Martin Stellman, and Franc Roddam, based on the album "Quadrophenia" by Pete Townshend. (V, W)

2773. QUARTET. (Gaumont-1981-James Ivory-N/R). Screenplay by Ruth Prawer Jhabvala, from the book by Jean Rhys; Harper & Row, 1975, 186p. (LACOPL, LAT, Q, V)

2774. QUEEN OF THE GYPSIES. (Sovexportfilm-1979-Emil Lotyanu-N/R). Screenplay written by Emil Lotyanu, based on a legend by Maxim Gorky. (W)

2775. QUERELLE. (Gaumont-1982-Rainer Werner Fassbinder-R). Screenplay by Rainer Werner Fassbinder, from the book by Jean Genet; Grove Press, 1974, 276p. (LACOPL, LAT, V)

2776. QUEST FOR FIRE. (20th Century-Fox-1981-Jean-Jacques Annaud-R). Screenplay by Gerard Brach, inspired by the novel by J. H. Rosny; Pantheon, 1967. (BFI, HR, LACOPL, LAT, Q, V, W)

2777. THE QUIET DUEL. (Daiei-1983-Akira Kurosawa-N/R). Screenplay by Akria Kurosawa and Senkichi Taniguchi, based on a play by Kazuo Kikuta. (W)

2778. QUINTET. (20th Century-Fox-1979-Robert Altman-R). Screenplay by Frank Barhydt, Robert Altman, and Patricia Resnick. (Q, V, W)

2779. R.S.V.P. (Platinum Pictures-1984-John and Lem Amero-N/R). Screenplay by LaRue Watts. (V)

2780. RABBIT TEST. (Avco Embassy-1978-Joan Rivers-PG).
       Screenplay by Joan Rivers and Jay Redack. (V, W)

       LA RABIA see THE RAGE

2781. RABID. (New World Pictures-1977-David Cronenberg-G).
       Screenplay by David Cronenberg. (V)

2782. RACE D'EP. (Little Sisters-1982-Lionel Soukas-N/R).
       Screenplay by Nicole Deschaumes. (W)

2783. RACE FOR YOUR LIFE, CHARLIE BROWN. (Paramount-
       1977-Bill Melendez-G). Screenplay by Charles M. Schulz,
       based on his "Peanuts" characters; Holt, Rinehart & Winston,
       1978, 126p. (LACOPL, V)

2784. RACE WITH THE DEVIL. (20th Century-Fox-1975-Jack
       Starrett-PG). Screenplay by Lee Frost and Wes Bishop.
       (Q, W)

2785. RACING WITH THE MOON. (Paramount-1984-Richard
       Benjamin-PG). Screenplay by Steven Kloves. (V)

2786. RACQUET. (Cal-Am Productions-1979-David Winters-R).
       Screenplay by Steve Michaels and Earle Doud. (W)

2787. RADIO ON. (British Film Institute/Road Movies Film
       Production-1979-Christopher Petit-N/R). Screenplay by
       Christopher Petit and Heidi Adolph. (V, W)

2788. RAFFERTY AND THE GOLD DUST TWINS. (Warner Bros.-
       1975-Dick Richards-R). Screenplay by John Kaye. (W)

       LA RAGAZZA DI TRIESTE see THE GIRL FROM TRIESTE

2789. THE RAGE. (Jose Maria Form/P. C. Teide-1979-Eugeni
       Anglada-N/R). Screenplay by Eugeni Anglada. (V)

2790. RAGGEDY MAN. (Universal-1981-Jack Fisk-PG). Screen-
       play by William D. Wittliff. (LAT, Q, V, W)

2791. RAGING BULL. (United Artists-1980-Martin Scorsese-R).
       Screenplay by Paul Schrader and Mardik Martin, from the
       book Raging Bull by Jake La Motta with Joseph Carter and
       Peter Savage; Prentice Hall, 1970, 218p. (BFI, FD, HR,
       LACOPL, LAT, NYT, Q, V, W)

2792. RAGING DRAGON. (Bedford Entertainment-1982-N/R). No
       production credits available. (W)

2793. RAGTIME. (Paramount-1981-Milos Forman-PG). Screenplay
       by Michael Weller, based on the E. L. Doctorow novel;

Random House, 1975, 270p. (BFI, HR, LACOPL, LAT, Q, V, W)

RAICES DE SANGRE see ROOTS OF BLOOD

2794. RAIDERS OF THE LOST ARK. (Paramount-1981-Steven Spielberg-PG). Screenplay by Lawrence Kasdan, story by George Lucas and Philip Kaufman; novelization by Campbell Black; Ballantine, 1984, 192p. (HR, LACOPL, LAT, NYT, Q, V, W)

2795. RAIN AND SHINE. (New Yorker-1978-Ferenc Andras-N/R). Screenplay by Ferenc Andras, Geza Beremenyi, and Akos Kertesz. (W)

2796. RAISE THE TITANIC. (Associated Film Distribution-1980-Jerry Jameson-PG). Screenplay by Adam Kennedy, adapted by Eric Hughes, from the novel by Clive Cussler; Viking Press, 1976, 312p. (LACOPL, Q, V, W)

RAMBO SFIDA LA CITTA see SYNDICATE SADISTS

2797. RANCHO DELUXE. (United Artists-1975-Frank Perry-R). Screenplay by Thomas McGuane. (Q, W)

2798. THE RAPE KILLER. (Joseph Brenner-1976-Dacosta Carayan-R). Screenplay by Telly Livadas. (W)

2799. RAPE OF INNOCENCE. (New Line Cinema-1976-Yves Boisset-N/R). Screenplay by Jean-Pierre Bastid and Michel Martens, adapted by Yves Boisset and Jean Curtelin. (W)

2800. RAPE OF LOVE. (Quartet Films-1979-Yannick Bellon-N/R). Screenplay by Yannick Bellon. (LAT, W)

2801. THE RASCALS. (Quartet Films-1982-Bernard Revon-R). Screenplay by Bernard Revon, Didier Bouquet-Nadaud, in collaboration with Michel Zemer and Claude de Givray. (V, W)

2802. THE RATS. (Golden Communications-1982-Robert Clouse-N/R). Screenplay by Charles Eglee, based on the novel by James Herbert; New American Library, 1974, 204p. (LACOPL, V)

2803. RATTLERS. (Boxoffice International-1976-John McCauley-PG). Screenplay and story by Jerry Golding. (W)

2804. RAVAGERS. (Columbia-1979-Richard Compton). Screenplay by Donald S. Sanford, based on the novel Path to Savagery by Robert Edmond Alter. (V, W)

2805. RAW FORCE. (American Panorama-1982-Edward Murphy-R).
       Screenplay by Edward Murphy. (V, W)

2806. THE RAZOR'S EDGE. (Columbia-1984-John Byrum-PG-13).
       Screenplay by John Byrum and Bill Murray, based on the
       novel by W. Somerset Maugham; Doubleday, 1944. (BFI,
       HR, LACOPL, LAT, NYT, V)

2807. REACHING OUT. (PAR Films-1983-Pat Russell-R). Screen-
       play written by Pat Russell. (V, W)

2808. REAL LIFE. (Paramount-1979-Albert Brooks-PG). Screen-
       play by Albert Brooks, Monica Johnson, and Harry Shearer.
       (Q, V, W)

2809. REAL LIFE. (Bedford-1984-Francis Megahy-N/R). Screen-
       play by Francis Megahy and Bernie Cooper. (V)

2810. REBELLION IN PATAGONIA. (Tricontinental-1977-Hector
       Olivera-N/R). Screenplay by Osvaldo Bayer, Fernando
       Ayala, and Hector Olivera, based on The Avengers of Tragic
       Patagonia by Osvaldo Bayer. (W)

2811. RECKLESS. (MGM/UA-1984-James Foley-R). Screenplay by
       Chris Columbus. (V)

2812. RECOMMENDATION FOR MERCY. (Cinema Shares Interna-
       tional-1976-Murray Markowitz-R). Screenplay by Fabian
       Jennings, Joel Weisenfeld, and Murray Markowitz. (W)

2813. RECORD CITY. (American International-1978-Dennis
       Steinmetz-PG). Screenplay by Ron Friedman. (W)

2814. RED DAWN. (MGM/UA-1984-John Milius-PG-13). Screenplay
       by Kevin Reynolds and John Milius. (HR, LAT, NYT, V)

2815. RED DUST. (ICAIC Productions-1982-Jesus Diaz-N/R).
       Screenplay by Jesus Diaz. (V, W)

2816. RED MONARCH. (Enigma-1983-Jack Gold-N/R). Screenplay
       by Charles Wood. (V)

2817. RED, WHITE AND ZERO. (Entertainment Marketing-1979-
       Lindsay Anderson, Peter Brook, Tony Richardson-N/R).
       Screenplay by Shelagh Delany, Peter Brook, and Tony
       Richardson. (W)

2818. THE REDEEMER. (Dimension-1978-Constantine S. Gochis-
       N/R). Screenplay by William Vernick. (W)

2819. REDNECK. (International Amusements-1975-Silvio Narizzano-
       N/R). Screenplay by Win Wells. (W)

2820. REDNECK COUNTY. (Group I Films-1979-Richard Robinson-
       R). Screenplay by B. W. Sandefur. (W)

2821. REDS. (Paramount-1981-Warren Beatty-PG). Screenplay by
       Warren Beatty and Trevor Griffiths. (BFI, HR, LAT, Q,
       V, W)

2822. REFINEMENTS IN LOVE. (Hollywood International-1975-
       Carlos Tobalina-X). Screenplay credits not available. (W)

2823. REFLECTIONS. (Court House Films-1984-Kevin Billington-
       N/R). Screenplay by John Banville. (V)

2824. REFLECTIONS (DRY SUMMER). (Hittite-1975-Ulvi Dogan &
       Ismail Metin-B&W-N/R). Screenplay by Necati Cumali and
       Jim Lehner. (W)

2825. REFLECTIONS FROM A BRASS BED. (Hemisphere-1976-
       Richard Clausen-R). Screenplay by Richard Clausen. (W)

2826. REFUGE. (Separate Dreams Co.-1981-Huck Fairman-N/R).
       Screenplay by Huck Fairman and Luther Sperberg. (V)

       REIFEZEUGNIS see FOR YOUR LOVE ONLY

2827. THE REINCARNATION OF PETER PROUD. (American
       International-1975-J. Lee Thompson-R). Screenplay by Max
       Ehrlich, based on his novel; Bobbs, 1974, 287p. (LACOPL,
       W)

2828. THE RELUCTANT GUNFIGHTER. (Bangkok Scope-1977-
       Anumat Bunnag-N/R). Story and screenplay by Gan Roong-
       kan. (V)

2829. REMEMBER MY NAME. (Columbia-1978-Alan Rudolph-R).
       Screenplay by Alan Rudolph. (V, W)

2830. RENALDO & CLARA. (Circuit Films-1978-Bob Dylan-N/R).
       Screenplay by Bob Dylan. (V, W)

2831. RENDEZVOUS WITH ANNE. (Leo Productions-1976-Lowell
       Pickett-X). Screenplay by Lowell Pickett. (W)

2832. RENE THE CANE. (AMLF-1977-Francis Girod-N/R). Screen-
       play by Francis Girod and Jacques Rouffio, from the book
       by Roger Borniche. (V)

2833. REPLAY. (Quartet Films-1978-Michel Drach-N/R). Screen-
       play by Pierre Uytterhoven and Michel Drach, based on a
       book by Dominique St. Alban. (LAT, W)

       REPO see ZERO TO SIXTY

2834. REPO MAN. (Universal-1984-Alex Cox-R). Screenplay by
       Alex Cox. (V)

2835. REPORT TO THE COMMISSIONER. (United Artists-1975-
       Milton Katselas-PG). Screenplay by Abby Mann and Ernest
       Tidyman, based on a novel by James Mills; Farrar, 1972,
       184p. (LACOPL, Q, W)

2836. THE RESCUERS. (Buena Vista-1977-Wolfgang Reitherman-G).
       Screenplay and story by Larry Clemmons, Ken Anderson,
       Vance Gerry, David Michener, Burny Mattinson, Frank
       Thomas, Fred Lucky, Ted Berman, and Dick Sebast, sug-
       gested by The Rescuers--Little, Brown, 1959--and Miss
       Bianca--Little, Brown, 1962--by Margery Sharp. (LACOPL,
       Q, V)

2837. RESTLESS. (Joseph Brenner-1978-Yorgo Pan Cosmatos-R).
       Screenplay by Yorgo Pan Cosmatos. (W)

2838. RESURRECTION. (Universal-1980-Daniel Petrie-PG).
       Screenplay by Lewis John Carlino, novelization by George
       Gipe; Pocket Books, 1980. (LACOPL, Q, V, W)

       RETENEZ MOI ... OU JE FAIS UN MALHEUR see TO
       CATCH A COP

       THE RETRIEVERS see HOT AND DEADLY

2839. RETURN FROM WITCH MOUNTAIN. (Buena Vista-1978-John
       Hough-G). Screenplay by Malcolm Marmorstein, based on
       characters created by Alexander Key. (Q, V, W)

2840. THE RETURN OF A MAN CALLED HORSE. (United Artists-
       1976-Irvin Kershner-PG). Screenplay by Jack DeWitt, based
       on character from A Man Called Horse by Dorothy M. John-
       son. (Q, W)

2841. THE RETURN OF CAPTAIN INVINCIBLE. (Seven Keys Film
       Dist.-1983-Philippe Mora-N/R). Screenplay by Steve de
       Souza and Andre Gaty. (V, W)

2842. THE RETURN OF MARTIN GUERRE. (European International-
       1983-Daniel Vigne-N/R). Screenplay written by Daniel Vigne
       and Jean-Claude Carriere. (LAT, W)

2843. THE RETURN OF THE GRANDMASTERS. (Marvin-1982-
       Joseph Kuo-R). Screenplay credits not available. (W)

2844. THE RETURN OF THE JEDI. (20th Century-Fox-1983-Richard
       Marquand-PG). Screenplay by Lawrence Kasdan and George
       Lucas; novelization by James Kahn; Ballantine, 1983, 181p.
       (LACOPL, LAT, V)

2845. RETURN OF THE MASTER KILLER. (World Northal-1982-Liu
       Chia-Liang-R). No screenplay credits available. (W)

2846. RETURN OF THE PANTHER. (In-Frames Films-1976-Wu Ma-
       R). Screenplay credits not available. (W)

2847. THE RETURN OF THE PINK PANTHER. (United Artists-
       1975-Blake Edwards-G). Screenplay by Frank Waldman and
       Blake Edwards. (Q, W)

2848. RETURN OF THE SECAUCUS SEVEN. (Libra-1980-John
       Sayles-N/R). Screenplay by John Sayles. (V, W)

2849. THE RETURN OF THE STREETFIGHTER. (New Line-1975-
       Shigehiro Ozawa-R). Screenplay by Koji Takada and Steve
       Autrey. (W)

2850. THE RETURN OF THE TALL BLOND MAN WITH ONE BLACK
       SHOE. (Lanir-1976-Yves Robert-R). Screenplay by Yves
       Robert and Francis Veber. (W)

2851. RETURN TO BOGGY CREEK. (777-1978-Tom Moore-G).
       Screenplay by Dave Woody. (W)

2852. RETURN TO CAMPUS. (Cinepix-1975-Harold Cornsweet-
       N/R). Written by Harold Cornsweet. (W)

2853. RETURN TO MACON COUNTY. (American International-1975-
       Richard Compton-PG). Screenplay by Richard Compton. (W)

2854. THE RETURNING. (Willow Films-1983-Joel Bender-N/R).
       Screenplay by Patrick Nash. (V)

2855. REUBEN, REUBEN. (20th Century-Fox-1983-Robert Ellis
       Miller-R). Screenplay by Julius J. Epstein, from a novel by
       Peter de Vries. (BFI, HR, LAT, NYT, V, W)

       REVENGE see TERROR FROM UNDER THE HOUSE

2856. REVENGE OF THE CHEERLEADERS. (Monarch-1976-Richard
       Lerner-R). Screenplay by Ted Greenwald, Ace Baandage,
       and Nathaniel Dorsky. (W)

2857. REVENGE OF THE NERDS. (20th Century-Fox-1984-Jeff
       Kanew-R). Screenplay by Steve Zacharias and Jeff Buhai,
       from a story by Tim Metcalfe, Miguel Tejada-Flores, Steve
       Zacharias, and Jeff Buhai. (V)

2858. REVENGE OF THE NINJA. (MGM/UA-1983-Sam Firstenberg-
       R). Screenplay by James R. Silke. (W)

2859. REVENGE OF THE PATRIOTS. (World Northal-1981-R). No
production credits available. (W)

2860. REVENGE OF THE PINK PANTHER. (United Artists-1978-
Blake Edwards-PG). Screenplay by Frank Waldman, Ron
Clark, and Blake Edwards, based on a story by Blake Ed-
wards. (Q, V, W)

2861. REVENGE OF THE SHOGUN WOMEN. (21st Century Distri-
bution-1982-Mei Chung Chang-N/R). Screenplay by Lin
Huang Kun and Terry Chambers. (V, W)

2862. REVENGE SQUAD. (ComWorld-1983-Chuck Braverman-PG).
Screenplay by Don Enright, based on the novel $80 to Stam-
ford by Lucille Fletcher; Random House, 1975, 151p.
(LACOPL, W)

2863. RHINESTONE. (20th Century-Fox-1984-Bob Clark-PG).
Screenplay by Phil Alden Robinson and Sylvester Stallone,
from a screen story by Phil Alden Robinson, based on the
song "Rhinestone Cowboy" by Larry Weiss. (V)

2864. RICH AND FAMOUS. (MGM/UA-1981-George Cukor-R).
Screenplay by Gerald Ayres, based on the play Old Ac-
quaintance by John Van Druten; Random House, 1941, 181p.
(BFI, HR, LACOPL, LAT, V, W)

2865. RICH KIDS. (United Artists-1979-Robert M. Young-PG).
Screenplay by Judith Ross; novelization by H. B. Gilmour.
(LACOPL, Q, V, W)

2866. THE RIDDLE OF THE SANDS. (Rank Film Dist.-1979-Tony
Maylam). Screenplay by Tony Maylam and John Bailey,
based on a novel by Erskine Childers; Dodd, 1940. (LACOPL,
V)

2867. RIDE A WILD PONY. (Buena Vista-1976-Don Chaffey-G).
Screenplay by Rosemary Anne Sisson, from the novel A
Sporting Proposition by James Aldridge; Little, Brown,
1973, 206p. (LACOPL, W)

2868. RIGHT OF WAY. (Schaefer/Karpf Productions-1983-George
Schaefer-N/R). Screenplay by Richard Lees, based on his
play. (V)

2869. THE RIGHT STUFF. (Ladd Co./Warner Bros.-1983-Philip
Kaufman-PG). Screenplay by Philip Kaufman, based on the
book by Tom Wolfe; Farrar, Straus, and Giroux, 1979, 436p.
(BFI, FD, HR, LACOPL, LAT, Q, V)

2870. LES RIPOUX. (AMLF-1984-Claude Zidi-N/R). Screenplay

by Claude Zidi and Didier Kaminka, from an original story idea by Simon Mickael. (V)

2871. RIPPED-OFF. (Cinema Shares International-1975-Franco Prosperi-R). Screenplay credits not available. (W)

2872. RISING DAMP. (ITC-1980-Joe McGrath-N/R). Screenplay by Eric Chappell. (V)

2873. RISKY BUSINESS. (Geffen Co./Warner Bros.-1983-Paul Brickman-R). Screenplay by Paul Brickman. (LAT, V)

2874. RITUALS. (Aquarius-1978-Peter Crane-R). Screenplay by Ian Sutherland. (BFI, W)

2875. THE RITZ. (Warner Bros.-1976-Richard Lester-PG). Screenplay by Terence McNally, based on his play of the same title. (Q, W)

2876. RIVALS. (World Entertainment-1979-Lyman Dayton-PG). Screenplay by Keith Merrill. (W)

2877. THE RIVER. (Universal-1984-Mark Rydell-PG-13). Screenplay by Robert Dillon and Julian Barry, based on a story by Robert Dillon; novelization by Robert Dillon; Berkley Books, 1984, 272p. (HR, LACOPL, LAT, NYT, V)

2878. THE RIVER NIGER. (Cine Artist-1976-Krishna Shah-R). Screenplay by Joseph A. Walker, from his play of the same title; Hill, 1973, 177p. (LACOPL, W)

2879. THE RIVER RAT. (Paramount-1984-Tom Rickman-PG). Screenplay by Tom Rickman. (V)

2880. ROAD GAMES. (Avco Embassy-1981-Richard Franklin-PG). Screenplay by Everett DeRoche. (V, W)

2881. ROADHOUSE 66. (Atlantic Releasing-1984-John Mark Robinson-R). Screenplay by Galen Lee and George Simpson, from a story by Galen Lee. (V)

2882. ROADIE. (United Artists-1980-Alan Rudolph-PG). Screenplay by Big Boy Medlin and Michael Ventura, based on a story by Big Boy Medlin, Michael Ventura, Zalman King, and Alan Rudolph. (V, W)

2883. THE ROADS OF EXILE. (Corinth-1981-Claude Goretta-N/R). Screenplay by Georges Haldas and Claude Goretta. (LAT, V, W)

2884. ROAR. (Filmways Australasian Distributors-1981-Noel

Marshall-N/R). Screenplay by Noel Marshall, with additional material by Ted Cassidy. (BFI, V)

2885. ROARING FIRE. (New Line-1982-Norry Suzuki-R). Screenplay by Norry Suzuki. (W)

2886. ROBBERS IN THE ZOO. (Concorde Film-1984-Christ Stuur-N/R). Screenplay by Felix Thijssen and Annie van den Oever, based on a book by Ciny Peppelenbosch. (V)

2887. ROBERT ET ROBERT. (Quartet Films-1979-Claude Lelouch-N/R). Screenplay by Claude Lelouch. (W)

2888. ROBIN AND MARIAN. (Columbia-1976-Richard Lester-PG). Screenplay by James Goldman. (Q, W)

2889. ROCKERS. (Rockers Film Corp.-1978-Theodoros Bafaloukos-N/R). Screenplay by Theodoros Bafaloukos. (V)

2890. ROCK 'N' ROLL HIGH SCHOOL. (New World-1979-Allan Arkush-PG). Screenplay by Richard Whitley, Russ Dvonch, and Joseph McBride, based on a story by Allan Arkush and Joe Dante. (V, W)

2891. ROCKY. (United Artists-1976-John G. Avildsen-PG). Screenplay by Sylvester Stallone; novelization by Sylvester Stallone; Ballantine Books, 1982. (BFI, HR, LACOPL, LAT, Q, V, W)

2892. ROCKY II. (United Artists-1979-Sylvester Stallone-PG). Screenplay by Sylvester Stallone; novelization by Sylvester Stallone; Ballantine Books, 1979, 180p. (HR, LACOPL, LAT, Q, V, W)

2893. ROCKY III. (MGM/UA-1982-Sylvester Stallone-PG). Screenplay by Sylvester Stallone; novelization by Sylvester Stallone; Ballantine Books, 1982. (HR, LACOPL, LAT, Q, V, W)

2894. THE ROCKY HORROR PICTURE SHOW. (20th Century-Fox-1975-Jim Sharman-R). Screenplay by Jim Sharman and Richard O'Brien. (W)

2895. THE ROGUE. (Group I-1976-Gregory Simpson-R). Screenplay credits not available. (W)

LE ROI ET L'OISEAU see THE KING AND THE MOCKING-BIRD

2896. THE ROLE. (Blaze Film Enterprises-1978-Shyam Benegal-N/R). Screenplay by Shyam Benegal. (V)

2897.   ROLLER BOOGIE. (United Artists-1979-Mark L. Lester-PG).
        Screenplay by Barry Schneider, from an original story by
        Irwin Yablans. (V, W)

2898.   ROLLERBABIES. (Classic-1976-Carter Stevens-X). Screen-
        play by Wesson Smith. (W)

2899.   ROLLERBALL. (United Artists-1975-Norman Jewison-R).
        Screenplay by William Harrison. (Q, W)

2900.   ROLLERCOASTER. (Universal-1977-James Goldstone-PG).
        Screenplay by Richard Levinson and William Link, based on
        a story by Sanford Sheldon, Richard Levinson, and William
        Link, suggested by a Tommy Cook story. (Q, V)

2901.   ROLLING THUNDER. (American International-1977-John
        Flynn-R). Screenplay by Paul Schrader and Heywood Gould.
        (Q, W)

2902.   ROLLOVER. (Orion/Warner Bros.-1981-Alan J. Pakula-R).
        Screenplay by David Shaber, story by David Shaber, Howard
        Kohn, and David Weir. (LAT, Q, W)

2903.   ROMANCING THE STONE. (20th Century-Fox-1984-Robert
        Zemeckis-PG). Screenplay by Diane Thomas; novelization by
        Joan Wilder; Avon, 1984, 261p. (LACOPL, V)

2904.   ROMANTIC COMEDY. (MGM/UA-1983-Arthur Hiller-PG).
        Screenplay by Bernard Slade, based on the play by Bernard
        Slade. (LAT, V)

2905.   THE ROMANTIC ENGLISHWOMAN. (New World-1975-Joseph
        Losey-R). Screenplay by Tom Stoppard and Thomas Wise-
        man, based on the novel by Thomas Wiseman; Putnam, 1972,
        319p. (LACOPL, Q, W)

2906.   ROOMMATES. (Platinum Pictures-1982-Chuck Vincent-N/R).
        Screenplay by Chuck Vincent and Rick Marx. (V)

2907.   ROOSTER COGBURN. (Universal-1975-Stuart Millar-PG).
        Screenplay by Martin Julien, suggested by characters in the
        novel True Grit by Charles Portis; Simon & Schuster, 1968.
        (LACOPL, Q, W)

2908.   ROOTS OF BLOOD. (Azteca-1979-Jesus Salvador Trevino-
        N/R). Screenplay by Jesus Salvador Trevino. (V)

2909.   ROOTS OF EVIL. (World Northal-1982-Christian Anders-R).
        Screenplay by Christian Anders. (W)

2910.   THE ROSE. (20th Century-Fox-1979-Mark Rydell-R).

Screenplay by Bill Kerby and Bo Goldman, based on a story
by Bill Kerby; novelization by Leonore Fleischer; Warner
Books, 1979. (FD, HR, LACOPL, Q, V, W)

2911. ROSEBUD. (United Artists-1975-Otto Preminger-PG).
Screenplay by Eric Lee Preminger, additional dialogue by
Marjorie Kellogg, based on the novel by Joan Hemingway
and Paul Bonnecarrere; Morrow, 1974, 277p. (FD, HR,
LACOPL, Q, V, W)

2912. ROSELAND. (Cinema Shares International-1977-James Ivory-
PG). Screenplay by Ruth Prawer Jhabvala. (Q, W)

ROSEMARY'S KILLER see THE PROWLER

2913. ROUGH CUT. (Paramount-1980-Donald Siegel-PG). Screen-
play by Francis Burns, based on Derek Lambert's Touch the
Lion's Paw; Saturday Review Press, 1975, 272p. (LACOPL,
Q, V, W)

ROUGH TREATMENT see WITHOUT ANESTHESIA

2914. ROYAL FLASH. (20th Century-Fox-1975-Richard Lester-PG).
Screenplay by George MacDonald Fraser, based on his novel;
Knopf, 1970, 257p. (LACOPL, W)

2915. THE RUBBER GUN. (Schuman-Katzka-1978-Allan Moyle-N/R).
Screenplay by Steve Lack. (W)

2916. RUBY. (Dimension Pictures-1977-Curtis Harrington-R).
Screenplay by George Edwards and Barry Schneider. (V)

2917. RUCKUS. (New World-1981-Max Kleven-PG). Screenplay
by Max Kleven. (W)

2918. RUDE BOY. (Michael White-1980-Jack Hazan and David
Mingay-R). Screenplay by David Mingay, Ray Gange, and
Jack Hazan. (V, W)

2919. RUM RUNNER. (Libert Films International-1976-Robert
Enrico-R). Screenplay by Pierre Pelegri and Robert Enrico,
from the book by J. Porcheral. (W)

2920. RUMBLE FISH. (Universal-1983-Francis Ford Coppola-R).
Screenplay by S. E. Hinton and Francis Ford Coppola, based
on S. E. Hinton's novel; Delacorte Press, 1975, 122p.
(LACOPL, LAT, V, W)

2921. RUMOURS OF GLORY. (Extra Modern Productions-1983-
Martin Lavut-N/R). No screenplay credits available. (V)

2922.   RUN AFTER ME UNTIL I CATCH YOU. (Silverstein-1979-
Robert Pouret-PG). Screenplay by Nicole De Buron and
Robert Pouret. (W)

2923.   RUN FOR THE ROSES. (Kodiak Films-1978-Henry Levin-PG).
Screenplay by Joseph G. Prieto and Mimi Avins. (V)

2924.   RUN, RABBIT, RUN. (Horizon-1975-Roger Fritz-R).
Screenplay credits not available. (W)

2925.   RUN, WAITER, RUN. (IFEX-1983-Ladislav Smoljak-N/R).
Screenplay by Zdenek Sverak. (W)

2926.   RUNAWAY. (Tri-Star-1984-Michael Crichton-PG-13). Screenplay by Michael Crichton. (V)

2927.   THE RUNNER STUMBLES. (Stanley Kramer-1979-Stanley
Kramer-PG). Screenplay by Milan Stitt, based on his Broadway play. (Q, V, W)

2928.   RUNNERS. (Hanstoll-1983-Charles Sturridge-N/R). Screenplay by Stephen Poliakoff. (BFI, V)

2929.   RUNNIN' AFTER LOVE. (Bauer International-1980-Carlos
Hugo Christensen-N/R). Screenplay by Carlos Hugo
Christensen. (W)

2930.   RUNNING. (Universal-1979-Steven Hilliard Stern-PG).
Screenplay by Steven Hilliard Stern; novelization by
Leonore Fleischer. (LACOPL, Q, V, W)

2931.   RUNNING BRAVE. (Englander Prods. Inc.-1983-D. S.
Everett-N/R). Screenplay by Henry Bean and Shirl Hendryx.
(LAT, V, W)

2932.   RUNNING HOT. (New Line Cinema-1984-Mark Griffiths-
N/R). Screenplay by Mark Griffiths. (V)

        LA RUPTURE see THE BREAKUP

2933.   RUSH. (Cinema Shares International-1984-Anthony Richmond
aka Tonino Ricci-N/R). Screenplay by Tito Carpi. (V)

2934.   RUSSIAN ROULETTE. (Avco Embassy-1975-Lou Lombardo-
PG). Screenplay by Tom Ardies, Stanley Mann, and Arnold
Margolin, based on the novel Kosygin Is Coming by Tom
Ardies; Doubleday, 1974, 207p. (LACOPL, Q, W)

2935.   S.O.B. (Lorimar/Paramount-1981-Blake Edwards-R).
Screenplay by Blake Edwards. (LAT, Q, V, W)

2936. S.O.S. (Mammoth-1975-Jim Buckley-X). Screenplay by Jim
       Buckley. (W)

2937. SACRIFICE. (Joseph Brenner-1980-Umberto Lenzi-R).
       Screenplay credits not available. (W)

2938. SAFARI EXPRESS. (Joseph Green-1980-Duccio Tessari-PG).
       Screenplay by Mario Amendola, Bruno Corbucci, Duccio
       Tessari, Gianfranco Clerici, and Antonio Exacoustos. (W)

2939. SAFARI 3000. (MGM/UA-1982-Harry Hurwitz-PG). Screen-
       play by Michael Harreschou, from a story by Jules Levy,
       Arthur Gardner, and Michael Harreschou. (W)

2940. THE SAGA OF DRACULA. (International Amusements-1975-
       Leon Klimovsky-R). Screenplay credits not given. (W)

2941. SAHARA. (MGM/UA-1983-Andrew V. McLaglen). Screen-
       play by James R. Silke. (V)

2942. THE SAILOR WHO FELL FROM GRACE WITH THE SEA.
       (Avco Embassy-1976-Lewis John Carlino-R). Screenplay by
       Lewis John Carlino, based on the novel by Yukio Mishima;
       Knopf, 1965. (LACOPL, Q, W)

2943. ST. HELENS. (Parnell-1981-Ernest Pintoff-PG). Screen-
       play by Peter Bellwood and Larry Ferguson. (V, W)

2944. ST. IVES. (Warner Bros.-1976-J. Lee Thompson-PG).
       Screenplay by Barry Beckerman, based on the novel The
       Procane Chronicle by Oliver Bleeck; Morrow, 1971, 221p.
       (LACOPL, Q, W)

2945. SAINT JACK. (New World Pictures-1979-Peter Bogdanovich-
       R). Screenplay by Howard Sackler, Paul Theroux, and
       Peter Bogdanovich, based on a novel by Paul Theroux;
       Houghton, 1973, 247p. (LACOPL, V, W)

2946. THE SALAMANDER. (ITC Films International-1983-Peter
       Zinner-N/R). Screenplay by Robert Katz, from a novel by
       Morris West; Morrow, 1973, 355p. (LACOPL, V, W)

2947. SALLY AND FREEDOM. (Scandinavia Today-1982-Gunnel
       Lindblom-N/R). Screenplay by Margareta Garpe and Gunnel
       Lindblom. (W)

2948. SALTY. (Saltwater-1975-Ricou Browning-G). Screenplay
       by Ricou Browning and Jack Cowden. (W)

2949. SALUT L'ARTISTE. (Exxel-1976-Yves Robert-N/R). Screen-
       play by Jean-Loup Dabadie and Yves Robert. (W)

SAM MARLOW, PRIVATE EYE see THE MAN WITH BOGART'S FACE

2950. SAME TIME, NEXT YEAR. (Universal-1978-Robert Mulligan-PG). Screenplay by Bernard Slade, based on his play; novelization by Linda Stewart; Dell, 1978, 174p. (HR, LACOPL, LAT, Q, V, W)

2951. SAMMY SOMEBODY. (Athena-1976-Joseph Adler-R). Screenplay credits not available. (W)

2952. SAMMY STOPS THE WORLD. (Special Event Entertainment-1979-Mel Shapiro-N/R). Book, music and lyrics by Leslie Bricusse and Anthony Newley (from Stop the World I Want to Get Off). (V)

2953. SAM'S SON. (Invictus Entertainment-1984-Michael Landon-PG). Screenplay by Michael Landon. (V)

2954. THE SANDGLASS. (Polish Corp-1983-Wojciech J. Has-N/R). Screenplay credits not given, based on the story "The Sanitorium Under the Sign of the Hourglass" by Bruno Schulz. (W)

2955. SANTI AND VEENA. (Hollywood Film Release-1976-San Pestonji-N/R). Screenplay by Maroot and Vijit Koonabut. (V)

2956. SAO BERNARDO. (Unifilm-1980-Leon Hirszman-N/R). Screenplay by Leon Hirszman. (W)

2957. SASQUATCH. (North American Film Enterprises-1978-Ed Ragozzini-N/R). Screenplay by Edward H. Hawkins, based on a story by Ronald B. Olson. (Q, V, W)

2958. SASSY SUE. (Boxoffice International-1975-Buckalew-X). Screenplay by Buckalew. (W)

SATANIC RITES OF DRACULA see COUNT DRACULA AND HIS VAMPIRE BRIDE

2959. SATAN'S BREW. (Albatros/Trio Film-1976-Rainer Werner Fassbinder-N/R). Screenplay by Rainer Werner Fassbinder. (V)

2960. SATAN'S CHILDREN. (Sterling International-1975-Joe Wiezycki-R). Screenplay by Gary Garrett. (W)

2961. SATAN'S MISTRESS. (Motion Picture Marketing-1982-James Polakof-R). Screenplay by James Polakof and Beverley Johnson. (V, W)

2962. SATAN'S SLAVE. (Crown International-1979-Norman J.
       Warren-R). Screenplay by David McGillivray. (W)

       SATANSBRATEN see SATAN'S BREW

2963. SATURDAY NIGHT AT THE BATHS. (Buckley Bros.-1975-
       David Buckley-R). Screenplay by Franklin Dhedouri and
       David Buckley. (W)

2964. SATURDAY NIGHT FEVER. (Paramount-1977-John Badham-
       R). Screenplay by Norman Wexler, based on the story by
       Nik Cohn; novelization by H. B. Gilmour; Bantam Books,
       1977, 182p. (BFI, HR, LACOPL, LAT, NYT, Q, V, W)

2965. SATURDAY NIGHT SPECIAL. (Robert Pentroff-1976-Sam
       Bloch-X). Screenplay by Joel Seigal. (W)

2966. SATURDAY THE 14TH. (New World Pictures-1981-Howard R.
       Cohen-PG). Screenplay by Howard R. Cohen, based on a
       story by Jeff Begun. (LAT, V)

2967. SATURN 3. (Associated Film Distribution-1980-Stanley
       Donen-R). Screenplay by Martin Amis, from a story by
       John Barry. (HR, LAT, V, W)

2968. SAVAGE ABDUCTION. (Cinemation-1975-John Lawrence-R).
       Screenplay by John Lawrence. (W)

2969. SAVAGE HARVEST. (20th Century-Fox-1981-Robert Collins-
       PG). Screenplay by Robert Blees, Robert Collins, based on
       a story by Ralph Helfer and Ken Noyle. (LAT, Q, V, W)

2970. THE SAVAGE HUNT OF KING STAKH. (IFEX-1982-Valery
       Rubinchik-N/R). Screenplay by Vladimir Korotkevich and
       Valery Rubinchik. (W)

2971. SAVAGE STREETS. (Motion Picture Marketing-1984-Danny
       Steinmann-R). Screenplay by Norman Yonemoto and Danny
       Steinmann. (V)

2972. SAVAGE WEEKEND. (Cannon Films-1983-David Paulsen-R).
       Screenplay by David Paulsen. (V, W)

2973. SAVANNAH SMILES. (Gold Coast Films-1982-Pierre DeMoro-
       PG). Screenplay by Mark Miller. (LAT, V, W)

2974. SCALPEL. (Avco Embassy-1978-John Grissmer-PG). Screen-
       play by John Grissmer, from a story by Joseph Weintraub.
       (W)

2975. SCALPS. (21st Century Distribution-1983-Fred Olen Ray-R).
       Screenplay by Fred Olen Ray. (V, W)

2976. SCANDAL. (Entertainment Marketing-1980-Akira Kurosawa-
       N/R). Screenplay by Akira Kurosawa and Ryuzo Kikushima.
       (W)

       SCANDALO see SUBMISSION

2977. SCANDALOUS. (Orion-1984-Rob Cohen-PG). Screenplay by
       Rob Cohen and John Byrum, story by Larry Cohen. (V)

2978. SCANNERS. (Avco Embassy-1981-David Cronenberg-R).
       Screenplay by David Cronenberg; novelization by Leon
       Whiteson; Tower, 1981. (LACOPL, Q, V, W)

2979. THE SCAR. (Cherdkhai-1981-Cherd Songsri-N/R). Screen-
       play by Tom Tatree and Raperpron. (V)

2980. SCARED TO DEATH. (Lone Star-1981-William Malone-R).
       Screenplay by William Malone. (W)

2981. SCARFACE. (Universal-1983-Brian DePalma-R). Screenplay
       by Oliver Stone; novelization by Paul Monette; Berkley
       Books, 1983, 311p. (LACOPL, LAT, V)

       LA SCARLATINE see SCARLET FEVER

2982. SCARLET FEVER. (UGC-1984-Gabriel Aghion-N/R). Screen-
       play by Gabriel Aghion. (V)

2983. SCARRED. (Seymour Borde & Associates-1984-Rose Marie
       Turko-R). Screenplay by Rose Marie Turko. (V)

2984. SCAVENGER HUNT. (20th Century-Fox-1980-Michael Schultz-
       PG). Screenplay by Steven A. Vail and Henry Harper, from
       a story by Steven A. Vail. (Q, V, W)

2985. THE SCENIC ROUTE. (New Line Cinema-1979-Mark Rappaport-
       N/R). Screenplay by Mark Rappaport. (W)

2986. SCENT OF A WOMAN. (United Artists-1976-Dino Risi-R).
       Screenplay by Ruggero Macari and Dino Risi, based on a
       novel by Giovanni Arpino. (W)

       SCHATJES! see DARLINGS!

2987. SCHIZO. (Niles International-1978-Peter Walker-R). Screen-
       play by David McGillivray. (W)

2988. SCHIZOID. (Cannon Group-1980-David Paulsen-R). Screen-
       play by David Paulsen. (V, W)

2989. SCHOOL FOR SWINGERS. (New Line-1975-John Weeram-X).
       Screenplay credits not available. (W)

2990. SCHOOL GIRL BRIDE. (American International-1975-R).
       Screenplay credits not available. (W)

2991. SCORCHY. (American International-1976-Hikmet Avedis-R).
       Screenplay by Hikmet Avedis. (W)

2992. SCOTT JOPLIN. (Universal-1977-Jeremy Paul Kagan-PG).
       Screenplay by Christopher Knopf. (V, W)

2993. SCREAM FOR HELP. (Lorimar-1984-Michael Winner-N/R).
       Screenplay by Tom Holland. (V)

2994. SCREAMERS. (New World-1982-Sergio Martino-R). Screen-
       play by Sergio Donati, Cesare Frugoni, and Sergio Martino.
       (V)

2995. SCREAMS OF A WINTER NIGHT. (Dimension-1979-James L.
       Wilson-PG). Screenplay by Richard H. Wadsack. (V, W)

2996. SCREWBALLS. (New World-1983-Rafal Zielinski-R). Screen-
       play by Jim Wynorski and Linda Shayne. (V, W)

2997. SCUM. (World Northal-1980-Alan Clarke-N/R). Screenplay
       by Roy Minton. (V, W)

       SCUM OF THE EARTH see POOR WHITE TRASH: PART 2

2998. THE SEA GYPSIES. (Warner Bros.-1978-Stewart Raffill-G).
       Screenplay by Stewart Raffill. (HR, Q, V, W)

2999. SEA OF ROSES. (Embrafilmo-Unifilm-1980-Ana Carolina-N/R).
       Screenplay by Ana Carolina. (V)

3000. THE SEA WOLVES. (Paramount/Lorimar-1981-Andrew V.
       McLaglen-PG). Reginald Rose wrote the screenplay, based
       on Boarding Party by James Leasor; Houghton-Mifflin, 1979,
       203p. (LACOPL, W)

       SEABO see BUCKSTONE COUNTY PRISON

3001. SEARCH AND DESTROY. (Film Ventures International-1981-
       William Fruet-PG). Screenplay by Don Enright. (V, W)

3002. THE SECOND AWAKENING OF CHRISTA KLAGES. (New
       Line-1979-Margarethe von Trotta-N/R). Screenplay by
       Margarethe von Trotta and Luisa Francia. (W)

3003. A SECOND CHANCE. (United Artists Classics-1981-Claude
       Lelouch-PG). Screenplay by Claude Lelouch. (LAT, W)

3004. THE SECOND COMING OF EVE. (Liberty-1975-Mac Ahlberg-
       X). No screenplay credits given. (W)

3005. SECOND-HAND HEARTS. (Lorimar/Paramount-1981-Hal
Ashby-PG). Screenplay by Charles Eastman. (LAT, Q,
V, W)

3006. THE SECOND SHIFT. (Marcusfilm-1980-Lasse Glomm-N/R).
Screenplay by Lasse Glomm, from stories by Espen Hraa-
vardsholm. (V)

3007. SECOND THOUGHTS. (Universal-1983-Lawrence Turman-PG).
Screenplay by Steve Brown, from a story by Steve Brown
and Terry Louise Fisher. (LAT, V, W)

3008. LE SECRET. (Cinema National-1975-Robert Enrico-N/R).
Screenplay by Pascal Jardin, from the novel Le Compagnon
Indesirable by Francis Ry, adapted by Robert Enrico and
Pascal Jardin. (W)

3009. THE SECRET DIARY OF SIGMUND FREUD. (TLC-1984-
Danford B. Greene-N/R). Screenplay by Roberto Mitrotti
and Linda Howard. (V)

3010. SECRET HONOR: THE LAST TESTAMENT OF RICHARD M.
NIXON. (Sandcastle 5-1984-Robert Altman-N/R). Screenplay by Donald Freed and Arnold M. Stone. (V)

3011. THE SECRET LIFE OF PLANTS. (Paramount-1978-Walon
Green-N/R). Screenplay by Peter Tompkins, Walon Green,
and Michael Braun, based on the book The Secret Life of
Plants by Peter Tompkins and Christopher Bird. (V)

3012. THE SECRET OF NIMH. (MGM/UA-1982-Don Bluth-G).
Screenplay and story adaptation by Don Bluth, John
Pomeroy, Gary Goldman, and Will Finn, based on the novel
Mrs. Frisby and the Rats of NIMH by Robert C. O'Brien;
Atheneum, 1971, 233p. (LACOPL, Q, V, W)

3013. SECRET OF NAVAJO CAVE. (Epoh-1976-James T. Flocker-
G). Screenplay credits not available. (W)

3014. THE SECRET OF YOLANDA. (1982-Yoel Silberg-R). Screenplay by Eli Tavor and Yoel Silberg. (BFI)

3015. SECRETS. (Lone Star Pictures International-1978-Philip
Saville-R). Screenplay by Rosemary Davies, from a story
by Philip Saville. (V, W)

3016. SECRETS. (Samuel Goldwyn Co.-1984-Gavin Millar-R).
Screenplay by Noella Smith. (V)

3017. THE SEDUCTION. (Embassy-1982-David Schmoeller-R).
Screenplay by David Schmoeller. (LAT, Q, V, W)

3018. THE SEDUCTION OF JOE TYNAN. (Universal-1979-Jerry Schatzberg-R). Screenplay by Alan Alda, novelization by Richard Cohen; Dell, 1979. (LACOPL, Q, V, W)

3019. THE SEDUCTION OF LYNN CARTER. (1975-X). No production credits available. (W)

SEED OF INNOCENCE see TEEN MOTHER

3020. SEEDS OF EVIL. (KKI-1981-Jim Kay-R). Screenplay by Jim Kay. (V)

3021. SEEMS LIKE OLD TIMES. (Columbia-1980-Jay Sandrich-PG). Screenplay by Neil Simon. (Q, V, W)

DIE SEHNSUCHT DER VERONIKA VOSS see VERONIKA VOSS

SEISHUN ZANKOKU MONOGATARI see CRUEL STORY OF YOUTH

3022. SELF-SERVICE SCHOOLGIRLS. (Hemisphere-1976-R). No production credits available. (W)

3023. SEMI-TOUGH. (United Artists-1977-Michael Ritchie-R). Screenplay by Walter Bernstein, based on the novel by Dan Jenkins; Atheneum, 1972, 307p. (LACOPL, Q, W)

3024. THE SENATOR LIKES WOMEN. (Horizon-1975-Lucio Fulci-R). Screenplay credits not available. (W)

3025. THE SENDER. (Paramount-1982-Roger Christian-R). Screenplay by Thomas Baum. (V)

SENILITA see CARELESS

3026. THE SENIORS. (Cinema Shares-1978-Rod Amateau-R). Screenplay by Stanley Shapiro. (W)

3027. SENSATIONS. (Pic American-1975-Alberto Ferro aka Lasse Braun-X). Screenplay by Alberto Ferro (aka Lasse Braun). (W)

3028. THE SENSUOUS ASSASSIN. (New Line-1975-Leonard Kiegel-N/R). No screenplay credits available. (W)

3029. THE SENSUOUS NURSE. (Mid-Broadway-1979-Nello Rossati-R). Screenplay credits not available. (W)

3030. THE SENSUOUS SICILIAN. (Medusa-1975-Marco Vicario-R). Screenplay by Marco Vicario, from the novel by Vitaliano Brancati; Dompiani, 1944. (LACOPL, W)

3031. THE SENSUOUS THREE. (Group I-1975-Steve Amberg-R).
       No screenplay credits available. (W)

3032. A SENTIMENTAL STORY. (Lenfilm-1976-Igor Maslennikov-
       N/R). Screenplay by Igor Maslennikov, based on the novel
       by Vera Panova. (V)

3033. THE SENTINEL. (Universal-1977-Michael Winner-R). Screen-
       play by Jeffrey Konvitz and Michael Winner, based on the
       novel by Jeffrey Konvitz; Ballantine, 1974, 278p. (HR,
       LACOPL, Q, V)

3034. SEPARATE WAYS. (Crown International-1981-Howard Avedis-
       R). Screenplay by Leah Appel, story by Leah Appel, How-
       ard Avedis, and Marlene Schmidt. (V, W)

3035. SGT. PEPPER'S LONELY HEARTS CLUB BAND. (Universal-
       1978-Michael Schultz-PG). Screenplay by Henry Edwards;
       novelization by Henry Edwards; Pocket Books, 1978. (HR,
       LACOPL, LAT, Q, V, W)

       SERGEANT STEINER see BREAKTHROUGH

3036. SERIAL. (Paramount-1980-Bill Persky-R). Screenplay by
       Rich Eustis, Michael Elias, based on the novel by Cyra
       McFadden; Knopf, 1977, 111p. (LACOPL, Q, V, W)

3037. SERIE NOIRE. (Gaumont-1982-Alain Corneau-N/R). Screen-
       play and adaptation by Georges Perec and Alain Corneau,
       based on A Hell of a Woman by Jim Thompson. (W)

3038. THE SERPENT'S EGG. (Paramount-1977-Ingmar Bergman-R).
       Screenplay by Ingmar Bergman; Pantheon, 1977, 123p.
       (LACOPL, Q, W)

3039. SERVANT AND MISTRESS. (New Line Cinema-1978-Bruno
       Gatillon-N/R). Screenplay by Frantz-Andre Burghuet and
       Dominique Fabre. (W)

       SESION CONTINUA see DOUBLE FEATURE

3040. SEVEN. (American International-1979-Andy Sidaris-R).
       Screenplay by William Driskill and Robert Baird, from a
       story by Andy Sidaris. (V, W)

3041. SEVEN ALONE. (Doty-Dayton-1975-Earl Bellamy-G).
       Screenplay by Douglas Day Stewart and Eleanor Lamb,
       based on the book On to Oregon by Honore Morrow; Mor-
       row, 1926. (LACOPL, W)

3042. SEVEN BEAUTIES. (Cinema 5-1976-Lina Wertmuller-R).

Screenplay by Lina Wertmuller; screenplay in <u>The Screen-plays of Lina Wertmuller</u>; Quadrangle, 1977, 334p. (HR, LACOPL, Q, V, W)

3043. THE SEVEN BROTHERS MEET DRACULA. (Dynamite Entertainment Inc.-1979-Roy Ward Baker-R). Screenplay by Ron Houghton. (V, W)

3044. SEVEN DOORS OF DEATH. (Aquarius-1983-Louis Fuller-R). Screenplay by Roy Corchoran. (W)

SEVEN GRAVES FOR ROGAN <u>see</u> A TIME TO DIE

3045. SEVEN-MAN ARMY. (Shaw Brothers-1976-Chang Cheh-N/R). Screenplay by I. Kuang and Chang Cheh. (W)

3046. THE SEVEN PER-CENT SOLUTION. (Universal-1976-Herbert Ross-PG). Screenplay by Nicholas Meyer, based on his novel; Dutton, 1974, 253p. (LACOPL, Q, V)

3047. SEVENTEEN AND ANXIOUS. (Martin-1975-Zybnek Brynych-R). Screenplay credits not available. (W)

3048. SEVERAL INTERVIEWS ON PERSONAL MATTERS. (IFEX/ Sovexportfilm-1982-Lana Gogoberidze-N/R). Screenplay by Zaura Arsenaschvili, Erlom Akhvlediani, and Lana Gogoberidze. (W)

3049. SEX AND THE FRENCH SCHOOLGIRL. (Aquarius-1975-Pierre Unia-X). No screenplay credits available. (W)

3050. SEX CLINIC GIRLS. (Alex Robbins-1975-Alex Robbins-X). Screenplay credits not available. (W)

3051. SEX DEMON. (J.D.G.-1975-J. C. Cricket-X). Screenplay by J. C. Cricket. (W)

3052. SEX WISH. (Bonefide-1976-X). No production credits available. (W)

3053. SEX WITH A SMILE. (Surrogate-1976-Sergio Martino-R). No screenplay credits available. (W)

3054. SEXTEEN. (Mad Dog-1975-Peter Locke-X). No screenplay credits available. (W)

3055. SEXTETTE. (Crown International-1979-Ken Hughes). Screenplay by Herbert Baker, based on the play <u>Sextette</u> by Mae West. (BFI, V, W)

3056. SEXTOOL. (Halsted/Brown-1975-Taylor Brown-X). No screenplay credits available. (W)

3057. SEXUAL COMMUNICATION. (Hollywood International-1975-Albert Irving-X). Screenplay by Albert Irving. (W)

3058. SEXUAL ECSTASY OF THE MACUMBA. (Hollywood International-1975-Jeremiah Schlotter-X). Screenplay credited to Mike Merino and Susane Foughtz. (W)

3059. SEXUAL KUNG FU IN HONG KONG. (Hollywood International-1975-Carlos Tobalina-X). Screenplay written by Lawrence Samuelson, adapted by Carlos Tobalina. (W)

3060. SEXUAL SENSORY PERCEPTION. (Hollywood International-1975-Jack Mattis & Martin Margulies-X). Screenplay written by Jack Mattis & Martin Margulies, with additional material by Larry Hilbrand. (W)

3061. SHADOW OF ANGELS. (Albatross/Artcofilm-1983-Daniel Schmid-N/R). Screenplay by Daniel Schmid and Rainer Werner Fassbinder, from Fassbinder's play. (W)

3062. SHADOW OF THE HAWK. (Columbia-1976-George McCowan-PG). Screenplay by Norman Thaddeus Vane and Herbert J. Wright, story by Peter Jensen, Lynette Cahill, and Norman Thaddeus Vane. (W)

THE SHADOW WARRIOR see KAGEMUSHA

3063. SHADOWMAN. (New Line Cinema-1975-Georges Franju-PG). Screenplay by Jacques Champreux. (W)

3064. THE SHAGGY D.A. (Buena Vista-1976-Robert Stevenson-G). Screenplay by Don Tait, suggested by The Hound of Florence by Felix Salten; Simon & Schuster, 1930. (LACOPL, Q, V)

3065. SHAMPOO. (Columbia-1975-Hal Ashby-R). Screenplay by Robert Towne and Warren Beatty. (Q, W)

3066. SHANGHAI JOE. (United International-1976-Mario Caiano-R). Screenplay credits not available. (W)

3067. SHANGHAI LIL AND THE SUN LUCK KID. (Bardene International-1975-Chu-Ko Chin-Yung, Yang Ching-Chen-N/R). Screenplay by Yang Ching-Chen and Chang Hsin-i. (W)

3068. THE SHAPE OF THINGS TO COME. (Film Ventures-1980-George McCowan). Screenplay by Martin Lager. (V, W)

3069. SHARKS' TREASURE. (United Artists-1975-Cornel Wilde-PG). Screenplay by Cornel Wilde. (W)

233 Sharky's

3070. SHARKY'S MACHINE. (Orion/Warner Bros.-1981-Burt Reynolds-R). Screenplay by Gerald Di Pego, based on the novel by William Diehl; Delacorte Press, 1978. (BFI, LACOPL, LAT, Q, V, W)

3071. SHE CAME TO THE VALLEY. (R.G.V. PICTURES-1979-Albert Band-PG). Screenplay by Frank Ray Perilli and Albert Band, based on the novel by Cleo Dawson. (W)

3072. SHE DANCES ALONE. (D.H.D. Enterprises-1981-Robert Dornhelm-N/R). Screenplay by Paul Davis. (V, W)

3073. SHEBA, BABY. (American International-1975-William Girdler-PG). Screenplay by William Girdler, story by William Girdler and David Sheldon. (W)

3074. SHEENA. (Columbia-1984-John Guillermin-PG). Screenplay by David Newman and Lorenzo Semple Jr., story by David Newman and Leslie Stevens. (V)

3075. SHEILA LEVINE IS DEAD AND LIVING IN NEW YORK. (Paramount-1975-Sidney J. Furie-PG). Screenplay by Kenny Solms and Gail Parent, based on the novel by Gail Parent; Putnam, 1972, 223p. (HR, LACOPL, LAT, Q, V, W)

3076. SHENANIGANS. (Jacoby-1977-Joseph Jacoby-N/R). Screenplay by Joseph Jacoby. (V)

3077. SHERLICK HOLMES. (Webster-1976-Tim McCoy-X). Screenplay credits not available. (W)

3078. THE SHILLINGBURY BLOWERS. (Inner Circle-1980-Val Guest-N/R). Screenplay by Francis Essex. (V)

3079. THE SHINING. (Warner Bros.-1980-Stanley Kubrick-R). Screenplay by Stanley Kubrick and Diane Johnson, based on the novel by Stephen King; New American Library, 1977, 447p. (LACOPL, Q, V, W)

3080. SHOCK TREATMENT. (20th Century-Fox-1981-Jim Sharman-PG). Screenplay by Richard O'Brien and Jim Sharman, additional ideas by Brian Thomson. (Q, LAT, V, W)

3081. SHOCK WAVES. (Joseph Brenner-1980-Ken Wiederhorn-PG). Screenplay by John Harrison and Ken Wiederhorn. (V, W)

3082. SHOGUN ASSASSIN. (New World-1980-Robert Houston-R). Screenplay by Robert Houston, David Weisman, and Kazuo Koike, based on an original story by Kazuo Koike and Goseki Kojima. (V, W)

3083. SHOOT. (Avco Embassy-1976-Harvey Hart-R). Screenplay
       by Dick Berg, from the novel by Douglas Fairbairn; Double-
       day, 1973, 152p. (LACOPL, Q, V, W)

3084. SHOOT THE MOON. (MGM/UA-1982-Alan Parker-R).
       Screenplay by Bo Goldman. (LAT, Q, V)

3085. THE SHOOTING PARTY. (Corinth Films-1981-Emil Loteanu-
       N/R). Screenplay by Emil Loteanu, based on a novel by
       Anton Chekhov, in Best Known Works; Blue Ribbon Books,
       1929. (LACOPL, LAT, W)

3086. THE SHOOTIST. (Paramount-1976-Don Siegel-PG). Screen-
       play by Miles Hood Swarthout and Scott Hale, based on a
       novel by Glendon Swarthout; Doubleday, 1975, 186p. (HR,
       LACOPL, Q, V, W)

3087. SHORT EYES. (Paramount-1977-Robert M. Young-R).
       Screenplay by Miguel Pinero, from his play; Hill & Wang,
       1975, 127p. (LACOPL, W)

3088. SHORTCUTS. (IFEX-1983-Jiri Menzel-N/R). Screenplay by
       Bohumil Hrabal and Jiri Menzel. (W)

3089. THE SHOUT. (Films Incorporated-1979-Jerzy Skolimowski-
       R). Screenplay by Michael Austin and Jerzy Skolimowski,
       from a story by Robert Graves. (W)

3090. SHOUT AT THE DEVIL. (American International-1976-Peter
       Hunt-PG). Screenplay by Wilbur Smith, Alistair Reid, and
       Stanley Price, from the novel by Wilbur Smith. (Q, W)

3091. SHRIEK OF THE MUTILATED. (Film Brokers Ltd.-1976-
       Michael Findlay-R). Screenplay by Ed Kelleher and Ed
       Adlum. (W)

       SHUSSHO IWAI see THE WOLVES

3092. THE SIBERIAD. (IFEX/Satra Film Corp./Sovexportfilm-1979-
       Andrei Mikhalkov Konchalovsky-N/R). Screenplay by
       Valentjob and Andrei Mikhalkov Konchalovsky. (W)

3093. SIDECAR RACERS. (Universal-1975-Earl Bellamy-PG).
       Screenplay by Jon Cleary. (Q, W)

3094. SIDEWINDER 1. (Avco Embassy-1977-Earl Bellamy-PG).
       Screenplay by Nancy Voyles Crawford and Thomas McMahon.
       (Q, V)

3095. SIDNEY SHELDON'S BLOODLINE. (Paramount-1979-Terence
       Young-R). Screenplay by Laird Koenig, based on the novel

by Sidney Sheldon; Morrow, 1978, 444p. (HR, LACOPL, LAT, Q, V, W)

3096. THE SIGN OF FOUR. (Mapleton Films-1983-Desmond Davis-N/R). Screenplay by Charles Pogue. (V)

3097. SIGNAL 7. (Don Taylor-1984-Rob Nilsson-N/R). Screenplay by Rob Nilsson. (V)

3098. SIGNUM LAUDIS. (IFEX-1983-Martin Holly-N/R). Screenplay by Vladimir Kalina and Jiri Krizan. (W)

3099. SILENCE OF THE NORTH. (Universal-1981-Allan Winton King-N/R). Screenplay by Patricia Louisiana Knop, based on a book by Olive Fredrickson and Ben East. (V)

3100. SILENT MADNESS. (Almi Pictures-1984-Simon Nuchtern-N/R). Screenplay by Robert Zimmerman and William P. Milling, with additional dialog by Nelson de Mille. (V)

3101. SILENT MOVIE. (20th Century-Fox-1976-Mel Brooks-PG). Screenplay by Mel Brooks, Ron Clark, Rudy DeLuca, and Barry Levinson, from a story by Ron Clark. (Q, W)

3102. SILENT NIGHT, DEADLY NIGHT. (Tri-Star-1984-Charles E. Sellier-R). Screenplay by Michael Hickey, based on a story by Paul Caimi. (V)

3103. THE SILENT ONE. (Gibson Films-1984-Yvonne Mackay-N/R). Screenplay by Ian Mune, from the novel by Joy Crowley. (V)

3104. THE SILENT PARTNER. (EMC Film Corp.-1979-Daryl Duke-R). Screenplay by Curtis Hanson, based on Anders Bodelson's novel Think of a Number. (V, W)

3105. SILENT RAGE. (Columbia-1982-Michael Miller-R). Screenplay by Joseph Fraley. (Q, V, W)

3106. SILENT SCREAM. (American Cinema Releasing-1980-Denny Harris-R). Screenplay by Ken Wheat, Jim Wheat, and Wallace C. Bennett. (V, W)

3107. THE SILENT STRANGER. (MGM-1975-Vance Lewis-PG). Screenplay by Vincenzo Cerami and Giancarlo Ferrando, from a story by Tony Anthony. (W)

3108. SILHOUETTES. (Primi Piani Enterprises-1982-Giuseppe Murolo-N/R). Screenplay by David Weiss, Giuseppe Murolo, and Russell Firestone; script consultant, Ken Friedman. (V, W)

3109. SILKWOOD. (20th Century-Fox-1983-Mike Nichols-R). Nora Ephron and Alice Arlen wrote the screenplay. (HR, LAT, V)

3110. SILVER BEARS. (Columbia-1978-Ivan Passer-PG). Screenplay by Peter Stone, based on the novel by Paul E. Erdman; Scribner's, 1974, 260p. (LACOPL, W)

3111. SILVER CITY. (Limelight-1984-Sophia Turkiewicz-N/R). Screenplay by Thomas Keneally, Sophia Turkiewicz. (V)

3112. SILVER DREAM RACER. (Almi-1983-David Wickes-PG). Screenplay by David Wickes. (V, W)

3113. SILVER STREAK. (20th Century-Fox-1976-Arthur Miller-PG). Screenplay by Colin Higgins. (HR, LAT, Q, V)

3114. SIMON. (Orion-1980-Marshall Brickman-PG). Screenplay authored by Marshall Brickman. (Q, V, W)

3115. A SIMPLE STORY. (Quartet Films-1979-Claude Sautet-N/R). Screenplay by Claude Sautet and Jean-Loup Dabadie. (W)

3116. SIMPLY IRRESISTIBLE. (Essex-1983-Edwin Brown-R). Screenplay by Sandra Winters and Edwin Brown. (W)

3117. SINBAD AND THE EYE OF THE TIGER. (Columbia-1977-Sam Wanamaker-G). Screenplay by Beverley Cross, from a story by Beverley Cross and Ray Harryhausen; novelization by John Ryder Hall; Pocket Books, 1977. (LACOPL, Q, V)

3118. THE SINS OF RACHEL. (R. A. Enterprises-1975-Richard Fontaine-R). Screenplay by Ann Noble. (W)

3119. SIP THE WINE. (Liberty Street-1976-Dan Caldwell-X). Screenplay credits not available. (W)

3120. SIR HENRY AT RAWLINSON END. (Charisma Films-1980-Steve Roberts-N/R). Screenplay by Vivian Stanshall and Steve Roberts. (V, W)

3121. THE SISTER-IN-LAW. (Crown International-1975-Joseph Ruben-R). Screenplay by Joseph Ruben. (W)

3122. SISTER STREET FIGHTER. (New Line-1976-Kazuhiko Yamaguchi-R). Screenplay by Norifumi Suzuki. (W)

3123. SISTERS, OR THE BALANCE OF HAPPINESS. (Cinema 5-1982-Margarethe von Trotta-N/R). Screenplay by Margarethe von Trotta, Martje Grohmann, and Luisa Francia. (W)

3124. SITTING DUCKS. (United Film Dist.-1979-Henry Jaglom-R). Screenplay by Henry Jaglom. (Q, V, W)

3125. SIX CAR STUD. (Zodiac-1975-Mike Taylor-N/R). No screen-
       play credits available. (W)

3126. SIX PACK. (20th Century-Fox-1982-Daniel Petrie-PG).
       Screenplay by Mike Marvin and Alex Matter. (Q, V, W)

3127. SIX PACK ANNIE. (American International-1975-Graydon F.
       David-R). Screenplay by Norman Winksi, David Kidd, and
       Wil David. (W)

3128. SIX WEEKS. (Universal-1982-Tony Bill-PG). Screenplay
       written by David Seltzer, based on the novel by Fred Mus-
       tard Stewart; Arbor House, 1976, 202p. (HR, LACOPL,
       LAT, NYT, V, W)

3129. SIXTEEN. (United International-1976-Tiziano Longo-R).
       No screenplay credits available. (W)

3130. SIXTEEN CANDLES. (Universal-1984-John Hughes-PG).
       Screenplay by John Hughes. (V)

3131. SIXTH AND MAIN. (National Cinema-1977-Christopher Cain-
       N/R). Screenplay credits not available. (V)

3132. SKATEBOARD. (Universal-1978-George Gage-PG). Screen-
       play by Richard A. Wolf and George Gage, based on a story
       by Richard A. Wolf. (V, W)

3133. SKATETOWN, U.S.A. (Columbia-1979-William A. Levey-PG).
       Screenplay by Nick Castle, based on a story by William A.
       Levey, Lorin Dreyfuss, and Nick Castle. (V, W)

3134. THE SKIP TRACER. (G. G. Communications-1979-Zale Dalen-
       PG). Screenplay credits not available. (W)

3135. SKY RIDERS. (20th Century-Fox-1976-Douglas Hickox-PG).
       Screenplay written by Jack Dewitt, Stanley Mann, and Garry
       Michael White. (W)

3136. THE SLAP. (Silver Screen Enterprises-1976-Claude Pinoteau-
       PG). Screenplay by Jean-Loup Dabadie and Claude Pinoteau.
       (W)

3137. SLAP IN THE FACE. (Horizon-1975-Rolf Thiele-R). Screen-
       play credits not available. (W)

3138. SLAP SHOT. (Universal-1977-George Roy Hill-R). Screen-
       play by Nancy Dowd. (Q, V)

3139. SLAPSTICK OF ANOTHER KIND. (Entertainment Releasing
       Co.-1984-Steve Paul-PG). Screenplay by Steven Paul, based
       on Kurt Vonnegut's novel Slapstick. (V)

3140.   THE SLASHER.   (William Mishkin-1975-Robert Montero-R).
Screenplay by Lou Angelli, Robert Montero, and I. Fasant.
(W)

3141.   SLAUGHTER IN SAN FRANCISCO.   (World Northal-1981-
William Lowe-R).   Screenplay by William Lowe.   (V)

3142.   SLAUGHTERDAY.   (Intercontinental-1981-Peter Patzak-R).
Screenplay by Peter Patzak, Walter Kindler, and Ossi
Bronner.   (W)

3143.   A SLAVE OF LOVE.   (Cinema 5-1978-Nikita Mikhalkov-N/R).
Screenplay by Friedrikh Gorenstein and Andrei Mikhalkov
Konchalovsky.   (W)

3144.   SLAVE OF THE CANNIBAL GOD.   (New Line Cinema-1979-
Sergio Martino-R).   Screenplay credits not available.   (W)

3145.   THE SLAYER.   (21st Century Distribution-1982-J. S.
Cardone-R).   Screenplay by J. S. Cardone and William R.
Ewing.   (V, W)

3146.   SLAYGROUND.   (Universal-1984-Terry Bedford-R).   Screenplay by Trevor Preston, from a novel by Richard Stark.
(V)

3147.   SLEEPAWAY CAMP.   (United Film Distribution Co.-1983-
Robert Hiltzik-R).   Screenplay by Robert Hiltzik.   (V, W)

3148.   SLEEPING DOGS.   (Sator-1982-Roger Donaldson-N/R).
Screenplay by Ian Mune and Arthur Baysting, story by
Karl Stead.   (LAT, W)

3149.   THE SLIPPER AND THE ROSE.   (Universal-1976-Bryan
Forbes-G).   Screenplay by Bryan Forbes, Robert B. Sherman, and Richard M. Sherman.   (Q, W)

3150.   SLIPUP.   (Slip-Art-1975-Harold Hindgrind-X).   Screenplay
by Harold Hindgrind.   (W)

3151.   SLITHIS.   (Fabtrax-1978-Stephen Traxler-PG).   Screenplay
by Stephen Traxler.   (W)

3152.   SLOW ATTACK.   (New Yorker Films-1983-Reinhard Hauff-
N/R).   Screenplay by Burkhard Driest.   (W)

3153.   SLOW DANCING IN THE BIG CITY.   (United Artists-1978-
John G. Avildsen-PG).   Screenplay by Barra Grant; novelization by Barra Grant; Warner Books, 1978.   (Q, V, W)

3154.   SLUMBER PARTY '57.   (Cannon Group-1977-William A. Levey-

R). Screenplay by Frank Farmer, from a story by William A.
Levey. (V, W)

3155. THE SLUMBER PARTY MASSACRE. (Pacific Film Release-
1982-Amy Jones-R). Screenplay by Rita Mae Brown. (V, W)

3156. SMALL CHANGE. (New World-1976-Francois Truffaut-PG).
Screenplay by Francois Truffaut and Suzanne Schiffman.
(Q, W)

3157. A SMALL CIRCLE OF FRIENDS. (United Artists-1980-Rob
Cohen-R). Screenplay by Ezra Sacks. (Q, V, W)

3158. A SMALL TOWN IN TEXAS. (American International-1976-
Jack Starrett-PG). Screenplay by William Norton. (W)

3159. SMASH PALACE. (Aardvark Films-1981-Roger Donaldson-
N/R). Screenplay by Roger Donaldson, Peter Hansard, and
Bruno Lawrence. (V)

3160. SMILE. (United Artists-1975-Michael Ritchie-PG). Screenplay by Jerry Belson. (Q, W)

3161. SMILE ORANGE. (Knuts-1976-Trevor D. Rhone-PG).
Screenplay by Trevor Rhone. (W)

3162. SMITHEREENS. (New Line-1982-Susan Seidelman-N/R).
Screenplay by Ron Nystwaner and Susan Seidelman. (W)

3163. SMOKE IN THE WIND. (Gamalex-1975-Joseph Kane-N/R).
Screenplay by Eric Allen. (W)

3164. SMOKEY AND THE BANDIT. (Universal-1977-Hal Needham-
PG). Screenplay by James Lee Barrett, Charles Shyer, and
Alan Mandel, from a story by Hal Needham and Robert L.
Levy. (HR, LAT, Q, V)

3165. SMOKEY AND THE BANDIT II. (Universal-1980-Hal Needham-
PG). Screenplay by Jerry Belson and Brock Yates, from a
story by Michael Kane, based on characters created by Hal
Needham and Robert L. Levy. (Q, V, W)

3166. SMOKEY AND THE BANDIT, PART 3. (Universal-1983-Dick
Lowry-PG). Screenplay by Stuart Birnbaum, David Dashev,
based on characters created by Hal Needham and Robert L.
Levy. (W)

3167. SMOKEY AND THE GOODTIME OUTLAWS. (Howco Interna-
tional-1978-Alex Grasshoff-PG). Screenplay by Frank Dobbs
and Bob Walsh, story by Jesse Turner. (W)

3168. SMOKEY AND THE HOTWIRE GANG. (NMD-1979-Anthony
       Cardoza-PG). Screenplay by T. Gary Cardoza. (W)

3169. SMOKEY BITES THE DUST. (New World-1981-Charles B.
       Griffith-PG). Screenplay by Max Apple, based on a story
       by Brian Williams. (LAT, V, W)

3170. SMOOTH VELVET, RAW SILK. (Dimension-1978-Brunello
       Rondi-R). Screenplay credits not available. (W)

3171. SMORGASBORD. (Warner Bros.-1983-Jerry Lewis-PG).
       Screenplay by Jerry Lewis and Bill Richmond. (V)

3172. SNAKE FIRST FIGHTER. (21st Century-1981-Chin Hsin-R).
       Screenplay credits not available. (LAT, W)

3173. SNAKE FIST VS. THE DRAGON. (21st Century-1980-R).
       No production credits available. (W)

3174. SNAP-SHOT. (Filmways Australasian-1979-Simon Wincer-
       N/R). Screenplay by Chris and Everett De Roche. (V)

       SNAPSHOT see THE DAY AFTER HALLOWEEN

3175. SO FINE. (Warner Bros.-1981-Andrew Bergman-R).
       Screenplay by Andrew Bergman. (BFI, LAT, Q, V, W)

3176. SO LONG, STOOGE. (AMLF-1983-Claude Berri-N/R).
       Screenplay by Claude Berri and Alain Page, from a novel
       by Alain Page. (V)

3177. SO SAD ABOUT GLORIA. (Libert Films International-1975-
       Harr Thomason-PG). Screenplay credits not available. (W)

3178. SODOM AND GOMORRAH--THE LAST SEVEN DAYS.
       (Mitchell Brothers-1975-Jim Mitchell & Artie Mitchell-X).
       Screenplay by Billy Boyer. (W)

3179. SOGGY BOTTOM U.S.A. (Gaylord-1982-Ted Flicker-PG).
       Screenplay by Eric Edson, Stephen C. Burnham, and Joy
       N. Houck Jr., from a story by Hal L. Harrison Jr. (W)

3180. THE SOLDIER. (Embassy-1982-James Glickenhaus-N/R).
       Screenplay by James Glickenhaus. (V, W)

3181. SOLDIER OF ORANGE. (Rank Film Organization-1979-Paul
       Verhoeven-N/R). Screenplay by Gerard Soeteman, Kees
       Holierhoek, and Paul Verhoeven. (V, W)

3182. A SOLDIER'S STORY. (Columbia-1984-Norman Jewison-PG).
       Screenplay by Charles Fuller, based on his play A Soldier's
       Play; Hill & Wang, 1982, 100p. (HR, LACOPL, LAT, V)

3183. SOME KIND OF HERO. (Paramount-1982-Michael Pressman-R).
       Screenplay by James Kirkwood and Robert Boris, based on
       the novel by James Kirkwood; Crowell, 1975, 399p.
       (LACOPL, Q, V)

3184. SOME LIKE IT COOL. (PRO International-1979-Francois
       Legrand aka Franz Antel-R). Screenplay by Joshua Sinclair
       and Tom Priman. (W)

3185. SOMEBODY KILLED HER HUSBAND. (Columbia-1978-Lamont
       Johnson-PG). Screenplay by Reginald Rose; novelization by
       Clyde B. Phillips; Jove, 1978. (LACOPL, Q, V, W)

3186. SOMETHING SHORT OF PARADISE. (American International-
       1979-David Helpern Jr.-PG). Screenplay by Fred Barron.
       (V, W)

3187. SOMETHING TO HIDE. (Atlantic-1976-Alistair Reid-N/R).
       Screenplay by Alistair Reid, based on a novel by Nicholas
       Monsarrat. (W)

3188. SOMETHING WICKED THIS WAY COMES. (Buena Vista-
       1983-Jack Clayton-PG). Screenplay by Ray Bradbury, based
       on his novel; Knopf, 1983, 145p. (HR, LACOPL, LAT, V)

3189. SOMEWHERE IN TIME. (Universal-1980-Jeannot Szwarc-PG).
       Screenplay by Richard Matheson, from his novel Bid Time
       Return; Viking, 1975, 277p. (HR, LACOPL, LAT, Q, V, W)

3190. SOMEWHERE, SOMEONE. (NEF/French Embassy-1979-Yannick
       Bellon-N/R). Screenplay by Yannick Bellon. (W)

3191. SONATA OVER THE LAKE. (Latvian Film Studio-1976-Gunar
       Tcelinski & Varis Brasla-N/R). Screenplay by R. Ezer,
       based on his novel The Well. (V)

       SONEZAKI SHINJU see THE LOVE SUICIDES AT SONEZAKI

3192. SONGWRITER. (Tri-Star-1984-Alan Rudolph-R). Screenplay
       by Bud Shrake. (V)

3193. SOPHIE'S CHOICE. (Universal-AFD-1982-Alan J. Pakula-R).
       Screenplay by Alan J. Pakula, based on the novel by William
       Styron; Random House, 1979, 515p. (HR, LACOPL, LAT,
       NYT, V, W)

3194. SORCERER. (Universal-Paramount-1977-William Friedkin-PG).
       Screenplay by Walon Green, from the novel The Wages of
       Fear by Georges Arnaud. (Q, V)

3195. SORCERESS. (New World-1983-Brian Stuart-R). Screenplay
       by Jim Wynorski. (V, W)

SOSKEN PA GUDS JORD see CHILDREN OF THE EARTH

3196. SOUL BROTHERS OF KUNG FU. (Cinema Shares Interna-
tional-1978-Hwa I. Hung-R). Screenplay credits not available. (W)

SOUNDER, PART 2 see PART 2, SOUNDER

3197. SOUNDS FROM THE MOUNTAINS. (Corinth Films-1980-
Mikio Naruse-N/R). Screenplay by Yoko Mizuki, from a
novel by Yasunari Kawabata. (W)

3198. SOUP DU JOUR. (ART-1975-Beau Buchanan-X). Screenplay credits not available. (W)

3199. SOUP FOR ONE. (Warner Bros.-1982-Jonathan Kaufer-R).
Screenplay by Jonathan Kaufer. (Q, V, W)

SOUP TO NUTS see WAITRESS

3200. SOUPCON. (Roy Durham/Jeffie Pike-1980-Jean-Charles
Tacchella-N/R). Screenplay by Jean-Charles Tacchella.
(W)

3201. SOUPERMAN. (Unique-1976-Fred Lincoln-X). No screenplay credits available. (W)

3202. SOURDOUGH. (Film Saturation Inc.-1977-Martin J.
Spinelli-G). Screenplay by Lewis N. Turner and Martin J.
Spinelli, from a story by Rod Perry. (V, W)

3203. SOUTHERN COMFORT. (20th Century-Fox-1981-Walter Hill-
R). Screenplay by Michael Kane, Walter Hill, and David
Giler. (LAT, Q, V, W)

SOUVENIRS, SOUVENIRS see MEMORIES, MEMORIES

3204. SPACE RAIDERS. (New World-1983-Howard R. Cohen-PG).
Screenplay by Howard R. Cohen. (LAT, V, W)

3205. SPACED OUT. (Miramax-1981-Norman J. Warren-R).
Screenplay by Andrew Payne. (V)

3206. SPACEHUNTER: ADVENTURES IN THE FORBIDDEN ZONE.
(Columbia-1983-Lamont Johnson-PG). Screenplay by Edith
Rey, David Preston, Dan Goldberg, and Len Blum, from a
story by Stewart Harding and Jean LaFleur. (LAT, V, W)

3207. SPACESHIP. (LAMI-1983-Bruce Kimmel-PG). Screenplay by
Bruce Kimmel. (W)

3208.   SPANISH FLY. (Emerson-1976-Bob Kellett-R). No screen-
        play credits available. (W)

3209.   SPARKLE. (Warner Bros.-1976-Sam O'Steen-PG). Screen-
        play by Joel Schumacher, story by Joel Schumacher and
        Howard Rosenman. (W)

3210.   SPARTACUS. (Corinth-1979-Yuri Grigorovich & V. Derbenev-
        N/R). Screenplay credits not available. (W)

3211.   SPASMO. (Libra-1976-Umberto Lenzi-N/R). Screenplay
        credits not available. (W)

3212.   SPASMS. (Producers Distribution Co.-1984-William Fruet-R).
        Screenplay by Don Enright, from the novel Death Bite by
        Michael Maryk and Brent Monahan. (V)

        SPAWN OF THE SLITHIS see SLITHIS

        THE SPAWNING see PIRANHA II

3213.   A SPECIAL DAY. (Cinema 5-1977-Ettore Scola-N/R).
        Screenplay and story by Ruggero Maccari, Ettore Scola,
        and Maurizio Costanzo. (Q, W)

3214.   SPECIAL SECTION. (Universal-1975-Costa Gavras-PG).
        Screenplay by Jorge Semprun and Costa-Gavras, from the
        work of Herve Villere. (Q, W)

3215.   SPECIAL TREATMENT. (New Yorker-1982-Goran Paskaljevic-
        N/R). Screenplay by G. Paskaljevic and Dusan Kovacevic.
        (W)

3216.   THE SPECIALIST. (1975-Frank Agrama-R). Screenplay
        credits not available. (W)

3217.   THE SPECIALIST. (Crown International-1975-Hikmet Avedis-
        R). Screenplay by Ralph B. Potts, Marlene Schmidt, and
        Hikmet Avedis, based on Come Now the Lawyers by Ralph B.
        Potts. (W)

3218.   SPECIALTY HOUSE. (Pyramid II-1975-C. E. Munger-X).
        Screenplay by Joseph Dreury. (W)

3219.   SPEEDTRAP. (First Artists-Intertamar-1978-Earl Bellamy-
        PG). Screenplay by Stuart A. Segal and Walter M. Spear,
        based on a story by Fred Mintz and Henry C. Parke. (W)

3220.   SPETTERS. (Samuel Goldwyn Co.-1981-Paul Verhoeven-R).
        Screenplay by Gerard Soeteman. (BFI, LAT, V, W)

3221. SPHINX. (Orion/Warner Bros.-1981-Franklin J. Schaffner-
       PG). Screenplay by John Byrum, from the novel by Robin
       Cook. (Q, V, W)

3222. THE SPIDERS. (Images Film-1979-Fritz Lang-N/R). Screen-
       play by Fritz Lang. (W)

3223. SPIKEY'S MAGIC WAND. (Different Strokes-1975-X). No
       production credits available. (W)

3224. SPINAL TAP. (Embassy-1984-Rob Reiner-R). Screenplay
       by Christopher Guest, Michael McKean, Harry Shearer, and
       Rob Reiner. (V)

3225. THE SPIRIT OF SEVENTY-SEX. (Artemis-1976-Ricki Krelmn-
       X). Screenplay by Ricki Krelmn. (W)

3226. THE SPIRIT OF THE BEE-HIVE. (Janus-1976-Victor Erice-
       N/R). Screenplay by Victor Erice and Angel Fernandez San-
       tos. (NYT, W)

3227. SPIRIT OF THE WIND. (Raven Pictures-1980-Ralph Liddle-
       N/R). Screenplay by Ralph Liddle and John Logue. (W)

3228. SPLASH. (Touchstone-1984-Ron Howard-PG). Screenplay
       by Lowell Ganz, Babaloo Mandel, and Bruce Jay Friedman,
       from a story by Bruce Jay Friedman, based on a story by
       Brian Grazer. (V)

3229. SPLATTER UNIVERSITY. (Troma Team-1984-Richard W.
       Haines-R). Screenplay by Richard W. Haines, John Michaels,
       and Michael Cunningham. (V)

3230. SPLIT IMAGE. (Orion/Polygram-1982-Red Kotcheff-R).
       Screenplay by Scott Spencer, Robert Kaufman, and Robert
       Mark Kamen. (V)

3231. SPLITTING UP. (Harlekijn Holland Film-1981-Herman van
       Veen-N/R). Screenplay by Herman van Veen, from his
       original story. (V)

3232. SPLITZ. (Film Ventures International-1984-Domonic Paris-
       N/R). Screenplay by Domonic Paris, Bianca Littlebaum,
       Harry Azorin, and Kelly Van Horn. (V)

3233. SPOILED CHILDREN. (Corinth-1981-Bertrand Tavernier-
       N/R). Screenplay by Charlotte Dubreuil, Christine Pascal,
       and Bertrand Tavernier. (LAT, V, W)

3234. SPRING BREAK. (Columbia-1983-Sean S. Cunningham-R).
       Screenplay by David Smilow. (LAT, V, W)

3235. SPRING FEVER. (Comworld Pictures-1983-Joseph L. Scanlan-
       PG). Screenplay by Stuart Gillard and Fred Stefan. (V, W)

3236. THE SPY WHO LOVED ME. (United Artists-1977-Lewis
       Gilbert-PG). Screenplay by Christopher Wood and Richard
       Maibaum; novelization by Christopher Wood; Warner, 1977,
       206p. (HR, LACOPL, LAT, NYT, Q, V)

3237. THE SQUEEZE. (Maverick-1980-Anthony M. Dawson-N/R).
       Screenplay by Simon O'Neil, Marc Princi, and Paul Costello.
       (LAT, V, W)

3238. SQUEEZE PLAY. (Troma Inc.-1981-Samuel Weil-R). Screen-
       play by Haim Pekelis, with additional material provided by
       Charles Kaufman. (V, W)

3239. SQUIRM. (American International-1976-Jeff Lieberman-R).
       Screenplay by Jeff Lieberman. (W)

3240. STACY'S KNIGHTS. (Crown International-1983-Jim Wilson-
       PG). Screenplay by Michael Blake. (W)

3241. STALKER. (Media Transactions-1978-Andrei Tarkovsky-N/R).
       Screenplay by Arkady and Boris Strugatzky, based on their
       novel Picnic by the Roadside. (LAT, W)

       DER STAND DER DINGE see THE STATE OF THINGS

3242. STAND UP VIRGIN SOLDIERS. (Warner Bros.-1977-Norman
       Cohen-N/R). Screenplay by Leslie Thomas, based on his
       novel of the same title. (V)

       LA STANZA DEL VESCOVO see THE BISHOP'S BEDROOM

3243. THE STAR CHAMBER. (20th Century-Fox-1983-Peter Hyams-
       R). Screenplay by Roderick Taylor and Peter Hyams. (V)

       STAR CHILD see SPACE RAIDERS

3244. STAR 80. (Ladd Co./Warner Bros.-1983-Bob Fosse-R).
       Screenplay by Bob Fosse, based in part on Death of a
       Playmate by Teresa Carpenter. (LAT, V)

3245. A STAR IS BORN. (Warner Bros.-1976-Frank Pierson-R).
       Screenplay by John Gregory Dunne, Joan Didion, and Frank
       Pierson, based on a story by William Wellman and Robert
       Carson. (V)

3246. STAR TREK--THE MOTION PICTURE. (Paramount-1979-
       Robert Wise-G). Screenplay by Harold Livingston, based
       on a story by Alan Dean Foster. (Q, V, W)

3247. STAR TREK II: THE WRATH OF KHAN. (Paramount-1982-
       Nicholas Meyer-PG). Screenplay by Jack B. Sowards, story
       by Harve Bennett and Jack B. Sowards, based on the tele-
       vision series "Star Trek" created by Gene Roddenberry.
       (HR, LAT, V, W)

3248. STAR TREK III: THE SEARCH FOR SPOCK. (Paramount-
       1984-Leonard Nimoy-PG). Screenplay by Harve Bennett,
       based on "Star Trek" television series created by Gene Rod-
       denberry; novelization by Vonda McIntyre; Pocket Books,
       1984, 292p. (HAR, LACOPL, LAT, V)

3249. STAR WARS. (20th Century-Fox-1977-George Lucas-PG).
       Screenplay by George Lucas. (V)

3250. STARBIRD AND SWEET WILLIAM. (Howco International-
       1976-Jack B. Hivley-G). Screenplay by Axel Gruenberg.
       (W)

3251. STARCRASH. (New World-1979-Lewis Coates-PG). Screen-
       play by Lewis Coates and Nat Wachsberger. (V, W)

3252. STARDUST. (Columbia-1975-Michael Apted-R). Screenplay
       by Ray Connolly. (W)

3253. STARDUST MEMORIES. (United Artists-1980-Woody Allen-
       PG). Screenplay by Woody Allen. (Q, V, W)

3254. STARHOPS. (First American Films-1978-Barbara Peeters-
       N/R). Screenplay by Dallas Meredith. (HR, V, W)

3255. STARK RAVING MAD. (Independent Artists-1983-George F.
       Hood-PG). Screenplay credits not available. (W)

3256. THE STARLETS. (Quadravision International-1976-David
       Summers & Joseph Tebber-X). Screenplay by M. C. Von
       Hellen. (W)

3257. STARMAN. (Columbia-1984-John Carpenter-PG). Screen-
       play by Bruce A. Evans and Raynold Gideon; novelization
       by Alan Dean Foster; Warner Books, 1984, 280p. (HR,
       LACOPL, LAT, NYT, V)

3258. STARSHIP INVASIONS. (Warner Bros.-1978-Ed Hunt-PG).
       Screenplay by Ed Hunt. (W)

3259. STARSTRUCK. (Cinecom International-1982-Gillian Armstrong-
       N/R). Screenplay by Stephen MacLean. (W)

3260. STARTING OVER. (Paramount-1979-Alan J. Pakula-R).
       Screenplay by James L. Brooks, based on the novel by

Dan Wakefield; Delacorte Press, 1973, 290p. (HR,
LACOPL, Q, V, W)

3261. THE STATE OF THINGS. (Gray City-1982-Wim Wenders-
N/R). Screenplay by Wim Wenders and Robert Kramer.
(V, W)

3262. STATELINE MOTEL. (International Cinefilm-1976-Maurizio
Lucidi-R). Screenplay credits not available. (W)

3263. STATION. (Toho-1982-Vasuo Furuhata-N/R). Screenplay
by So Kuramoto. (W)

3264. A STATION FOR TWO. (?-1983-Eldar Ryazanov-N/R).
Screenplay by Emil Braginsky and Eldar Ryazanov. (BFI)

3265. STAY AS YOU ARE. (New Line Cinema-1979-Alberto Lattuada-
N/R). Screenplay by Alberto Lattuada and Enrico Oldoini,
story by Paolo Cavara and Enrico Oldoini. (W)

3266. STAY HUNGRY. (United Artists-1976-Bob Rafelson-R).
Screenplay by Charles Gaines and Bob Rafelson, based on
a novel by Charles Gaines; Doubleday, 1972, 262p. (Q, W)

3267. STAYING ALIVE. (Mishkin-1979-Robert A. Endelson-R).
Screenplay by Straw Weisman. (W)

3268. STAYING ALIVE. (Paramount-1983-Sylvester Stallone-PG).
Screenplay by Sylvester Stallone and Norman Wexler, based
on characters created by Nik Cohn; novelization by Leonore
Fleischer; Pocket Books, 1983, 190p. (BFI, HR, LACOPL,
LAT, V, W)

3269. STEEL. (World-Northal Films-1980-Steven Carver-N/R).
Screenplay by Leigh Chapman. (V, W)

3270. THE STEEPLE-CHASE. (IFEX-1983-Jaroslav Soukup-N/R).
Screenplay by Miroslav Vaic and Jaroslav Soukup. (W)

3271. THE STEPFORD WIVES. (Columbia-1975-Bryan Forbes-PG).
Screenplay by William Goldman, from the novel by Ira Levin;
Random House, 1972, 145p. (Q, W)

3272. THE STEPPE. (Mosfilm-1978-Sergei Bondarchuk-N/R).
Screenplay by Sergei Bondarchuk. (V, W)

3273. STEPPING OUT. (Scandinavia Today-1982-Esben Hoilund
Carlsen-N/R). Screenplay by Nils Schou. (W)

3274. STEREO. (Emergent Films Ltd.-1984-David Cronenberg-
N/R). Screenplay by David Cronenberg. (V)

3275. STERNSTEIN MANOR. (Public Cinema-1980-Hans Geissendor-fer-N/R). Screenplay by Ludwig Anzengruber. (W)

3276. STEVIE. (First Artists-1978-Robert Enders-N/R). Screen-play by Hugh Whitemore, based on his play and the works of Stevie Smith. (LAT, V, W)

3277. STEVIE, SAMSON AND DELILAH. (Libert Films International-1975-Steve Hawkes-G). Screenplay credits not available. (W)

3278. STILL OF THE NIGHT. (MGM/UA-1982-Robert Benton-PG). Screenplay by Robert Benton, from a story by David New-man and Robert Benton; novelization by Robert Alley; Ballantine Books, 1982, 224p. (LACOPL, V)

3279. STILL SMOKIN'. (Paramount-1983-Thomas Chong-R). Screen-play by Thomas Chong and Cheech Marin. (W)

3280. THE STILTS. (Emiliano Piedra-1984-Carlos Saura-N/R). Screenplay by Carlos Saura and Fernando Fernan Gomez. (V)

3281. THE STING II. (Universal-1983-Jeremy Paul Kagan-PG). Screenplay by David S. Ward. (LAT, V)

3282. STINGRAY. (AVCO Embassy-1978-Richard Taylor-PG). Screenplay by Richard Taylor. (W)

3283. STIR. (Hoyts Distribution-1980-Stephen Wallace-R). Screen-play by Bob Jewson. (LAT, V)

3284. STIR CRAZY. (Columbia-1980-Sidney Poitier-R). Screenplay by Bruce Jay Friedman. (Q, V, W)

3285. THE STONE BOY. (TLC Films-1984-Chris Cain-PG). Screenplay by Gina Beriault. (V)

3286. STONY ISLAND. (World-Northal-1978-Andrew Davis-PG). Screenplay by Andrew Davis and Tamar Hoffs. (V)

3287. STOP THE WORLD--I WANT TO GET OFF. (Special Event Entertainment-1978-Mel Shapiro-N/R). Screenplay by Leslie Bricusse and Anthony Newley. (W)

3288. STORIES FROM A FLYING TRUNK. (EMI-1979-Christine Edzard-N/R). Screenplay by Christine Edzard, from three stories by Hans Christian Andersen: "The Kitchen," "The Little Match Girl," and "Little Ida." (V)

3289. STORM BOY. (South Australian Film Corp.-1976-Henri

Safran-N/R). Screenplay by Sonia Borg, from a novel by
Colin Thiele. (LAT, V)

3290. STORMTROOPERS. (CIDIF-1977-Salvatore Samperi-N/R).
Screenplay by Renato Pozzetto and Cochi Ponzoni. (V)

3291. STORY OF A LOVE AFFAIR. (New Yorker-1975-Michelangelo
Antonioni-N/R). Screenplay by Michelangelo Antonioni,
Daniele d'Anza, Silvio Giovaninetti, and Francesco Maselli.
(W)

3292. THE STORY OF ADELE H. (New World-1975-Francois Truffaut-PG). Screenplay by Francois Truffaut, Jean Gruault,
Suzanne Schiffman, and Frances V. Guille; English adaptation by Jan Dawson; screenplay published by Grove Press,
1976, 191p. (LACOPL, Q, V, W)

3293. THE STORY OF JOANNA. (Blueberry Hill-1975-Gerard
Damiano-X). Screenplay by Gerard Damiano. (W)

3294. THE STORY OF O. (Allied Artists-1975-Just Jaeckin-X).
Screenplay by Sebastien Japrisot, based on the novel by
Pauline Reage. (W)

3295. STRAIGHT TIME. (Warner Bros.-1978-Ulu Grosbard-R).
Screenplay by Alvin Sargent, Edward Bunker, and Jeffrey
Boam, based on Edward Bunker's novel No Beast So Fierce;
Woodhill, 1975, 192p. (LACOPL, Q, V, W)

3296. A STRAITLACED GIRL. (Parafrance-1977-Michel Lang-N/R).
Screenplay by Michel Lang, from the book by Claire Gallois.
(V)

3297. A STRANGE AFFAIR. (Parafrance-1982-Pierre Granier-
Deferre-N/R). Screenplay by Pierre Granier-Deferre,
Christopher Frank, and Jean-Marc Roberts, from the novel
Affaires Etrangeres by Jean-Marc Roberts. (V)

3298. STRANGE BREW. (MGM/UA-1983-Dave Thomas-PG). Screenplay by Dave Thomas, Rick Moranis, and Steven De Jarnatt.
(LAT, V, W)

3299. STRANGE INVADERS. (Orion-1983-Michael Laughlin-PG).
Screenplay by William Condon and Michael Laughlin. (LAT,
V, W)

3300. STRANGE MASQUERADE. (Pike Films-1980-Pal Sandor-N/R).
Screenplay by Zsuzsa Toth. (W)

3301. STRANGE SHADOWS IN AN EMPTY ROOM. (American
International-1977-Martin Herbert-R). Screenplay by
Vincent Mann and Frank Clark. (V)

3302. STRANGE THINGS HAPPEN AT NIGHT. (Clark-1978-R).
No production credits available. (W)

3303. THE STRANGER AND THE GUNFIGHTER. (Columbia-1976-
Anthony Dawson-PG). Screenplay and story by Barth Jules
Sussman. (W)

3304. A STRANGER IS WATCHING. (MGM/UA-1982-Sean S.
Cunningham-R). Screenplay written by Earl Mac Rauch and
Victor Miller, based on a novel by Mary Higgins Clark;
Simon and Schuster, 1977, 314p. (LACOPL, Q, V, W)

3305. STRANGER'S KISS. (Orion Classics-1983-Matthew Chapman-
N/R). Screenplay written by Matthew Chapman and Blaine
Novak, based on a story by Blaine Novak. (V)

3306. STREAMERS. (United Artists Classics-1983-Robert Altman-
R). Screenplay by David Rabe, based on his play. (LAT,
V)

3307. STREET GIRLS. (New World-1975-Michael Miller-R). Screenplay by Barry Levinson and Michael Miller. (W)

3308. STREET PEOPLE. (American International-1976-Maurice
Lucidi-R). Screenplay by Ernest Tidyman and Randall
Kleiser. (W)

3309. THE STREETFIGHTER'S LAST REVENGE. (New Line Cinema-
1979-R). No production credits available. (W)

3310. STREETS OF FIRE. (Universal/RKO Pictures-1984-Walter
Hill-PG). Screenplay by Walter Hill and Larry Gross. (V)

3311. STRIKING BACK. (Film Ventures International-1981-William
Fruet-R). Screenplay by Don Enright. (W)

3312. STRIPES. (Columbia-1981-Ivan Reitman-R). Screenplay by
Len Blum, Dan Goldberg, and Harold Ramis. (LAT, Q, V,
W)

3313. STROKER ACE. (Universal-1983-Hal Needham-PG).
Screenplay by Hugh Wilson and Hal Needham, based on the
novel Stand on It by William Neely and Robert K. Ottum;
Little, Brown, 1973, 294p. (HAR, LACOPL, LAT, V, W)

3314. STRONG MEDICINE. (Film Forum-1981-Richard Foreman-
N/R). Screenplay by Richard Foreman. (W)

3315. STRONGER THAN THE SUN. (BBC Productions-1980-Michael
Apted-N/R). Screenplay by Stephen Poliakoff. (V)

3316. THE STRONGEST MAN IN THE WORLD. (Buena Vista-1975-
Vincent McEveety-G). Screenplay by Joseph L. McEveety
and Herman Groves. (W)

3317. STROSZEK. (New Yorker-1977-Werner Herzog-N/R). Screenplay written by Werner Herzog. (V)

3318. STRYKER. (New World Pictures-1983-Cirio H. Santiago-R).
Screenplay by Howard R. Cohen. (LAT, V, W)

3319. STUCK ON YOU. (Troma-1983-Michael Herz and Samuel
Weil-R). Screenplay by Stuart Strutin, Warren Leight, Don
Perman, Darren Kloomok, Melanie Mintz, Anthony Gittleson,
Duffy Ceaser Magesis, Michael Herz, and Lloyd Kaufman.
(V, W)

3320. STUCKEY'S LAST STAND. (Royal Oak Film Corp-1980-
Lawrence G. Goldfarb-PG). Screenplay by Lawrence G.
Goldfarb. (V, W)

3321. THE STUD. (Trans-American-1979-Quentin Masters-N/R).
Screenplay by Jackie Collins, from her novel. (BFI, W)

3322. STUD BROWN. (Cinemation Industries-1975-Al Adamson-
N/R). Screenplay credits not available. (W)

3323. THE STUD FARM. (New Yorker-1982-Andras Kovacs-N/R).
Screenplay by Andras Kovacs, based on a novel by Istvan
Gall. (W)

3324. STUDENT BODIES. (Paramount-1981-Mickey Rose-R).
Screenplay by Mickey Rose. (LAT, Q, V, W)

3325. THE STUDENT BODY. (Surrogate-1976-Gus Trikonis-R).
Screenplay by Hubert Smith. (W)

3326. THE STUNT MAN. (Melvin Simon-1980-Richard Rush-R).
Screenplay by Lawrence B. Marcus, adaptation by Richard
Rush, based on the novel by Paul Brodeur. (V, W)

3327. STUNTS. (New Line Cinema-1977-Mark L. Lester-PG).
Screenplay by Dennis Johnson and Barney Cohen, from a
story by Raymond Lofaro, Robert Shaye, and Michael
Harpster. (V)

STURMTRUPPEN see STORMTROOPERS

3328. SUBMISSION. (Joseph Brenner-1977-Salvatore Samperi-R).
Screenplay by Ottavio Jemma and Salvatore Samperi. (V, W)

3329. SUBWAY RIDERS. (Hep Pictures-1981-Amos Poe-N/R).
Screenplay by Amos Poe. (V, W)

3330. SUCCESS IS THE BEST REVENGE. (DeVere and Gaumont-
       1984-Jerzy Skolimowski-N/R). Screenplay by Michael Lyndon
       and Jerzy Skolimowski. (V)

3331. SUDDEN FURY. (Scotia American-1975-D. Brian Damude-PG).
       Screenplay by D. Brian Damude. (W)

3332. SUDDEN IMPACT. (Warner Bros.-1983-Clint Eastwood-R).
       Screenplay by Joseph C. Stinson, story by Earl E. Smith
       and Charles B. Pierce, based on characters created by Harry
       Julian Fink and Rose M. Fink. (LAT, W)

3333. SUMMER AFFAIR. (Transvue-1982-George S. Casorati-R).
       Screenplay by George S. Casorati. (W)

3334. SUMMER CAMP. (Seymour Borde & Assoc.-1979-Chuck
       Vincent-R). Screenplay by Avrumie Schnitzer, based on a
       story by Mark Borde and Avrumie Schnitzer. (V, W)

3335. SUMMER LOVERS. (Filmways-1982-Randal Kleiser-R).
       Screenplay by Randal Kleiser. (Q, V, W)

3336. SUMMER OF LAURA. (Stu Segall-1976-David Davidson-X).
       Screenplay credits not available. (W)

3337. SUMMER OF SECRETS. (Greater Union Film Distributors-
       1976-Jim Sharman-N/R). Screenplay by John Aitken. (V)

3338. SUMMER PARADISE. (Cinema 5-1978-Gunnel Lindblom-N/R).
       Screenplay by Ulla Isaksson and Gunnel Lindblom, based on
       a novel by Ulla Isaksson. (W)

       A SUMMER RAIN see SUMMER SHOWERS

3339. SUMMER SCHOOL TEACHERS. (New World-1975-Barbara
       Peeters-R). Screenplay by Barbara Peeters. (W)

3340. SUMMER SHOWERS. (Unifilm-1980-Carlos Diegues-N/R).
       Screenplay by Carlos Diegues. (V, W)

3341. SUMMERTIME. (Massimo Mazzuco-1983-Massimo Mazzuco-N/R).
       Screenplay by Massimo Mazzuco and Michelle Reedy. (V)

3342. SUNBURN. (Paramount-1979-Richard C. Sarafian-PG).
       Screenplay by John Daly, Stephen Oliver, James Booth,
       based on the book The Bind by Stanley Ellin; Random
       House, 1970, 312p. (LACOPL, Q, V, W)

3343. SUNBURST. (Cinema Financial of America-1975-James
       Polakof-R). Screenplay credits not available. (W)

3344. SUNDAY IN THE COUNTRY. (American International-1975-
John Trent-R). Screenplay by Robert Maxwell and John
Trent, story by David Main. (W)

3345. A SUNDAY IN THE COUNTRY. (MLF-1984-Bertrand
Tavernier-N/R). Screenplay by Bertrand and Colo Taver-
nier, based on the novella Monsieur L'admiral Va Bientot
Mourir by Pierre Bost. (V)

3346. SUNDAY LOVERS. (United Artists-1981-Bryan Forbes,
Edouard Molinaro, Dino Risi, Gene Wilder-R). Screenplay
by Leslie Bricusse, Francis Veber, Age and Scarpelli, and
Gene Wilder. (Q, V, W)

3347. THE SUNDAY WOMAN. (20th Century-Fox-1976-Luigi
Comencini-R). Screenplay by Age and Scarpelli, based on
a novel by Fruttero and Lucentini; Harcourt, 1973, 408p.
(LACOPL, Q, W)

3348. SUNNYSIDE. (American International-1979-Timothy Galfas-
R). Screenplay by Timothy Galfas and Jeff King, from a
story by Jeff King and Robert L. Schaffel. (V, W)

3349. SUNSET COVE. (Cal-Am-1978-Al Adamson-R). Screenplay
by Cash Maintenant and Budd Donnelly. (W)

3350. THE SUNSHINE BOYS. (United Artists-1975-Herbert Ross-
PG). Screenplay by Neil Simon, from his play of the same
title; Random House, 1973, 108p. (HR, LACOPL, LAT,
NYT, Q, V, W)

3351. SUNSHINE RUN. (First American-1979-Chris Robinson-PG).
Screenplay by Chris Robinson. (W)

3352. EL SUPER. (Max Mambru Films-1979-Leon Ichaso and Orlando
Jimenez-Leal-N/R). Screenplay by Manuel Arce and Leon
Ichaso, based on the play by Ivan Acosta. (V, W)

3353. SUPER BUG. (Allied Artists-1975-G). No production credits
available. (W)

3354. SUPER DRAGON. (In-Frame-1976-Kin Lung-PG). No screenplay credits available. (W)

3355. SUPER FUZZ. (Avco Embassy-1981-Sergio Corbucci-PG).
Screenplay by Sergio Corbucci and Sabatino Ciuffini. (LAT,
V, W)

3356. THE SUPER-JOCKS. (Joseph Brenner-1980-Emil Nofal & Ray
Sargeant-R). Screenplay by Emil Nofal. (W)

3357. SUPER MANCHU. (Capital-1975-Wu Min Msiung-R). No
       screenplay credits available. (W)

3358. SUPER POWER. (Transmedia Distribution Corp.-1981-Lin
       Chan Wai-R). Screenplay credits not available. (W)

3359. SUPER SEAL. (Epoh-1976-Michael Dugan-G). Screenplay by
       Victor Lundin and Joshua Smith. (W)

3360. SUPER STOOGES VS. THE WONDER WOMEN. (Shaw Brothers-
       1975-Al Bradley-N/R). Screenplay by Aldo Crudo and Alfonso
       Brescia. (W)

3361. THE SUPER WEAPON. (Howard Mahler-1976-PG). Screenplay
       by Norbert Albertson. (W)

3362. SUPERCOCK. (Hagen-Wayne-1975-Gus Trikonis-PG). Screen-
       play by Michael Laton. (W)

3363. SUPERGIRL. (Tri-Star-1984-Jeannot Szwarc-PG).
       Screenplay by David Odell, based on the comic-strip char-
       acter. (V)

3364. SUPERMAN. (Warner Bros.-1978-Richard Donner-PG).
       Screenplay by Mario Puzo, David Newman, Leslie Newman,
       and Robert Benton, based on characters created by Jerry
       Siegel and Joe Shuster. (Q, V, W)

3365. SUPERMAN II. (Warner Bros.-1981-Richard Lester-PG).
       Screenplay by Mario Puzo, David Newman, and Leslie New-
       man, from a story by Mario Puzo. (LAT, Q, V, W)

3366. SUPERMAN III. (Warner Bros.-1983-Richard Lester-PG).
       Screenplay by David Newman and Leslie Newman, based on
       the characters created by Jerry Siegel and Joe Shuster.
       (BFI, LAT, W)

3367. SUPERSONIC MAN. (Topar-1980-Juan Piquer-N/R). Screen-
       play by Sebastian Moi and Juan Piquer. (W)

3368. SUPERVIXENS. (RM Films International-1975-Russ Meyer-
       X). Screenplay by Russ Meyer. (W)

3369. SURF II. (International Film Marketing-1984-Randall Badat-
       R). Screenplay by Randall Badat. (V)

3370. SURFER GIRLS. (Essex-1976-Boots McCoy-X). Screenplay
       credits not available. (W)

3371. THE SURROGATE. (Cinepix-1984-Don Carmody-N/R).
       Screenplay by Don Carmody and Robert Geoffrain. (V)

3372.   SURVIVAL RUN. (Film Ventures International-1980-Larry
        Spiegel-R). Screenplay by Larry Spiegel and G. M. Cahill,
        based on a story by G. M. Cahill and Frederic Shore. (V,
        W)

3373.   SURVIVE! (Paramount-1976-Rene Cardona Jr.-R). Screen-
        play written by Rene Cardona Jr., based on a book by Clay
        Blair Jr.; Berkley Publishing Corp., 1973, 280p. (HR,
        LACOPL, V, W)

3374.   THE SURVIVORS. (Columbia-1983-Michael Ritchie-R).
        Screenplay by Michael Leeson. (W)

3375.   SUSANA. (Plexus-1983-Luis Bunuel-N/R). Screenplay by
        Jaime Salvador, based on a novel by Manuel Reachi. (W)

3376.   LES SUSPECTS. (S. J. International-1976-Michel Wyn-PG).
        Screenplay by Michel Wyn, Paul Andreota, and Michel Sales,
        from a book by Paul Andreota. (W)

3377.   SUZANNE. (Ambassador-1980-Robin Spry-N/R). Screenplay
        by Robin Spry and Ronald Sutherland, based on the novel
        Snow Lark by Ronald Sutherland. (V)

3378.   THE SVEN KLANG QUINTET. (Swedish Film Institute/
        Europa Film/Stockholm Film-1976-Stellan Olsson-N/R).
        Screenplay by Henric Holmberg and Ninne Olsson. (V)

3379.   SWAMP THING. (Embassy-1982-Wes Craven-PG). Screen-
        play by Wes Craven, based on DC Comics characters. (HR,
        LAT, Q, V, W)

3380.   SWANN IN LOVE. (Gaumont-1984-Volker Schlondorff-R).
        Screenplay by Peter Brook, Jean-Claude Carriere, Marie-
        Helene Estienne, and Volker Schlondorff, based on Marcel
        Proust's Un Amour de Swann. (V)

3381.   THE SWAP. (Cannon Group-1980-John Shade-R). Screen-
        play by John C. Broderick. (W)

3382.   SWAP MEET. (Dimension-1979-Brice Mack-R). Screenplay
        by Steve Krantz. (V, W)

3383.   THE SWARM. (Warner Bros.-1978-Irwin Allen-PG). Screen-
        play by Stirling Silliphant, based on a novel by Arthur Her-
        zog; Simon & Schuster, 1974, 256p. (LACOPL, Q, V, W)

3384.   SWASHBUCKLER. (Universal-1976-James Goldstone-R).
        Screenplay by Jeffrey Bloom, story by Paul Wheeler. (Q,W)

3385.   SWEATER GIRLS. (Mirror-1978-Don Jones-R). Screenplay by
        Don Jones and Neva Friedenn. (W)

3386. SWEE' PEA. (Sumit-1983-Peter Del Monte-N/R). Screenplay by Bernardino Zapponi and Peter Del Monte. (W)

3387. SWEENEY. (EMI-1977-David Wickes-N/R). Screenplay by Ranald Graham, based on a television series created by Ian Kennedy Martin. (V)

3388. SWEET CAKES. (SFC-1976-Hans Johnson-X). Screenplay credits not available. (W)

3389. THE SWEET CREEK COUNTY WAR. (Key International-1979-J. Frank James-PG). Screenplay by J. Frank James. (V, W)

3390. SWEET DIRTY TONY. (Marvin-1981-Chuck Workman-N/R). Screenplay by Chuck Workman. (W)

3391. SWEET HOURS. (Elias Querejeta-1982-Carlos Saura-N/R). Screenplay by Carlos Saura. (V)

3392. SWEET MOVIE. (Biograph-1975-Dusan Makevejev-N/R). Screenplay credits not available. (W)

3393. SWEET REVENGE. (United Artists-1976-Jerry Schatzberg-PG). Screenplay by B. J. Perla and Marilyn Goldin, from a story by B. J. Perla. (Q, W)

3394. SWEET SIXTEEN. (CI Films of California-1983-Jim Sotos-R). Screenplay by Erwin Goldman. (V, W)

3395. SWEET WILLIAM. (World-Northal-1982-Claude Whatham-N/R). Screenplay by Beryl Bainbridge, from her novel. (LAT, V, W)

3396. SWEET WOMAN. (Lenfilm-1976-Vladimir Fetin-N/R). Screenplay by Iren Velenbovskaia. (V)

3397. SWEPT AWAY ... BY AN UNUSUAL DESTINY IN THE BLUE SEA OF AUGUST. (Cinema 5-1975-Lina Wertmuller-R). Screenplay by Lina Wertmuller. (Q, W)

3398. SWING SHIFT. (Warner Bros.-1984-Jonathan Demme-PG). Screenplay by Rob Morton. (V)

3399. THE SWINGIN' MODELS. (Hemisphere-1975-Ilja von Anutroff-R). Screenplay credits not available. (W)

3400. THE SWINGING BARMAIDS. (Premiere-1975-Gus Trikonis-R). Screenplay by Charles B. Griffith. (W)

3401. THE SWINGING COEDS. (Omni-1976-Ross Meyers-R). Screenplay by Candy Clifford Diehl. (W)

3402. SWINGING TEACHER. (Worldwide Entertainment-1976-David Feldshuh-R). Screenplay by Kathy Fehn. (W)

3403. SWISS BANK ACCOUNT. (American Films Ltd.-1975-Robert Anderson-PG). Screenplay by Kevin Davis. (W)

3404. SWITCHBLADE SISTERS. (Centaur-1975-Jack Hill-R). Screenplay by F. X. Maier. (W)

3405. THE SWORD AND THE SORCERER. (Group 1-1982-Albert Pyun-R). Screenplay by Albert Pyun, Thomas Karnowski, and John Stuckmeyer. (V, W)

3406. THE SWORD OF THE BARBARIANS. (Cannon Releasing-1983-Michael E. Lemick-R). Screenplay by Pietro Regnoli. (V, W)

3407. SWORD OF THE VALIANT. (Cannon Releasing-1984-Stephen Weeks-PG). Screenplay by Stephen Weeks, Philip M. Breen, and Howard C. Pen. (V)

3408. SWORDKILL. (Empire Pictures-1984-Larry Carroll-N/R). Screenplay by Tim Curnen. (V)

3409. SYMPTOMS. (Bryanston-1976-Joseph Larraz-R). Screenplay by Joseph Larraz and Stanley Miller. (W)

3410. SYNDICATE SADISTS. (Summit Associated Ltd.-1983-Umberto Lenzi-R). Screenplay by Vincenzo Mannino. (V)

3411. TNT JACKSON. (New World-1975-Cirio Santiago-R). Screenplay by Dick Miller and Ken Metcalfe. (W)

3412. TABLE FOR FIVE. (Warner Bros.-1983-Robert Lieberman-PG). Screenplay by David Seltzer. (V)

3413. TAG. (New World Pictures-1982-Nick Castle-PG). Screenplay written by Nick Castle. (V)

3414. TAKE A HARD RIDE. (20th Century-Fox-1975-Anthony M. Dawson-PG). Screenplay by Eric Bercovici and Jerry Ludwig. (W)

3415. TAKE ALL OF ME. (Group 1 International-1978-Luigi Cozzi). Screenplay by Luigi Cozzi, Michele Delle Aie, Daniele Giudice, and Sonia Molteni. (V, W)

3416. TAKE DOWN. (Buena Vista-1979-Keith Merrill-PG). Screenplay by Keith Merrill and Eric Hendershot, based on a story idea by Eric Hendershot. (Q, V, W)

3417. TAKE IT OR LEAVE IT. (Nutty Stiff-1983-Dave Robinson-

N/R). Screenplay by Dave Robinson and Phil MacDonald.
(V)

3418. TAKE IT TO THE LIMIT. (Variety International Pictures-
1980-Peter Starr-PG). Written by Charles Michael Lorre and
Peter Starr. (W)

3419. TAKE ONE. (Reel-to-Real-1977-Wakefield Poole-X). No
screenplay credits available. (V)

3420a. TAKE THIS JOB AND SHOVE IT. (Avco Embassy-1981-Gus
Trikonis-PG). Screenplay by Barry Schneider, story by
Jeffrey Bernini, Barry Schneider, based on a song by David
Allan Coe. (LAT, Q, V, W)

3420b. THE TAKE-OFF. (IFEX/Sovexportfilm-1982-Savva Kulish-
N/R). Screenplay by Oleg Osetinsky. (W)

3420c. THE TAKERS. (Boxoffice International-1975-Carlos Montoya-
X). Screenplay credits not available. (W)

3421a. TALES FROM THE VIENNA WOODS. (Cinema 5-1981-
Maximilian Schell-N/R). Screenplay by Christopher Hampton,
Maximilian Schell, based on the play by Odon von Horvath.
(W)

3421b. TALES OF ORDINARY MADNESS. (Fred Baker-1983-Marco
Ferreri-N/R). Screenplay by Marco Ferreri, Sergio Amidei,
and Anthony Foutz, based on short stories by Charles Bu-
kowski. (W)

3421c. TANK. (Lorimar/Universal-1984-Marvin Chomsky-PG).
Screenplay by Dan Gordon. (V)

3422a. THE TANNER STEEL MILL. (Westdeutscher Rundfunk-1976-
Marianne Luedcke & Ingo Kratisch-N/R). Screenplay by
Peter Stripp, based on Felix Pinner's novel. (V)

DIE TANNERHUETTE see THE TANNER STEEL MILL

3422b. TANYA. (Boxoffice International-1976-Nate Rogers-N/R).
No screenplay credits available. (W)

3422c. TANYA'S ISLAND. (IFEX-Fred Baker-1980-Alfred Sole-R).
Screenplay by Pierre Brousseau. (V, W)

3423a. TAPESTRY OF PASSION. (Essex-1976-Alan B. Colberg-X).
Screenplay by Alan B. Colberg and Billy Thornberg, from a
story by Alan B. Colberg. (W)

3423b. TAPS. (20th Century-Fox-1981-Harold Becker-PG).

Screenplay written by Darryl Ponicsan and Robert Mark
Kamen, based on Devery Freeman's novel Father Sky, as
adapted by James Lineberger; Morrow, 1979, 216p. (BFI,
HR, LACOPL, LAT, NYT, Q, V, W)

3423c. TARGET: HARRY. (ABC Pictures International-1980-Henry
Neill aka Roger Corman-R). Screenplay by Bob Barbash.
(V, W)

3424a. TARZ & JANE & BOY & CHEETA. (Fine Brothers/Ded
Films-1976-Hans Johnson-X). Screenplay credits not available. (W)

3424b. TARZAN, THE APE MAN. (MGM/United Artists-1981-John
Derek-R). Screenplay by Tom Rowe, Gary Goddard, based
on characters created by Edgar Rice Burroughs; Grosset,
1914. (BFI, LACOPL, LAT, Q, V, W)

3424c. A TASTE OF SIN. (Ambassador Pictures-1983-Ulli Lommel-
R). Screenplay by Ulli Lommel, John P. Marsh, Ron Norman. (V, W)

3425a. THE TASTE OF THE SAVAGE. (World Wide-1975-Alberto
Mariscal-R). Screenplay credits not available. (W)

3425b. TATTOO. (20th Century-Fox-1981-Bob Brooks-R). Screenplay by Joyce Bunuel. (LAT, Q, V, W)

3425c. THE TATTOO CONNECTION. (World Northal-1979-Lee Tso-
Nam-R). Screenplay by Luk Pak Sang. (W)

3426a. TATTOOED DRAGON. (World Northal-1981-R). No production credits available. (W)

3426b. TAXI DRIVER. (Columbia-1976-Martin Scorsese-R). Screen-
play by Paul Schrader; novelization by Richard M. Elman and
Paul Schrader, Bantam Books, 1976, 147p. (HR, LACOPL,
LAT, Q, V, W)

TAXI TO THE JOHN see TAXI ZUM KLO

3426c. TAXI ZUM KLO. (Promovision International-1981-Frank
Rripploh-N/R). Screenplay by Frank Rripploh. (BFI, LAT,
V, W)

TCHAO PANTIN see SO LONG, STOOGE

3427a. THE TEACHER. (Tricontinental-1978-Octavio Cortazar-N/R).
Screenplay by Luis R. Noguera, from a story by Octavio
Cortazar. (W)

3427b. TEACHERS. (United Artists-1984-Arthur Hiller-R). Screen-play by W. R. McKinney. (V)

3427c. TEAM-MATES. (Independent International-1978-Steven Jacobson-R). Screenplay by Jennifer Lawson. (W)

3428a. TEEN MOTHERS. (Cannon Group-1980-Boaz Davidson-R). Screenplay by Stuart Krieger. (W)

3428b. TEENAGE CHEERLEADER. (Mature-1975-X). No production credits available. (W)

3428c. TEENAGE HITCHHIKERS. (NMD-1975-Gerri Sedley-R). Screenplay by Rod Whipple. (W)

3429a. TEENAGE LOVERS. (1975-X). No production credits avail-able. (W)

3429b. TEENAGE MILKMAID. (Monarch-1975-Roberta Findlay-X). Screenplay by Roberta Findlay. (W)

3429c. TEENAGE SEX THERAPY. (Art Mart-1976-Buzz Richards-X). Screenplay credits not available. (W)

3430. TEENAGE TEASERS. (Intercontinental-1981-Jack Angel-R). Screenplay credits not available. (W)

3431. TEENAGE TRAMP. (NMD-1975-Anton Holden-R). Screenplay credits not available. (W)

3432. TEENAGE TWINS. (MSW-1976-Carter Stevens-X). Screen-play by Al Hazard. (W)

3433. TELEFON. (United Artists-1977-Don Siegel-PG). Screen-play by Peter Hyams, Stirling Silliphant, based on a novel by Walter Wager; Macmillan, 1975, 206p. (HR, LACOPL, LAT, Q, W)

3434. TELL ME A RIDDLE. (Filmways-1980-Lee Grant-PG). Screenplay by Joyce Eliason and Alev Lytle, based on Tillie Olsen's novella. (V, W)

3435. TELL THEM JOHNNY WADD IS HERE. (Freeway-1976-Bob Chinn-X). Screenplay by Robert Mathews. (W)

3436. THE TEMPEST. (Boyd's Co.-1979-Derek Jarman-N/R). Screenplay by Derek Jarman, from the play by William Shakespeare; Cambridge University Press, 1965, 117p. (LACOPL, V, W)

3437. TEMPEST. (Columbia-1982-Paul Mazursky-PG). Screenplay by Paul Mazursky and Leon Capetanos. (Q, V)

3438. THE TEMPTER. (Avco Embassy-1978-Alberto de Martino-R).
       Screenplay by Alberto de Martino, Vincenzo Mannino, and
       Gianfranco Clerici. (V, W)

3439. 10. (Orion/Warner Bros.-1979-Blake Edwards-R). Screen-
       play by Blake Edwards. (HR, LAT, Q, V, W)

3440. TEN LITTLE INDIANS. (Avco Embassy-1975-Peter Collinson-
       PG). Screenplay by Peter Welbeck, based on a novel by
       Agatha Christie; Dodd, Mead, 1978, 264p. (W)

3441. 10 TO MIDNIGHT. (Cannon Group-1983-J. Lee Thompson-
       R). Screenplay by William Roberts. (LAT, V)

3442. 10 VIOLENT WOMEN. (New American Films-1984-Ted V.
       Mikels-R). Screenplay by James Gordon White and Ted V.
       Mikels. (V, W)

3443. THE TENANT. (Paramount-1976-Roman Polanski-R). Screen-
       play by Roman Polanski and Gerard Brach, based on a novel
       by Roland Topor; Doubleday, 1966. (LACOPL, Q, W)

3444. TENDER COUSINS. (Crown International-1982-David Hamilton-
       R). Screenplay by Josiane Leveque and Claude D'Anna, from
       a story by Pascal Laine. (W)

3445. TENDER DRACULA. (Scotia American-1975-). No produc-
       tion credits available. (W)

3446. TENDER FLESH. (Brut-1976-Laurence Harvey-R). Screen-
       play by Wallace C. Bennett. (W)

3447. TENDER MERCIES. (EMI-1982-Bruce Beresford-PG).
       Screenplay by Horton Foote. (LAT, V)

       TENDRES COUSINES see TENDER COUSINS

3448. TENT OF MIRACLES. (Embrafilme-1979-Nelson Pereira dos
       Santos-N/R). Screenplay by Nelson Pereira dos Santos,
       based on a novel by Jorge Amado; Knopf, 1971, 380p.
       (LACOPL, W)

3449. TERESA THE THIEF. (World Northal-1979-Carlo Di Palma-
       N/R). Screenplay by Age, Scarpelli, and Dacia Maraini,
       based on the novel Memoirs of a Thief by Dacia Maraini.
       (W)

3450. THE TERMINATOR. (Orion-1984-James Cameron-R). Screen-
       play by James Cameron and Gale Anne Hurd. (V)

3451. TERMS OF ENDEARMENT. (Paramount-1983-James L. Brooks-
       PG). Screenplay by James L. Brooks, based on a novel by

Larry McMurtry; Simon & Schuster, 1975, 410p. (BFI, HR,
LACOPL, LAT, V, W)

3452. TERROR. (Crown International-1979-Norman J. Warren-R).
Screenplay by David McGillivray, from a story by Les Young
and Moira Young. (V, W)

3453. TERROR FROM UNDER THE HOUSE. (Hemisphere-1976-
Sidney Hayers-PG). Screenplay by John Kruse. (W)

3454. TERROR HOUSE. (Intercontinental-1976-Bud Townsend-PG).
Screenplay by Allen J. Actors. (W)

3455. TERROR IN THE WOODS. (American International-1975-
Massimo Dallamano-R). No screenplay credits available. (W)

3456. TERROR ON TOUR. (Intercontinental World Distributing-
1983-Don Edmonds-N/R). Screenplay by Del Lekus. (V)

3457. TERROR TRAIN. (20th Century-Fox-1980-Roger Spottiswoode-
R). Screenplay by T. Y. Drake. (Q, V, W)

3458. THE TERRORISTS. (20th Century-Fox-1975-Casper Wrede-
N/R). Screenplay by Paul Wheeler. (W)

3459. THE TERRY FOX STORY. (20th Century-Fox-1983-Ralph L.
Thomas-N/R). Screenplay by Edward Hume, from a story
by John and Rose Kastner. (W)

3460. TESS. (Columbia-1979-Roman Polanski-R). Screenplay by
Roman Polanski, Gerard Brach and John Brownjohn, based
on the novel Tess of the D'Urbervilles by Thomas Hardy;
Norton, 1965. (BFI, HR, LACOPL, LAT, Q, V, W)

3461. TESTAMENT. (Paramount-1983-Lynne Littman-PG). Screenplay by John Sacret Young, from the story "The Last Testament" by Carol Amen. (LAT, V)

3462. TEX. (Buena Vista-1982-Tim Hunter-PG). Screenplay by
Charlie Haas and Tim Hunter, based on the novel by S. E.
Hinton; Dell, 1979, 191p. (HR, LACOPL, Q, V)

3463. TEXAS DETOUR. (Cinema Shares International-1978-Hikmet
Avedis-R). Screenplay written by Hikmet Avedis. (W)

3464. TEXAS LIGHTNING. (Film Ventures International-1981-Gary
Graver-R). Screenplay by Gary Graver. (W)

3465. THANK GOD IT'S FRIDAY. (Columbia-1978-Robert Klane-
PG). Screenplay by Barry Armyan Bernstein. (W)

3466. THAT CHAMPIONSHIP SEASON. (Cannon Film-1982-Jason
       Miller-R). Screenplay by Jason Miller; Penguin, 1984, 144p.
       (HR, LACOPL, LAT, V, W)

3467. THAT LADY FROM RIO. (Carioca-1976-Amanda Barton-X).
       Screenplay written by Amanda Barton. (W)

3468. THAT LUCKY TOUCH. (Allied Artists-1975-Christopher
       Miles-PG). Screenplay by John Briley, based on an idea by
       Moss Hart. (W)

3469. THAT OBSCURE OBJECT OF DESIRE. (First Artists-1977-
       Luis Bunuel-R). Screenplay by Luis Bunuel, with the col-
       laboration of Jean-Claude Carriere, from the book by Pierre
       Louys. (V)

3470. THAT SINKING FEELING. (Minor Miracle Film Cooperative-
       1979-Bill Forsyth-N/R). Screenplay by Bill Forsyth. (V)

3471. THAT SUMMER! (Columbia-1979-Harley Cokliss-N/R).
       Screenplay by Janey Preger, based on a story by Tony
       Attard. (V)

3472. THAT'S THE WAY OF THE WORLD. (United Artists-1975-
       Sig Shore-PG). Screenplay by Robert Lipsyte, from his
       original story. (W)

3473. THEIR ONLY CHANCE. (Ellman-1978-J. David Siddon-N/R).
       Screenplay by J. David Siddon. (W)

3474. THEMROC. (Libra-1980-Claude Faraldo-N/R). Screenplay
       written by Claude Faraldo. (W)

3475. THERE GOES THE BRIDE. (Vanguard Releasing Inc.-1980-
       Terence Marcel-PG). Screenplay by Ray Cooney and Terence
       Marcel, from a play by Ray Cooney. (V, W)

3476. THEY ALL LAUGHED. (20th Century-Fox-1981-Peter
       Bogdanovich-PG). Screenplay by Peter Bogdanovich.
       (BFI, LAT, V, W)

3477. THEY CALL ME BRUCE? (Film Ventures International-1982-
       Elliott Hong-PG). Screenplay by David Randolph, Johnny
       Yune, Elliott Hong, and Tim Clawson. (HR, LAT, V, W)

3478. THEY CAME FROM WITHIN. (Trans-America-1976-David
       Cronenberg-R). Screenplay by David Cronenberg. (W)

3479. THEY DON'T WEAR BLACK TIE. (New Yorker-1983-Leon
       Hirszman-N/R). Screenplay by Gian-Francesco Guarnieri
       and Leon Hirszman. (W)

3480. THEY WENT THAT-A-WAY AND THAT-A-WAY. (International Picture Show-1978-Edward Montagne and Stuart E. McGowan-PG). Screenplay by Tim Conway. (V, W)

3481. THEY'RE COMING TO GET YOU. (Independent International-1976-Sergio Martino-R). No screenplay credits available. (W)

3482. THEY'RE PLAYING WITH FIRE. (New World-1984-Howard Avedis-R). Screenplay by Howard Avedis and Marlene Schmidt. (V)

THE THIEF see IL LADRONE

3483. THIEF. (United Artists-1981-Michael Mann-R). Screenplay by Michael Mann, based on The Home Invaders by Frank Hohimer. (W)

3484. THIEF OF HEARTS. (Paramount-1984-Douglas Day Stewart-R). Screenplay by Douglas Day Stewart. (V)

3485. THIEVES. (Paramount-1977-John Berry-PG). Screenplay by Herb Gardner, based on his play. (Q, V)

3486. THE THIN LINE. (New Yorker-1981-Michal Bat-Adam-N/R). Screenplay by Michal Bat-Adam. (LAT, W)

3487. THE THING. (Universal-1982-John Carpenter-R). Screenplay by Bill Lancaster, based on the story "Who Goes There?" by John W. Campbell Jr. (Q, V, W)

3488. THINGS ARE TOUGH ALL OVER. (Columbia-1982-Thomas K. Avildsen-R). Screenplay written by Richard (Cheech) Marin and Tommy Chong. (Q, V, W)

3489. THINK DIRTY. (Quartet-1978-Jim Clark-R). Screenplay by Marty Feldman. (W)

3490. THE THIRD GENERATION. (New Yorker-1980-Rainer Werner Fassbinder-N/R). Screenplay by Rainer Werner Fassbinder. (W)

3491. THIRST. (New Line/Marvin-1981-Rod Hardy-R). Screenplay by John Pinkney. (W)

3492. THE THIRSTY DEAD. (International Amusements-1975-Terry Becker-PG). Screenplay credits not available. (W)

13 NUNS see REVENGE OF THE SHOGUN WOMEN

3493. THE THIRTY-NINE STEPS. (1979-Don Sharp-PG). Screen-

play by Michael Robson, based on the novel by John Buchan;
Dutton, 1958, 145p. (LACOPL, V, W)

3494. THIS IS ELVIS. (Warner Bros.-1981-Malcolm Leo & Andrew
Solt-PG). Screenplay by Malcolm Leo and Andrew Solt.
(HR, LAT, Q, V, W)

THIS IS SPINAL TAP see SPINAL TAP

3495. THIS TIME I'LL MAKE YOU RICH. (Avco Embassy-1975-
Frank Kramer-PG). Screenplay credits not available. (W)

3496. THOSE LIPS, THOSE EYES. (United Artists-1980-Michael
Pressman-R). Screenplay by David Shaber. (Q, V, W)

3497. THOU SHALT NOT KILL ... BUT ONCE. (In-Frame Films-
1975-Au Yeung Chuen-R). No screenplay credits available.
(W)

3498. 3 A.M. (Westwood-1976-Robert McCallum-X). Screenplay
by Tony Trelos. (W)

3499. THREE BULLETS FOR A LONG GUN. (Marron-1975-Peter
Henkel-PG). Screenplay and story by Beau Brummell and
Keith van der Wat. (W)

3500. THREE DAYS OF THE CONDOR. (Paramount-1975-Sydney
Pollack-R). Screenplay by Lorenzo Semple Jr., and David
Rayfiel, based on a novel by James Grady; Norton, 1974,
192p. (HR, LACOPL, Q, V, W)

THREE FOR THE MONEY see WIN, PLACE OR STEAL

3501. THREE SHADES OF FLESH. (Today-1976-Hans Christian-X).
No screenplay credits available. (W)

3502. THE THREE SISTERS. (NTA-1977-Paul Bogart-N/R).
Screenplay by Randall Jarrel, from the play by Anton Chek-
hov, as staged by Lee Strasberg; Macmillan, 1969, 160p.
(LACOPL, W)

3503. 3 WOMEN. (20th Century-Fox-1977-Robert Altman-PG).
Screenplay by Robert Altman, based on his dream. (HR,
LAT, Q, V, W)

3504. THROUGH THE LOOKING GLASS. (Mture-1976-Jonas
Middleton-X). Screenplay written by Ronald Wertheim. (W)

3505. THUNDER AND LIGHTNING. (20th Century-Fox-1977-Corey
Allen-PG). Screenplay by William Hjortsberg. (V)

3506. THE THURSDAY MORNING MURDERS. (Aurora International-
       1976-Michael Nahay-R). Screenplay by Michael Nahay. (W)

3507. TI-CUL TOUGAS. (Nu-Image Film-1977-Jean-Guy Noel-N/R).
       Screenplay written by Jean-Guy Noel. (V)

3508. TICKET OF NO RETURN. (Public Cinema-1982-Ulrike
       Ottinger-N/R). Screenplay written by Ulrike Ottinger. (W)

3509. TICKET TO HEAVEN. (United Artists Classics-1981-R. L.
       Thomas-PG). Screenplay by R. L. Thomas and Anne Came-
       ron, based on the book Moonwebs by Josh Freed. (LAT, W)

3510. TIDAL WAVE. (New World-1975-Shiro Moritani-PG). Screen-
       play and story by Shinobu Hashimoto. (W)

3511. TIFFANY JONES. (Cineworld-1976-Pete Walker-R). Screen-
       play by Alfred Shaughnessy. (W)

3512. TIGER FROM HONG KONG. (Monarch-1978-Chang I-R).
       Screenplay credits not available. (W)

3513. TIGHTROPE. (Warner Bros.-1984-Richard Tuggle-R).
       Screenplay by Richard Tuggle. (V)

3514. THE TIGRESS. (New World-1978-Jean Lafleur-R). Screen-
       play by Marven McGara. (W)

3515. TILL DEATH. (Cougar-1978-Walter Stocker-PG). Screen-
       play by Gregory Dana. (W)

3516. TILL MARRIAGE DO US PART. (Franklin Media-1979-Luigi
       Comencini-R). Screenplay by Luigi Comencini and Ivo Perilli.
       (W)

3517. TILT. (Warner Bros.-1979-Rudy Durand-PG). Screenplay
       by Rudy Durand and Donald Cammell, based on a story by
       Rudy Durand; novelization by James Creech III; Dell, 1978,
       188p. (LACOPL, V, W)

3518. TIM. (Satori-1981-Michael Pate-N/R). Screenplay by Michael
       Pate, from the novel by Colleen McCullough; Harper, 1974,
       248p. (LACOPL, W)

3519. TIMBER TRAMPS. (Howco International-1975-PG). Screen-
       play by Chuck Keen. (W)

3520. TIME AFTER TIME. (Orion-Warner Bros.-1979-Nicholas
       Meyer-PG). Screenplay by Nicholas Meyer, based on a
       story by Karl Alexander and Steve Hayes; novelization by
       Karl Alexander; Delacorte Press, 1979, 341p. (HR, LACOPL,
       Q, V, W)

3521. TIME BANDITS. (Avco Embassy-1981-Terry Gilliam-PG).
       Screenplay by Michael Palin and Terry Gilliam. (LAT, Q,
       V, W)

3522. TIME FOR REVENGE. (Televicine-1983-Adolfo Aristarain-
       N/R). Screenplay by Adolfo Aristarain. (W)

3523. TIME SLIP. (Toei-1981-Kosei Saito-N/R). Screenplay by
       Toshio Kaneda, from a story by Ryo Hanamura. (V)

3524. A TIME TO DIE. (Almi-1983-Matt Cimber-R). Screenplay
       by John Goff, Matt Cimber, and William Russell, from a
       story by Mario Puzo. (V, W)

3525. TIME WALKER. (New World-1982-Tom Kennedy-PG). Screen-
       play by Karen Levitt and Tom Friedman. (W)

3526. TIMERIDER. (Jensen-Farley-1983-William Dear-PG). Screen-
       play by William Dear and Michael Nesmith. (V)

3527- TIMES SQUARE. (AFD Films-1980-Alan Mayle-R). Screen-
  28. play by Jacob Brackman, based on a story by Alan Mayle
       and Leanne Unger. (Q, V, W)

3529. THE TIN DRUM. (Argos Films-1979-Volker Schlondorff-N/R).
       Screenplay by Jean-Claude Carriere, Franz Seitz, and Volker
       Schlondorff, based on the book by Gunter Grass; Vintage
       Books, 1964, 591p. (LACOPL, Q, V, W)

3530. TIN MAN. (Goldfarb Distributors Inc.-1983-John G.
       Thomas-N/R). Screenplay by Bishop Holiday. (V)

3531. TINTORERA. (United Film-1978-Rene Cardona Jr.-R).
       Screenplay credits not given; based on a novel by Ramon
       Bravo. (W)

3532. TITLE SHOT. (Cinepax-1982-N/R). Screenplay by John
       Saxton, story by Richard Gabourie. (W)

3533. TO ALL A GOODNIGHT. (Intercontinental World Distribu-
       tion Corp.-1980-David Hess-N/R). Screenplay by Alex Rebar.
       (V)

3534. TO AN UNKNOWN GOD. (Elias Quereleta-1982-Jaime Chavarri-
       N/R). Screenplay written by Elias Quereleta and Jaime
       Chavarri, based on a script by Francisco J. Lucio. (W)

3535. TO BE OR NOT TO BE. (20th Century-Fox-1983-Alan
       Johnson-PG). Screenplay by Thomas Meehan and Ronny
       Graham, based on a film directed by Ernest Lubitsch and
       written by Edwin Justus Mayer. (LAT, V)

3536. TO CATCH A COP. (Gaumont-1984-Michel Gerard-N/R). Screenplay by Michel Gerard, David Milhaud, and Jean-Francois Navarre. (V)

3537. TO FORGET VENICE. (Quartet Films-1980-Franco Brusati-N/R). Screenplay by Franco Brusati and Jaja Fiastri, story by Franco Brusati. (W)

3538. TO HEX WITH SEX. (RAF Industries-1975-Simon Nuchtern-N/R). Screenplay credits not available. (W)

3539. TO LOVE, PERHAPS TO DIE. (Finest-1975-R). No production credits available. (W)

3540. TO REMEMBER OR TO FORGET. (IFEX/Sovexportfilm-1982-Janis Streich-N/R). Screenplay written by Oleg Rudnev. (W)

3541. TO THE STARS BY HARD WAYS. (IFEX/Sovexportfilm-1982-Richard Victorov-N/R). Screenplay by Kir Bulychev and Richard Victorov. (W)

3542. TODO MODO. (Nu-Image-1980-Elio Petri-N/R). Screenplay by Elio Petri and Berto Pelosso. (V, W)

3543. TOM HORN. (Warner Bros.-1980-William Wiard-R). Screenplay by Thomas McGuane and Bud Shrake, based on Life of Tom Horn, Government Scout and Interpreter by Tom Horn; University of Oklahoma Press, 1964, 277p. (LACOPL, Q V, W)

3544. THE TOM MACHINE. (National Film School-1981-Paul Bamborough-N/R). Screenplay by Paul Bamborough. (V)

3545. TOM THUMB. (Paramount-1976-Michel Boisrond-G). Screenplay by Marcel Julian. (W)

3546. TOMMY. (Columbia-1975-Ken Russell-PG). Screenplay by Ken Russell, based on the musical drama by Pete Townshend. (Q, W)

3547. TOMORROW NEVER COMES. (Rank Film Distributors-1978-Peter Collinson-N/R). Screenplay by David Pursall, Jack Seddon, and Sydney Banks. (W)

3548. TOMORROW'S CHILDREN. (Unite Trois-1976-Jean Pourtale-N/R). Screenplay by Jean Pourtale, Frank Vialle, and Raymond Lepoutre. (V)

3549. TONGUE. (J & A Productions-1976-K. B.-X). Screenplay credits not available. (W)

3550. TONIGHT FOR SURE. (Kino International-1982-Francis Ford Coppola-N/R). Screenplay by Francis Ford Coppola. (V, W)

3551. TONITE ... I LOVE YOU. (Hollywood International-1975-Carlos Tobalina-X). No screenplay credits available. (W)

3552. TOO FAR TO GO. (Zoetrope-1982-Fielder Cook-PG). Screenplay by William Hanley, from stories by John Updike. (W)

3553. TOO HOT TO HANDLE. (L. Kirtman-1976-James Beckley-X). No screenplay credits available. (W)

3554. TOO HOT TO HANDLE. (Derio Productions-1978-Don Schain-R). Screenplay by J. Michael Sherman and Don Buday. (W)

3555. TOO SHY TO TRY. (Quartet-1983-Pierre Richard-PG). Screenplay by Pierre Richard, Jean-Jacques Annaud, and Alain Godard. (W)

3556. THE TOOLBOX MURDERS. (Cal-Am Release-1978-Dennis Donnelly-R). Screenplay by Robert Easter and Ann N. Kindberg. (V, W)

3557. TOOTSIE. (Columbia-1982-Sydney Pollack-PG). Screenplay written by Larry Gelbart and Murray Schisgal, from a story by Don McGuire and Larry Gelbart. (HR, LAT, NYT, Q, V, W)

3558. TOP SECRET. (Paramount-1984-Jim Abrahams, David Zucker & Jerry Zucker-PG). Screenplay written by Jim Abrahams, David Zucker, Jerry Zucker, and Martyn Burke. (V)

3559. TOPELE. (Risto-1975-Leo Filler-G). Screenplay based on a story by Sholom Aleichem. (W)

3560. TORCHLIGHT. (Film Ventures International-1984-Tom Wright-N/R). Story and screenplay by P. S. Martin and Eliza Moorman. (V)

3561. THE TORMENTED. (21st Century-1978-Mario Gariazzo-R). Screenplay credits not available. (W)

3562. TOUCH AND GO. (Libra Films-1975-Philippe De Broca-PG). Screenplay and dialogue by Jean-Loup Dabadie. (W)

3563. A TOUCH OF GENIE. (808 Pictures-1975-X). Screenplay credits not available. (W)

3564. TOUCHED. (Lorimar-1983-John Flynn-N/R). Screenplay written by Lyle Kessler. (LAT, V, W)

3565. TOUCHED BY LOVE. (Columbia-1980-Gus Trikonis-PG).
Hesper Anderson based her screenplay on the book To Elvis
with Love by Lena Canada; Everest House, 1978, 178p.
(LACOPL, Q, V, W)

3566. TOUCHED IN THE HEAD. (Bauer International-1977-Jacques
Doillon-N/R). Screenplay by Jacques Doillon and Philippe
Defrance. (W)

3567. TOUGH ENOUGH. (20th Century-Fox-1983-Richard O.
Fleischer-PG). Screenplay written by John Leone. (LAT,
V, W)

3568. THE TOURIST TRAP. (Compass International/Manson
International-1979-David Schmoeller-PG). Screenplay by
David Schmoeller and J. Larry Carroll. (V, W)

3569. TOWER OF LOVE. (Boxoffice International-1975-George
Drazich-N/R). Screenplay by Harriet Foster. (W)

3570. TOWING. (United International-1978-Maura Smith-PG).
Screenplay by Maura Smith. (W)

3571. THE TOWN THAT DREADED SUNDOWN. (American International Pictures-1977-Charles B. Pierce-R). Screenplay by
Earl E. Smith. (Q, V)

3572. THE TOY. (Show-Biz Co.-1978-Francis Veber-N/R).
Screenplay by Francis Veber. (V, W)

3573. THE TOY. (Columbia-1982-Richard Donner-PG). Screenplay by Carol Sobieski, based on a film by Francis Veber.
(HR, LAT, V)

3574. TOY SOLDIERS. (New World Pictures-1984-David Fisher-R).
Screenplay by David Fisher and Walter Fox. (V)

3575. THE TRACE. (Fox-Hachette-1983-Bernard Favre-N/R).
Screenplay written by Bernard Favre and Bertrand
Tavernier. (V)

3576. TRACKDOWN. (United Artists-1976-Richard T. Heffron-R).
Screenplay by Paul Edwards, from a story by Ivan Nagy.
(W)

3577. TRADING PLACES. (Paramount-1983-John Landis-R).
Screenplay by Timothy Harris and Herschel Weingrod.
(HR, LAT, V, W)

THE TRAFFIC JAM see L'INGORGO

3578. TRAIL OF THE PINK PANTHER. (MGM/UA-1982-Blake
       Edwards-PG). Screenplay by Frank Waldman, Tom Waldman,
       Blake Edwards, and Geoffrey Edwards, based on a story
       by Blake Edwards. (HR, LAT, V, W)

3579. TRAIN RIDE TO HOLLYWOOD. (Taylor-Laughlin-1975-
       Charles Rondeau-G). Screenplay by Dan Gordon. (W)

3580. THE TRANS-SIBERIAN EXPRESS. (International Film
       Exchange/Satra Film Corp./Sovexportfilm-1979-Eldar
       Urazbayev-N/R). No screenplay credits available. (W)

3581. THE TRAP DOOR. (B Movies-1980-Beth B and Scott B-
       N/R). Screenplay by Beth B and Scott B. (W)

3582. THE TRAP OF COUGAR MOUNTAIN. (Manson-1976-G).
       Production credits not available. (W)

3583. TRAP THEM AND KILL THEM. (Megastar Pictures-1984-
       Joe D'Amato aka Aristide Massaccesi-N/R). Screenplay
       written by Romano Scandariato and Aristide Massaccesi.
       (V)

3584. TRAPPED. (Panorama-1982-Matthew Patrick-N/R). Screen-
       play written by Julio Torresoto. (LAT, W)

3585. TREASURE OF MATECUMBE. (Buena Vista-1976-Vincent
       McEveety-G). Screenplay by Don Tait, based on A Journey
       to Matecumbe by Robert Lewis Taylor; McGraw-Hill, 1961.
       (LACOPL, V, W)

3586. TREASURE OF THE FOUR CROWNS. (Cannon-1983-
       Ferdinando Baldi-PG). Screenplay by Lloyd Battista, Jim
       Bryce, and Jerry Lazarus, from a story by Tony Petitto and
       Gene Quintano. (BFI, V, W)

3587. THE TREE OF KNOWLEDGE. (Scandinavia Today-1982-Nils
       Malmros-N/R). Screenplay by Nils Malmros and Fred Cryer.
       (W)

3588. THE TREE OF WOODEN CLOGS. (Gaumont/Sacis/New
       Yorker-1979-Ermanno Olmi-N/R). Screenplay by Ermanno
       Olmi. (W)

       THE TREK OF LIFE see YOL

3589. TRENCHCOAT. (Buena Vista-1983-Michael Tuchner-PG).
       Screenplay by Jeffrey Price and Peter Seaman. (HR, LAT,
       V, W)

3590. TRIBUTE. (20th Century-Fox-1980-Bob Clark-PG).

Screenplay written by Bernard Slade, based on his stage
play. (Q, V, W)

3591. TRICK OR TREATS. (Lone Star Pictures International-1982-
Gary Graver-R). Screenplay by Gary Graver. (V, W)

3592. TRIP WITH THE TEACHER. (Crown International-1975-Earl
Barton-R). Screenplay by Earl Barton. (W)

3593. TRIUMPHS OF A MAN CALLED HORSE. (Jensen Farley-
1984-John Hough-PG). Screenplay by Ken Blackwell and
Carlos Aured, based on a story by Jack DeWitt and a char-
acter by Dorothy M. Johnson. (V)

3594. TRON. (Buena Vista-1982-Steven Lisberger-PG). Screenplay by Steven Lisberger, from his original story; novelization by Brian Daley; Ballantine Books, 1982, 173p. (HR,
LACOPL, LAT, Q, V, W)

3595. THE TROUBLE WITH YOUNG STUFF. (1976-Odus Hamlin-X).
Screenplay written by Odus Hamlin. (W)

3596. THE TROUPE. (Eastways Prods.-1981-Avi Nesher-N/R).
Screenplay by Avi Nesher. (V)

3597. THE TROUT. (Gaumont-1982-Joseph Losey-N/R). Screenplay written by Monique Lange and Joseph Losey, from the
book by Roger Vailland; Gallimard, 1964, 247p. (LACOPL,
LAT, V, W)

3598. TRUCKIN'. (Dimensions-1975-Ken Handler-PG). Screenplay written by Michael Thomas. (W)

3599. TRUCKIN' MAN. (Preacherman-1975-Will Zens-R). Screenplay credits not available. (W)

3600. TRUE CONFESSIONS. (United Artists-1981-Ulu Grosbard-R).
Screenplay written by John Gregory Dunne and Joan Didion,
based on the novel by John Gregory Dunne; Dutton, 1977.
(HR, LACOPL, LAT, NYT, Q, V, W)

LA TRUITE see THE TROUT

3601. TUCK EVERLASTING. (Coe Films-1981-Frederick King
Keller-N/R). Screenplay written by Stratton Rawson, Fred
A. Keller, Frederick King Keller, and Jim Bisco, based on
the novel by Natalie Babbitt. (W)

3602. TULIPS. (Avco Embassy-1981-Stan Ferris-N/R). Screenplay by Fred Sappho. (V)

3603. TUNNELVISION. (World Wide Films-1976-Brad Swirnoff and Neil Israel-R). Screenplay written by Neil Israel and Michael Mislove. (W)

LES TURLUPINS see THE RASCALS

3604. THE TURNING POINT. (20th Century-Fox-1977-Herbert Ross-PG). Screenplay by Arthur Laurents. (Q, W)

3605. TURUMBA. (Les Blank/Flower Films-1984-Kidlat Tahimik-N/R). Screenplay written by Kidlat Tahimik. (V)

3606. TUSK. (Yang Film/Films 21-1980-Alejandro Jodorowsky-N/R). Screenplay by Nick Niciphor, Jeffrey O'Kelly, and Alejandro Jodorowsky, based on the novel, "Poo Lorn of the Elephant," by Reginald Campbell. (V)

3607. 24 FIREMAN'S STREET. (Unifilm-1982-Istvan Szabo-N/R). Screenplay by Istvan Szabo. (W)

3608. 26 DAYS IN THE LIFE OF DOSTOYEVSKY. (IFEX/Sovexportfilm-1982-Alexander Zarkhi-N/R). Screenplay written by Vladimir Vladimirov and Pavel Finn. (LAT, W)

3609. TWICE UPON A TIME. (Ladd Co./Warner Bros.-1983-John Korty and Charles Swenson-PG). Screenplay by John Korty, Charles Swenson, Suella Kennedy and Bill Couturie, based on a story by John Korty. (V, W)

3610. TWILIGHT TIME. (MGM/UA-1983-Goran Paskaljevic-PG). Screenplay by Goran Paskaljevic, Flip David, Dan Tana, and Rowland Barber. (V, W)

3611. TWILIGHT ZONE--THE MOVIE. (Warner Bros.-1983-John Landis-PG). Screenplay written by John Landis, based on the television series created by Rod Serling; novelization by Robert Bloch; Warner Books, 1983, 205p. (HR, LACOPL, LAT, NYT, V, W)

3612. TWILIGHT'S LAST GLEAMING. (Allied Artists-1977-Robert Aldrich-R). Screenplay by Ronald M. Cohen and Edward Huebsch, based on the novel Viper Three by Walter Wager; Macmillan, 1971, 257p. (LACOPL, Q, V)

3613. THE TWIN. (AAA Release-1984-Yves Robert-N/R). Screenplay by Yves Robert, Elizabeth Rappeneau, and Boris Bergman, based on Donald Westlake's novel Two Much; Evans, 1975, 286p. (LACOPL, V)

3614. TWINKLE, TWINKLE, KILLER KANE. (UFD-1980-William

Peter Blatty-R). Screenplay by William Peter Blatty, based on his novel; Doubleday, 1966. (LACOPL, W)

3615. TWO AGAINST THE LAW. (Joseph Green-1976-Jose Giovanni-N/R). Screenplay by Jose Giovanni. (W)

3616. TWO CHAMPIONS OF DEATH. (World Northal-1982-Chang Cheh-R). Screenplay credits not available. (W)

3617. TWO-MINUTE WARNING. (Universal-1976-Larry Peerce-R). Screenplay written by Edward Hume, based on the novel by George La Fountaine; Coward, 1975, 223p. (HR, LACOPL, LAT, Q, V, W)

3618. TWO OF A KIND. (20th Century-Fox-1983-John Herzfeld-PG). Screenplay by John Herzfeld. (HR, LAT, V, W)

3619. TWO STAGE SISTERS. (Tianma Film Studio-1981). Screenplay by Lin Gu, Xu Jin, and Xie Jin. (V)

3620. 2076 OLYMPIAD. (Aragon Production Co.-1977-James R. Martin-N/R). Screenplay by James R. Martin. (V)

3621. 2010. (MGM/UA-1984-Peter Hyams-PG). Screenplay written by Peter Hyams, based on the novel by Arthur C. Clarke; Ballantine Books, 1982, 291p. (HR, LACOPL, LAT, NYT, V)

3622. THE TWO WORLDS OF ANGELITA. (First Run Features-1983-Jane Morrison-N/R). Screenplay written by Jose Manuel Torres Santiago, Rose Rosenblatt, and Jane Morrison. (V, W)

3623. UFORIA. (Universal-1984-John Binder-N/R). Screenplay by John Binder. (V)

3624. THE ULTIMATE WARRIOR. (Warner Bros.-1976-Robert Clouse-R). Screenplay by Robert Clouse. (W)

3625. UNCLE JOE SHANNON. (United Artists-1978-Joseph C. Hanwright-PG). Screenplay written by Burt Young; novelization by Tom Albrandi; Pinnacle Books, 1978. (LACOPL, Q, V, W)

3626. UNCLE SCAM. (New World Pictures of Philadelphia-1981-Tom Pileggi & Michael Levanios Jr.-N/R). Screenplay by Tom Pilong, Michael Levanios Jr., Tom Pileggi, and Joe Ryan. (V, W)

3627. UNCOMMON VALOR. (Paramount-1983-Ted Kotcheff-R). Screenplay by Joe Gayton. (LAT, V)

3628. UNDER FIRE. (Orion-1983-Roger Spottiswoode-R). Screenplay by Ronald Shelton and Clayton Frohman, from a story
by Clayton Frohman. (LAT, V, W)

3629. UNDER THE FLAG OF THE RISING SUN. (Toho-1982-Kinji
Fukasaku-N/R). Kaneto Shindo wrote the screenplay, based
on a story by Shoji Yuki. (W)

3630. UNDER THE RAINBOW. (Orion/Warner Bros.-1981-Steve
Rash-PG). Pat McCormick, Harry Hurwitz, Martin Smith,
Pat Bradley, and Fred Bauer wrote the screenplay, from a
story by Fred Bauer and Pat Bradley. (LAT, Q, V, W)

3631. UNDER THE VOLCANO. (Universal-1984-John Huston-R).
Screenplay by Guy Gallo, from the novel by Malcolm Lowry;
Lippincott, 1965. (HR, LACOPL, LAT, V)

3632. UNDERCOVERS HERO. (United Artists-1975-Roy Boulting-
R). Screenplay by Leo Marks and Roy Boulting. (Q, W)

3633. UNDERGROUND ACES. (Filmways-1981-Robert Butler-PG).
Screenplay by Jim Carabatsos, Lenore Wright, and Andrew
Peter Marin. (W)

3634. UNDERGROUND U.S.A. (New Cinema-1980-Eric Mitchell-
N/R). Screenplay by Eric Mitchell. (W)

3635. UNFAITHFULLY YOURS. (20th Century-Fox-1984-Howard
Zieff-PG). Screenplay by Valerie Curtin, Barry Levinson,
and Robert Klane, based upon a screenplay by Preston
Sturges. (V)

3636. UNFINISHED BUSINESS. (Zebra-1984-Don Owen-N/R).
Screenplay by Don Owen. (V)

3637. AN UNFINISHED PIECE FOR PLAYER PIANO. (Corinth-
1982-Nikita Mikhalkov-N/R). Screenplay by Nikita Mikhalkov
and Alexander Adabashyan, from the novel Platonov by Anton
Chekhov; Hill, 1964, 195p. (LACOPL, W)

3638. UNIDENTIFIED FLYING ODDBALL. (Buena Vista-1979-Russ
Mayberry-G). Don Tait wrote the screenplay, based on
Mark Twain's novel A Connecticut Yankee in King Arthur's
Court; Dodd, Mead, 1960, 450p. (HR, LACOPL, LAT, NYT,
V, W)

3639. UNION CITY. (Kinesis-1980-Mark Reichert-PG). Screenplay
by Mark Reichert, from a story by Cornell Woolrich. (LAT,
V, W)

3640. AN UNMARRIED WOMAN. (20th Century-Fox-1978-Paul

Mazursky-R). Paul Mazursky wrote the screenplay; novelization by Carol Hill. (LACOPL, Q, V, W)

3641. THE UNSEEN. (World Northal-1981-Peter Foleg-R). Screenplay by Michael L. Grace. (V, W)

3642. UNTIL SEPTEMBER. (MGM/UA-1984-Richard Marquand-R). Screenplay by Janice Lee Graham. (V)

3643. UP! (RM Films International-1976-Russ Meyer-X). Screenplay by B. Callum, from an original story by Russ Meyer. (V, W)

3644. UP FROM THE DEPTHS. (New World-1979-Charles B. Griffith-N/R). Alfred Sweeney wrote the screenplay. (V, W)

3645. UP IN SMOKE. (Paramount-1978-Lou Adler-R). Cheech Marin and Thomas Chong wrote the original screenplay. (Q, V, W)

3646. UP THE ACADEMY. (Warner Bros.-1980-Robert Downey-R). Screenplay by Tom Patchett and Jay Tarses. (Q, V, W)

3647. UP THE CREEK. (Orion-1984-Robert Butler-R). Screenplay by Jim Kouf. (HR, LAT, V)

3648. UP YOUR ALLEY. (Group 1-1975-Art Lieberman-R). No screenplay credits available. (W)

3649. THE UPPERCRUST. (Satel-Film/Bayside Films-1982-Peter Patzak-N/R). Screenplay by Helmut Zenker and Peter Patzak. (V, W)

3650. THE URANIUM CONSPIRACY. (Noah Films-1978-Menahem Golan-N/R). Screenplay by David Paulsen, based on a story by Y. Ben-Porath. (V)

3651. URBAN COWBOY. (Paramount-1980-James Bridges-PG). Screenplay by James Bridges and John Aaron Latham, based on John Aaron Latham's story "Ballad of the Urban Cowboy: America's Search for True Grit," in Esquire Magazine, September 12, 1978, pp. 21-30. (HR, LACOPL, LAT, NYT, Q, V, W)

3652. USED CARS. (Columbia-1980-Robert Zemeckis-R). Screenplay by Robert Zemeckis and Bob Gale. (V, W)

UTILITIES see GETTING EVEN

3653. VALENTINA. (International Film Exchange-1982-Gleb Panfilov-N/R). Screenplay written by Glen Panfilov. (W)

VALENTINE see SEPARATE WAYS

3654.   VALENTINO. (United Artists-1977-Ken Russell-R). Screenplay by Ken Russell and John Byrum. (HR, LAT, V, W)

THE VALLEY see THE VALLEY OBSCURED BY CLOUDS

3655.   VALLEY GIRL. (Atlantic Releasing Corp.-1983-Martha
Coolidge-R). Screenplay written by Wayne Crawford and
Andrew Lane. (HR, LAT, V, W)

3656.   THE VALLEY OBSCURED BY CLOUDS. (Michael Kaplan/
Circle Associates-1981-Barbet Schroeder-N/R). Screenplay
written by Barbet Schroeder, adaptation and dialog by Paul
Gegauff and Barbet Schroeder. (W)

3657.   VAMPIRE HOOKERS. (Capricorn Three-1978-Cirio H.
Santiago-R). Screenplay by Howard Cohen. (W)

3658.   VAMPYRES. (Cambist-1975-Joseph Larraz-X). Screenplay
by D. Daubeney. (W)

3659.   VAN NUYS BLVD. (Crown International-1979-William Sachs-
R). Screenplay by William Sachs. (HR, LAT, V, W)

3660.   VANESSA. (Intercontinental Releasing Corp.-1977-Hubert
Frank-X). Screenplay by Joos De Ridder. (V)

3661.   VASSILY AND VASSILISA. (IFEX/Sovexportfilm-1982-Irina
Poplavskaya-N/R). Screenplay by Vassily Solovyov. (W)

3662.   VELVET SMOOTH. (Howard Mahler-1976-Michael Fink-R).
Screenplay credits not available. (W)

3663.   VENGEANCE IS MINE. (Shochiku Co. Ltd.-1980-Shohei
Imamura-N/R). Screenplay by Masaru Baba, based on the
book by Ryuzo Saki. (V)

3664.   VENGEANCE OF THE ZOMBIES. (International Amusements-
1975-Leon Klimovsky-R). Screenplay credits not available.
(W)

3665.   VENOM. (Paramount-1982-Piers Haggard-R). Screenplay by
Robert Carrington, from a novel by Alan Scholefield; Morrow, 1977. (BFI, LACOPL, LAT, Q, V)

VERDICT see JURY OF ONE

3666.   THE VERDICT. (20th Century-Fox-1982-Sidney Lumet-R).
Screenplay written by David Mamet, based on the novel by
Barry Reed; G. K. Hall, 1980, 476p. (BFI, HR, LACOPL,
LAT, NYT, Q, V, W)

3667. VERONIKA VOSS. (Laura Film/Tango Film-1982-Rainer
       Werner Fassbinder-N/R). Screenplay written by Rainer
       Werner Fassbinder. (V)

3668. VERONIQUE OR THE SUMMER OF MY 13TH YEAR. (Levitt-
       Pickman-1976-Claudine Guillemin-N/R). Screenplay written
       by Claudine Guillemin. (W)

3669. VICE SQUAD. (Avco Embassy-1982-Gary A. Sherman-R).
       Screenplay by Sandy Howard, Kenneth Peters, and Robert
       Vincent O'Neil. (HR, LAT, Q, V, W)

3670. VICTOR/VICTORIA. (MGM/UA-1982-Blake Edwards-PG).
       Screenplay by Blake Edwards, based on the film Viktor und
       Viktoria (UFA, 1933) conceived by Hans Hoemburg, written
       and directed by Rheinhold Schuenzel. (BFI, HR, LAT, NYT,
       Q, V, W)

3671. VICTORY. (Lorimar/Paramount-1981-John Huston-PG).
       Screenplay by Evan Jones and Yabo Yablonsky, from a
       story by Yabo Yablonsky, Djordje Milicevic, and Jeff Ma-
       guire. (LAT, Q, V, W)

3672. VICTORY MARCH. (Summit-1983-Marco Bellocchio-N/R).
       Screenplay by Marco Bellocchio and Sergio Bazzini. (W)

       VIDAS see LIVES/SURVIVORS

3673. VIDEO VIXENS. (Troma-1983-Ronald Sullivan-R). Screen-
       play written by Joel Gross. (W)

3674. VIDEODROME. (Universal-1983-David Cronenberg-R).
       Screenplay written by David Cronenberg. (V, W)

3675. VIGIL. (John Maynard-1984-Vincent Ward-N/R). Screen-
       play by Vincent Ward and Graeme Tetley. (V)

3676. VIGILANTE. (Artists Releasing Corp.-1982-William Lustig-
       R). Screenplay written by Richard Vetere. (LAT, V, W)

3677. VIGILANTE FORCE. (United Artists-1976-George Armitage-
       PG). Screenplay written by George Armitage. (W)

3678. THE VILLAIN. (Columbia-1979-Hal Needham-PG). Screen-
       play by Robert G. Kane. (Q, V, W)

3679. VINCENT, FRANCOIS, PAUL AND THE OTHERS. (Joseph
       Green-1976-Claude Sautet-N/R). Screenplay by Jean-Loup
       Dabadie, Claude Neron, and Claude Sautet. (W)

3680. THE VIOLATION OF CLAUDIA. (Lustig Prods.-1977-William

B. Lustiog-X). Screenplay written by Sally McKinley and
Travis Webb. (V)

3681. THE VIOLENT PROFESSIONALS. (Scotia American-1975-
Fernando DeLeo-R). Screenplay credits not available. (W)

3682. VIOLETTE. (Gaumont/New Yorker-1978-Claude Chabrol-R).
Screenplay by Odile Barski, Herve Bromberger, and
Frederic Grendel, adaptation and dialog by Odile Barski,
from the book by Jean-Marie Fitere. (W)

3683. VIRGIN AND THE LOVER. (Kemal International-1976-Kemal
Horulu-X). Screenplay by Kenneth Schwartz. (W)

3684. VIRGIN SNOW. (Snow Ball-1976-Dexter Eagle-X). No
screenplay credits available. (W)

3685. THE VIRGIN WITCH. (Joseph Brenner-1978-Ray Austin-R).
Screenplay by Klaus Vogel. (W)

3686. VIRILITY. (Athena/Coliseum-1976-Paolo Cavara-R). Screenplay by Gian Paolo Callegari. (W)

3687. VIRUS. (Haruki Kadokawa Films-1980-Kinji Fukasaku-N/R).
Screenplay by Koji Takada, Gregory Kanpp, and Kinji
Fukasaku, based on the novel by Sakyo Komatsu. (V)

3688. VISITING HOURS. (20th Century-Fox-1982-Jean Claude
Lord-R). Screenplay written by Brian Taggert. (Q, V, W)

3689. THE VISITOR. (International Picture Show-1979-Michael J.
Paradise-R). Screenplay by Lou Comici and Robert Bundy,
from an original story by Michael J. Paradise and Ovidio
Assonitis. (W)

3690. VIVA ITALIA. (Cinema 5-1978-Mario Monicelli, Dino Risi,
and Ettore Scola-N/R). Screenplay written by Age, Scarpelli, Ruggero Maccari, and Bernardino Zapponi. (V, W)

3691. VIVA KNIEVEL! (Warner Bros.-1977-Gordon Douglas-PG).
Screenplay written by Antonio Santillan and Norman Katkov.
(HR, Q, V, W)

3692. VIVE LA SOCIALE! (Fox Hachette-1983-Gerard Mordillat-
N/R). Screenplay by Gerard Mordillat, Jacques Audiard,
and Louis-Charles Sirjacq. (V)

VIVEMENT DIMANCHE see LET IT BE SUNDAY

3693. VOICE OVER. (Welsh Arts-1983-Chris Monger-N/R). Screenplay written by Chris Monger. (W)

3694. VOICES. (United Artists-1979-Robert Markowitz-PG).
Screenplay by John Herzfeld. (Q, V, W)

VOKZAL DLYA DVOIKH see A STATION FOR TWO

3695. VOODOO BLACK EXORCIST. (Horizon-1975-Manuel Cano-R).
Screenplay credits not available. (W)

3696. VOODOO HEARTBEAT. (TWI National-1975-Charles Nizet-R).
Screenplay by Charles Nizet. (W)

3697. VORTEX. (B Movies-1982-Scott B and Beth B-N/R).
Screenplay by Beth B and Scott B. (LAT, V, W)

VOSHOJDENIE see THE ASCENT

3698. VOYAGE EN DOUCE. (New Yorker-1981-Michel Deville-N/R).
Screenplay by Michel Deville, Francois-Regis Bastide,
Camille Bourniqueld, Muriel Cerf, Jean Chalon, Pierrette
Grainville, Yves Navarre, Jacques Perry, Maurice Pons,
Beatrice Privat, Suzanne Prou, Frederic Rey, Dominique
Rolin, and Isaure de Saint-Pierre. (LAT, W)

3699. VOYAGE OF THE DAMNED. (Avco Embassy-1976-Stuart
Rosenberg-PG). Screenplay written by Steve Shagan and
David Butler, based on the book by Gordon Thomas and
Max Morgan-Witts; Stein, 1974, 317p. (HR, LACOPL, LAT,
Q, V, W)

3700. THE VULTURES. (Canadian Film Development Corp.-1978-
Jean-Claude Lebrecque-N/R). Screenplay by Robert Gurik.
(BFI)

3701. W. C. FIELDS AND ME. (Universal-1976-Arthur Hiller-PG).
Screenplay by Bob Merrill, based on a book by Carlotta
Monti and Cy Rice; Prentice-Hall, 1971, 227p. (HR,
LACOPL, Q, V, W)

3702. W. W. AND THE DIXIE DANCEKINGS. (20th Century-Fox-
1975-John G. Avildsen-PG). Screenplay by Thomas Rickman.
(W)

3703. THE WACKIEST WAGON TRAIN IN THE WEST. (Topar-1976-
G). No production credits available. (W)

3704. WACKO. (Jensen Farley-1983-Greydon Clark-PG). Screenplay by Dana Olsen, Michael Spound, M. James Kauf Jr.,
and David Greenwalt. (W)

3705. WAGNER. (Alan Landsburg-1983-Tony Palmer-N/R). Screenplay written by Charles Wood. (LAT, V, W)

3706. WAITING FOR GAVRILOV. (IFEX-1983-Pyotr Todorovsky-
N/R). Screenplay written by Sergei Bodrov. (W)

3707. WAITRESS. (Troma-1982-Samuel Weil and Michael Herz-R).
Screenplay by Michael Stone, with additional material written by Charles Kaufman. (LAT, V)

3708. WALK PROUD. (Universal-1979-Robert Collins-PG). Screenplay by Evan Hunter; novelization by Evan Hunter; Dell,
1979, 212p. (LACOPL, Q, V, W)

WALKING TALL, PART 2 see PART 2, WALKING TALL

3709. WALTZ ACROSS TEXAS. (Atlantic Releasing Corp.-1983-
Ernest Day-PG). Screenplay written by Bill Svanoe. (LAT,
V, W)

3710. WANDA NEVADA. (United Artists-1979-Peter Fonda-PG).
Screenplay by Dennis Hackin. (W)

3711. WANDA, THE WICKED WARDEN. (Bernie Jacon-1979-Jess
Franco-R). Screenplay credits not available. (W)

3712. THE WANDERERS. (Orion/Warner Bros.-1979-Philip Kaufman-
R). Screenplay by Rose Kaufman, Philip Kaufman, based on
the novel by Richard Price; Houghton, 1974, 239p.
(LACOPL, Q, V, W)

3713. WAR AND PEACE. (TeleCulture-1983-N/R). Screenplay by
Heinrich Boll, based on From the Standpoint of the Infantry
by Alexander Kluge. (W)

3714. WAR GAMES. (MGM/UA-1983-John Badham-PG). Screenplay by Lawrence Lasker and Walter F. Parkes. (BFI, HR,
LAT, V)

3715. WAR GODDESS. (American International-1975-Terence
Young-R). Screenplay by Richard Aubrey, from a story by
Robert Graves and Richard Aubrey. (W)

3716. WAR OF THE WIZARDS. (21st Century Distribution-1983-
Richard Caan and Sam Arikawa-PG). Screenplay written
by F. Kenneth Lin. (V, W)

3717. WAR OF THE WORLDS--NEXT CENTURY. (Polish Corp.
Productions-1981-Piotr Szulkin-N/R). No screenplay credits
available. (V)

3718. WARLORDS OF ATLANTIS. (Columbia-1978-Kevin Connor-
PG). Screenplay written by Brian Hayles. (V, W)

WARLORDS OF THE 21st CENTURY see BATTLETRUCK

3719. THE WARRIORS. (Paramount-1979-Walter Hill-R). Screenplay by David Shaber and Walter Hill, based on the novel
by Sol Yurick; Holt, 1965, 189p. (HR, LACOPL, Q, V, W)

3720. WARRIORS OF THE WASTELAND. (New Line Cinema-1984-
Enzo Girolami Castellari-R). Screenplay by Tito Carpi and
Enzo Girolami Castellari, from an original story by Tito Carpi.
(V)

3721. WASHINGTON B.C. (First American-1979-Fred Levinson-PG).
Screenplay by Larry Spiegel and Phil Dusenberry. (W)

3722. WATCH OUT, WE'RE MAD. (Columbia-1976-Marcello Fondato-
G). Screenplay by Marcello Fondato and Francesco Scar-
maglia, based on a story by Marcello Fondato. (W)

3723. THE WATCHER IN THE WOODS. (Buena Vista-1980-John
Hough-PG). Screenplay by Brian Clemens, Harry Spalding,
and Rosemary Anne Sisson, based on Florence Engel Randall's novel; Atheneum, 1976, 229p. (LAT, V, W)

3724. THE WATER BABIES. (Pethurst International-1979-Lionel
Jeffries-N/R). Screenplay by Michael Robson, based on a
book by Charles Kingsley; Dutton, 1957, 284p. (LACOPL,
V)

3725. WATERSHIP DOWN. (Avco Embassy-1978-Martin Rosen-PG).
Screenplay by Martin Rosen, from a novel by Richard Adams;
Macmillan, 1972, 429p. (LACOPL, Q, V, W)

3726. THE WATTS MONSTER. (Dimension-1979-William Crain-R).
Screenplay by Larry LeBron. (V, W)

3727. WAVELENGTH. (New World Pictures-1983-Mike Gray-PG).
Screenplay by Mike Gray. (V, W)

3728. WE ALL LOVED EACH OTHER SO MUCH. (Cinema 5-1977-
Ettore Scola-N/R). Screenplay by Age, Scarpelli, and
Ettore Scola. (W)

3729. WE OF THE NEVER NEVER. (Triumph Films-1983-Igor
Auzins-G). Screenplay by Peter Schreck, based on the
book by Jeannie Gunn; Hutchinson & Co., n.d. (BFI,
LACOPL, LAT, W)

3730. WE WILL ALL MEET IN PARADISE. (First Artists-1978-
Yves Robert-PG). Screenplay by Jean-Loup Dabadie, from
a story by Jean-Loup Dabadie and Yves Robert. (W)

3731. A WEDDING. (20th Century-Fox-1978-Robert Altman-PG).
A screenplay by John Considine, Patricia Resnick, Allan

Nicholls, and Robert Altman, from a story by Robert Altman
and John Considine. (Q, V, W)

3732. WEEKEND PASS. (Crown International-1984-Lawrence
Bassoff-R). Screenplay written by Lawrence Bassoff. (V)

3733. A WEEK'S VACATION. (Biograph International-1982-Bertrand
Tavernier-N/R). Screenplay by Bertrand Tavernier, Colo
Tavernier, and Marie-Francoise Hans. (W)

3734. WELCOME HOME, BROTHER CHARLES. (Crown International-
1975-Jamac Fanaka-R). Screenplay written by Jamac Fanaka.
(W)

WELCOME TO ARROW BEACH see TENDER FLESH

3735. WELCOME TO L.A. (United Artists-1976-Alan Rudolph-R).
Screenplay by Alan Rudolph. (Q, V, W)

3736. WET ROCK. (Variety Films-1975-X). No screenplay credits
available. (W)

3737. WHAT CHANGED CHARLEY FARTHING? (Stirling Gold-1976-
Sidney Hayers-PG). Screenplay written by David Pursall
and Jack Seddon. (W)

3738. WHEN A STRANGER CALLS. (Columbia-1979-Fred Walton-
R). Screenplay by Steve Feke and Fred Walton. (Q, V, W)

3739. WHEN A WOMAN CALLS. (Tania-1975-William Haddington Jr.-
X). Screenplay written by Luigi di Gaspany. (W)

3740. WHEN JOSEPH RETURNS. (New Yorker-1983-Zsolt Kezdi-
Kovacs-N/R). Screenplay by Zsolt Kezdi-Kovacs. (W)

3741. WHEN TAEKWONDO STRIKES. (World Northal-1981-R). No
production credits available. (W)

3742. WHEN TIME RAN OUT. (Warner Bros.-1980-James Goldstone-
PG). Screenplay by Carl Foreman and Stirling Silliphant,
based on the novel The Day the World Ended by Gordon
Thomas and Max Morgan-Witts; Stein, 1969, 306p. (LACOPL,
Q, V, W)

3743. WHEN YOU COMIN' BACK, RED RYDER? (Columbia-1979-
Milton Katselas-R). Screenplay by Mark Medoff, based on
his play of the same title; White, 1974, 120p. (LACOPL, Q,
V, W)

3744. WHERE IS PARSIFAL? (Terence Young-1984-Henri Helman-
N/R). Berta Dominguez qrote this original screenplay. (V)

3745.   WHERE THE BOYS ARE '84. (Tri-Star Pictures-1984-Hy
        Averbach-R). Screenplay written by Stu Krieger and Jeff
        Burkhart, suggested by Glendon Swarthout's novel; Random
        House, 1960. (HR, LACOPL, LAT, V)

3746.   WHERE THE BUFFALO ROAM. (Universal-1980-Art Linson-
        R). Screenplay written by John Kaye. (V, W)

3747.   WHERE THE GREEN ANTS DREAM. (Werner Herzog
        Filmproduktion-1984-Werner Herzog-N/R). Screenplay writ-
        ten by Werner Herzog. (V)

3748.   WHERE THE RED FERN GROWS. (Doty-Dayton-1975-Norman
        Tokar-G). Screenplay by Douglas Day Stewart and Eleanor
        Lamb; based on the novel by Wilson Rawls; Doubleday, 1961.
        (LACOPL, W)

3749.   WHERE THERE'S SMOKE. (Libra-1975-Andre Cayatte-N/R).
        Screenplay by Andre Cayatte, adaptation and dialog by
        Andre Cayatte and Pierre Dumayet. (W)

3750.   WHERE TIME BEGAN. (International Picture Show-1978-
        Juan Piquer-G). Screenplay by Juan Piquer and Carlos
        Puerto, based on a novel by Jules Verne. (W)

3751.   WHERE'S WILLIE. (Taurus-1978-John Florea-G). Screen-
        play written by Frank Koomen, Ann Koomen, and Alan Cas-
        sidy, from an original story by William H. White. (W)

3752.   WHIFFS. (20th Century-Fox-1975-Ted Post-PG). An origi-
        nal screenplay by Malcolm Marmorstein. (W)

3753.   THE WHISTLE BLOWERS. (Dielst-1975-Milton Vickers-X).
        No screenplay credits available. (W)

3754.   THE WHITE BUFFALO. (United Artists-1977-J. Lee
        Thompson-PG). Screenplay by Richard Sale, based on his
        novel; Simon & Schuster, 1975, 253p. (LACOPL, V)

3755.   THE WHITE DELUSION. (The Movies-1984-Adriaan
        Ditvoorst-N/R). Adriaan Ditvoorst wrote this original
        screenplay. (V)

3756.   WHITE DOG. (Paramount-1982-Samuel Fuller-PG). Screen-
        play by Samuel Fuller and Curtis Hanson, based on the
        story by Romain Gary. (V)

3757.   WHITE LINE FEVER. (Columbia-1975-Jonathan Kaplan-PG).
        Screenplay by Ken Friedman and Jonathan Kaplan. (Q, W)

3758.   THE WHITE LIONS. (Alan Landsburg-1983-Mel Stuart-PG).

Screenplay written by Corey Blechman and Peter Dixon, from a book by Chris McBride, White Lions of Timbavati; Paddington Press, 1977. (LACOPL, V)

3759. THE WHITE SHIP. (Kirghizfilm-1978-Bolotbek Shamshiev-N/R). Screenplay based on a story by Chinghiz Aitmatov. (W)

3760. WHITE SLAVERY IN NEW YORKER. (Independent-1976-X). No production credits available. (W)

3761. WHO? (Lorimar-1982-Jack Gould-PG). Screenplay by Jack Gould, from a novel by Algis Budrys. (W)

3762. WHO DARES WINS. (Rank Film Distributors-1982-Ian Sharp-N/R). Screenplay by Reginald Rose, based on an original story by George Markstein. (V)

WHO FELL ASLEEP? see DEADLY GAMES

3763. WHO HAS SEEN THE WIND. (Cinema World-1980-Allan King-N/R). Screenplay by Patricia Watson, from the novel by W. O. Mitchell; Little, Brown, 1947. (LACOPL, W)

3764. WHO IS KILLING THE GREAT CHEFS OF EUROPE? (Warner Bros.-1978-Ted Kotcheff-PG). Screenplay by Peter Stone, based on the book Someone Is Killing the Great Chefs of Europe by Nan and Ivan Lyons; Harcourt Brace Jovanovich, 1976, 236p. (HR, LACOPL, Q, V, W)

3765. THE WHOLE SHOOTIN' MATCH. (Cinema Perspectives-1979-Eagle Pennell-N/R). Screenplay by Eagle Pennell and Lin Sutherland. (W)

3766. WHO'LL STOP THE RAIN. (United Artists-1978-Karel Reisz-N/R). Screenplay by Judith Roscoe and Robert Stone, from the novel Dog Soldiers by Robert Stone; Houghton, 1974, 342p. (HR, LACOPL, W)

3767. WHOLLY MOSES! (Columbia-1980-Gary Weis-PG). Screenplay by Guy Thomas. (Q, V, W)

3768. WHOSE CHILD AM I? (Brian Distributing Corp.-1976-Lawrence Britten-R). Screenplay by James Stevens. (W)

3769. WHOSE LIFE IS IT ANYWAY? (United Artists/MGM-1981-John Badham-R). Screenplay by Brian Clark and Reginald Rose, based on the stage play by Brian Clark. (LAT, Q, V, W)

3770. WHY NOT! (New Line Cinema-1979-Coline Serreau-N/R). Screenplay written by Coline Serreau. (W)

3771.   WHY ROCK THE BOAT? (Columbia-1975-John Howe-N/R).
        Screenplay by William Weintraub, from his novel. (W)

3772.   WHY SHOOT THE TEACHER? (Quartet Films-1980-Silvio
        Narizzano-N/R). Screenplay by James De Felice, from the
        novel of the same name by Max Braithwaite. (W)

3773.   WHY WOULD I LIE? (MGM/UA-1980-Larry Peerce-PG).
        Screenplay by Peter Stone, based on the novel The Fabri-
        cator by Hollis Hodges; Crown, 1976, 183p. (LACOPL, Q,
        V, W)

3774.   THE WICKED LADY. (Cannon Group-1983-Michael Winner-
        N/R). Screenplay by Michael Winner and Leslie Arliss, with
        additional dialog by Gordon Glennon and Aimee Stuart, based
        on The Life and Death of the Wicked Lady Skelton by Mag-
        dalen King-Hall; Rinehart, 1946. (HR, LACOPL, LAT, V, W)

3775.   THE WICKER MAN. (Warner Bros.-1975-Robin Hardy-R).
        Screenplay by Anthony Shaffer; novel by Robin Hardy and
        Anthony Shaffer; Crown, 1978. (LACOPL, W)

3776.   WIDE OPEN MARRIAGE. (Cambist-1975-Quirin Steiner-X).
        Screenplay credits not available. (W)

3777.   WIFEMISTRESS. (Quartet Films-1979-Marco Vicario-R).
        Screenplay by Rodolfo Sonego. (W)

3778.   THE WILBY CONSPIRACY. (United Artists-1975-Ralph
        Nelson-PG). Screenplay by Rod Amateau and Harold Neben-
        zal, based on a novel by Peter Driscoll; Lippincott, 1972,
        324p. (HR, LACOPL, Q, W)

3779.   THE WILD DUCK. (New Yorker-1977-Hans W. Geissendorfer-
        N/R). Screenplay by Hans W. Geissendorfer, based on the
        play by Henrik Ibsen; Norton, 1968, 226p. (LACOPL, W)

3780.   THE WILD DUCK. (Orion-1983-Henri Safran-N/R). Screen-
        play by Henri Safran, Peter Smalley, and John Lind, based
        on the play by Henrik Ibsen; Norton, 1968, 226p. (LACOPL,
        V, W)

        WILD GAME see JAIL BAIT

3781.   THE WILD GEESE. (Allied Artists-1978-Andrew V. McLaglen-
        R). Screenplay by Reginald Rose, based on the novel of
        the same name by Daniel Carney. (W)

3782.   THE WILD GOOSE CHASE. (EDP-1976-Claude Zidi-N/R).
        Screenplay by Claude Zidi. (W)

3783.   WILD HONEY. (Shermart-1975-Don Edmonds-X). Screenplay
        by Don Edmonds. (W)

3784.   WILD HORSES. (Endeavour-1983-Derek Morton-N/R).
        Screenplay by Kevin O'Sullivan. (V)

3785.   WILD HUNTING OF KING STAKH. (Sovexportfilm-1980-
        Valeri Roubintchik-N/R). Screenplay by Vladimir Korot-
        kevitch. (V)

3786.   THE WILD LIFE. (Universal-1984-Art Linson-R). Screen-
        play by Cameron Crowe. (V)

3787.   THE WILD MCCULLOCHS. (American International-1975-
        Max Baer-PG). Screenplay by Max Baer. (W)

3788.   THE WILD PARTY. (American International-1975-James
        Ivory-R). Screenplay by Walter Marks, based on a poem
        by Joseph Moncure March. (Q, W)

3789.   THE WILD SIDE. (New World Pictures-1983-Penelope
        Spheeris-N/R). Screenplay by Penelope Spheeris. (V)

3790.   WILD STYLE. (First Run Features-1983-Charlie Ahearn-
        N/R). Screenplay written by Charlie Ahearn. (BFI, LAT,
        V, W)

3791.   WILDCAT WOMEN. (Parliament-1976-R). No production
        credits available. (W)

3792.   WILDERNESS FAMILY PART 2. (Pacific International
        Enterprises-1978-Frank Zuniga-G). Screenplay by Arthur
        Dubs. (W)

3793.   DER WILLI BUSCH REPORT. (Almi Cinema 5-1982-Niklaus
        Schilling-N/R). Screenplay written by Niklaus Schilling.
        (W)

3794.   WILLIE & PHIL. (20th Century-Fox-1980-Paul Mazursky-R).
        Screenplay by Paul Mazursky, novelization by Joyce Thomp-
        son Steele; Avon, 1980. (LACOPL, Q, V, W)

3795.   WILLIE AND SCRATCH. (Libert Films International-1975-
        Robert J. Emery-R). Screenplay written by Robert J.
        Emery. (W)

3796.   WIN, PLACE OR STEAL. (Cinema National-1975-Richard
        Bailey-PG). Screenplay by Anthony Monaco and Richard
        Bailey. (W)

3797.   THE WIND AND THE LION. (United Artists-1975-John
        Milius-PG). Screenplay by John Milius. (Q, W)

3798. THE WIND IN MY POCKET. (IFEX-1983-Jaroslav Soukup-
      N/R). Screenplay by Jaroslav Soukup and Miroslav Valc.
      (W)

3799. WINDOWS. (United Artists-1980-Gordon Willis-R). Screen-
      play by Barry Siegel, novelization by H. B. Gilmour.
      (LACOPL, Q, V, W)

3800. THE WINDS OF AUTUMN. (Howco International-1976-Charles
      B. Pierce-PG). Screenplay written by Earl E. Smith. (W)

3801. WINDS OF CHANGE. (Sanrio-1979-Takashi-PG). Narration
      written by Norman Corwin, based on Ovid's Metamorphoses;
      Viking Press, 1958, 461p. (LACOPL, W)

3802. WINDWALKER. (Pacific International Enterprises-1980-Kieth
      Merrill-PG). Screenplay by Ray Goldrup, from the novel by
      Blaine M. Yorgason. (V, W)

3803. WINDY CITY. (Warner Bros.-1984-Armyan Bernstein-R).
      Screenplay written by Armyan Bernstein. (V)

      THE WINGED SERPENT see Q: QUETZALCOATL

3804. WINSTANLEY. (British Film Institute-1979-Kevin Brownlow
      and Andrew Molle-B&W-N/R). Screenplay credits not avail-
      able; based on the novel Comrade Jacob by David Caute.
      (W)

3805. WINTER FLIGHT. (Enigma-1984-Roy Battersby-N/R).
      Screenplay by Alan Janes. (V)

3806. WINTER HAWK. (Howco International-1975-Charles B.
      Pierce-PG). Screenplay written by Charles B. Pierce. (W)

3807. WINTER HEAT. (Claude Goddard-1976-Claude Goddard-X).
      No screenplay credits available. (W)

3808. WINTER KILLS. (Avco Embassy-1979-William Richert-R).
      Screenplay by William Richert, based on the novel of the
      same name by Richard Condon; Dial Press, 1974, 304p.
      (LACOPL, Q, V, W)

3809. WINTER OF OUR DREAMS. (Satori-1982-John Duigan-N/R).
      Screenplay by John Duigan. (BFI, W)

3810. WISE BLOOD. (New Line Cinema-1980-John Huston-N/R).
      Screenplay by Benedict Fitzgerald, from the novel by
      Flannery O'Connor; Farrar, 1962. (LACOPL, W)

3811. WISHBONE CUTTER. (Howco International-1978-Earl E.
      Smith-PG). Screenplay written by Earl E. Smith. (W)

3812. WITCH HUNT. (Scandinavia Today-1982-Anja Breien-N/R).
       Screenplay written by Anja Breien. (W)

3813. THE WITCH WHO CAME FROM THE SEA. (Moonstone-1976-
       Matt Cimber-R). Screenplay by Robert Thom. (W)

3814. WITHOUT A TRACE. (20th Century-Fox-1983-Stanley R.
       Jaffe-PG). Screenplay by Beth Gutcheon, based on her
       novel Still Missing; Putnam, 1981, 364p. (BFI, LACOPL, V)

3815. WITHOUT ANESTHESIA. (New Yorker-1982-Andrzej Wajda-
       N/R). Screenplay written by Agnieszka Holland and Andrzej
       Wajda. (W)

3816. WITHOUT WARNING. (Filmways-1980-Greydon Clark-R).
       Screenplay by Lyn Freeman, Daniel Grodnik, Ben Nett, and
       Steve Mathis. (V, W)

3817. THE WITNESS. (Libra-1982-Peter Basco-N/R). Screenplay
       by Peter Basco. (W)

       DE WITTE WAAN see THE WHITE DELUSION

3818. THE WIZ. (Universal-1978-Sidney Lumet-G). Screenplay by
       Joel Schumacher, from The Wonderful Wizard of Oz by L.
       Frank Baum; based on the musical play The Wiz, with book
       by William F. Brown and music and lyrics by Charlie Smalls;
       Dutton, 1965, 147p. (HR, LACOPL, LAT, NYT, Q, V, W)

       WO DIE GRUNEN AMEISEN TRAUMEN see WHERE THE
       GREEN ANTS DREAM

       WOJNA SWIATOW--NASTEPNE STULECIE see WAR OF THE
       WORLD--NEXT CENTURY

3819. WOLFEN. (Orion/Warner Bros.-1981-Michael Wadleigh-R).
       Screenplay by David Eyre and Michael Wadleigh, based on a
       novel by Whitley Strieber; Bantam Books, 1981, 275p.
       (LACOPL, LAT, Q, V, W)

3820. THE WOLVES. (Public-1982-Hideo Gosha-N/R). Screenplay
       by Kei Tasaka. (W)

3821. THE WOMAN ACROSS THE WAY. (Giorgos Panoussopoulos
       Ltd./Greek Film Center/Greka Film-1983-Giorgos Panoussop-
       oulos-N/R). Screenplay written by Giorgos Panoussopoulos,
       Philippos Drakontaidis, and Petros Tatsopoulos. (V)

3822. A WOMAN AT HER WINDOW. (SNC-1976-Pierre Granier-
       Deferre-N/R). Screenplay by Jorge Semprun and Pierre
       Granier-Deferre, from the book by Pierre Drieu La Rochelle.
       (V, W)

3823. A WOMAN BETWEEN DOG & WOLF. (Gaumont-1979-Andre
       Delvaux-N/R). Screenplay by Ivo Michiels and Andre
       Delvaux. (V)

3824. A WOMAN FOR ALL MEN. (General Film Corp.-1975-Arthur
       Marks-R). Screenplay credits not available. (W)

3825. THE WOMAN HUNT. (New World-1975-Eddie Romero-R).
       Screenplay credits not available. (W)

3826. THE WOMAN IN RED. (Orion-1984-Gene Wilder-PG-13).
       Screenplay written by Gene Wilder, based on Un Elephant
       Ca Trompe Enormement by Jean-Loup Dabadie and Yves
       Robert. (HR, LAT, NYT, V)

3827. WOMAN IN THE RAIN. (Boxoffice International-1976-Paul
       Hunt-PG). Screenplay credits not available. (W)

3828. THE WOMAN INSIDE. (20th Century-Fox-1981-Joseph Van
       Winkle-R). Screenplay by Joseph Van Winkle. (V, W)

3829. A WOMAN LIKE EVE. (Sigma Films B.V.-1980-Nouchka van
       Brakel-N/R). Screenplay by Nouchka van Brakel. (V)

3830. THE WOMAN NEXT DOOR. (United Artists Classics-1981-
       Francois Truffaut-N/R). Screenplay by Francois Truffaut,
       Suzanne Schiffman, and Jean Aurel. (LAT, V, W)

3831. A WOMAN WITHOUT LOVE. (Televicine International-1983-
       Luis Bunuel-N/R). Screenplay by Jaime Salvador, based on
       the novel Pierre et Jean by Guy de Maupassant; Brentano,
       1899, 335p. (LACOPL, V)

3832. A WOMAN'S DECISION. (Tinc-1978-Krzysztof Zanussi-N/R).
       Screenplay by Krzysztof Zanussi. (W)

3833. WOMBLING FREE. (Satori Entertainment-1984-Lionel
       Jeffries-N/R). Screenplay by Lionel Jeffries, based on a
       book and BBC television series by Elizabeth Beresford. (V)

3834. WOMEN. (New Yorker-1979-Marta Meszaros-N/R). Screen-
       play by Ildiko Korody, Joszef Balasz, and Geza Beremenyi.
       (W)

3835. WOMEN FOR SALE. (Independent International-1975-Ernest
       Farmer-R). Screenplay credits not available. (W)

       WON TON TON, THE DOG WHO SAVED HOLLYWOOD.
       (Paramount-1976-Michael Winner-PG). Screenplay by Arnold
       Schulman and Cy Howard. (Q, W)

3837. THE WONDERFUL CROOK. (New Yorker-1977-Claude
Goretta-N/R). An original screenplay by Claude Goretta.
(W)

3838. WORDS AND MUSIC. (AAA-1984-Elie Chouraqui-N/R).
Screenplay written by Elie Chouraqui. (V)

3839. THE WORLD ACCORDING TO GARP. (Warner Bros.-1982-
George Roy Hill-R). Screenplay written by Steve Tesich,
based on the novel by John Irving; Dutton, 1978, 437p.
(HR, LACOPL, LAT, Q, V, W)

3840. THE WORLD IS FULL OF MARRIED MEN. (New Realm-1979-
Robert Young-R). Screenplay by Jackie Collins, with addi-
tional dialog by Terry Howard; based on a novel by Jackie
Collins; World Publishing Co., 1968, 223p. (LACOPL, V, W)

3841. THE WORLD OF DRUNKEN MASTER. (Marvin-1982-Joseph
Kuo-R). Screenplay by Tien Shan Hsi. (W)

3842. WORLDS APART. (Scanlon-1980-Barbara Noble-N/R).
Screenplay by Amos Kollek, from his novel Don't Ask Me If
I Love; M. Evans, 1971, 292p. (LACOPL, W)

3843. THE WORLD'S GREATEST LOVER. (20th Century-Fox-1977-
Gene Wilder-PG). Screenplay by Gene Wilder; novelization
by Chris Greenburg; Ace Books, 1977. (LACOPL, Q, W)

3844. THE WORM EATERS. (New American-1981-Herb Robins-N/R).
Screenplay by Herb Robins, from a story by Nancy Kapner.
(V, W)

3845. WOYZECK. (New Yorker-1980-Werner Herzog-N/R). Screenplay written by Werner Herzog, from the play by Georg
Buchner. (V, W)

3846. THE WRESTLING QUEEN. (Harnell-1975-PG). No production credits available. (W)

3847. THE WRONG DAMN FILM. (Davidson-1975-Carson Davidson-
N/R). Screenplay by Carson Davidson. (W)

3848. WRONG IS RIGHT. (Columbia-1982-Richard Brooks-R).
Screenplay by Richard Brooks, based on the novel The Bet-
ter Angels by Charles McCarry; Dutton, 1979, 282p.
(LACOPL, Q, V)

3849. THE WRONG MOVE. (Bauer International-1979-Wim Wenders-
N/R). Screenplay by Peter Handke. (W)

3850. WUTHERING HEIGHTS. (Plexus-1983-Luis Bunuel-N/R).

Screenplay by Luis Bunuel, Arduino Maiuri, and Julio Alejandro de Castro; based on Emily Bronte's novel; Norton, 1963, 325p. (LACOPL, W)

3851. X-RAY. (Cannon-1981-Boaz Davidson-N/R). Screenplay by Marc Behm, from a story by Boaz Davidson. (BFI)

3852. XALA. (New Yorker-1976-Ousmane Sembene-N/R). Screenplay by Ousmane Sembene, based on his novel; L. Hill & Co., 1976, 114p. (LACOPL, W)

3853. XANADU. (Universal-1980-Robert Greenwald-PG). Richard Christian Danus and Marc Reid Rubel wrote this screenplay; novelization by Richard Christian Danus; Jove, 1980. (LACOPL, Q, V, W)

XI YING MEN see THE IN-LAWS (1983)

3854. XICA. (Embrafilme/Unifilm-1982-Carlos Diegues-N/R). Screenplay by Carlos Diegues and Joao Felicio dos Santos. (W)

3855. XTRO. (New Line Cinema-1983-Harry Bromley Davenport-R). Screenplay by Robert Smith and Iain Cassie, based upon an original script by Michel Parry and Harry Bromley Davenport. (LAT, V, W)

3856. THE YAKUZA. (Warner Bros.-1975-Sydney Pollack-R). Screenplay by Paul Schrader and Robert Towne, from a story by Leonard Schrader. (Q, W)

3857. YANKS. (Universal-1979-John Schlesinger-R). Screenplay by Colin Welland and Walter Bernstein; novelization by Christine Sparks; Dell Books, 1979, 235p. (HR, LACOPL, LAT, NYT, Q, V, W)

3858. THE YEAR OF LIVING DANGEROUSLY. (MGM/UA-1982-Peter Weir-PG). Screenplay by David Williamson, Peter Weir, and C. J. Koch, based on the novel by C. J. Koch; Penguin, 1983, 304p. (HR, LACOPL, LAT, V)

3859. THE YEAR OF THE HARE. (Filminor-1979-Risto Jarva-N/R). Screenplay by Arto Paasilinna, Risto Jarva, and Kullervo Kukkasjarvi. (V)

3860. YELLOWBEARD. (Orion-1983-Mel Damski-PG). An original screenplay written by Graham Chapman, Peter Cook, and Bernard McKenna. (BFI, LAT, V, W)

3861. YENTL. (MGM/UA-1983-Barbra Streisand-PG). Screenplay written by Jack Rosenthal and Barbra Streisand, based on

<u>Yentl, the Yeshiva Boy</u> by Isaac Bashevis Singer; Farrar, Straus, Giroux, 1983, 58p. (BFI, HR, LACOPL, LAT, NYT, V, W)

3862. YES, GIORGIO. (MGM/UA-1982-Franklin J. Schaffner-PG). Screenplay by Norman Steinberg, suggested by the novel by Anne Piper. (HR, LAT, NYT, V, W)

3863. YESTERDAY'S HERO. (EMI-1979-Neil Leifer-N/R). Screenplay by Jackie Collins. (V)

LES YEUX DES OISEAUX see EYES OF THE BIRDS

3864. YOL. (Triumph Films-1982-Serif Goren-PG). An original screenplay written by Yilmaz Guney. (V, W)

3865. YOR, THE HUNTER FROM THE FUTURE. (Columbia-1983-Anthony M. Dawson aka Antonio Margheriti-PG). Screenplay by Robert Bailey, and Anthony M. Dawson (aka Antonio Margheriti), from the novel by Juan Zanotto and Ray Collins. (LAT, V, W)

3866. YOU AND ME. (Filmmakers International-1975-David Carradine-N/R). Screenplay and story by Robert Henderson. (W)

3867. YOU ARE NOT ALONE. (Steen Herdel-1981-Lasse Nielsen and Ernest Johansen-N/R). Screenplay written by Lasse Nielsen and Bent Peterson. (W)

3868. YOU BETTER WATCH OUT. (Edward R. Pressman-1980-Lewis Jackson-N/R). Screenplay written by Lewis Jackson. (V, W)

3869. YOU LIGHT UP MY LIFE. (Columbia-1977-Joseph Brooks-PG). Screenplay written by Joseph Brooks. (HR, LAT, NYT, Q, V, W)

3870. YOU TAKE THE KIDS. (IFEX-1983-Marie Polednakova-N/R). Screenplay written by Marie Polednakova, from her original screen story. (W)

3871. YOUNG AND WILD. (Boxoffice International-1975-Dwayne Avery-R). Screenplay credits not given. (W)

3872. YOUNG CASANOVA. (Seaberg-1975-Max Pecas-X). Screenplay by Max Pecas and Michel Vocoret. (W)

3873. THE YOUNG CYCLE GIRLS. (Peter Perry-1979-Peter Perry-R). Screenplay originally written for the screen by John Arnoldy. (V, W)

3874. THE YOUNG DIVORCEES. (Monarch-1975-Laurance E.
       Mascott-X). Screenplay written by Holly Mascott. (W)

3875. YOUNG DOCTORS IN LOVE. (20th Century-Fox-1982-Garry
       Marshall-R). Screenplay by Michael Elias and Rich Eustis.
       (Q, V, W)

3876. YOUNG LADY CHATTERLEY. (PRO International-1977-Alan
       Roberts-X). Screenplay written by Steve Michaels. (V)

3877. THE YOUNG PASSIONS. (Hollywood International-1975-
       Bobby Davis-X).

3878. THE YOUNG PLAYTHINGS. (Associated Films-1975-Joe
       Sarno-R). Screenplay credits not available.

3879. YOUNG WARRIORS. (Cannon-1983-Lawrence D. Foldes-R).
       Screenplay written by Lawrence D. Foldes and Russell W.
       Colgin. (BFI, V, W)

3880. YOUNGBLOOD. (American International-1978-Noel Nosseck-
       R). Screenplay written by Paul Carter Harrison. (W)

3881. YOUR HEAVEN, MY HELL. (Athena-1976-Rafaello R.
       Marchent-PG). Screenplay credits not available. (W)

3882. YOUR TURN, MY TURN. (New Yorker-1979-Francois
       Letterier-PG). Screenplay written by Daniele Thompson,
       Francoise Dorin, and Francois Leterrier, from a novel by
       Francoise Dorin. (W)

       LOS ZANCOS see THE STILTS

3883. ZAPPED! (Embassy-1982-Robert J. Rosenthal-R). Screen-
       play by Bruce Rubin and Robert J. Rosenthal. (HR, LAT,
       Q, V, W)

3884. ZELIG. (Orion/Warner Bros.-1983-Woody Allen-PG).
       Screenplay written by Woody Allen. (LAT, V)

       ZERKALO see THE MIRROR

3885. ZERO TO SIXTY. (First Artists-1978-Don Weis-PG).
       Screenplay by W. Lyle Richardson, from a story by Peg
       Shirley and Judith Bustany. (W)

3886. ZIG-ZAG. (Peppercorn/Wormser-1975-Laszlo Szabo-R).
       Screenplay by Laszlo Szabo. (W)

3887. ZOMBIE. (Jerry Gross Organization-1980-Lucio Fulci-X).
       Screenplay and story by Elisa Briganti. (V, W)

3888. ZOOT SUIT. (Universal-1981-Luis Valdez-R). Screenplay
       by Luis Valdez, based on his original play. (HR, LAT, Q,
       V, W)

3889. ZORRO, THE GAY BLADE. (20th Century-Fox-1981-Peter
       Medak-PG). Screenplay by Hal Dresner, based on charac-
       ters created by Johnston M. McCulley; story by Hal Dres-
       ner, Greg Alt, Don Moriarty, and Bob Randall. (BFI, HR,
       LAT, Q, V, W)

3890. LES ZOZOS. (Bauer International-1977-Pascal Thomas-N/R).
       Screenplay by Pascal Thomas and Roland Duval. (W)

3891. ZULU DAWN. (American Cinema-1980-Douglas Hickox-PG).
       Screenplay written by Cy Endfield and Anthony Storey.
       (W)

       ZWISCHEN ZWEI KRIEGEN see BETWEEN TWO WARS

INDEX

Davis, Ivan 1663
Davis, Kenn 2440
Davis, Kevin 3403
Davis, Mary 2187, 2699
Davis, Ossie 714
Davis, Paul 3072
Davis, Robin 1683
Davis, Walt 829
Dawson, Anthony M. 3865
Dawson, Cleo 3071
Dawson, Jan 3292
Day, Gerry 300
Dayton, Lyman 2695
Deal, Morris 1578
Deane, Hamilton 944
De Antonio, Emile 1726
Dear, William 3526
Dearden, James 665
De Arminan, Jaime 2384
De Bello, John 162
DeBernardi, Piero 249, 287, 640, 1124, 1420, 2346, 2538
DeBevoise, Allen 410, 411
de Bosio, Gianfranco 2308
De Broca, Philippe 816, 2131, 2720
De Buron, Nicole 2922
De Camp, L. Sprague 683
DeCapite, Raymond 1511
DeCaro, Lucio 1210
Decaux, Alain 2261
de Chalonge, Christian 2143
de Christofaro, Ron 2541
de Concini, Ennio 1836, 1950, 2121
De Felice, James 3772
DeFelitta, Frank 164, 1051
Defoe, Daniel 2151
Defrance, Philippe 3566
de Givray, Claude 2801
de Gregorio, Eduardo 551
Dehlavi, Jamil 334
De Jarnatt, Steven 3298
Delabriere, Patrick 1287
de La Fourchardiere, Georges 594
De La Loma, Jose Antonio 694
Delaney, Shelagh 2817
de la Parra, Pim 2558
DeLaurentis, Robert 2028
Delay, Claude 564

Dell, Gabriel 2169
Dell, Wanda 2196
Del Monte, Peter 3386
DeLuca, Rudy 548, 1571, 3101
de Lussanet, Paul 814
Delvaux, Andre 3823
de Martino, Alberto 614, 3438
de Martino, Aldo 614, 711
de Mille, Nelson 3100
Demme, Jonathan 1162
Demy, Jacques 919
DeNegri, Giuliani G. 2424
Denmark, Wilston 1813
Dennis, Charles 730, 937, 1170
Dent, Arthur 2032
Denuziere, Maurice 2061
de Oliveira, Manoel 97
Deon, Michel 2767
de Ossio, Maria L. 2527
De Palma, Brian 344, 363, 966, 1600
Derbenev, Vadim 1777
Derek, John 371, 1121
de Renzy, Alex 1153, 2686
De Ridder, Joos 3660
DeRita, Massimo 124, 333, 2575
Derloshon, Jerry 1977
De Roche, Chris 788, 3174
De Roche, Everett 788, 1509, 2633, 2880, 3174
De Salzmann, Jeanne 2222
Deschaumes, Nicole 2782
Desegonzac, Edouard 544
De Simone, Tom 578
Desmond, Dick 1049
des Olbes, Claude 1028
de Souza, Steve 1247, 2841
Detiege, David 455, 767, 2051
de Troyes, Chretien 2644
de Turenne, Henri 1243
Deville, Michel 930, 3698
DeVito, Ralph 819, 1114
Devlin, Don 1513
Devore, Christopher 1021, 1263
Devore, Gary 184, 911
de Vos, Pieter 1366
De Vries, Peter 2855
De Vries, Theun 1366